T0075771

Country of Origin: United States

Springer
the language of science

Thank you for your order! An invoice is being mailed separately. F
For more information on our products and for new book annc

Reference#	4500107860	

Ship to:

BAKER & TAYLOR BOOKS
501 S GLADIOLUS STREET

Tel: 8154722444

MOMENCE   IL   609541799

United States

Quantity	ISBN	Title
3	9781461417699	Genetic Programming Theory and Practice IX
3	Total quantity enclosed	

Claim Policy:
Claims regarding this shipment must be confirmed in writing and received by us within thirty
days of the invoice date. Please call our toll-free number if assistance is required.

Book Return Policy
Returns are accepted within two months of invoice date. Returns of products that were purchased
for resale are accepted within twelve months of invoice date. Please enclose a copy of our invoice
or packing slip when you send your return to expedite processing and avoid a possible 10%
penalty. For your protection, returns should be sent by a traceable method. We are not
responsible for product returned that does not belong to us.

4500107860

Packing List

ease call 800-SPRINGER (1-800-777-4643) if assistance is required.
ncements, please visit us at springeronline.com/springeralerts.

Customer Order Date	01/31/2012

YRC Collect

0000575442

Purchase Order: MOM2525553

	Author/Editor
	Rick Riolo

US returns to:
Springer Returns Dept
c/o IPS
1210 Ingram Drive
Chambersburg, PA 17202

Canadian returns to:
Springer
c/o Georgetown Terminal Warehouse
34 Armstrong Avenue
Georgetown, Ontario L7G 4R9

Rick Riolo, Ekaterina Vladislavleva and Jason H. Moore (Eds.)

Genetic Programming Theory and Practice IX

Genetic and Evolutionary Computation Series

Series Editors

David E. Goldberg
Consulting Editor
IlliGAL, Dept. of General Engineering
University of Illinois at Urbana-Champaign
Urbana, IL 61801 USA
Email: deg@uiuc.edu

John R. Koza
Consulting Editor
Medical Informatics
Stanford University
Stanford, CA 94305-5479 USA
Email: john@johnkoza.com

For other titles published in this series, go to
http://www.springer.com/series/7373

Rick Riolo • Ekaterina Vladislavleva • Jason H. Moore
Editors

Genetic Programming Theory and Practice IX

Foreword by Una-May O'Reilly

 Springer

Editors
Rick Riolo
Center for the Study of Complex
Systems (CSCS)
University of Michigan
Ann Arbor, Michigan
USA
rlriolo@umich.edu

Ekaterina Vladislavleva
Evolved Analytics Europe BVBA
Wijnegem
Belgium

Jason H. Moore
Institute for Quantitative
Biomedical Sciences
Dartmouth Medical School
Lebanon, New Hampshire
USA

ISSN 1932-0167
ISBN 978-1-4614-1769-9   e-ISBN 978-1-4614-1770-5
DOI 10.1007/978-1-4614-1770-5
Springer New York Dordrecht Heidelberg London

Library of Congress Control Number: 2011940166

© Springer Science+Business Media, LLC 2011
All rights reserved. This work may not be translated or copied in whole or in part without the written
permission of the publisher (Springer Science+Business Media, LLC, 233 Spring Street, New York,
NY 10013, USA), except for brief excerpts in connection with reviews or scholarly analysis. Use in
connection with any form of information storage and retrieval, electronic adaptation, computer software,
or by similar or dissimilar methodology now known or hereafter developed is forbidden.
The use in this publication of trade names, trademarks, service marks, and similar terms, even if they
are not identified as such, is not to be taken as an expression of opinion as to whether or not they are
subject to proprietary rights.

Printed on acid-free paper

Springer is part of Springer Science+Business Media (www.springer.com)

Contents

Contributing Authors   vii

Preface   xi

Foreword   xiii

Genetic Programming Theory and Practice 2010: An Introduction   xv
Ekaterina Vladislavleva, Jason H. Moore and Rick Riolo

1
What's in an Evolved Name? The Evolution of Modularity via Tag-Based   1
Reference
Lee Spector, Kyle Harrington, Brian Martin, Thomas Helmuth

2
Let the Games Evolve!   17
Moshe Sipper

3
Novelty Search and the Problem with Objectives   37
Joel Lehman and Kenneth O. Stanley

4
A Fine-Grained View of Phenotypes and Locality in Genetic Programming   57
James McDermott, Edgar Galván-Lopéz and Michael O'Neill

5
Evolution of an Effective Brain-Computer Interface Mouse via Genetic   77
Programming with Adaptive Tarpeian Bloat Control
Riccardo Poli, Mathew Salvaris, and Caterina Cinel

6
Improved Time Series Prediction and Symbolic Regression with Affine   97
Arithmetic
Cassio Pennachin, Moshe Looks and J. A. de Vasconcelos

7
Computational Complexity Analysis of Genetic Programming - Initial   113
Results and Future Directions
Frank Neumann, Una-May O'Reilly and Markus Wagner

8

Accuracy in Symbolic Regression 129
Michael F. Korns

9

Human-Computer Interaction in a Computational Evolution System for the 153
Genetic Analysis of Cancer
Jason H. Moore, Douglas P. Hill, Jonathan M. Fisher, Nicole Lavender, and La Creis Kidd

10

Baseline Genetic Programming: Symbolic Regression on Benchmarks for 173
Sensory Evaluation Modeling
Pierre-Luc Noel, Kalyan Veeramachaneni and Una-May O'Reilly

11

Detecting Shadow Economy Sizes With Symbolic Regression 195
Philip D. Truscott and Michael F. Korns

12

The Importance of Being Flat – Studying the Program Length Distributions 211
of Operator Equalisation
Sara Silva and Leonardo Vanneschi

13

FFX: Fast, Scalable, Deterministic Symbolic Regression Technology 235
Trent McConaghy

Index 261

Contributing Authors

Caterina Cinel is a Principal Research Officer in the School of Computer Science and Electronic Engineering of the University of Essex, UK (ccinel@essex.ac.uk).

Edgar Galván-Lopéz is a Research Fellow in the School of Computer Science and Statistics at Trinity College University, Ireland (edgar.galvan@tcd.ie).

Jonathan Fisher is a software engineer in the Institute for Quantitative Biomedical Sciencesat Dartmouth Medical School, USA (jonathan.fisher@Dartmouth.edu).

Kyle Harrington is a Ph.D. Candidate in the School of Computer Science at Brandeis University, a member of the CI lab at Hampshire College, and a visiting scholar at the University of Massachusetts, Amherst (kyleh@cs.brandeis.edu).

Thomas Helmuth is a graduate student in the Computer Science Department at the University of Massachusetts, Amherst, MA, USA (thelmuth@cs.umass.edu).

Douglas Hill is a software engineer in the Institute for Quantitative Biomedical Sciencesat Dartmouth Medical School, USA (douglas.hill@Dartmouth.edu).

La Creis Kidd is an Associate Professor of Pharmacology and Toxicology at the University of Louisville, USA (lrkidd01@louisville.edu).

Michael F. Korns is Chief Technology Officer at Freeman Investment Management, Henderson, Nevada, USA (mkorns@korns.com).

Nicole Lavender is a graduate student in Pharmacology and Toxicology at the University of Louisville, USA (nalave01@louisville.edu).

Joel Lehman is a Ph.D. Candidate in the Department of Electrical Engineering and Computer Science at the University of Central Florida, USA (lehman.154@gmail.com).

Moshe Looks is a software designer and researcher at Google Inc., USA (madscience@google.com).

Brian Martin is an undergraduate student at Hampshire College, Amherst, MA, USA (btm08@hampshire.edu).

Trent McConaghy is co-founder and Chief Scientific Officer of Solido Design Automation Inc., which makes variation-aware IC design software for top-tier semiconductor firms. He is based in Vancouver, Canada. (trent_mcconaghy@yahoo.com).

James McDermott is a Research Fellow in the Evolutionary Design and Optimization group, Computer Science and Artificial Intelligence Laboratory, Massachusetts Institute of Technology, USA (jmmcd@csail.mit.edu).

Jason H. Moore is the Third Century Professor of Genetics and Director of the Institute for Quantitative Biomedical Sciences at Dartmouth Medical School, USA (Jason.H.Moore@Dartmouth.edu).

Frank Neumann is a Senior Lecturer in the School of Computer Science at the University of Adelaide, Australia (frank.neumann@adelaide.edu.au)

Pierre-Luc Noel is a graduate student at E.T.H. Zurich pursuing a Master's degree in Engineering. He completed his thesis requirement as a guest of the Evolutionary Design and Optimization Group, CSAIL, MIT.

Michael O'Neill is Director of the Natural Computing Research and Applications group, University College Dublin, Ireland (m.oneill@ucd.ie).

Una-May O'Reilly is leader of the Evolutionary Design and Optimization Group and Principal Research Scientist at the Computer Science and Artificial Intelligence Laboratory (CSAIL), Massachusetts Institute of Technology, USA (unamay@csail.mit.edu).

Cassio Pennachin is a graduate student at Universidade Federal de Minas Gerais, Belo Horizonte, MG, Brazil (pennachin@ufmg.br).

Riccardo Poli is a Professor of Computer Science in the School of Computer Science and Electronic Engineering of the University of Essex, UK (rpoli@essex.ac.uk).

Rick Riolo is Director of the Computer Lab and Associate Research Scientist in the Center for the Study of Complex Systems at the University of Michigan, USA (rlriolo@umich.edu).

Mathew Salvaris is a Senior Research Officer in the School of Computer Science and Electronic Engineering of the University of Essex, UK (mssalv@essex.ac.uk).

Sara Silva is a senior researcher of the KDBIO (Knowledge Discovery and Bioinformatics) group at INESC-ID Lisboa, Technical University of Lisbon, Portugal, and an invited researcher of the ECOS (Evolutionary and Complex Systems) group at CISUC, University of Coimbra, Portugal (sara@kdbio.inesc-id.pt).

Moshe Sipper is a Professor of Computer Science at Ben-Gurion University, Israel (sipper@cs.bgu.ac.il).

Lee Spector is a Professor of Computer Science in the School of Cognitive Science at Hampshire College, Amherst, MA, USA (lspector@hampshire.edu).

Kenneth Stanley is an Assistant Professor in the Department of Electrical Engineering and Computer Science at the University of Central Florida, USA (kstanley@eecs.ucf.edu).

Leonardo Vanneschi is an Assistant Professor of Computer Science at the Department of Informatics, Systems and Communication (D.I.S.Co.) of the University of Milano-Bicocca, Italy, and an Associate Researcher of the KD-BIO (Knowledge Discovery and Bioinformatics) group of INESC-ID Lisboa, Technical University of Lisbon, Portugal (vanneschi@disco.unimib.it).

João A. de Vasconcelos is a professor of Electrical Engineering at Universidade Federal de Minas Gerais, Belo Horizonte, MG, Brazil (joao@cpdee.ufmg.br).

Kalyan Veeramachaneni is a post-doctoral associate at the Computer Science and Artificial Intelligence Laboratory, MIT. He received his Ph.D in Electrical Engineering from Syracuse University in December, 2009.

Ekaterina Vladislavleva is a Chief Data Scientist at Evolved Analytics, founder at Evolved Analytics Europe, and a Guest Lecturer in the Department of Mathematics and Computer Science at the University of Antwerp, Belgium (katya@evolved-analytics.com).

Markus Wagner is a Ph.D. Candidate in the School of Computer Science at the University of Adelaide, Australia (markus.wagner@adelaide.edu.au)

Preface

The work described in this book was first presented at the Nineth Workshop on Genetic Programming, Theory and Practice, organized by the Center for the Study of Complex Systems at the University of Michigan, Ann Arbor, May 12-14, 2011. The goal of this workshop series is to promote the exchange of research results and ideas between those who focus on Genetic Programming (GP) theory and those who focus on the application of GP to various real-world problems. In order to facilitate these interactions, the number of talks and participants was small and the time for discussion was large. Further, participants were asked to review each other's chapters *before* the workshop. Those reviewer comments, as well as discussion at the workshop, are reflected in the chapters presented in this book. Additional information about the workshop, addendums to chapters, and a site for continuing discussions by participants and by others can be found at http://cscs.umich.edu/gptp-workshops/ .

We thank all the workshop participants for making the workshop an exciting and productive three days. In particular we thank the authors, without whose hard work and creative talents, neither the workshop nor the book would be possible. We also thank our keynote speaker Steve Grand, creator of the artificial life computer game *Creatures*, independent researcher, software developer and writer, who is now working on a new project, *GRANDROIDS*. Steve's talk inspired a great deal of discussion among the participants throughout the workshop, and his comments on other presentations and the ensuing discussions were always insightful.

The workshop received support from these sources:

- The Center for the Study of Complex Systems (CSCS);

- John Koza, Third Millennium Venture Capital Limited;

- Michael Korns;

- Mark Kotanchek, Evolved Analytics;

- Jason Moore, Computational Genetics Laboratory at Dartmouth College;

- Conor Ryan, Biocomputing and Developmental Systems Group, Computer Science and Information Systems, University of Limerick;

- Babak Hodjat and Genetic Finance LLC;

- Bill Worzel and Genetics Squared;

- Stu Card and Critical Technologies, Inc; and

- Trent McConaghy.

We thank all of our sponsors for their kind and generous support for the workshop and GP research in general.

A number of people made key contributions to running the workshop and assisting the attendees while they were in Ann Arbor. Foremost among them was Howard Oishi, who makes GPTP workshops run smoothly with his diligent efforts before, during and after the workshop itself. After the workshop, many people provided invaluable assistance in producing this book. Special thanks go to Stefan Sirakov, who did a wonderful job working with the authors, editors and publishers to get the book completed very quickly. Jennifer Maurer and Melissa Fearon provided invaluable editorial efforts, from the initial plans for the book through its final publication. Thanks also to Springer for helping with various technical publishing issues.

RICK RIOLO, EKATERINA (KATYA) VLADISLAVLEVA
AND JASON MOORE

Foreword

In springtime, for 5 of the 9 past years, I have been drawn to Ann Arbor, Michigan, where it has been my privilege and pleasure to participate in my favorite annual meeting: Genetic Programming, From Theory to Practice. This meeting has been my favorite since its inception in 2002. Part of its allure is the extraordinary mix of people it brings to the meeting table: theoreticians and practitioners of genetic programming join to communicate their progress, exchange their ideas, engage the latest technological challenges and open up to voice their assessments, experiences, goals and visions. This year we were very privileged to learn of Steve Grand's GRANDROID project and be on the receiving end of his insightful observations of our presentations and discussions.

This meeting is unique because it brings genetic programming theoreticians and practitioners together with a purpose: to bridge the gap between them. Genetic programming theory faces fundamental challenges associated with multiple aspects of the algorithm: its stochasticity, complex representations and operators, to name just a few. But, theoreticians continue to make progress as demonstrated by chapters in this volume. Genetic programming practitioners enjoy the freedom to explore numerous algorithmic designs and they turn to theory to provide them with clear explanations and deep though simple insights. Within this volume you will find numerous chapters presenting the best of current genetic programming practice. I welcome all readers to this latest exciting, 9th, volume in the GPTP workshop series.

Una-May O'Reilly
Principal Research Scientist
Computer Science and Artificial Intelligence Laboratory (CSAIL)
Massachusetts Institute of Technologyi, USA
June, 2011

Genetic Programming Theory and Practice 2010: An Introduction

Ekaterina Vladislavleva[1], Jason H. Moore[2], and Rick Riolo[3]

[1]*Evolved Analytics Europe BVBA, Belgium;* [2]*Dartmouth Medical School, Dartmouth College, U.S.A.;* [3]*Center for Study of Complex Systems, University of Michigan, U.S.A.*

Keywords: genetic programming, symbolic regression, automatic programming, program induction

1.   The workshop

The 2011 workshop on Genetic Programming in Theory and Practice was hosted by the Center for the Study of Complex Systems of the University of Michigan for the ninth time. According to many participants the last two years were the best ever for GPTP. The number of presented chapters was lower in 2011 compared with the previous years, but the attendance was as usual, which is a good indication of the added value of GPTP discussions.

In 2011 we planned even more time for discussions compared to previous years (both, talk-related and general), invited more new people to the GPTP community, and introduced a new feature for facilitating debates after chapter presentations. Each presentation was followed by a 10-minute commentary by the two reviewer groups, who reflected on how and whether the work presented in the chapter could be used in their own research, and what are interesting new directions of potential collaboration.

In workshop format, the ratio of presentation time versus discussion time has reached a current global optimum in 2011. Despite the differences in the backgrounds among all participants, despite a high fraction of new presenters (which was one of the highest this year), despite the differences in everybody's goals – discussions and debates in 2011 have undoubtedly achieved a new level of depth. Respectful disagreements showed a new level of collective effort to achieve consensus. Constructiveness and openness of suggestions about the future formats of the workshop proved the strong self-imposed commitment of GPTPers to maintain the high quality of debates, diversity of topics and impact of the results.

This year the workshop opened with a wonderful keynote address of Steve Grand on designing complex self-organizing phenotypes capable of planning, hoping, speculating or dreaming–"Do Grandroids dream of electric sheep?"[1]. Steve, the creator of a computer game called Creatures, is currently working on

---

[1] See http://cscs.umich.edu/PmWiki/Farms/GPTP-11/field.php?n=Main.PublicPages

re-designing his complex virtual creatures with genetically designed nervous and bio-chemical systems with the goal of implementing imagination (consciousness) using artificial neurons. In his provocative talk Steve impressed the audience with his holistic approach to designing virtual life, emphasized the tremendous challenges in designing life-like creatures (e.g. visual invariance), and hypothesized about the essential characteristics necessary for a good design - self-organizing maps and a balance between a goal-oriented anticipation-intention-attention system (Yang) and a reality-based sensation-feedback system (Yin).

Steve Grand's talk, albeit not directly about genetic programming, gave a kick-start to critical, constructive, and reflective discussions on the past, present and future of the field of AI, EC and GP.

In three days starting from May 12 we listened to thirteen chapter presentations with recent results on GP in practice and in theory. Many discussions this year could be split into discussions on general-purpose GP and GP symbolic regression for data fitting. We summarize the main themes presented and discussed this year below.

Important topics in general purpose GP were (with references to relevant GPTP chapters in parentheses):

- Modularity and subsequently the scalability of GP (Spector et al.; Moore et al.);

- Foundations of evolvability of GP (see Moore et al for a strategy of co-evolving operators in GP);

- Theoretical results on computational complexity in GP (Neumann et al.);

- Theoretical understanding of operators locality for phenotypes (McDermott et al.);

- Human competitive results achieved with GP (Sipper);

- The need for important high-impact problems that can be solved with GP (Moore et al.; Korns; Truscott and Korns);

- The need for multiple search and selection criteria (Silva et al., Moore et al., McConaghy);

- The risks of search stagnation with rigid objectives and risks of cutting off paths to the solutions (Stanley et al.; Spector et al., Looks et al.);

- The need for novelty (Stanley et al.);

- The foundations of empowering GP search with expert knowledge (Moore et al., Poli et al., Sipper);

GP symbolic regression (SR) has always been an important and well-represented subfield in GPTP workshops, and this year as in previous years half of the chapters were devoted to it. Symbolic regression as a mode of genetic programming enjoys all the challenges of general purpose GP mentioned above as well as some additional questions historically raised for symbolic regression (SR) problems:

- How to guarantee reproducibility of SR? (Korns; McConaghy);

- How to validate SR results for problems where no single answer exists (O'Reilly et al.);

- How to measure and control genotypic complexity? Did we solve the bloat problem? (Silva et al., Poli et al.);

- How to control phenotypic complexity? Can we identify, monitor, and avoid over-fitting? (Silva et al.);

- How to guarantee operator locality (local adaptation) to pursue a continuous evolution of accuracy? (Korns);

- Is there a unified comprehensive collection of hard SR benchmarks? (O'Reilly et al.; Korns);

- Do we have a machine learning envy? Why is SR not accepted as a standard off-the-shelf data fitting approach? Should we make comparison studies of SR with common machine learning approaches and (regularized) linear regression? Or is symbolic regression in a different league (as a hypothesis and insight-generating system in the presence of expert knowledge)? Should we solve somebody else's (ML) problems or we need to identify our own unique problems and solve them (with or without SR)? (McConaghy, Korns).

Research on symbolic regression generated a lot of controversy during the discussions this year. The goal of the discussions was to accept and understand the symbolic regression paradox. On the one hand, the SR technology emerged as a simple illustration (almost a side effect) of genetic programming where an individual's genotype is coded as a parse tree of variable length and the goal of the search is data fitting. On the other hand, it is generally accepted as the most successful, and definitely most researched mode of genetic programming (it is definitely more successful than the true goal of GP - automatic programming). The fraction of scientific results being published on symbolic regression and its applications is very large compared to the total amount of results on GP, but more and more of these publications report on successful application of SR to real-life problems rather than on substantial algorithmic improvements to SR via GP.

The feeling of many people in SR community is that the field has become mature. The technology has demonstrated competitive advantage in many industries – financial, mining, chemical, food, and in many sciences - mathematics, social sciences, medical sciences. Despite obvious and well accepted scalability issues to massive data sets (computational complexity grows nonlinearly with the number of driving input variables), the range of problems where SR can be successfully applied is still vast (here we talk about problems with hundreds of dimensions and hundreds to millions of records).

A natural worry about a technology becoming successful and gaining industrial strength is the fear of scientific stagnation. This fear in one way or another was expressed this year in the discussions. Steve Grand expressed a provocative hypothesis reflecting on one of the discussions–Artificial intelligence (AI) started as a field aimed to understand human intelligence, but it quickly converged (and stagnated) to the natural language processing problems (because of high initial success of the latter). What if Genetic Programming, started as a field to implement automated programming, will, like AI, converge (and stagnate) to symbolic regression?

While SR produces human-competitive results in many application areas, application of Automated programming with GP is still very far from maturity. The overall consensus is that the real challenges are lying in the original GP arena.

A suggestion to ban symbolic regression from GPTP for next year to give room to results from other fields on program evolution generated a lot of controversy. Symbolic regression is "paying the bills" and is therefore the main focus of several groups of GPTP participants. However, the suggestion emphasized the generally acknowledged thirst for results on general-purpose GP, and GP for automated programming.

Another interesting idea was that symbolic regression and automated programming are just the two ends of a continuum of problems relevant for genetic programming: from Symbolic Regression to Evolution of executable variable length structures to Automatic Programming. And while the 'simplest' application of GP to data fitting, SR, is well studied and reasonably understood, more effort must be put into the rest of the continuum, i.e., problems where a solution is a computer program.

The search for such problems should be one of the goals for future GPTP workshops.

2.   Participant Reflections: Goals, Results, Challenges and Directions

To better understand GPTP participants' views of their research and how it fits with and is served by GPTP workshops and the GP field in general, with an eye toward continually improving GPTP workshops in future, we solicited more detailed feedback from GPTP-2011 participants, including their ideas on four important questions:

1. What is the main motivating scientific question related to the use of GP in your own work?

2. What are the useful ideas that came out of the talks and discussions this year?

3. What are the current GP challenges in retrospect of the talks and discussions at GPTP this year?

4. What are the Theory and Practice directions in GP that you would like to see pursued at future workshops?

We appreciate all the insightful responses the participants gave to these questions and are happy to share them here.

Question 1: What is the main motivating scientific question related to the use of GP in your own work?

–How can GP be enhanced to support the flexible evolution of programs with complex modular architectures? *Lee Spector*

–In our work on brain computer interfaces we used GP because we needed to solve very difficult problems for which there is virtually not previous design wisdom that can be applied. We turned to GP after having used semi-linear transformations, such as wavelet transforms and support vector machines, which gave reasonable results, but were particularly sensitive to noise and artifacts. *Riccardo Poli and Mathew Salvaris*

–Near-term: Can I ship it? Longer-term: How can GP help to make a large positive impact on the world? Specific questions that are a surrogate of this Q: How can I use GP towards achieving a billion dollars or a Nobel? *Trent McConaghy*

– GP is not *used* in our work; GP *is* our work. In other words, the focus of our work is not on applications using GP, but it is on how to better understand and improve the functioning of GP. So the probably ever ending questions that we try to answer are: can GP be improved? How? *Leonardo Vanneschi, Sara Silva*

– GP offers a platform to help answer the question of whether evolutionary computation can serve as an engine for open-ended discovery and innovation. *Ken Stanley*

– The major breakthrough (or quantum leap) in my mind would be the application of GP to the world of software in general; more specifically, using GP to evolve software. Harman (2010) wrote that, "...despite its current widespread use, there was, within living memory, equal skepticism about whether compiled code could be trusted. If a similar change of attitude to evolved code occurs over time...". Possibly, just as compilers are as common as the cold today, and nobody looks at compiled code (well, I guess unless you're one of the few compiler writers...), all of us implicitly trusting compiled code, there could be a day when evolution goes ubiquitous. Then, evolved code will go the same way as compiled code: We'll merrily evolve away — and simply put to use... *Moshe Sipper*

– How a system is able to learn a symbolic executable function that can be used as a classifier or model and how to embed this system into a larger framework that can optimize? How the embarrassingly parallel nature of GP can leverage it to become a solution method of choice for very large (exascale) distributed machine learning problems? *Una-May O'Reilly*

– I am interested in Symbolic Regression to answer questions that have previously proven to be insoluble in Social Science Research. I am also interest in the use of Abstract Expression Grammars that will allow a genetic search process to take place which will be probabilistic and yet guided by one or more socio-economic theories. *Philip Truscott*

– When dealing with hard search problems, the choice of representation can be the difference between success and failure. A badly-behaved mapping from genotype to fitness can cause search to fail. In our research we attempt to understand the behaviour of the genotype to fitness mapping. *James McDermott*

– I'm interested in applications of GP in domains where there are no clear optima but where finding many diverse local optima is desired. To this end, I'm interested in GP as a perpetual local optima finder that scales in quality and speed with distributed processing power. *Babak Hodjat*

– How can I transform GP from a black box algorithm that understands nothing about my complex problems to a competent algorithm that solves problems as I would if I had sufficient time to tinker? *Jason Moore*

–What are the limits of using GP/SR to extract relationships from real world data? How does this compare to learnability using other machine learning techniques? Can we get our algorithms to the point that they become ubiquitous? *Guido Smits*

Question 2: What are the useful ideas that came out of the talks and discussions this year?

One of the goals of GPTP workshops is to invite GPTP practitioner and theorists to get together to share the most recent and best working ideas about the nots and bolts of GP. GPTP publications of previous years as well as the current volume are a very illustrative example that idea spreading actually works. We asked this question to estimate the impact of presentations on the future work of GPTP-2011 participants.

– Many things... including John Holland's comments about the evolution of tag matching mechanisms in nature, Trent's new non-GP approach to symbolic regression, meta-evolutionary ideas that came out of a conversation with Ken Stanley, developments in other approaches to program induction mentioned by Moshe Looks. *Lee Spector*

– It's a long list, everything was invigorating! Near-term: Pennachin et al. on affine arithmetic. Hodjat's cool hack for cheap cloud resources. Longer-term: The talks on modularity (Spector; Stanley and Lehman), software synthesis / games (Spector; Sipper), and BCI (Poli et al), raised the most questions for me. And of course my own talk on a non-GP approach to a "traditional" GP problem *Trent McConaghy*

– We very much liked the idea of optimizing novelty in a GP population, presented by Lehman and Stanley. In particular, we believe in the effectiveness of the idea in case of premature convergence when standard fitness is used. We would also try to implement a multi-objective system optimizing usual fitness and novelty together and test them on our applications. *Silva and Vannecshi*

– Discussions of the role of diversity maintenance in evolutionary algorithms at GPTP inspired my co-author Joel Lehman and I to consider some potential future research directions. *Ken Stanley*

– The most relevant work to my own was Lee's. Creating named objects (variables) is something we could definitely use too. *Moshe Sipper*

– I may reconsider different representations such as stacks though I am still intimidated by the complexity of PushGP. Maybe linear GP. I will remind myself to make sure I am attending to population diversity. I want to try out Triple Shot or FFX and evaluate where it is superior and inferior to GPSR. I would implement the affine arithmetic if a need for its benefits arise in my problem domains. *Una-May O'Reilly*

– I was very interested in Trent's "Triple Shot" presentation and I would like to see a comparison of that approach with Symbolic Regression on some specific problems in a future paper to more fully understand the difference. *Philip Truscott*

– At GPTP this year some novel representations were described: we would be interested in investigating their genotype-fitness mappings. There was discussion of information-theoretic distances, a key tool in describing mapping behaviour. Some of the bloat control methods discussed have already been implemented in our current software. *James McDermott*

– I was quite interested in the application of novelty search in increasing diversity in a GP run. I liked the idea of a multi-layered GP where the reproduction functions are also evolved. In the same presentation, I liked the very pragmatic introduction of human expert interjection in the evolutionary process. The discussions on module evolution were interesting and gave me some ideas as to how to implement them in my system. The AA+ method presented was also interesting. *(Babak Hodjat)*

– I was very inspired by the outstanding presentations and the informative discussions. There were three things that I found particularly interesting. First, I was fascinated by Steve Grand's idea to develop artificial life with a consciousness. What does this mean for GP (and life in general) if he succeeds? Second, I found Lee Spector's use of tags to be intriguing. The role of tags in my own work needs to be fleshed out but I think it has great potential. Finally, I very much liked Ken Stanley's work on novelty search. He generated a lot of useful discussion at the workshop. *Jason Moore*

–The discussions on 'novelty' and the development of 'modularity' were quite interesting. It's always nice to have an out-of-the-box keynote that is provocative and makes you put things in a different perspective. *Guido Smits*

Question 3: What are the current GP challenges in retrospect of the talks and discussions at GPTP this year?

Another goal of GPTP workshops is to be a representation of state-of-the-art technological solutions in theory and practice of GP. Because we believe that state-of-the-art solutions are always delivered as a response to well-stated research challenges, we've been trying to formulate and publish these challenges in GPTP volumes. The goals and interests in GPTP community are very diverse, as illustrated by the answers on the main motivating scientific question. Another related question to ask is whether researchers with such diverse interests are faced with the common challenges (challenges which are fundamental to GP). The answers of collective conscience of GPTP are below: (Our own opinion as well as a summary of answers will follow in the last section of this Introduction.)

– Too hard to summarize! But I guess one thing is that I think that our biggest challenges, long term, relate not to specialized GP subsets/applications such as symbolic regression (as useful as these may be, and of course there are still important challenges in these areas too) but rather to the evolution of broader classes of useful computer programs. *Lee Spector*

– How can we make GP in general a technology? What are the most fruitful areas for GP research? What "traditional" GP problems are amenable to a completely different approach? *Trent McConaghy*

– Michael Korns had a good point on this: some problems are still difficult to solve with GP, even though their formulation is amazingly simple... a more deep understanding of the reasons why a problem is easy or hard to solve by GP is one of our main challenges. Compared to the past, when difficulty studies were just done on training data, we wish to extend the study to the generalization ability of GP to out-of-sample data. Last but not least, we wish to not limit the study to symbolic regression, but to extend it to other kinds of problems. *Leonardo Vannecshi and Sara Silva)*

– The main challenge for GP is to broaden its scope sufficiently to attract the interest of communities outside the traditional GP community. *Ken Stanley*

– Obviously, symbolic regression going automatic and commercial was the biggest theme this year... *Moshe Sipper*

– We need to review and possibly revise our "raison d'etre" with respect to our motivation to learn executable expressions and whether using evolutionary models for our search algorithm (i.e. a population and crossover) is important or coincidental? Are we still interested in program search? Or is program construction (by FFT) sufficient for our goals?

We appear ready to push into automatic programming research community domains and might be able to use GPTP as a means of driving the automatic programming GP capability up.

We are always in need of integrating modeling problems from outside of GPSR into the fold. *Una-May O'Reilly*

– I think the development of GP software is clearly a fascinating topic that is only at the start of what I think will be a long and fruitful life in research. I think some kind of Web site or organization that explains what the different Symbolic Regression packages can (and cannot do) will be a big plus for the users. I also think we could stimulate further research by publishing a "challenge file" that with various data sets that contain difficult symbolic regression problems. The file should be freely downloadable from a Web site and the challenges should have no noise so the "winners" know they have reached a solution immediately. *Philip Truscott*

– We believe that the biggest challenge for GP is a principled method of explaining why GP works for some problems and fails for others. The proposal of a suite of simple, difficult symbolic regression problems was a response to this. There was also an emphasis on clever hacks that make GP, especially symbolic regression, run more efficiently. All GP practitioners should be interested in the potential and the limits of such approaches. *James McDermott*

– I was somewhat surprised by what sounded like existential debates surrounding GP at the workshop. This is usually the mark of a young science still in search of a niche. I think the problem is much less that the merits of GP have yet to be articulated well, but that GP has yet to prove it's unique value in a noteworthy application area. I think we should work on making GP immediately synonymous with a certain application area, and the articulation and attention will follow. *Babak Hodjat*

– For the last few years I have been encouraged by the progress at GPTP on using GP to solve complex problems. This year, for the first time, I felt like we had taken a step backwards with the realization that GP, as currently implemented, has trouble with certain classes of complex problems. This is a natural speed bump for any computational intelligence method and I am confident that new and novel approaches will be introduced in the coming years to keep us moving forward. *Jason Moore*

– Still the original goal of automatic programming and the associated representations and fitness functions seem to be the biggest challenge. It seems the community is ready to reemphasize these aspects. *Guido Smits*

Question 4: What are the Theory and Practice directions in GP that you would like to see pursued at future workshops?

– I personally value the breadth of perspectives that we get from newcomers and from people from outside of GP. I really enjoyed the keynote this year (and subsequent, related conversations) and also the contributions of some of the "first timers." *Lee Spector*

– Works asking questions / problems like: (1) questions where GP can shed insight into the nature of evolution, complexity, or software, (2) novel problems where GP is the only currently known technique to solve it, (3) questions about the GP computational process, (4) problems where GP is one of many possible techniques to solve a problem, and benchmarks indicate that GP is competitive or best. In particular I would love to see more work on scalable estimation of distribution algorithms, software synthesis, and novel problems. *Trent McConaghy*

– A simple theoretical framework that can allow people that are not expert in our field to have a quick intuition on how and why GP works. A more sophisticated GP framework that can be used for applications, with the possibility of choosing among many pre-defined methods (standard GP, multi-optimization, operator equalization, fitness sharing, multi-population, etc.), or even better a framework that chooses among these methods automatically. *Sara Silva and Leonardo Vanneschi* – I think it would be very important to look at the issue of generalisation in GP. *Riccardo Poli*

– It would be interesting to discuss genetic encodings, such as indirect encoding and morphogenesis, and the implications of different such encodings for GP. *Ken Stanley*

– More on program evolution and induction. *Moshe Sipper*

– The new theory showed complexity results for ORDER and MAJORITY with 1+1 Hillclimbing with a mutation operator. How does a population affect these results? How does complexity control affect these results? Can we explore the relationship of GP to bayesian networks, stochastic search heuristics community? *Una-May O'Reilly*

– I have glanced at papers that cover using GP as a design tool for physical products. I would like to hear more about research in this area. *Philip Truscott*

– In future workshops, we would welcome further fundamental work on representational issues, in particular on principled methods of choosing the right representation for each problem. *James McDermott*

– I'm interested in massive distribution, and any theoretical analysis of the quality and performance improvement of such distribution. *Babak Hodjat*

– Large-scale application of competent GPs to real-world complex problems. *Jason Moore*

– What are the kinds of objective functions we need to get true GP that is broadly applicable to automatic programming and solving design problems? What are the consequences of open-ended evolution, speciation, niching, morphogenesis, self-organisation etc. *Guido Smits*

3.   Summary–Where we've been, work to be done

GPTP workshops are one-track invitation only events designed to high-light state-of-the-art GP results for theory and practice while maintaining the small size of the group (people should fit into one room at a round table). Every year in autumn we invite 13 to 16 people or groups to submit a chapter addressing one of the current challenges in the field of GP or reporting a substantial improvement in efficiency or effectiveness of GP evolution. In addition we also publish a call for chapters to solicit two to three chapters with important results that we overlooked while creating the list of invitees. We as the organizers are striving to create and facilitate the friendly atmosphere at GPTP where people would be motivated to share and objectively evaluate each other's results, review the global state of the field, identify the missing pieces, and make a passionate collective effort to develop the field of GP further.

We are happy to see that GPTP community has become so united and yet stayed very diverse over the last nine years (which is arguably ac characteristic of a community of very good friends or family members). The discussions have reached a new level intellectual depth and excitement—people are acquainted with each other's work, we speak each other's language, we have formulated our joint goals to push GP towards success, to prevent stagnation, and to facilitate dialogue.

One of important observation this year was that GPTP'ers seem to care more about development of the full range of GP applications and theory, rather than just caring about publishing/presenting their own work. For example, some people doing symbolic regression suggested that next year's GPTP (of more regularly if the need be) be completely devoted to program evolution without symbolic regression results at all. We will not ban SR from future workshops, but will respond to the unanimous quest for results in "hard-core" GP by changing the ratio of SR vs General-purpose (non SR) GP in GPTP-2012.

There is still lots of work to be done in general purpose GP. The present state of GP in theory and in practice is challenged by an "insufficient" amount of applications of GP to evolution of executable expressions (beyond symbolic regression), the need for scalability and a unified list of "hard" benchmarks of GP in it's currently most successful symbolic regression mode, the need for research on program evolution, the unsolved yet question on evolvability, and the need to back GP up with theoretical results.

The commonly acknowledged "blind spot" or missing piece this year was morphogenesis. How to understand the expressive powers of morphogenesis? What makes genes exploit the regularity in the environment?

Since the beginning of artificial evolution we have not moved much closer to an open-ended evolution, and understanding evolvability. What if artificial evolution does not work for that? Where does GP end and A-life begins?

Another controversial set of questions revolved around the question: Does search need an objective other than the search for novelty? Or is search is inherently multi-objective and there is a continuum of objectives, including novelty? Might it be that the "open-endedness" of artificial evolution is doomed because it is related to the problem of expressing the true search and continuum of objectives in a limited set?

Many more questions remain to be answered:

- How to do program synthesis and program transformation? How to define problems where a solution is a computer program? What kinds of executable architectures should we be evolving?

- Where is inherent parallelism of GP? Should we get everybody to run GP on a cloud?

- Who does not want to get 1 billion people to use GP? Is GP on smart phones a solution?

- Can evolutionary biology help GP?

- What are opportunities of GP as a science? Is it even possible to obtain computational complexity results for the simplest GP incarnation - symbolic regression?

- Do we still want to understand natural evolution? Do we still want to understand how brain works?

- If we ever get to Automated Programming, how long will it be to get to Automated Design?

We want to see these questions addressed in the future GPTP workshops and will do our best to provide all conditions necessary for fruitful discussions regarding these questions. Please, contact us, if you are interested in presenting work related to questions above in GPTP-2012.

As for GPTP 2011 it was yet another enjoyable, energetic, envigorating, and intellectually challenging event where old friends met, new minds shined, and essential questions were asked. We are grateful to all sponsors and acknowledge the importance of their contributions to such an intellectually productive and regular event. The workshop is generously founded and sponsored by the University of Michigan Center for the Study of Complex Systems (CSCS) and receives further funding from the following people and organizations: Michael Korns , Bill Worzel of Genetics Squared, John Koza of Third Millenium, Babak Hodjat of Genetic Finance LLC, Mark Kotanchek of Evolved Analytics, Jason Moore of the Computational Genetics Laboratory of Dartmouth College, Conor Ryan of the Biocomputing and Developmental Systems Group of the University of Limerick, Trent McConaghy and Stu Card of Critical Technologies Inc.

We thank all the participants of GPTP-2011 for a wonderful workshop! Let's keep it this way!

Chapter 1

WHAT'S IN AN EVOLVED NAME?
THE EVOLUTION OF MODULARITY VIA
TAG-BASED REFERENCE

Lee Spector[*†], Kyle Harrington[‡], Brian Martin[*], Thomas Helmuth[†]

[*]*Cognitive Science, Hampshire College, Amherst, MA, 01002 USA.*

[†]*Computer Science, University of Massachusetts, Amherst, MA, 01003 USA.*

[‡]*Computer Science, Brandeis University, Waltham, MA, 02453 USA.*

Abstract

Programming languages provide a variety of mechanisms to associate names with values, and these mechanisms play a central role in programming practice. For example, they allow multiple references to the same storage location or function in different parts of a complex program. By contrast, the representations used in current genetic programming systems provide few if any naming mechanisms, and it is therefore generally not possible for evolved programs to use names in sophisticated ways. In this chapter we describe a new approach to names in genetic programming that is based on Holland's concept of tags. We demonstrate the use of tag-based names, we describe some of the ways in which they may help to extend the power and reach of genetic programming systems, and we look at the ways that tag-based names are actually used in an evolved program that solves a robot navigation problem.

Keywords: genetic programming, modularity, names, tags, stack-based genetic programming, Push programming language, PushGP

1.   Programming with Names

It would be hard to imagine a modern computer programming language that did not allow programmers to name data objects and functional modules. Indeed, even the simplest assembly languages allow programmers to label defined code and data and then, later, to use those labels to refer to the defined items. The binding of names is also a fundamental operation in the interpretation of lambda expressions, which provide the semantic foundations of programming language theory.

Certainly for any task that lends itself to hierarchical, modular decomposition, a programmer will want to assign names to modules and to use those names to allow modules to refer to one another. Because we can expect most complex real-world problems to fit this description to some extent—as Simon put it, hierarchy is "one of the central structural schemes that the architect of complexity uses" (Simon, 1969)—we can understand why naming is such an important element of programming language design.

Indeed, naming is so important that language designers accommodate it even though it complicates both language and compiler design in a variety of ways. The grammars of most programming languages fail to be fully context free because name definitions and uses must match, and special measures must be taken to ensure program validity and the proper handling of name references in the context of language-specific rules for name scope and extent.

The concept of a "name" is not, however, completely straightforward. A great many subtleties in the use of names have been noted by philosophers of language and logic over millennia, with seminal contributions to the theory of names having been made by Aristotle, John Stuart Mill, Gottlob Frege, Bertrand Russell, and others. Many of these theories consider names to be abbreviated descriptions, a characterization that might apply to binding forms in declarative languages such as Prolog, but which does not seem to apply to names as used in imperative or functional programming languages. Arguably the most significant recent work was done by Saul Kripke, whose *Naming and Necessity* breaks from the tradition of description-based theories of names and presents a causal theory that accounts for proper names as "rigid designators" (Kripke, 1972). While natural languages and programming languages are quite different, aspects of Kripke's theory do seem to apply to names in imperative and functional programming languages as well. The key insight is that a name is associated with a referent through an act of "dubbing" or "baptism," after which the name will designate the referent.[1]

How does this concept of naming apply to programming practice? In most programming languages the programmer can use definitions to perform the "dubbing" action, after which the defined names can be used to refer to the values provided in the definitions. Names may also occur within named values, of course, and these will in turn refer to values that were associated with those names in previous definitions. The use of a name that has not been defined is generally an error that halts compilation or execution; this has implications for the evolution of name-using programs, as discussed below. Additional compli-

---

[1] Kripke's theory is considerably more complicated than this, and is expressed in terms of his "possible world semantics." We will not be concerned with these complications here.

cations are introduced when the same name is defined more than once; different programming languages deal with this issue in different ways, expressed through the languages' rules for scope and extent.

What about names in genetic programming? In the simplest traditional genetic programming systems, such as that described in (Koza, 1992), no explicit facilities for naming are provided. In systems with automatically defined, functions, such as that described in (Koza, 1994), evolving programs define and use names for functions and their arguments but the numbers and types of names are specified in advance by the human who is using the system; they do not arise from the genetic programming process. In systems with "architecture-altering operations," like that described in (Koza et al., 1999), the number and types of names do indeed emerge from the evolutionary process but only through the use of considerably more complicated program variation operators that must ensure that calls to functions match their definitions and that all names are defined before they are used. Furthermore, the programs produced by these systems can only use names in certain pre-defined ways; for example, they cannot dynamically redefine names as they run, as many programs written by humans do.

However, even in the simplest traditional genetic programming systems one can include functions in the function set that provide name-like capabilities. Perhaps the most straightforward of these is "indexed memory," in which "write" and "read" functions store and retrieve values by integer indices (Teller, 1994). In a sense, indexed memory provides a naming scheme in which names are integers and in which undefined names refer to a default value (e.g. zero). The standard indexed memory scheme does not permit the naming of code, but one could imagine simple extensions that would allow this.

Of course, there are now many other forms of genetic programming, and different opportunities for naming may arise in each of them. Any system that permits the evolution of modules of any kind must have some way of referring to the modules that have been defined, and such systems will therefore have to have some capabilities or conventions for naming (Koza, 1990; Koza, 1992; Angeline and Pollack, 1993; Kinnear, Jr., 1994; Spector, 1996; Bruce, 1997; Racine et al., 1998; Roberts et al., 2001; Li et al., 2005; Jonyer and Himes, 2006; Hornby, 2007; Hemberg et al., 2007; Walker and Miller, 2008; Shirakawa and Nagao, 2009; Wijesinghe and Ciesielski, 2010). Some other systems use forms of reference based on pattern matching (Ray, 1991), which bear some similarities to the tag-based naming scheme that we present below. However, we do not believe that any of these systems have demonstrated the full gains that we should expect from capabilities for the flexible evolution of complex modular architectures .

In this chapter we describe work on a new technique for naming that is based on "tags" as described by Holland (Holland, 1993; Holland, 1995). Tags have been used in a variety of contexts, most notably in work on the evolution of cooperation (e.g. (Riolo et al., 2001; Spector and Klein, 2006; Soule, 2011)), but their use for naming in genetic programming is new. We will argue that this new technique provides powerful new capabilities.

Although tag-based names can conceivably be used in many kinds of genetic programming systems, our work to date has been conducted with PushGP, a genetic programming system that evolves programs expressed in the Push programming language. We will therefore next present the core concepts of Push, including the facilities for naming that have long existed in Push but which have never been shown to be useful for program evolution. We will then introduce tags and describe how they may be used to name modules in various kinds of genetic programming systems, with a focus on their implementation in PushGP. Following the description of the technique we discuss recent results that demonstrate the utility of tag-based modularity on standard problems, and we look in detail at the ways that tags are actually used in evolved programs. We conclude with a number of directions for future work.

2.   Push and Push Names

The Push programming language was designed for use in evolutionary computation systems, as the language in which evolving programs are expressed (Spector, 2001; Spector and Robinson, 2002a; Spector et al., 2005). It is a stack-based language in which a separate stack is used for each data type, with instructions taking their arguments from—and leaving their results on—stacks of the appropriate types. This allows instructions and literals to be intermixed regardless of type without jeorardizing execution safety. Instructions act as "no-ops" (that is, they do nothing) if they find insufficient arguments on stacks. Push implementations now exist in C++, Java, JavaScript, Python, Common Lisp, Clojure, Scheme, Erlang, and R. Many of these are available for free download from the Push project page.[2]

In Push "code" is itself a data type. A variety of powerful capabilities are supported by the fact that Push programs can manipulate their own code on the "exec" stack, which stores the actual execution queue of the program during execution, and on the "code" stack, which stores code but is otherwise treated as any other data stack. Push programs can transform their own code in ways that produce the effects of automatically defined, functions (Koza, 1992; Koza, 1994) or automatically defined, macros (Spector, 1996) without pre-specification of the number of modules and without more complex mechanisms such as architecture-altering operations (Koza et al., 1999). Push supports the evolution of recursion, iteration, combinators, co-routines, and novel

---

[2]http://hampshire.edu/lspector/push.html

control structures, all through combinations of the built-in code-manipulation instructions. PushGP, the genetic programming system used for the work presented below, was designed to be as simple and generic as possible (e.g. it has no automatically defined functions, strong typing mechanisms, or syntactic constraints) aside from using Push as the language for evolving programs, but it can nonetheless produce programs with all of the features described above because of the expressive power of the Push language itself.

Push supports several forms of program modularity that do *not* involve naming. For example, a Push program can use standard stack-manipulation instructions on the exec stack (e.g. `exec.dup`, which duplicates the top element of the exec stack, and `exec.rot`, which rotates the top three items on the exec stack) to cause sub-programs to be executed multiple times, providing a form of modular code reuse. More exotic forms of nameless modularity can be implemented by manipulating code in arbitrary ways prior to execution, using Push's full suite of code manipulation instructions that were inspired by Lisp's list manipulation functions (including versions of `car`, `cdr`, `list`, `append`, `subst`, etc.). Push also includes versions of the K, S and Y *combinators* in combinatory logic (Schönfinkel, 1924; Curry and Feys, 1958), each of which performs a specific transformation on the exec stack to support the concise expression of arbitrary recursive functions. These mechanisms have been shown to support the evolution of programs with evolved control structures that are in some senses modular and that solve a wide range of problems. For example, even before the introduction of the exec stack manipulation instructions (which appeared with "Push 3" in 2005 (Spector et al., 2005)) Push's code manipulation mechanisms had been shown to automatically produce modular solutions to parity problems (Spector and Robinson, 2002a) and to induce modules in response to a dynamic, fitness environment (Spector and Robinson, 2002b). More recent work, using Push 3, has produced solutions to a wide range of standard problems (including list reversal, factorial regression, Fibonacci regression, parity, exponentiation, and sorting (Spector et al., 2005)) along with the production of human-competitive results in quantum circuit design (Spector, 2004) and pure mathematics (Spector et al., 2008).

But what about named modules? Push includes a data type for names, along with instructions for associating names with values and for retrieving named values, but the use of names has never been evident in evolved programs. One can write Push programs that use names by hand, but such programs have not readily emerged from genetic programming runs. This has been an issue of concern to the Push development team, and consequently the details of the ways in which Push handles names have been revised and refined several times over the history of the project. The current version of the language specification, for Push 3 (Spector et al., 2004), allows names to be defined and used quite parsimoniously.

For example, consider this program fragment from (Spector et al., 2005):

```
(times2 exec.define (2 integer.*))
```

Because `times2` is not a pre-defined Push instruction and does not yet have a defined value the interpreter will push it onto the name stack when it is processed. When `exec.define` is processed it will pop the name stack and associate the popped name (`times2`) with the item that is then on top of the exec stack (which will then be (`2 integer.*`); the exec stack will also be popped). Subsequent references to `times2`, unless they are quoted, will cause the value (`2 integer.*`) to be pushed onto the exec stack, with the effect that `times2` will act as a named subroutine for doubling the number on top of the integer stack. Of course one could do the same thing with any arbitrarily complex module code.

However, even though the Push 3 naming scheme is both powerful and parsimonious we have rarely seen it used in significant ways in evolved programs. Why? Our most recent thinking on this question has focused on the difficulty of matching name definitions and references, which depends in part on the number of names in circulation and in part on the details of the genetic programming system's code generation and variation algorithms. Concerning the former, one faces a dilemma because the best way to promote the matching of definitions and references is to provide only a small number of names, but doing so would also limit the complexity of the name-based modular architectures that can possibly evolve, which is antithetical to our research and development goals. A variety of approaches to this dilemma might be envisioned, and we have explored options such as gradually increasing the number of available names over the course of a genetic programming run. But the measures that we have taken have not been particularly effective. One can also envision a variety of modifications to code generation and variation algorithms that would encourage or enforce the proper matching of name definitions and references, for example by adding definition and reference expressions to programs only in matched pairs and by repairing mismatches after crossover. Such approaches deserve study, but we are more interested in approaches that allow name-use strategies to emerge more naturally from the evolutionary process, without putting constraints on the ways in which names can be used and without requiring the re-engineering of the overarching evolutionary algorithm.[3]

This is the context within which we turn to the concept of tags, to provide a mechanism for naming and reference that is more suited to use in genetic programming systems.

---

[3] It is particularly desirable to avoid constraints on code generation and variation in meta-genetic programming systems and autoconstructive evolution systems, in which code generation and variation algorithms are themselves subject to random variation and selection. But we think it is desirable to do this even in the context of standard genetic programming with hand-designed code generation and variation algorithms.

3.   Tags

John Holland, in his work on general principles of complex adaptive systems, has presented an abstraction of a wide variety of matching, binding, and aggregation mechanisms based on the concept of a "tag" (Holland, 1993; Holland, 1995). A tag in this context is an initially meaningless identifier that can come to have meaning through the matches in which it participates. Holland provides several examples of tag-like mechanisms in human societies and in biological systems, including banners or flags used by armies and "the 'active sites' that enable antibodies to attach themselves to antigens" (Holland, 1995, p. 13). In some but not all of the examples of tag usage presented by Holland and others the matching of tags may be inexact, with binding occurring only if the degree of match exceeds a specified threshold, or with the closest matching candidate being selected for binding. This inexact matching will be crucial for the application to genetic programming that we present below.

One of the areas in which the concept of tags has been applied by several researchers is the study of the evolution of cooperation. For example, in the model of Riolo, Cohen, and Axelrod, one agent will donate to a second agent if difference between the tags of the two agents is less than the "tolerance" threshold of the donor (Riolo et al., 2001). In this model, and the related models that have subsequently been developed by others (Spector and Klein, 2006; Soule, 2011), tags and tolerances are allowed to change over evolutionary time. These studies show that the existence of a tagging mechanism can have major effects on the features of the systems that evolve, sometimes permitting the evolution of cooperation in contexts in which it would not otherwise emerge.

How can tags be used to address the issues described in the previous section, concerning the use of names in genetic programming? We suggest that tags be incorporated into genetic programming systems by providing mechanisms that allow programs to tag values (including values that contain executable code), along with mechanisms that allow for the retrieval and possible execution of tagged values. Tags differ from names in this context because we can allow inexact tag matching, and because this can better facilitate the coordination of "name definitions" (now "tagging" operations) and "name references" (now tag-based retrieval operations, also called "tag references"). In particular, we can specify that a tag reference will always recall the value with the closest matching tag. This will ensure that as long as *any* value has been tagged *all* subsequent tag references will retrieve *some* value. As more values are tagged with different tags, the values retrieved by particular tag references may change because there may be different closest matches at different times.[4] But at almost

---

[4]The set of tagged values will grow dynamically during program execution, as tagging instructions are executed. In addition, new tagging instructions may be added to programs over evolutionary time by

all times—except when no tagging actions have yet been performed—each tag reference will retrieve some tagged value. If our current thinking about the evolutionary weakness of ordinary names is correct then tag-based names, with "closest match" retrieval, should make it easier to evolve programs that make significant use of named (actually tagged) modules.

Versions of this general tagging scheme might be applied to a wide range of genetic programming systems. One implementation choice that must be made for any application concerns the representation of tags. In biology tags may be complex, structured objects, while in applications to the evolution of cooperation they have often been floating-point numbers with tag matching based on numerical differences.[5] In our work on tag-based modules in genetic programming we have used an even simpler representation in which tags are positive integers and tag matching is based on a ceiling function. We say that the closest match for a reference to tag t_{ref}, among all tags t_{val} that have been used to tag values, is the tag $t_{val} \geq t_{ref}$ for which $t_{val} - t_{ref}$ is minimal if at least some $t_{val} \geq t_{ref}$, or the smallest t_{val} if all $t_{val} < t_{ref}$. This means that if there is no exact match then we "count up" from the referenced tag until we find a tag that has been used to tag a value, wrapping back to zero if the referenced tag is greater than all of the tags that have been used.

Another implementation choice concerns the relation between tags, the instructions that tag values, and the instructions that use tags to retrieve values. It would be possible to treat tags as first-class data items, and to write tagging and tag reference instructions to take these data items as arguments. For the sake of parsimony, however, we have opted instead to embed tags within the tagging and tag reference instruction names so that, for example, an instruction such as tag.float.123 would be used to tag a floating-point value with the tag "123" and an instruction such as tagged.123 would be used to retrieve the value that has been tagged with the tag closest to "123."

In the context of these implementation decisions we can consider further steps required to provide tagging in various types of genetic programming systems. In the simplest traditional genetic programming systems, which represent programs as Lisp-style symbolic expressions and which do not include any facilities for automatically defined functions, we might support calls to one-argument functions of the form tag.i, which would act to tag the code in their argument positions with the tags embedded in their names (and presumably return some constant value or the results of evaluating their arguments), and also zero-argument functions of the form tagged-i, which would act as branches

---

mutation and by other genetic operators. Such events may cause a tag reference to refer to a different value than it referred to previously.

[5] In some of the work in this area tags are points in a multi-dimensional space, with matching determined by Euclidean distance (Spector and Klein, 2006).

to the code with the closest matching tag (or presumably return some constant value if no code had yet been tagged). The system's code generation routines would have to be modified to produce such function calls, and the program execution architecture would have to be modified to support an execution step limit that prevents unbounded recursion. This particular implementation would only allow the tagging of zero-argument functions, but it might nonetheless have utility.

Systems that already support automatically defined, functions and architecture-altering operations present different opportunities, and we might begin by simply replacing function names with tags, both in definitions and in calls. This would allow us to drop many of the measures that must ordinarily be taken in such systems to ensure that all calls refer to defined functions, since calls would refer to the function with the closest matching tag (or to some default function if no function has yet been defined). Measures would still have to be taken to ensure that the numbers of arguments in calls match the numbers of parameters of definitions, but initial experiments might be conducted with settings that mandate a single, constant number of parameters for all automatically defined functions.

In the context of Push it is quite simple to define even more general and powerful tagging and tag-reference mechanisms. Each tagging instruction, of the form `tag.<type>.`i, pops the stack of the specified type and associates the popped value with the specified tag. As with all other Push instructions, if the needed value is not on the specified stack then the instruction does nothing. Tagging instructions specifying a type of "code" or "exec" can be used to tag bodies of code, which can be used as named (tagged) code modules that take any number of arguments and return any number of values. Instructions of the form `tagged.`i retrieve the value with the closest matching tag and push it onto the exec stack. If the value is a literal of some type other than code then its execution will push it onto the appropriate stack, following the standard Push execution semantics. If the value is code then it will be executed. Additional instructions (not used here) of the form `tagged.code.`i retrieve tagged values to the code stack rather than the exec stack, allowing for further manipulation prior to execution. And additional instructions (also not used here) of the form `untag.`i can be used to remove tags from previously tagged values.

In previous work (Spector et al., 2011) we have demonstrated that tag usage readily emerges in runs of PushGP and that the availability of tags allows PushGP to scale well on problems such as the lawnmower problem, which Koza used to show that systems with automatically defined functions scaled better than those without them (Koza, 1994). In fact, the results showed that PushGP with tags scaled better than PushGP with combinators and exec stack manipulation instructions, which are the PushGP mechanisms that had previously been most effective in supporting the evolution of modularity. It is therefore clear that we have succeeded in our goal of developing a way to evolve programs using arbitrary named (tagged) values, and it is also clear that this capability does indeed enhance the power of genetic programming.

4.   What's in an Evolved Name?

Our prior work showed that tags can support the evolution of modularity and that this capability can allow a genetic programming system to scale well on problems that have regularities that can be exploited by modular programs (Spector et al., 2011). But in the prior work we did not study the modules that were actually produced by genetic programming. In the remainder of this chapter we take this additional step.

One of the problems to which we applied PushGP with tags in our prior work is the "dirt-sensing, obstacle-avoiding robot problem" (originally described in (Spector, 1996)). This problem is much like the lawnmower problem, in which one seeks a program that causes a robotic lawnmower to mow the grass in all of the squares in a "lawn" grid, but with the following modifications: the metaphor is changed from lawn mowing to mopping, there are irregularly placed objects through which the robot cannot move, and sensors are provided for dirt and for obstacles. Each program is tested on two grids with differently placed obstacles. The details of the problem specification and system configuration are not relevant to our purposes here, but the interested reader may consult (Spector et al., 2011).[6]

In one PushGP run on this problem, on an 8×12 grid, we evolved a successful program that had the modular calling structure shown in Figure 1-1 for one of the two obstacle placements on which it was tested, and the modular calling structure shown in Figure 1-2 for the other obstacle placement. Each of these figures was produced by tracing tag references dynamically during a run of an automatically simplified version of the evolved program, with each unique retrieved value being represented as a distinct node in the graph and with Module 0 being added to the graph to represent the entire program (with which execution starts). The thicknesses of the node outlines indicate the size of the code in the corresponding modules. Arrows between nodes indicate that the module at the tail of an arrow initiates a call of the module at the head of the arrow, and the numbers by the arrows indicate the number of times that such calls are made in a single execution of the program.

There are many interesting things to note about these diagrams. First it is interesting to note that they are different, which means that the program executes different code, with altered modular architectures, when it confronts different environments. But there are also many commonalities between the

---

[6]See also the source code and erratum note at http://hampshire.edu/lspector/tags-gecco-2011.

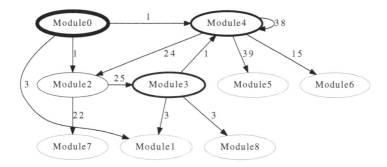

Figure 1-1. The modular calling structure of an evolved solution to the dirt-sensing, obstacle-avoiding robot problem when executed on one particular 8 × 12 grid.

two diagrams. In particular, each shows that module 4, which is relatively large and complex, is used as a main loop that makes many calls to Module 2 which in turn calls Module 3. Table 1-1 shows the actual code associated with each module, and while we have not presented enough details about the problem or instructions to explain this code completely, we can nonetheless see, for example, that Module 3 is the only one of the large and frequently called modules that performs obstacle sensing; we can therefore infer that it serves as something like a subroutine for obstacle avoidance.

In producing these diagrams we also noticed that this evolved program does not dynamically redefine any tagged modules after their first uses. That is, it is never the case that the same tag retrieves two different values at different times during the execution of the program. This is interesting in part because it is an emergent property that is not mandated by the tagging mechanism; programs that perform dynamic redefinition may be produced in other runs.

One other interesting observation regarding this solution is that it treats module boundaries in unconventional ways. For example, Module 3 ends with (if-dirty frog) which is *part* of a conditional expression. If the robot is facing a dirty grid location then frog will be executed, but if it is not then the first expression in the code that *follows* the call to Module 3—in this case this will be tagged.10, in Module 2—will be executed. Furthermore, if the robot is facing a dirty grid location then not only will frog be executed but also the call to tagged.10, which is not textually within the same module as the if-dirty conditional, will be skipped. This arrangement clearly has utility but it is quite unusual from the perspective of ordinary human programming practice.

5. Conclusions and Future Work

We have described a new technique for evolving programs that use name-like designators to refer to code and data modules, and we have situated this

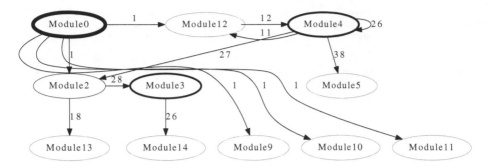

Figure 1-2. The modular calling structure of the same evolved solution to the dirt-sensing, obstacle-avoiding robot problem that produced the structure diagrammed in Figure 1-1 but, in this case, executed on a different 8 × 12 grid.

Table 1-1. Code modules retrieved by tag references in an automatically simplified version of an evolved solution to the 8 × 12s dirt-sensing, obstacle-avoiding robot problem. See (Spector et al., 2011) for full descriptions of the instructions used for this problem.

Module #	Tag #	Value
0	[main]	[omitted to conserve space]
1	242	mop
2	608	(tag.exec.489 frog left tagged.220 tagged.10)
3	238	((left) (if-obstacle (if-obstacle) (mop if-dirty if-obstacle left mop) (if-obstacle (left tagged.243 tagged.239 left)) tag.exec.770) (tagged.343) (if-dirty frog))
4	360	((mop mop (mop mop left mop tag.exec.143 v8a if-dirty if-dirty left tagged.435) (if-dirty) (tagged.662 tag.exec.91) (if-dirty mop)) (if-dirty if-dirty tagged.580) (tagged.336))
5	489	frog
6	695	if-obstacle
7	143	v8a
8	245	left
9	200	left
10	920	left
11	258	mop
12	770	tagged.343
13	90	mop
14	248	frog

new mechanism within the literature of related mechanisms that have been used in genetic programming. In previous work we demonstrated that this new mechanism, which is based on Holland's concept of tags, supports the evolution of modular programs and allows genetic programming to scale well on certain benchmark problems. Here we also exhibited the actual modular architectures produced by the system for the dirt-sensing, obstacle-avoiding robot problem . We believe that we have demonstrated that tags can support the evolution of programs with complex, modular architectures, and that they may therefore play an important role in the future application of genetic programming to complex, real-world problems.

We have outlined ways in which tags could be implemented genetic programming systems that evolve Lisp-like symbolic expressions, but we have only experimented with tag-based modularity in PushGP so far. An obvious area for future work is to implement and test versions of the technique in other kinds of genetic programming systems.

Among the other next steps that we would like to take are the tracing and analysis of tag usage over the course of evolutionary runs. We would expect tag usage to grow incrementally, and we would expect to see evolutionary transitions when new tags arise and "steal" references from pre-existing tags. We would also like to explore variations of the technique. For example, preliminary experiments in PushGP indicate that tag-based modules may arise even more readily if tagging instructions do not pop their arguments from their stacks, so that the insertion of a tagging instruction into a program is more likely to leave the functionality of the program unchanged until a tag reference instruction is later added; we would like to explore this variation more systematically. More ambitiously, would also like to investigate tag reference mechanisms that support more sophisticated notions of scope and extent, along with tag matching schemes in which the conditions for matching are themselves subject to variation and natural selection.[7]

Acknowledgments

Nathan Whitehouse, Daniel Gerow, Jaime Dávila, and Rebecca S. Neimark contributed to conversations in which some of the ideas used in this work were refined. Thanks also Jordan Pollack and the Brandeis DEMO lab for computational support, to the GPTP reviewers and discussion participants, and to Hampshire College for support for the Hampshire College Institute for Computational Intelligence.

This material is based upon work supported by the National Science Foundation under Grant No. 1017817. Any opinions, findings, and conclusions or

---

[7]As suggested by John Holland (personal communication).

recommendations expressed in this publication are those of the authors and do not necessarily reflect the views of the National Science Foundation.

References

Angeline, Peter J. and Pollack, Jordan (1993). Evolutionary module acquisition. In Fogel, D. and Atmar, W., editors, *Proceedings of the Second Annual Conference on Evolutionary Programming*, pages 154–163, La Jolla, CA, USA.

Bruce, Wilker Shane (1997). The lawnmower problem revisited: Stack-based genetic programming and automatically defined functions. In Koza, John R. et al., editors, *Genetic Programming 1997: Proceedings of the Second Annual Conference*, pages 52–57, Stanford University, CA, USA. Morgan Kaufmann.

Curry, H.B. and Feys, R. (1958). *Combinatory Logic*, 1.

Hemberg, Erik, Gilligan, Conor, O'Neill, Michael, and Brabazon, Anthony (2007). A grammatical genetic programming approach to modularity in genetic algorithms. In Ebner, Marc et al., editors, *Proceedings of the 10th European Conference on Genetic Programming*, volume 4445 of *Lecture Notes in Computer Science*, pages 1–11, Valencia, Spain. Springer.

Holland, J. (1993). The effect of labels (tags) on social interactions. Technical Report Working Paper 93-10-064, Santa Fe Institute, Santa Fe, NM.

Holland, J. H. (1995). *Hidden Order: How Adaptation Builds Complexity*. Perseus Books.

Hornby, G.S. (2007). Modularity, reuse, and hierarchy: measuring complexity by measuring structure and organization. *Complexity*, 13(2):50–61.

Jonyer, Istvan and Himes, Akiko (2006). Improving modularity in genetic programming using graph-based data mining. In Sutcliffe, Geoff C. J. and Goebel, Randy G., editors, *Proceedings of the Nineteenth International Florida Artificial Intelligence Research Society Conference*, pages 556–561, Melbourne Beach, Florida, USA. American Association for Artificial Intelligence.

Kinnear, Jr., Kenneth E. (1994). Alternatives in automatic function definition: A comparison of performance. In Kinnear, Jr., Kenneth E., editor, *Advances in Genetic Programming*, chapter 6, pages 119–141. MIT Press.

Koza, J. (1990). Genetic programming: A paradigm for genetically breeding populations of computer programs to solve problems. Technical Report STAN-CS-90-1314, Dept. of Computer Science, Stanford University.

Koza, John R. (1992). *Genetic Programming: On the Programming of Computers by Means of Natural Selection*. MIT Press, Cambridge, MA, USA.

Koza, John R. (1994). *Genetic Programming II: Automatic Discovery of Reusable Programs*. MIT Press, Cambridge Massachusetts.

Koza, John R., Andre, David, Bennett III, Forrest H, and Keane, Martin (1999). *Genetic Programming 3: Darwinian Invention and Problem Solving.* Morgan Kaufman.

Kripke, S. A. (1972). *Naming and Necessity.* Harvard University Press.

Li, Xin, Zhou, Chi, Xiao, Weimin, and Nelson, Peter C. (2005). Direct evolution of hierarchical solutions with self-emergent substructures. In *The Fourth International Conference on Machine Learning and Applications (ICMLA'05)*, pages 337–342, Los Angeles, California. IEEE press.

Racine, Alain, Schoenauer, Marc, and Dague, Philippe (1998). A dynamic lattice to evolve hierarchically shared subroutines: DL'GP. In Banzhaf, Wolfgang, Poli, Riccardo, Schoenauer, Marc, and Fogarty, Terence C., editors, *Proceedings of the First European Workshop on Genetic Programming*, volume 1391 of *LNCS*, pages 220–232, Paris. Springer-Verlag.

Ray, Thomas S. (1991). Is it alive or is it GA? In Belew, Richard K. and Booker, Lashon B., editors, *Proceedings of the Fourth International Conference on Genetic Algorithms (ICGA'91)*, pages 527–534, San Mateo, California. Morgan Kaufmann Publishers.

Riolo, R. L., Cohen, M. D., and Axelrod, R. (2001). Evolution of cooperation without reciprocity. *Nature*, 414:441–443.

Roberts, Simon C., Howard, Daniel, and Koza, John R. (2001). Evolving modules in genetic programming by subtree encapsulation. In Miller, Julian F. et al., editors, *Genetic Programming, Proceedings of EuroGP'2001*, volume 2038 of *LNCS*, pages 160–175, Lake Como, Italy. Springer-Verlag.

Schönfinkel, M. (1924). Über die bausteine der mathematischen logik. *Mathematische Annalen*, 92:307–316.

Shirakawa, Shinichi and Nagao, Tomoharu (2009). Graph structured program evolution with automatically defined nodes. In Raidl, Guenther et al., editors, *GECCO '09: Proceedings of the 11th Annual conference on Genetic and evolutionary computation*, pages 1107–1114, Montreal. ACM.

Simon, H.A. (1969). The architecture of complexity. In Simon, Herbert A., editor, *The Sciences of the Artificial*, pages 84–118. The MIT Press.

Soule, T. (2011). Evolutionary dynamics of tag mediated cooperation with multilevel selection. *Evolutionary Computation*, 19(1):25–43.

Spector, Lee (1996). Simultaneous evolution of programs and their control structures. In Angeline, Peter J. and Kinnear, Jr., K. E., editors, *Advances in Genetic Programming 2*, chapter 7, pages 137–154. MIT Press, Cambridge, MA, USA.

Spector, Lee (2001). Autoconstructive evolution: Push, pushGP, and pushpop. In Spector, Lee et al., editors, *Proceedings of the Genetic and Evolutionary Computation Conference (GECCO-2001)*, pages 137–146, San Francisco, California, USA. Morgan Kaufmann.

Spector, Lee (2004). *Automatic Quantum Computer Programming: A Genetic Programming Approach*, volume 7 of *Genetic Programming*. Kluwer Academic Publishers, Boston/Dordrecht/New York/London.

Spector, Lee, Clark, David M., Lindsay, Ian, Barr, Bradford, and Klein, Jon (2008). Genetic programming for finite algebras. In Keijzer, Maarten et al., editors, *GECCO '08: Proceedings of the 10th annual conference on Genetic and evolutionary computation*, pages 1291–1298, Atlanta, GA, USA. ACM.

Spector, Lee and Klein, Jon (2006). Multidimensional tags, cooperative populations, and genetic programming. In Riolo, Rick L., Soule, Terence, and Worzel, Bill, editors, *Genetic Programming Theory and Practice IV*, volume 5 of *Genetic and Evolutionary Computation*, chapter 15, pages –. Springer, Ann Arbor.

Spector, Lee, Klein, Jon, and Keijzer, Maarten (2005). The push3 execution stack and the evolution of control. In Beyer, Hans-Georg et al., editors, *GECCO 2005: Proceedings of the 2005 conference on Genetic and evolutionary computation*, volume 2, pages 1689–1696, Washington DC, USA. ACM Press.

Spector, Lee, Martin, Brian, Harrington, Kyle, and Helmuth, Thomas (2011). Tag-based modules in genetic programming. In *Proceedings of the Genetic and Evolutionary Computation Conference (GECCO-2011)*. To appear.

Spector, Lee, Perry, Chris, Klein, Jon, and Keijzer, Maarten (2004). Push 3.0 programming language description. Technical Report HC-CSTR-2004-02, School of Cognitive Science, Hampshire College, USA.

Spector, Lee and Robinson, Alan (2002a). Genetic programming and autoconstructive evolution with the push programming language. *Genetic Programming and Evolvable Machines*, 3(1):7–40.

Spector, Lee and Robinson, Alan (2002b). Multi-type, self-adaptive genetic programming as an agent creation tool. In Barry, Alwyn M., editor, *GECCO 2002: Proceedings of the Bird of a Feather Workshops, Genetic and Evolutionary Computation Conference*, pages 73–80, New York. AAAI.

Teller, Astro (1994). The evolution of mental models. In Kinnear, Kenneth E., editor, *Advances in Genetic Programming*, Complex Adaptive Systems, pages 199–220, Cambridge. MIT Press.

Walker, James Alfred and Miller, Julian Francis (2008). The automatic acquisition, evolution and reuse of modules in cartesian genetic programming. *IEEE Transactions on Evolutionary Computation*, 12(4):397–417.

Wijesinghe, Gayan and Ciesielski, Vic (2010). Evolving programs with parameters and loops. In *IEEE Congress on Evolutionary Computation (CEC 2010)*, Barcelona, Spain. IEEE Press.

Chapter 2

LET THE GAMES EVOLVE!

Moshe Sipper

Department of Computer Science, Ben-Gurion University, Beer-Sheva 84105, Israel

Abstract   I survey my group's results over the past six years within the game area, demonstrating continual success in evolving winning strategies for challenging games and puzzles, including: chess, backgammon, Robocode, lose checkers, simulated car racing, Rush Hour, and FreeCell.

Keywords: backgammon, chess, FreeCell, lose checkers, policy, RARS, Robocode, Rush Hour

> *It was on a bitterly cold night and frosty morning, towards the end of the winter of '97, that I was awakened by a tugging at my shoulder. It was Holmes. The candle in his hand shone upon his eager, stooping face, and told me at a glance that something was amiss.*
>
> *"Come, Watson, come!" he cried. "The game is afoot. Not a word! Into your clothes and come!"*
>
> Arthur Conan Doyle, "The Adventure of the Abbey Grange"

1.   GP is for Genetic Programming, GP is for Game Playing

Ever since the dawn of artificial intelligence (AI) in the 1950s games have been part and parcel of this lively field. In 1957, a year after the Dartmouth Conference that marked the official birth of AI, Alex Bernstein designed a program for the IBM 704 that played two amateur games of chess. In 1958, Allen Newell, J. C. Shaw, and Herbert Simon introduced a more sophisticated chess program (beaten in thirty-five moves by a ten-year-old beginner in its last official game played in 1960). Arthur L. Samuel of IBM spent much of the fifties working on game-playing AI programs, and by 1961 he had a checkers program that could play rather decently. In 1961 and 1963 Donald Michie described a simple trial-and-error learning system for learning how to play Tic-

Tac-Toe (or Noughts and Crosses) called MENACE (for Matchbox Educable Noughts and Crosses Engine).

Why do games attract such interest? "There are two principal reasons to continue to do research on games," wrote (Epstein, 1999). "First, human fascination with game playing is long-standing and pervasive. Anthropologists have catalogued popular games in almost every culture... Games intrigue us because they address important cognitive functions... The second reason to continue game-playing research is that some difficult games remain to be won, games that people play very well but computers do not. These games clarify what our current approach lacks. They set challenges for us to meet, and they promise ample rewards."

Studying games may thus advance our knowledge in both cognition and artificial intelligence, and, last but not least, games possess a competitive angle which coincides with our human nature, thus motivating both researcher and student alike.

During the past few years there has been an ever-increasing interest in the application of computational intelligence techniques in general, and evolutionary algorithms in particular, within the vast domain of games. I happened to stumble across this trend early on and decided to climb aboard the gamesome boat while it was still not too far from the harbor.

The year 2005 saw the first *IEEE Symposium on Computational Intelligence and Games*, which went on to become an annually organized event. The symposia's success and popularity led to their promotion from symposium to conference in 2010, and also spawned the journal *IEEE Transactions on Computational Intelligence and AI in Games* in 2009. In 2008, a journal showcase of evolutionary computation in games seemed to be the right thing to do—so we did it (Sipper and Giacobini, 2008).

In this paper I survey my group's results over the past six years within the game area, demonstrating continual success in evolutionarily tackling hard games and puzzles. The next section presents our earliest results in three games: chess, backgammon, and Robocode. Section 3 delineates the application of GP to evolving lose checkers strategies. In Section 4 we apply GP to a single-player game—a puzzle—known as Rush Hour. Sections 5 and 6 summarize results obtained for FreeCell and RARS (Robot Auto Racing Simulator), respectively. Finally, we end with concluding remarks in Section 7.[1]

---

[1]Caveat lector: Given the limited space and my intended coverage some sections are less detailed than others. Full details can, of course, be found in the references provided.

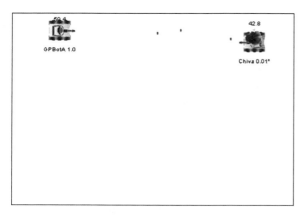

Figure 2-1 Robocode: GP bot (left) fights an enemy (right) to the death (and lives to tell the tale).

2. Genesis: A Wholly Trinity

Our ludic pursuit began in 2005 with the study of three games—chess, backgammon, and Robocode (Sipper et al., 2007):

1. **Backgammon.** The goal was to evolve a full-fledged player for the non-doubling-cube version of the game (Azaria and Sipper, 2005a; Azaria and Sipper, 2005b).

2. **Chess** (endgames). The goal was to evolve a player able to play endgames (Hauptman and Sipper, 2005a; Hauptman and Sipper, 2005b). While endgames typically contain but a few pieces, the problem of evaluation is still hard, as the pieces are usually free to move all over the board, resulting in complex game trees—both deep and with high branching factors. Indeed, in the chess lore much has been said and written about endgames.

3. **Robocode.** A simulation-based game in which robotic tanks fight to destruction in a closed arena (Figure 2-1). The programmers implement their robots in the Java programming language, and can test their creations either by using a graphical environment in which battles are held, or by submitting them to a central web site where online tournaments regularly take place. Our goal here was to evolve robocode players able to rank high in the international league (Shichel et al., 2005).

A strategy for a given player in a game is a way of specifying which choice the player is to make at every point in the game from the set of allowable choices at that point, given all the information that is available to the player at that point (Koza, 1992). The problem of discovering a strategy for playing a game can be viewed as one of seeking a computer program. Depending on the game, the program might take as input the entire history of past moves or just the current state of the game. The desired program then produces the next move as output. For some games one might evolve a complete strategy that addresses every situation tackled. This proved to work well with Robocode, which is a dynamic game, with relatively few parameters, and little need for past history.

Another approach (which can probably be traced back to (Samuel, 1959)) is to couple a current-state evaluator (e.g., board evaluator) with a next-move generator. One can go on to create a minimax tree, which consists of all possible moves, countermoves, counter-countermoves, and so on; for real-life games, such a tree's size quickly becomes prohibitive. Deep Blue, the famous machine chess player, and its offspring Deeper Blue, relied mainly on brute-force methods to gain an advantage over the opponent, by traversing as deeply as possible the game tree (Kendall and Whitwell, 2001). Although these programs achieved amazing performance levels, Chomsky criticized this aspect of game-playing research as being "about as interesting as the fact that a bulldozer can lift more than some weight lifter" (Chomsky, 1993). The approach we used with backgammon and chess was to derive a very shallow, *single-level* tree, and evolve "smart" evaluation functions. Our artificial player was thus created by combining an evolved board evaluator with a (relatively simple) program that generated all next-move boards (such programs can easily be written for backgammon and chess).

Thus, we used GP to evolve either complete game strategies (Robocode) or board-evaluation functions (chess, backgammon). Our results for these three games (which also garnered two HUMIE awards, in 2005 and 2007) are summarized below.

Backgammon.   We pitted our top evolved backgammon players against *Pubeval*, a free, public-domain board evaluation function written by Gerry Tesauro to serve as a common standardized benchmark. It is a linear function of the raw board information (number of checkers at each location), which represents a linear approximation to human play. The program became the *de facto* yardstick used by the growing community of backgammon-playing program developers. Our top evolved player was able to attain a win percentage of 62.4% in a tournament against Pubeval, about 10% higher than the previous top method. Moreover, several different evolved strategies were able to surpass the 60% mark, and most of them outdid all previous works.

Chess (endgames).   We pitted our top evolved chess-endgame players against two very strong external opponents: 1) A program we wrote ('Master') based upon consultation with several high-ranking chess players; 2) CRAFTY— a world-class chess program, which finished second in the 2004 World Computer Speed Chess Championship. Speed chess ("blitz") involves a time-limit per move, which we imposed both on CRAFTY and on our players. Not only did we thus seek to evolve good players, but ones that played well *and fast*.

Table 2-1. Percent of wins, material advantage without mating (having a higher point count than the opponent), and draws for best GP-EndChess player in a tournament against two top competitors.

	%Wins	%Advs	%Draws
Master	6.00	2.00	68.00
CRAFTY	2.00	4.00	72.00

Results are shown in Table 2-1. As can be seen, GP-EndChess managed to hold its own, and even win, against these top players.

Deeper analysis of the strategies developed (Hauptman and Sipper, 2005a) revealed several important shortcomings, most of which stemmed from the fact that they used deep knowledge and little search, typically developing only *one* level of the search tree. Simply increasing the search depth would not have solved the problem, since the evolved programs examined each board very thoroughly, and scanning many boards would have increased time requirements prohibitively. And so we turned to evolution to find an optimal way to overcome this problem: how to add more search at the expense of less knowledgeable (and thus less time-consuming) node evaluators, while attaining better performance. In (Hauptman and Sipper, 2007b) *we evolved the search algorithm itself*, focusing on the *Mate-In-N* problem: find a key move such that even with the best possible counterplays, the opponent cannot avoid being mated in (or before) move N. Our evolved search algorithms successfully solved several instances of the Mate-In-N problem, for the hardest ones developing 47% less game-tree nodes than CRAFTY. Improvement was thus not over the basic alpha-beta algorithm, but over a world-class program using all standard enhancements.

Finally, in (Hauptman and Sipper, 2007a), we examined a strong evolved chess-endgame player, focusing on the player's emergent capabilities and tactics in the context of a chess match. Using a number of methods, we analyzed the evolved player's building blocks and their effect on play level (e.g., comparison of evolved player's moves and CRAFTY's, study of play level of single terminals, disabling of terminals in evolved player, etc.). We concluded that evolution found combinations of building blocks that were far from trivial and could not be explained through simple combination—thereby indicating the possible *emergence* of complex strategies.

Robocode. A Robocode player is written as an event-driven Java program. A main loop controls the tank activities, which can be interrupted on various occasions, called *events*. The program was limited to four lines of code, as we were aiming for the HaikuBot category, one of the divisions of the international league with a four-line code limit.

We submitted our top evolved player to the online league. At its very first tournament it came in third, later climbing to first place of 28.[2] All other 27 programs—defeated by our evolved bot—were written by humans.

3.   You Lose, You Win

Many variants of the game of checkers exist, several of them played by a great number of people (including tournament play). Practically all checkers variants are two-player games that contain only two types of pieces set on an $n \times n$ board. The most well-known variant of checkers is American checkers. It offers a relatively small search space (roughly 10^{20} legal positions compared to the 10^{43}–10^{50} estimated for chess) with a relatively small branching factor. It is fairly easy to write a competent[3] computer player for American checkers using minimax search and a trivial evaluation function. The generic evaluation function for checkers is a piece differential that assigns extra value to kings on the board. This sort of player was used by (Chellapilla and Fogel, 2001) in their work on evolving checkers-playing programs.

American checkers shares its domain with another, somewhat less-popular variant of checkers, known as lose checkers. The basic rules of lose checkers are the same as American checkers (though the existence of different organizations may cause some difference in the peripheral rules). The objective, however, is quite different. A losing position for a player in American checkers is a winning position for that player in lose checkers and vice versa (i.e., one wins by losing all pieces or remaining with no legal move). (Hlynka and Schaeffer, 2006) observed that, unlike the case of American checkers, lose checkers lacks an intuitive state evaluation function. Surprisingly (and regrettably) the inverse of the standard, piece differential-based checkers evaluation function is woefully ineffective. In some cases lose checkers computer players rely solely on optimized deep search and an endgame state database, having the evaluation function return a random value for states not in the database.

To date, there has been limited research interest in lose checkers (Hlynka and Schaeffer, 2006; Smith and Sailer, 2004), leaving room for improvement.[4] The mere fact that it is difficult to hand-craft a good evaluation function for lose checkers allows for the claim that any good evaluation function is in fact human competitive. If capable human programmers resort to having their evalu-

---

[2]robocode.yajags.com/20050625/haiku-1v1.html

[3]We use "competent" to describe players that show a level of playing skill comparable to some human players (i.e., are not trivially bad) and yet do not exhibit the level of play of the strongest players (be they computer or human) available. As it is often hard to compare levels of play between different games, we find this fluid definition of "competence" to be suitable.

[4]American checkers was solved by (Schaeffer et al., 2007).

Table 2-2. Lose checkers: Basic domain-independent terminal nodes. F: floating point, B: boolean.

Node name	Return type	Return value
ERC()	F	Preset random number
False()	B	Boolean *false* value
One()	F	1
True()	B	Boolean *true* value
Zero()	F	0

Table 2-3. Lose checkers: Domain-specific terminal nodes that deal with board characteristics.

Node name	Type	Return value
EnemeyKingCount()	F	The enemy's king count
EnemeyManCount()	F	The enemy's man count
EnemeyPieceCount()	F	The enemy's piece count
FriendlyKingCount()	F	The player's king count
FriendlyManCount()	F	The player's man count
FriendlyPieceCount()	F	The player's piece count
KingCount()	F	FriendlyKingCount() – EnemeyKingCount()
KingFactor()	F	King factor value
ManCount()	F	FriendlyManCount() – EnemeyManCount()
Mobility()	F	The number of plies available to the player
PieceCount()	F	FriendlyPieceCount() – EnemeyPieceCount()

Table 2-4. Lose checkers: Domain-specific terminal nodes that deal with square characteristics. They all receive two parameters—X and Y—the row and column of the square, respectively.

Node name	Type	Return value
IsEmptySquare(X,Y)	B	True iff square empty
IsFriendlyPiece(X,Y)	B	True iff square occupied by friendly piece
IsKingPiece(X,Y)	B	True iff square occupied by king
IsManPiece(X,Y)	B	True iff square occupied by man

ation function return random values, then any improvement on random is worth noting.

We have recently applied GP to evolving good lose-checkers players (Benbassat and Sipper, 2010). The individuals in the population acted as board-evaluation functions, to be combined with a standard game-search algorithm such as alpha-beta. The value they returned for a given board state was seen as an indication of how good that board state was for the player whose turn it was to play.

We used strongly typed GP with two node types: Boolean and floating point. The terminal set comprised basic domain-independent nodes (Table 2-2) and domain-specific nodes. These latter are listed in two tables: Table 2-3 shows nodes describing characteristics that have to do with the board in its entirety, and Table 2-4 shows nodes describing characteristics of a certain square on the board. The function nodes are listed in Table 2-5.

Table 2-5. Lose checkers: Function nodes. F_i: floating-point parameter, B_i: Boolean parameter.

Node name	Type	Return value
AND(B_1,B_2)	B	Logical AND of parameters
LowerEqual(F_1,F_2)	B	True iff $F_1 \leq F_2$
NAND(B_1,B_2)	B	Logical NAND of parameters
NOR(B_1,B_2)	B	Logical NOR of parameters
NOTG(B_1,B_2)	B	Logical NOT of B_1
OR(B_1,B_2)	B	Logical OR of parameters
IFT(B_1,F_1,F_2)	F	F_1 if B_1 is true and F_2 otherwise
Minus(F_1,F_2)	F	$F_1 - F_2$
MultERC(F_1)	F	F_1 multiplied by preset random number
NullFuncJ(F_1,F_2)	F	F_1
Plus(F_1,F_2)	F	$F_1 + F_2$

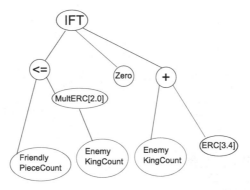

Figure 2-2. Lose checkers: Sample tree.

Figure 2-2 shows a sample tree, which returns 0 if the friendly piece count is less than or equal to double the number of enemy kings on the board, otherwise returning the number of enemy kings plus 3.4.

Aside from the standard two-point crossover we introduced a one-way crossover operator: randomly select a subtree in both participating individuals, and then insert a copy of the selected subtree from the first individual (donor) in place of the selected subtree from the second individual (receiver). The individual with higher fitness was always chosen to act as the donor. We also defined a form of local, minimally disruptive mutation, and used explicitly defined introns (Benbassat and Sipper, 2010).

As for fitness, evolving players faced two types of opponents: external "guides," and their own cohorts in the population (the latter known as coevolution). Two types of guides were implemented: a random player and an alpha-beta player. The random player chose a move at random and was used to test initial runs. The alpha-beta player searched up to a preset depth in the game tree and used an evaluation function returning a random value for game states for which there was no clear winner (in states where win or loss was evident the evaluation function returned an appropriate value). An individual's fitness value was proportional to its performance in a set of games against a mix of opponent guides and cohorts.

Our setup supported two different kinds of GP players. The first examined all legal moves and used the GP individual to assign scores to the different moves, choosing the one that scored highest. This method is essentially a minimax search of depth 1. The second kind of player mixed GP game-state evaluation with a minimax search. It used the alpha-beta search algorithm implemented for the guides, but instead of evaluating non-terminal states randomly it did so using the GP individual. This method added search power to our players but required more time.

(Benbassat and Sipper, 2010) presents a plethora of experiments we performed, the bottom line being the emergence of highly competent players. Our evolved alpha-beta players were able to beat opponent alpha-beta players that searched considerably deeper. To wit, our players were able not only to win— but to do so while expending far fewer computational resources (i.e., expansion of tree nodes).

4.   Help! I'm Stuck in the Parking Lot

Single-player games, or puzzles, have received much attention from the AI community for quite some time (e.g., (Hearn, 2006; Robertson and Munro, 1978)). Quite a few NP-Complete puzzles, though, have remained relatively neglected by researchers (see (Kendall et al., 2008) for a review).

Among these difficult games we find the Rush Hour puzzle.[5] The commercial version of this popular single-player game is played on a 6x6 grid, simulating a parking lot replete with several vehicles. The goal is to find a sequence of legal vehicular moves that ultimately clears the way for the red target car, allowing it to exit the lot through a tile that marks the exit (see Figure 2-3). Vehicles—of length two or three tiles—are restricted to moving either vertically or horizontally (but not both), they cannot vault over other vehicles, and no two vehicles may occupy the same tile at once. The generalized version of the game is defined on an arbitrary grid size, though the 6x6 board is sufficiently challenging for humans (we are not aware of humans playing, let alone solving, complex boards larger than 6x6).

How does one go about solving such a puzzle through computational means? A primary problem-solving approach within the field of AI is that of heuristic search. One of the most important heuristic search algorithms is iterative-

---

[5] The name "Rush Hour" is a trademark of Binary Arts, Inc. The game was originally invented by Nobuyuki Yoshigahara in the late 1970s.

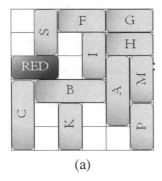 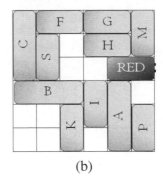

(a)   (b)

Figure 2-3. (a) A sample Rush Hour configuration. This is problem no. 9 of the problem set shipped with the standard version of the game by Binary Arts, Inc. (b) A possible goal state: the red car has reached the exit tile on the right-hand side of the grid.

deepening A* (IDA*) (Hart et al., 1968; Korf, 1985), which is widely used to solve single-player games. IDA* and similar algorithms are strongly based on the notion of approximating the distance of a given configuration (or *state*) to the problem's solution (or *goal*). Such approximations are found by means of a computationally efficient function, known as the *heuristic function*.

By applying the heuristic function to states reachable from the current ones considered it becomes possible to select more-promising alternatives earlier on in the search process, possibly reducing the amount of search effort (typically measured in number of nodes expanded) required to solve a given problem. The putative reduction is strongly tied to the quality of the heuristic function used: employing a perfect function means simply "strolling" onto the solution (i.e., no search de facto), while using a bad function could render the search less efficient than totally uninformed search, such as breadth-first search (BFS) or depth-first search (DFS).

In (Hauptman et al., 2009) we used GP to evolve heuristic functions for the Rush Hour puzzle. We first constructed a "brute-force," iterative-deepening search algorithm, along with several search enhancements—some culled from the literature, some of our own devise—but with no heuristic functions. As expected, this method worked well on relatively simple boards, and even solved most moderately difficult ones within reasonable bounds of space and time. However, when dealing with complex problems, this method yielded inadequate performance.

We moved on to hand-crafting several novel heuristics for this domain, which we then tested empirically. The effect of these heuristics on search efficiency was inconsistent, alternating between decreasing the number of nodes traversed by 70% (for certain initial configurations) and increasing this number by as much as 170% (for other configurations). It was clear at this point that using our heuristics correctly was a difficult task.

Table 2-6. Rush Hour: Terminal set of an individual program in the population. B:Boolean, R:Real or Integer. The upper part of the table contains terminals used both in *Condition* and *Value* trees, while the lower part regards *Condition* trees only.

Node name	Type	Return value
BlockersLowerBound	R	A lower bound on the number of moves required to remove blocking vehicles out of the red car's path
GoalDistance	R	Sum of all vehicles' distances to their locations in the deduced-goal board
Hybrid	R	Same as *GoalDistance*, but also add number of vehicles between each car and its designated location
$\{0.0, 0.1 \ldots, 1.0, 1, \ldots, 9\}$	R	Numeric terminals
IsMoveToSecluded	B	Did the last move taken position the vehicle at a location that no other vehicle can occupy?
IsReleasingMove	B	Did the last move made add new possible moves?
g	R	Distance from the initial board
PhaseByDistance	R	$g \div (g + DistanceToGoal)$
PhaseByBlockers	R	$g \div (g + BlockersLowerBound)$
NumberOfSiblings	R	The number of nodes expanded from the parent of the current node
DifficultyLevel	R	The difficulty level of the given problem, relative to other problems in the current problem set.

Enter GP. Our main set of experiments focused on evolving *combinations* of the basic heuristics devised—a form of hyper-heuristic search. We used the basic heuristics as building blocks in a GP setting, wherein individuals were embodied as ordered sets of search-guiding rules (or *policies*), the parts of which were GP trees. The effect on performance was profound: evolution proved immensely efficacious, managing to combine heuristics of highly variable utility into composites that were nearly always beneficial, and far better than each separate component.

Table 2-6 lists the heuristics and auxiliary functions we devised. Using these elemental blocks effectively is a difficult task, as it involves solving two major sub-problems:

1. Finding exact conditions regarding *when* to apply each heuristic (in order to avoid the strong inconsistent effect on performance mentioned above).

2. Combining several estimates to get a more accurate one. We hypothesized that different areas of the search space might benefit from the application of different heuristics.

As we wanted to embody both application conditions and combinations of estimates, we decided to evolve ordered sets of control rules, or *policies*. Policies typically have the following structure:

$RULE_1$: IF $Condition_1$ THEN $Value_1$

$\quad\cdot$

$RULE_N$: IF $Condition_N$ THEN $Value_N$
$DEFAULT$: $Value_{N+1}$

where $Condition_i$ and $Value_i$ represent conditions and estimates, respectively.

Policies are used by the search algorithm in the following manner: the rules are ordered such that we apply the first rule that "fires" (meaning its condition is true for a given board), returning its $Value$ part. If no rule fires, the value is taken from the last (default) tree: $Value_{N+1}$. Thus, individuals, while in the form of policies, are still board evaluators (or heuristics)—the value returned by the activated rule is an arithmetic combination of heuristic values, and is thus a heuristic value itself. This suits our requirements: rule ordering and conditions control when we apply a heuristic combination, and values provide the combinations themselves.

Thus, with N being the number of rules used, each individual in the evolving population contains N $Condition$ GP-trees and $N+1$ $Value$ GP-trees. After experimenting with several sizes of policies, we settled on $N = 5$, providing us with enough rules per individual, while avoiding "heavy" individuals with too many rules. The depth limit used both for the $Condition$ and $Value$ trees was empirically set to 5. The function set included $\{AND,OR,\leq,\geq\}$ for condition trees and $\{\times,+\}$ for value trees.

Fitness scores were obtained by performing full IDA* search with the given individual used as the heuristic function. For each solved board we assigned to the individual a score equal to the percentage of nodes reduced, compared to searching with no heuristics. For unsolved boards this score was 0. Scores were averaged over 10 randomly selected boards from the training set.

Our results (which garnered another HUMIE in 2009) proved excellent. Indeed, our success with 6x6 boards led us to evolve more problem instances, specifically, difficult 8x8 boards. Overall, evolved policies managed to cut the amount of required search to 40% for 6x6 boards and to 10% for 8x8 boards, compared to iterative deepening.

(Baum and Durdanovic, 2000) tackled Rush Hour with an artificial economy of agents and their best reported solver was able to solve 15 of the 40 standard problems (we solved all). Interestingly, they also tried a GP approach, noting, "We have tried several approaches to getting a Genetic Program to solve these problems, varying the instance presentation scheme and other parameters... it has never learned to solve any of the original problem set." Obviously, with the right GP approach, Rush Hour can be solved.

5.   Lunch Isn't Free—But Cells Are

A well-known, highly popular example within the domain of discrete puzzles is the card game of FreeCell. Starting with all cards randomly divided into k piles (called *cascades*), the objective of the game is to move all cards onto four different piles (called *foundations*)—one per suit—arranged upwards from the ace until the king. Additionally, there are initially empty cells (called *FreeCells*), whose purpose is to aid with moving the cards. Only exposed cards

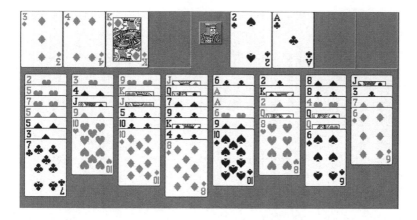

Figure 2-4. A FreeCell game configuration. Cascades: Bottom 8 piles. Foundations: 4 upper-right piles. FreeCells: 4 upper-left piles. Note that cascades are not arranged according to suits, but foundations are. Legal moves for current configuration: 1) moving 7♣ from the leftmost cascade to either the pile fourth from the left (on top of the 8♦), or to the pile third from the right (on top of the 8♡); 2) moving the 6♦ from the right cascade to the left one (on top of the 7♣); and 3) moving any single card on top of a cascade onto the empty FreeCell.

can be moved, either from FreeCells or foundations. Legal move destinations include: a home cell, if all previous (i.e., lower) cards are already there; empty FreeCells; and, on top of a next-highest card of opposite color in a cascade (Figure 2-4). FreeCell was proven by Helmert to be NP-Complete (Helmert, 2003). Computational complexity aside, many (oft-frustrated) human players (including the authors) will readily attest to the game's hardness. The attainment of a competent machine player would undoubtedly be considered a human-competitive result.

FreeCell remained relatively obscure until it was included in the Windows 95 operating system (and in all subsequent versions), along with 32,000 problems—known as *Microsoft 32K*—all solvable but one (this latter, game #11982, was proven to be unsolvable). Despite there being numerous FreeCell solvers available via the Web, few have been written up in the scientific literature. The best published solver to date was that of Heineman (Heineman, 2009), able to solve 96% of Microsoft 32K using a hybrid A* / hill-climbing search algorithm called *staged deepening* (henceforth referred to as the *HSD* algorithm). The HSD algorithm, along with a heuristic function, forms Heineman's FreeCell solver (we made a distinction between the HSD algorithm, the HSD heuristic, and the HSD solver—which includes both).

In (Elyasaf et al., 2011) we used a genetic algorithm to develop the strongest known heuristic-based solver for the game of FreeCell, substantively surpassing that of Heineman's. Along the way we devised several novel heuristics for

Table 2-7. FreeCell: List of heuristics used by the genetic algorithm. R: Real or Integer.

Node name	Type	Return value
HSDH	R	Heineman's staged deepening heuristic
NumberWellPlaced	R	Number of well-placed cards in cascade piles
NumCardsNotAtFoundations	R	Number of cards not at foundation piles
FreeCells	R	Number of free FreeCells and cascades
DifferenceFromTop	R	Average value of top cards in cascades minus average value of top cards in foundation piles
LowestHomeCard	R	Highest possible card value minus lowest card value in foundation piles
HighestHomeCard	R	Highest card value in foundation piles
DifferenceHome	R	Highest card value in foundation piles minus lowest one
SumOfBottomCards	R	Highest possible card value multiplied by number of suites, minus sum of cascades' bottom card

FreeCell (Table 2-7), many of which could be applied to other domains and games.

Combining several heuristics to get a more accurate one is considered one of the most difficult problems in contemporary heuristics research (Burke et al., 2010; Samadi et al., 2008). In (Elyasaf et al., 2011) we tackled a sub-problem, that of combining heuristics by *arithmetic* means, by summing their values or taking the maximal value. The problem of combining heuristics is difficult primarily because it entails traversing an extremely large search space of possible numeric combinations and game configurations. To tackle this problem we used a genetic algorithm.

Each individual comprised 9 real values in the range $[0, 1)$, representing a linear combination of all 9 heuristics listed in Table 2-7. Specifically, the heuristic value, H, designated by an evolving individual was defined as $H = \sum_{i=1}^{9} w_i h_i$, where w_i is the ith weight specified by the genome, and h_i is the ith heuristic shown in Table 2-7. To obtain a more uniform calculation we normalized all heuristic values to within the range $[0, 1]$ by maintaining a maximal possible value for each heuristic, and dividing by it. For example, *DifferenceHome* returns values in the range $[0, 13]$ (13 being the difference between the king's value and the ace's value), and the normalized values are attained by dividing by 13.

An individual's fitness score was obtained by performing full HSD search on deals (initial configurations) taken from the training set, with the individual used as the heuristic function. Fitness equaled the average search-node reduction ratio. This ratio was obtained by comparing the reduction in number of search nodes—averaged over solved deals—with the average number of nodes when searching with the original HSD heuristic (HSDH). For example, if the average reduction in search was by 70% compared with HSDH (i.e., 70% less nodes expanded on average), the fitness score was set to 0.7. If a given deal was not solved within 2 minutes (a time limit we set empirically), we assigned a fitness score of 0 to that deal.

To distinguish between individuals that did not solve a given deal and individuals that solved it but without reducing the amount of search (the latter case reflecting better performance than the former), we assigned to the latter a partial score of $(1 - FractionExcessNodes)/C$, where *FractionExcessNodes* is the fraction of excessive nodes (values greater than 1 were truncated to 1), and C is a constant used to decrease the score relative to search reduction (set empirically to 1000). For example, an excess of 30% would yield a partial score of $(1 - 0.3)/C$; an excess of over 200% would yield 0.

We used Hillis-style coevolution wherein a population of solutions coevolves alongside a population of problems (Hillis, 1990). The basic idea is that neither population should stagnate: as solvers become more adept at solving certain problems, these latter do not remain in the problem set (as with a simple GA) but are rather removed from the population of problems—which itself evolves. In this form of competitive coevolution the fitness of one population is inversely related to the fitness of the other population. Specifically, in our coevolutionary scenario the first population comprised the solvers and in the second population an individual represented a *set* of FreeCell deals.

And the winner was... GA-FreeCell. Our evolutionarily produced FreeCell solver significantly surpasses the best published solver to date by three distinct measures: 1) number of search nodes is reduced by 87%; 2) time to solution is reduced by 93%; and 3) average solution length is reduced by 41%. Our top solver is the best published FreeCell player to date, solving 98% of the standard Microsoft 32K problem set, and also able to beat high-ranking human players.

One of our best solvers is the following: (+ (* DifferenceToGoal 0.09) (* DifferenceToNextStepHome 0.01) (* FreeCells 0.0) (* DifferenceFromTop 0.77) (* LowestHomeCard 0.01) (* UppestHomeCard 0.08) (* NumOfArranged 0.01) (* DifferenceHome 0.01) (* BottomCardsSum 0.02)). (In other good solvers DifferenceFromTop was less weighty.)

How does our evolution-produced player fare against humans? The website www.freecell.net provides a ranking of human FreeCell players, listing solution time and win rate (alas, no data on number of boards examined by humans, nor on solution lengths). The site statistics, which we downloaded on April 12, 2011, included results for 76 humans who met our minimal-game requirement of 30K games—all but two of whom exhibited a win rate greater than 91%. Sorted according to number of games played, the no. 1 player played 147,219 games, achieving a win rate of 97.61%. This human is therefore pushed to the second position, with our top player (98.36% win rate) taking the first place. If the statistics are sorted according to win rate then our player assumes the no. 9 position. Either way, it is clear that when compared with strong, persistent, and consistent humans, GA-FreeCell emerges as a highly competitive player.

This work may well have pushed the limit of what has been done with evolution, FreeCell being one of the most difficult single-player domains (if not the most difficult) to which evolutionary algorithms have been applied to date.

6.   A Racy Affair

Controlling a moving vehicle is considered a complex problem, both in simulated and real-world environments. Dealing with physical forces, varying road conditions, unexpected opponent behavior, damage control, and many other factors, render the car-racing problem a fertile ground for artificial intelligence research.

In (Shichel and Sipper, 2011) we applied GP to creating car controller programs for the game of RARS—Robot Auto Racing Simulator, which is an open-source, car-race simulator. We chose RARS mainly because of its extensive human-written driver library, and the substantive amount of published works that describe machine-learning approaches applied to RARS—enabling us to perform significant comparisons between our results and both human- and machine-designed solutions.

A RARS controller is a C++ class with a single method, which receives the current race *situation* and determines the desired speed and wheel angle of the car. The simulation engine queries the controller approximately 20 times per "game second," and advances the car according to the returned decisions and physical constraints. The *situation* argument provides the agent (car controller) with detailed information about the current race conditions, such as current speed and direction, road curvature, fuel status, and nearby car positions.

Controlling the car is done by two actuators: speed and steering. The speed actuator specifies the desired speed of the car, while the steering actuator specifies the desired wheel angle. The simulation engine uses both values to calculate the involved physical forces and compute the car's movement. Extreme values, such as high speed or a steep steering angle, may result in slippage or skidding, and must be taken into consideration when crafting a controller.

Using GP to evolve driver controllers we created highly generalized game-playing agents, able to outperform most human-crafted controllers and all machine-designed ones on a variety of game tracks (Shichel and Sipper, 2011).

The evolved drivers demonstrated a high degree of generalization, enabling them to perform well on most tracks—including ones that were not used during the evolutionary process. We noted that using a complex track for fitness evaluation, coupled with a comprehensive yet simple set of genetic building blocks, contributed greatly to our controllers' generalization capabilities. We also analyzed the evolved code, observing the emergence of useful patterns, such as a time-to-crash indicator. Such patterns, not pre-coded into the system, were repeatedly used in the evolved individuals' code, acting as evolution-made genetic building blocks.

7.   In Conclusion... Evolution Rocks!

Our extensive experience shows that evolutionary algorithms, and in particular genetic programming, are able to parlay fragmentary human intuition into full-fledged winning strategies. Such algorithms are therefore a good candidate when confronted with the problem of finding a complex, successful game strategy or puzzle solver.

We believe that a major reason for our success in evolving winning game strategies is genetic programming's ability to readily accommodate human expertise. When tackling a new game we begin our experimentation with small sets of functions and terminals, which are then revised and added upon through our examination of evolved players and their performance. For example, (Sipper et al., 2007) described three major steps in the development of the evolutionary chess setup.

Genetic programming represents a viable means to automatic programming, and perhaps more generally to machine intelligence, in no small part due to its ability to "cooperate" with humans: more than many other adaptive-search techniques genetic programming's representational affluence and openness lend it to the ready imbuing of the designer's own intelligence within the genotypic language. While AI purists may wrinkle their noses at this, taking the AI-should-emerge-from-scratch stance, we argue that a more practical path to AI involves man-machine cooperation. Genetic programming, as evidenced herein, is a forerunning candidate for the 'machine' part.

AI practitioners sometimes overlook the important distinction between two phases of intelligence (or knowledge) development: 1) from scratch to a mediocre level, and 2) from mediocre to expert level. Traditional AI is often better at handling the first phase. Genetic programming allows the AIer to focus his attention on the second phase, namely, the attainment of true expertise. When aiming to develop a winning strategy, be it in games or any other domain, the genetic-programming practitioner will set his sights at the mediocre-to-expert phase of development, with the scratch-to-mediocre handled automatically during the initial generations of the evolutionary process. Although the designer is "imposing" his own views on the machine, this affords the "pushing" of the artificial intelligence frontier further out.

To summarize:

- Genetic programming has proven to be an excellent tool for automatically generating complex game strategies.

- A crucial advantage of genetic programming lies in its ability to incorporate human intelligence readily.

- As such, genetic programming is an excellent choice when complex strategies are needed, and human intelligence is there for the imbuing.

I evolve therefore I win.

"Why do you not solve it yourself, Mycroft? You can see as far as I."

"Possibly, Sherlock... No, you are the one man who can clear the matter up. If you have a fancy to see your name in the next honours list –"

My friend smiled and shook his head.

"I play the game for the game's own sake," said he.

Arthur Conan Doyle, "The Adventure of the Bruce-Partington Plans"

References

Azaria, Yaniv and Sipper, Moshe (2005a). GP-gammon: Genetically programming backgammon players. *Genetic Programming and Evolvable Machines*, 6(3):283–300. Published online: 12 August 2005.

Azaria, Yaniv and Sipper, Moshe (2005b). Using GP-gammon: Using genetic programming to evolve backgammon players. In Keijzer, Maarten et al., editors, *Proceedings of the 8th European Conference on Genetic Programming*, volume 3447 of *Lecture Notes in Computer Science*, pages 132–142, Lausanne, Switzerland. Springer.

Baum, E. B. and Durdanovic, I. B. (2000). Evolution of cooperative problem solving in an artificial economy. *Neural Computation*, 12:2743–2775.

Benbassat, Amit and Sipper, Moshe (2010). Evolving lose-checkers players using genetic programming. In *IEEE Conference on Computational Intelligence and Game*, pages 30–37, IT University of Copenhagen, Denmark.

Burke, E. K., Hyde, M., Kendall, G., Ochoa, G., Ozcan, E., and Woodward, J. R. (2010). A classification of hyper-heuristic approaches. In Gendreau, M. and Potvin, J-Y., editors, *Handbook of Meta-Heuristics 2nd Edition*, pages 449–468. Springer.

Chellapilla, K. and Fogel, D. B. (2001). Evolving an expert checkers playing program without using human expertise. *IEEE Transactions on Evolutionary Computation*, 5(4):422–428.

Chomsky, N. (1993). *Language and Thought*. Moyer Bell, Wakefield, RI.

Elyasaf, A., Hauptman, A., and Sipper, M. (2011). GA-FreeCell: Evolving solvers for the game of FreeCell. In *GECCO 2011: Proceedings of the Genetic and Evolutionary Computation Conference*, New York, NY, USA. ACM. (accepted).

Epstein, S. L. (1999). Game playing: The next moves. In *Proceedings of the Sixteenth National Conference on Artificial Intelligence*, pages 987–993. AAAI Press, Menlo Park, California USA.

Hart, P. E., Nilsson, N. J., and Raphael, B. (1968). A formal basis for heuristic determination of minimum path cost. *IEEE Transactions on Systems Science and Cybernetics*, 4(2):100–107.

Hauptman, A. and Sipper, M. (2007a). Emergence of complex strategies in the evolution of chess endgame players. *Advances in Complex Systems*, 10(suppl. no. 1):35–59.

Hauptman, Ami, Elyasaf, Achiya, Sipper, Moshe, and Karmon, Assaf (2009). GP-rush: using genetic programming to evolve solvers for the rush hour puzzle. In Raidl, Guenther et al., editors, *GECCO '09: Proceedings of the 11th Annual conference on Genetic and evolutionary computation*, pages 955–962, Montreal. ACM.

Hauptman, Ami and Sipper, Moshe (2005a). Analyzing the intelligence of a genetically programmed chess player. In Rothlauf, Franz, editor, *Late breaking paper at Genetic and Evolutionary Computation Conference (GECCO'2005)*, Washington, D.C., USA.

Hauptman, Ami and Sipper, Moshe (2005b). GP-endchess: Using genetic programming to evolve chess endgame players. In Keijzer, Maarten et al., editors, *Proceedings of the 8th European Conference on Genetic Programming*, volume 3447 of *Lecture Notes in Computer Science*, pages 120–131, Lausanne, Switzerland. Springer.

Hauptman, Ami and Sipper, Moshe (2007b). Evolution of an efficient search algorithm for the mate-in-N problem in chess. In Ebner, Marc et al., editors, *Proceedings of the 10th European Conference on Genetic Programming*, volume 4445 of *Lecture Notes in Computer Science*, pages 78–89, Valencia, Spain. Springer.

Hearn, R. A. (2006). *Games, puzzles, and computation*. PhD thesis, Massachusetts Institute of Technology, Dept. of Electrical Engineering and Computer Science.

Heineman, G. T. (2009). Algorithm to solve FreeCell solitaire games. Blog column associated with the book "Algorithms in a Nutshell book," by G. T. Heineman, G. Pollice, and S. Selkow, O'Reilly Media, 2008. http://broadcast.oreilly.com/2009/01/january-column-graph-algorithm.html.

Helmert, M. (2003). Complexity results for standard benchmark domains in planning. *Artificial Intelligence*, 143(2):219–262.

Hillis, D. W. (1990). Co-evolving parasites improve simulated evolution in an optimization procedure. *Physica D*, 42:228–234.

Hlynka, M. and Schaeffer, J. (2006). Automatic generation of search engines. In *Advances in Computer Games*, pages 23–38.

Kendall, G., Parkes, A., and Spoerer, K. (2008). A survey of NP-complete puzzles. *International Computer Games Association Journal (ICGA)*, 31:13–34.

Kendall, G. and Whitwell, G. (2001). An evolutionary approach for the tuning of a chess evaluation function using population dynamics. In *Proceedings of the 2001 Congress on Evolutionary Computation (CEC2001)*, pages 995–1002. IEEE Press.

Korf, R. E. (1985). Depth-first iterative-deepening: An optimal admissible tree search. *Artificial Intelligence*, 27(1):97–109.

Koza, John R. (1992). *Genetic Programming: On the Programming of Computers by Means of Natural Selection*. MIT Press, Cambridge, MA, USA.

Robertson, E. and Munro, I. (1978). NP-completeness, puzzles and games. *Utilas Mathematica*, 13:99–116.

Samadi, M., Felner, A., and Schaeffer, J. (2008). Learning from multiple heuristics. In Fox, Dieter and Gomes, Carla P., editors, *Proceedings of the Twenty-Third AAAI Conference on Artificial Intelligence (AAAI 2008)*, pages 357–362. AAAI Press.

Samuel, A. L. (1959). Some studies in machine learning using the game of checkers. *IBM Journal of Research and Development*, 3(3):210–229.

Schaeffer, J., Burch, N., Bjornsson, Y., Kishimoto, A., Muller, M., Lake, R., Lu, P., and Sutphen, S. (2007). Checkers is solved. *Science*, 317(5844):1518–1522.

Shichel, Y. and Sipper, M. (2011). GP-RARS: Evolving controllers for the Robot Auto Racing Simulator. *Memetic Computing*. (accepted).

Shichel, Yehonatan, Ziserman, Eran, and Sipper, Moshe (2005). GP-robocode: Using genetic programming to evolve robocode players. In Keijzer, Maarten et al., editors, *Proceedings of the 8th European Conference on Genetic Programming*, volume 3447 of *Lecture Notes in Computer Science*, pages 143–154, Lausanne, Switzerland. Springer.

Sipper, Moshe, Azaria, Yaniv, Hauptman, Ami, and Shichel, Yehonatan (2007). Designing an evolutionary strategizing machine for game playing and beyond. *IEEE Transactions on Systems, Man and Cybernetics, Part C: Applications and Reviews*, 37(4):583–593.

Sipper, Moshe and Giacobini, Mario (2008). Introduction to special section on evolutionary computation in games. *Genetic Programming and Evolvable Machines*, 9(4):279–280.

Smith, M. and Sailer, F. (2004). Learning to beat the world Lose Checkers champion using TDLeaf(λ).

Chapter 3

NOVELTY SEARCH AND THE PROBLEM WITH OBJECTIVES

Joel Lehman[1] and Kenneth O. Stanley[1]

[1]*Department of EECS, University of Central Florida, Orlando, Florida, USA;*

Abstract   By synthesizing a growing body of work in search processes that are not driven by explicit objectives, this paper advances the hypothesis that there is a fundamental problem with the dominant paradigm of objective-based search in evolutionary computation and genetic programming: Most *ambitious* objectives do not illuminate a path to themselves. That is, the gradient of improvement induced by ambitious objectives tends to lead not to the objective itself but instead to dead-end local optima. Indirectly supporting this hypothesis, great discoveries often are not the result of objective-driven search. For example, the major inspiration for both evolutionary computation and genetic programming, natural evolution, innovates through an open-ended process that lacks a final objective. Similarly, large-scale cultural evolutionary processes, such as the evolution of technology, mathematics, and art, lack a unified fixed goal. In addition, direct evidence for this hypothesis is presented from a recently-introduced search algorithm called novelty search. Though ignorant of the ultimate objective of search, in many instances novelty search has counter-intuitively outperformed searching directly for the objective, including a wide variety of randomly-generated problems introduced in an experiment in this chapter. Thus a new understanding is beginning to emerge that suggests that searching for a fixed objective, which is the reigning paradigm in evolutionary computation and even machine learning as a whole, may ultimately *limit* what can be achieved. Yet the liberating implication of this hypothesis argued in this paper is that by embracing search processes that are *not* driven by explicit objectives, the breadth and depth of what is reachable through evolutionary methods such as genetic programming may be greatly expanded.

Keywords: Novelty search, objective-based search, non-objective search, deception, evolutionary computation

1.   Introduction

Evolutionary computation (EC; De Jong, 2006; Holland, 1975) and genetic programming (GP; Koza, 1992) are algorithmic abstractions of natural evolution, inspired by nature's prolific creativity and the astronomical complexity of its products. Supporting such abstractions, evolutionary algorithms (EAs) have achieved impressive results, sometimes exceeding the capabilities of human design (Koza et al., 2003; Spector et al., 1999). Yet the ambitious goal of evolving artifacts with complexity comparable to those crafted by natural evolution remains daunting.

An interesting question is what prevents EAs from evolving artifacts with a functional complexity of the magnitude seen in biological organisms. There are many possible answers, each pointing to potential faults in current EAs. For example, representation, selection, or the design of problem domains could each possibly be the paramount issue preventing higher achievement in EC, and there are researchers who investigate ways of improving each of these components (Pelikan et al., 2001; Stewart, 2001). This paper focuses on *selection* and argues that the currently dominant objective-based selection paradigm significantly limits the potential of EAs.

This handicap results from a well-known problem facing EAs called deception (Goldberg, 1987): Sometimes a mutation increases fitness but actually leads *further* from the objective. That is, the fitness function in EC is a heuristic and thus there is no guarantee that increasing fitness actually decreases the distance to the objective of the search. The fundamental problem is that the stepping stones that lead to the objective may not resemble the objective itself. For example, humans bear little resemblance to their flatworm ancestors. In the words of John Stuart Mill, it is a fallacy to assume that the "conditions of a phenomenon must, or at least probably will, resemble the phenomenon itself." (Mill, 1846, p. 470). Yet this fallacy is the very *foundation* of typical fitness functions and thus ultimately limits their effectiveness.

In practice, researchers become accustomed to the fragility of fitness functions and learn certain rules of thumb that guide their efforts. One prominent such inductive rule is that the more ambitious the objective is, the less likely evolution will be able to solve it. This intuition, supported by experiments in this paper with increasingly difficult problems, highlights the critical problem undermining objective-based search: While we want to harness evolution to solve ambitious problems, the more ambitious the objective is, the less informative the gradient of the induced objective function will be. A provocative question is whether the quest for the objective itself sometimes precludes search from achieving anything remarkable. In other words, could ignoring the ultimate objective of search, or even searching entirely without an explicit objective, sometimes be a more viable approach to discovery?

A recent technique in EC called novelty, search (Lehman and Stanley, 2011; Lehman and Stanley, 2008) shows that indeed new opportunities for discovery arise once explicit objectives are abandoned: Contrary to intuition, searching without regard to the objective can often outperform searching explicitly for the objective. Instead of searching for the objective, novelty search only rewards individuals with functionality *different* from those that precede them in the search; inspired by nature's drive towards diversity, novelty search directly incentivizes novelty in lieu of any notion of progress. In a growing number of experiments, novelty search has successfully been applied to solving problems, often solving them more effectively than an algorithm searching directly for the objective (Lehman and Stanley, 2011; Risi et al., 2010; Lehman and Stanley, 2010a; Doucette, 2010; Mouret, 2009; Lehman and Stanley, 2010b). For example, an experiment introduced in this chapter demonstrates the advantages of novelty search in a wide variety of randomly-generated maze navigation problems.

However, novelty search provides but one example of a non-objective search, i.e. a search without a final explicit objective. A more prominent example is natural evolution itself, the process from which both EC and GP are inspired. While some might view reproduction as the goal of natural evolution, complex organisms such as ourselves are less efficient and slower to reproduce than simple single-celled creatures. Thus, what we might be tempted to characterize as progress in natural evolution is in fact quantitatively detrimental to the supposed objective of reproduction. That is, most innovation seen in natural evolution may result more from finding new ways of meeting life's challenges (i.e. founding new niches) than from simply optimizing reproductive fitness. Furthermore, nature does not aim at any single point or set of points in the space of organisms. In contrast, the objective in EC or GP is usually just such a point or set of points (e.g. the optimum or one of a set of optima).

Similarly, the evolution of mathematics, art, and technology are facilitated by exploration around recent discoveries, serendipity, and a plethora of diverse and conflicting individual objectives. That is, these human-driven processes of search also do not aim at any unified society-wide singular objective. Thus the types of search processes that continually innovate to produce radical advancements often lack a final predefined goal. This observation makes sense because a single fixed goal would either (1) be deceptive and therefore bring search to a point at which progress would effectively halt, or (2) if the goal is not so deceptive then innovation would cease once the goal is met.

The most awe-inspiring forms of search, which continually discover complex and interesting novelty, tend to build exploratively and incrementally upon prior innovations while lacking final objectives. When search is framed in this way, it is natural to ask, why is the typical approach in EC and GP to start from a random initial population and then to search narrowly towards a fixed goal?

While it does indeed succeed in some cases, such objective-based search does not scale to the most ambitious objectives, e.g., the ones that natural evolution is able to reach, because the objective-based search paradigm constrains evolution in a particularly restrictive way. That is, natural evolution succeeds because it divergently explores many ways of life while optimizing a behavior (i.e., reproduction) largely *orthogonal* to what is interesting about its discoveries, while objective-based search directly follows the gradient of improvement until it either succeeds or is too far deceived.

The main implication of the hypothesis advanced in this paper is that to reach truly ambitious goals, EAs may need to be modified to exploit richer gradients of information than estimated distance to a fixed objective. Behavioral novelty is one such gradient, yet although novelty search does outperform objective-based search in many deceptive problems, it too pales in comparison to the creative achievement of natural evolution. That is, there still remains much work to be done in developing powerful non-objective search algorithms. Thus, while illustrating the limitations of objective-based search may be a negative result, at the same time it also illuminates an exciting and potentially profound challenge for researchers in GP and EC: Through exploring the mostly untamed wilderness of non-objective search algorithms we may be able to finally devise truly creative algorithms that continually yield innovative complex artifacts. This paper reviews a spectrum of recent work that supports this view, ultimately building an argument in favor of a wider perspective for GP and EC.

2.   Deception

In this section we argue that deception is a deleterious fundamental property of ambitious objectives that paradoxically prevents such objectives from being reached when searching directly for them.

Investigating Deception

The motivation behind characterizing deception and problem difficulty is to understand what properties of problems may cause EAs to fail, so that such properties can potentially be remedied or avoided.

The original definition of deception (Goldberg, 1987) is based on the building blocks hypothesis, in which small genetic building blocks are integrated to form larger blocks (Holland, 1975). In the original conception, a problem is deceptive if lower-order building blocks, when combined, do not lead to a global optimum. Thus, in deceptive problems the fitness function may actively steer search away from exactly what is necessary to solve the problem.

Some alternative measures of problem difficulty attempt to quantify the ruggedness of the fitness landscape, motivated by the intuition that optimizing more rugged landscapes is more difficult (Weinberger, 1990). Importantly, because the fitness, landscape is induced by the objective function, the problem of ruggedness, presupposing reasonable settings for the EA, can be attributed to the objective function itself.

Interestingly, other researchers suggest that ruggedness is overemphasized and that neutral fitness plateaus (i.e., neutral networks) are key influences on evolutionary dynamics (Barnett, 2001; Stewart, 2001). However, even neutral networks suggest a deficiency in the objective function: By definition a neutral part of the search space contains no gradient information with respect to the objective function. That is, in a neutral network the compass of the objective function is ambiguous with respect to which way search should proceed.

In summary, there are many ways to consider, measure, and model the difficulty of problems for EAs. While in general the exact properties of a problem that make it difficult for EAs are still a subject of research, in this paper the term deception will refer to an intuitive definition of problem hardness: A deceptive problem is one in which a reasonable EA (with a reasonable representation, parameters, and search operators) will not reach the desired objective in a reasonable amount of time. That is, a deceptive problem is simply a problem in which following the gradient of the objective function leads to local optima.

It is important to note that this definition of deception is different from the traditional definition (Goldberg, 1987). This intuitive approach helps to isolate the general problem with particular objective functions because the word "deception" itself reflects a fault in the *objective function* (as opposed to in the algorithm itself): An objective function with the pathology of deceptiveness will *deceive* search by actively pointing the wrong way.

Mitigating Deception

Ideally, there would exist a silver bullet method immune to the problem of deception such that any objective would be reachable in a reasonable amount of time. Although it is impossible that any such general silver bullet method exists (Wolpert and Macready, 1995), researchers strive to create methods that can overcome deception in practice.

Common approaches in EC to mitigating deception are diversity, maintenance techniques (Mahfoud, 1995), building models that derive additional information from an imperfect fitness function (Pelikan et al., 2001), or accelerating search through neutral networks (Stewart, 2001). However, all of these techniques remain vulnerable to sufficiently uninformative objective functions.

In direct response to the problem of local optima when evolving towards sophisticated behaviors, some researchers incrementally evolve solutions by sequentially applying carefully crafted objective functions (Gomez and Miikkulainen, 1997). However, with ambitious objectives crafting an appropriate sequence of objectives may be difficult or impossible to achieve a priori. Additionally, the requirement of such intimate domain knowledge conflicts with the aspiration of *machine* learning.

In addition to single-objective optimization, there also exist evolutionary methods that optimize several objectives at once: Multi-Objective Evolutionary Algorithms (MOEAs) (Veldhuizen and Lamont, 2000). However, these MOEAs are not immune to the problem of deception (Deb, 1999), and adding objectives does not always make a problem easier (Brockhoff et al., 2007).

Another approach in EC related to deception is coevolution, wherein interactions between individuals contribute towards fitness. The hope is that continual competition between individuals will spark an evolutionary *arms race* in which the interactions between individuals continually creates a smooth gradient for better performance (Cliff and Miller, 1995). However, in practice such arms race often converge to situations analogous to local optima in standard objective-based search, e.g. mediocre stable-states, cycling between behaviors without further progress, or unbalanced adaptation where one species significantly out-adapts other competing species (Ficici and Pollack, 1998).

In summary, because deception is a significant problem in EC, there are *many* methods that have been designed to mitigate deception. However, while they may sometimes work, ultimately such methods do not cure the underlying pathology of the objective function that causes deception: The gradient of the objective function may be misleading or uninformative to begin with. Given a sufficiently uninformative objective function, it is an open question whether *any* method relying solely on the objective function will be effective. Thus an interesting yet sobering conclusion is that some objectives may be unreachable by direct objective-based search alone. Furthermore, as task complexity increases it is more difficult to successfully craft an appropriate objective function (Ficici and Pollack, 1998; Zaera et al., 1996). These insights match many EC practitioners' experience that the difficulty in ambitious experiments is often in crafting a sufficient fitness function. Thus the ultimate conclusion is that the more ambitious the experiment, the more likely it is that objective-based search will lead to mediocre local optima as opposed to the desired goal.

3.   Non-objective Search

If one accepts that there can be no general solution to the fundamental problem of deception in objective-based search (Wolpert and Macready, 1995), it becomes important to consider alternative paradigms such as searches in which there is no a priori fixed objective.

Interestingly, natural evolution, which inspires both EC and GP, is an example of such a non-objective search. That is, there is no final organism for which natural evolution searches. While competition between organisms may increase reproductive fitness, the complexity of biological organisms that we are tempted to attribute to selection is instead nearly always quantitatively *detrimental* to fitness. That is, large complex organisms reproduce slower and less efficiently than simple single-celled organisms. Indeed, some biologists have argued that selection pressure may not explain innovation (Gould, 1996; Lynch, 2007). The conclusion is that innovation may result more from accumulating novel ways of life (i.e. new niches) than from optimizing fitness.

Similarly, cultural evolutionary processes such as the evolution of mathematics, art, and technology also lack a single unified objective. That is, there is no fixed final theory of mathematics, no final transcendent pinnacle of art, and no final culminating technology that these systems singularly strive towards. Innovation in such systems branches from existing innovations by local search empowered by a diversity of differing individual goals and serendipitous discovery (Drexler and Minsky, 1986; Kelly, 2010, pp. 165–166).

Finally, an interesting, well-studied microcosm of open-ended innovation is provided by an online system called Picbreeder (Secretan et al., 2011) wherein users interactively evolve pictures that are represented as compositions of mathematical functions. During evolution, a user can publish a particular image to the Picbreeder website, where other users can see and rate it. Users can evolve images starting from a random initial population or they can start instead from any one of the images already published. Most evolution in this system happens through users branching from already-evolved pictures because they are more complex and visually appealing than random images. Thus, branching in Picbreeder fosters a collaborative system that leads to an accumulation of diverse, complex pictures. It is important to note that there is no overall drive to the system besides the wide-ranging individual preferences of the users.

Though there is no system-wide goal and no bias in the encoding towards particular classes of images, surprisingly, many pictures resembling real-world phenomena such as faces, cars, and butterflies have been evolved. That is, through collaborative interactive evolution users have discovered mathematical representations of recognizable images. Creating an interactive evolution system that can discover recognizable images is difficult, and is rare among such systems. Because the evolutionary history of all images is preserved by Picbreeder, one can trace the ancestors of such complex images all the way to their random origins in an initial population. Whereas one might guess that users discovered these images by intentionally selecting images that resemble them, interestingly, that is not the case. In fact, for most cases of complex images, the nearly-immediate predecessors to what looks like particular real-world objects do *not* resemble that same object (Figure 3-1). That is, the precursors to an image resembling a car were not chosen because they were car-like, but for some other aesthetic merit, mirroring biological exaptation. In fact, users are often frustrated when they try and fail to evolve towards a specific image class (Secretan et al., 2011), yet those image classes are still discovered – but only

Figure 3-1. **Deceptive Precursors.** Three pairs of related images evolved by users on Picbreeder are shown above. Each left image is a close evolutionary ancestor of the image to its right. The important insight is that the precursor pictures that are stepping stones to a particular image often do not resemble that final image.

when discovering them is *not* the goal. In other words, the success of Picbreeder at finding so many recognizable images results from of its lack of an overarching goal. Furthermore, (Woolley and Stanley, 2011) show that pictures evolved on Picbreeder cannot be re-evolved effectively by the same algorithm and encoding inside Picbreeder if those pictures are set as objectives for evolution.

The implication from reviewing these examples of non-objective searches is that the types of systems that foster open-ended innovation and lead to the accumulation of complex interesting artifacts tend to lack singular fixed objectives. While the evidence presented thus far has been inductive, the next section reviews novelty, search, a non-objective search algorithm that can be quantitatively compared in various domains to more traditional objective-based search. Thus novelty search provides an opportunity to test directly whether abandoning the single-minded search for the objective is ever beneficial.

4.   Novelty Search

Recall that the problem with the objective-based search paradigm that is common in EC models is that the objective function (e.g., the fitness function) does not necessarily reward the intermediate stepping stones that lead to the objective. These stepping stones often do not resemble the objective itself, especially as objectives become more ambitious, which makes it increasingly difficult to identify these stepping stones *a priori*.

The approach in novelty search (Lehman and Stanley, 2008; Lehman and Stanley, 2011), is to identify novelty as a *proxy* for stepping stones. That is, instead of searching for a final objective, the learning method rewards instances with functionality significantly different from what has been discovered before. Thus, instead of a traditional objective function, evolution employs a *novelty metric*. That way, no attempt is made to measure overall progress. In effect, such a process performs explicitly what natural evolution does passively, i.e., gradually accumulating novel forms that ascend the complexity ladder.

For example, in a biped locomotion domain, initial attempts might simply fall down. An objective function may explicitly *reward* falling the farthest, which is unrelated to the ultimate objective of walking and thus exemplifies a deceptive local optimum. In contrast, the novelty metric would reward simply falling down in a different way, regardless of whether it is closer to the objective behavior or not. After a few ways to fall are discovered, the only way to be rewarded is to find a behavior that does *not* fall right away. In this way, behavioral complexity rises from the bottom up. Eventually, to do something new, the biped would have to successfully walk for some distance even though it is not an objective.

Novelty search succeeds where objective-based search fails by rewarding the stepping stones. That is, anything that is genuinely different is rewarded and promoted as a jumping-off point for further evolution. While we cannot know which stepping stones are the right ones, if we accept that the primary pathology in objective-based search is that it cannot detect the stepping stones at all, then that pathology is remedied. This idea is also related to research in *curiosity seeking* in reinforcement learning (Schmidhuber, 2006).

Evolutionary algorithms like GP or neuroevolution (Yao, 1999) are well-suited to novelty search because the population of genomes that is central to such algorithms naturally covers a wide range of expanding behaviors. In fact, tracking novelty requires little change to any evolutionary algorithm aside from replacing the fitness function with a *novelty metric*.

The novelty metric measures how different an individual is from other individuals, thereby creating a constant pressure to do something new. The key idea is that instead of rewarding performance on an objective, the novelty search rewards diverging from prior behaviors. Therefore, novelty needs to be *measured*. There are many potential ways to measure novelty by analyzing and quantifying behaviors to characterize their differences. Importantly, like the fitness function, this measure must be fitted to the domain.

The novelty of a newly-generated individual is computed with respect to the *behaviors* (i.e., *not* the genotypes) of an *archive* of past individuals and the current population. The aim is to characterize how far away the new individual is from the rest of the population and its predecessors in *behavior space*, i.e., the space of unique behaviors. A good metric should thus compute the *sparseness* at any point in the behavior space. Areas with denser clusters of visited points are less novel and therefore rewarded less.

A simple measure of sparseness at a point is the average distance to the k-nearest neighbors of that point, where k is a fixed parameter that is determined experimentally. Intuitively, if the average distance to a given point's nearest neighbors is large then it is in a sparse area; it is in a dense region if the average distance is small. The sparseness ρ at point x is given by

$$\rho(x) = \frac{1}{k} \sum_{i=0}^{k} \text{dist}(x, \mu_i), \tag{3.1}$$

where μ_i is the ith-nearest neighbor of x with respect to the distance metric *dist*, which is a domain-dependent measure of behavioral difference between two individuals in the search space. The nearest neighbors calculation must take into consideration individuals from the current population and from the permanent archive of novel individuals. Candidates from more sparse regions of this behavioral search space then receive higher novelty scores. Note that this novelty space cannot be explored purposefully; it is not known *a priori* how to enter areas of low density just as it is not known a priori how to construct a solution close to the objective. Thus, moving through the space of novel behaviors requires exploration.

The current generation plus the archive give a comprehensive sample of where the search has been and where it currently is; that way, by attempting to maximize the novelty metric, the gradient of search is simply towards what is *new*, with no explicitly-specified objective within the search space.

Novelty search in general allows any behavior characterization and any novelty metric. Although generally applicable, novelty search is particularly suited to domains with deceptive fitness landscapes, intuitive behavioral characterization, and domain constraints on possible expressible behaviors. More generally, novelty search can be applied even when the experimenter has no clear objective in mind at all. For example, in some domains, rather than optimality, the aim may be to collect all the interesting behaviors in the space.

Once objective-based fitness is replaced with novelty, the underlying EA operates as normal, selecting the highest-scoring individuals to reproduce. Over generations, the population spreads out across the space of possible behaviors, continually ascending to new levels of complexity to create novel behaviors as the simpler variants are exhausted.

5.   Experiments with Novelty Search

There have been many successful applications of novelty search in EC (Lehman and Stanley, 2011; Risi et al., 2010; Goldsby and Cheng, 2010; Mouret, 2009; Lehman and Stanley, 2008; Lehman and Stanley, 2010a; Lehman and Stanley, 2010b; Doucette, 2010), both with GP (Doucette, 2010; Lehman and Stanley, 2010a; Goldsby and Cheng, 2010) and neuroevolution (Lehman and Stanley, 2011; Risi et al., 2010; Mouret, 2009; Lehman and Stanley, 2010b). This section reviews some such results to provide evidence that search can indeed function effectively without an explicit objective.

Novelty search was first introduced in a conference paper in 2008 (Lehman and Stanley, 2008) in which it was combined with the NEAT neuroevolution method (Stanley and Miikkulainen, 2002) and tested in a deceptive maze-navigation domain. In the harder of the two tested mazes, novelty search solved the maze in 39 out of 40 attempts (even though solving the maze was *not* the objective), while objective-based search nearly always failed (succeeding only three times out of 40 even though solving the maze *was* the objective). These results were also reproduced in combination with a multi-objective EA (Mouret,

2009). Novelty-related methods have also been shown beneficial in evolving plastic neural networks that learn from experience (Risi et al., 2010).

Novelty search was further applied to biped locomotion (Lehman and Stanley, 2011), a difficult control task that is popular within machine learning (Reil and Husbands, 2002). Though it was not looking directly for stable gaits, novelty search evolved controllers that traveled farther (4.04 meters, $sd = 2.57$) than solutions evolved by objective-based search (2.88 meters, $sd = 1.04$) on average over 50 runs of both methods. More dramatically, the *best* gait discovered by novelty search traveled 13.7 meters, while the best gait discovered by objective-based search traveled only 6.8 meters.

In GP, novelty search has worked successfully in the artificial ant benchmark (Lehman and Stanley, 2010a; Doucette, 2010), maze navigation (Lehman and Stanley, 2010a; Doucette, 2010), and in finding latent bugs in software models (Goldsby and Cheng, 2010). Novelty search with GP has outperformed standard objective-based search (Lehman and Stanley, 2010a; Doucette, 2010), proven less prone to program bloat (Lehman and Stanley, 2010a), and found more general solutions than objective-based search (Doucette, 2010).

Building on prior results in maze navigation with GP (Lehman and Stanley, 2010a; Doucette, 2010), the next section describes an experiment that investigates how the performance of novelty search and traditional objective-based search degrade with increasing problem complexity.

6.   Scaling Problem Complexity in Maze Navigation

A hypothesis advanced by this chapter is that as problems grow more difficult, the gradient defined by measuring distance to the objective becomes increasingly deceptive and thereby less informative. Thus as deceptiveness increases, non-objective search methods like novelty search may outperform more traditional objective-based search methods. However, while not susceptible to traditional deception, novelty search also is not guaranteed to consistently find *specific* objectives as problems become more complex.

Therefore, an interesting experiment is to compare how the relationship between problem complexity and performance varies in both traditional objective-based search and novelty search, which serves as an example of a non-objective search algorithm. Maze navigation is a natural choice of domain for such an investigation because it is a good model for search problems in general (Lehman and Stanley, 2011), because it is the basis for previous comparisons between novelty search and objective-based search (Lehman and Stanley, 2010a; Doucette, 2010; Lehman and Stanley, 2011; Mouret, 2009), and because it is easy to generate mazes of parameterized complexity.

Table 3-1. Parameters for the Maze Problem

Objective:	Find a robot that navigates the maze
Terminal set:	Left (turn left), Right (turn right), Move (move forward one square)
Functions set:	IfWallAhead (execute one of two child instructions based on whether there is a wall directly ahead), If-GoalAhead (execute one of two child instructions based on whether the goal is within a 90 degree cone projected outwards from where the robot is facing), Prog2 (sequentially execute the two child instructions)
Fitness cases:	One of 360 randomly-generated mazes
Wrapper:	Program repeatedly executed for 200 time steps
Population Size:	500
Termination:	Maximum number of generations = 200, 400 and 600

Experiment Description

The GP maze domain works as follows. A robot controlled by a genetic program must navigate from a starting point to an end point within a fixed amount of time. The task is complicated by occlusions and cul-de-sacs that prevent a direct route and create local optima in the fitness landscape. The robot can move forward, turn, and act conditionally based on whether there is a wall directly in front of it or not, or whether it is facing the general direction of the goal or not. The robot is successful in the task if it reaches the goal location. This setup is similar to previous GP maze navigation experiments (Lehman and Stanley, 2010a; Doucette, 2010). Table 3-1 describes the parameters of the experiment.

Objective fitness-based GP, which will be compared to novelty search, requires a fitness function to reward maze-navigating robots. Because the objective is to reach the goal, the fitness f is defined as the distance from the robot to the goal at the end of an evaluation: $f = b_f - d_g$, where b_f is the maximum distance possible and d_g is the distance from the robot to the goal. Given a maze with no deceptive obstacles, this fitness function defines a monotonic gradient for search. The constant b_f ensures that all individuals will have positive fitness.

GP with novelty search, on the other hand, requires a novelty metric to distinguish between maze-navigating robots. Defining the novelty metric requires careful consideration because it biases the search in a fundamentally different way than the fitness function. The novelty metric determines the behavior-space through which search will proceed. It is important that the type of behaviors that one hopes to distinguish are recognized by the metric.

As in prior maze navigation experiments (Lehman and Stanley, 2011; Lehman and Stanley, 2010a), the behavior of a navigator is defined as its ending position. The novelty metric is then the Euclidean distance between the ending positions of two individuals. For example, two robots stuck in the same corner appear similar, while one robot that simply sits at the start position looks very different from one that reaches the goal, though they are both equally viable to the novelty metric.

To compare how effectively fitness-based search and novelty search evolve navigational policies for increasingly complex maze problems, both search methods were tested on 360 randomly-generated mazes. These mazes were created by a recursive division algorithm (Reynolds, 2010), which divides an initally empty maze (i.e., without any interior walls) into two subareas by randomly adding a horizonal or vertical wall with a single randomly-located hole in it (which makes all open points reachable from any other open point in the maze). This process continues recursively within each subarea until no areas can be further subdivided without making the maze untraversable, or until the limit for subdivisions (chosen randomly between 2 and 50 for each maze in this experiment) is exceeded. The starting position of the maze navigating robot and the goal position it is trying to reach are also chosen randomly. Examples of mazes generated by such recursive division are shown in Figure 3-2.

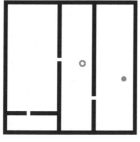

(a) Simple Maze Problem (b) More Complex Maze Problem

Figure 3-2. **Two randomly-generated maze problems created by the recursive division algorithm.** In both mazes, the filled circle represents the starting location and the unfilled circle represents the goal location. The maze shown in (a) has fewer subdivisions and a shorter optimal path to the goal than the maze shown in (b).

The length of the shortest possible path between the start and goal position was found to be a good heuristic for problem complexity. Intuitively, longer paths potentially require more complex navigational policies. In addition, increasing path length was highly correlated with decreasing performance for all of the search methods (adjusted $R^2 > 0.75$ for each method). Thus mazes were sampled such that 4 maze problems were chosen for each shortest-path length between 10 and 100. For each of the 360 mazes, 10 independent runs were conducted for both fitness-based search, novelty search, and GP with random selection. Random selection was considered as a control to differentiate novelty search from random exploration of the search space. Experiments were conducted with limits of 200, 400, and 600 generations. A given run was considered successful if a navigator was evolved that reached the goal within the time limit of 200 steps.

Results

The main result, as illustrated by Figures 3-3(a) and 3-3(b), is that novelty search solves significantly more instances of the generated maze problems ($p <$ 0.001, Fischer's exact test) and that it scales to solving more complex instances significantly better than objective fitness-based search or random search ($p <$ 0.001, the intercept values of the linear regression models are significantly different according to an ANCOVA test.) In addition, Figure 3-3(b) shows that novelty search better exploits additional evaluations than fitness-based search or random search. While random search may waste many evaluations with policies that are the same and fitness-based search may waste many evaluations attempting to escape from deceptive local optima, novelty search constantly incentivizes discovering new behaviors.

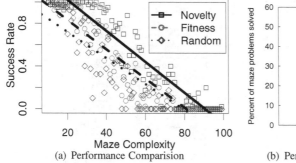
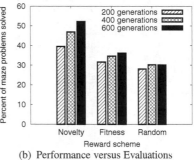

(a) Performance Comparision   (b) Performance versus Evaluations

Figure 3-3. **Reward scheme comparisons.** The effectiveness of novelty search, fitness-based search, and random search at solving problems of increasing complexity is plotted along with linear regressions in (a). Novelty search is the most effective although its performance also degrades with increasing problem complexity. Each plotted point is from ten runs, each lasting 600 generations. The effect on performance of varying the amount of generations for novelty search, fitness-based search, and random search is shown in (b). Novelty search exploits additional evaluations more effectively than fitness-based search or random search.

It is important to note that the performance of each of the three compared methods decreases with increasingly complex maze instances. Few instances are reliably solved by any of the methods with optimal path length greater than 80. Thus while novelty search may outperform the other methods in this domain, it too struggles to discover *specific* ambitious objectives from first principles;

this result tentatively supports the hypothesis that in some cases attempting to achieve specific objectives from a random starting point may ultimately be futile beyond a certain level of problem complexity.

This experiment and the previous section (which enumerated prior results with novelty search) offer strong empirical evidence that novelty search may often be a viable approach. Though such evidence of its effectiveness continues to accumulate, because it challenges the intuitive assumption that search should be driven by an objective, some skepticism of novelty search is a natural response, as addressed next.

7.   Common Objections to Novelty Search

Common objections to novelty search include: (1) that it is not general, (2) that it is ineffective if the space of behaviors to be explored becomes vast, (3) that maintaining a growing archive of past behaviors is too computationally expensive, and (4) that novelty itself is an objective and thus that novelty search is still an objective-based search.

7.1 Generality

Because maze-navigation is easily understood and makes a good model for search in general, it has often been used to illustrate properties of novelty search (Lehman and Stanley, 2010a; Lehman and Stanley, 2008; Lehman and Stanley, 2011; Mouret, 2009; Lehman and Stanley, 2010b). However, novelty search has also been applied to diverse domains such as biped walking (Lehman and Stanley, 2011), discovering latent bugs in software models (Goldsby and Cheng, 2010), T-mazes common in learning experiments with rats (Risi et al., 2010), and the artificial ant GP benchmark (Lehman and Stanley, 2010a). It has been combined with multi-objective search (Mouret, 2009) and applied with both neuroevolution and GP. Thus, while of course it will not always succeed in every domain, evidence of its generality as a viable tool in the toolbox of EC continues to accumulate.

7.2 Dimensionality

Though smaller behavior spaces can be more thoroughly explored, novelty search incentivizes the discovery of maximally different behaviors in any size of behavior space. Thus even in vast behavior spaces novelty search will expand to cover the space loosely, uncovering a wide variety of representative behaviors, some of which may be solutions to problems. For example, even when exploring a 400-dimensional behavior space constructed from considering nearly every point in the trajectory of a maze-navigating robot, novelty search still consistently discovers neural networks that solve mazes (Lehman and Stanley, 2011). Of course, it is possible to construct scenarios in which vast sections of the behavior space are uninteresting. However, search in such cases can be accelerated by restricting which behaviors are considered novel (Lehman and Stanley, 2010b).

7.3 Costs of Expanding the Archive

The purpose of the archive of previously novel behaviors in novelty search is to discourage backtracking by keeping track of where search has previously been in the behavior space. Though the archive in general grows slowly, because it grows continually over the course of evolution, it may eventually become computationally expensive to calculate the novelty of a new individual. However, kd-trees or other specialized data structures can reduce the computational complexity of such calculations, and experiments have shown that in practice it may often be possible to limit the size of the archive without harming novelty search's performance (Lehman and Stanley, 2011).

7.4 Novelty as an Objective

While some might say that rewarding novelty effectively means that novelty is just a special kind of objective, novelty is not an objective in the usual spirit of the word in EC. That is, for many years objectives in EC have been descriptions of *areas of the search space towards which evolution should be directed*. In other words, *objectives* describe where we want search to go. Yet novelty does *not* favor any particular part of the search space; instead, it is *relative* to what behaviors have been previously encountered, is constantly changing, and is largely orthogonal to the actual objective of the experiment. Thus while the semantics of the word *objective* are likely to continue to invite debate, drawing the distinction between novelty on the one hand and traditional objectives on the other is important because the purpose of scientific language is to *facilitate* drawing such distinctions rather than to obfuscate them. In fact, it could be argued that one reason that non-objective search has received so little attention until now is that a number of different incentives for search have been conflated as being one and the same when they are in fact fundamentally different. Thus language can help to extricate us from such misleading conflations.

The next section examines the larger implications of non-objective search.

8.   Implications

The success of novelty, search combined with the general tendency of systems that continually innovate to lack fixed objectives is that sometimes it is beneficial to *ignore* the objective rather than to seek it. Although this insight may at first appear strange or unsettling, the evidence suggests that the underlying assumption causing this discomfort, i.e., that searching for something is always the best way to find it, does not hold. That is, novelty search provides direct evidence that searching without knowledge of the objective can sometimes provide an advantage.

It is important to note that while novelty search is a viable alternative to objective-based search and has been shown to outperform it in non-trivial domains, it is no panacea and also so far falls short of natural evolution. However, as a new tool for EC and a working example of what can be gained from considering non-objective search, novelty search may inspire future research into more powerful EAs that can achieve more by not directly trying to do so.

That is, acknowledging that the prevailing paradigm of objective-based search is not the only way nor always the best way to guide search opens our minds to the possibilities of non-objective search, of which novelty search is only one example. Other examples of non-objective search include natural evolution and the cultural evolutions of math, art, and technology. These systems continually innovate and yield artifacts of increasing complexity though they are not guided by progress towards a fixed objective. New innovations in such objective-less systems typically branch exploratively outwards from prior innovations. This dynamic contrasts starkly with the objective paradigm in EC wherein evolution in any experiment almost always starts from an unstructured, random population and then evolves narrowly to a particular goal artifact.

The problem is that we often attribute the creativity and complexity of nature to *optimization* of reproductive fitness by natural selection. Thus the optimization process has become the key abstraction driving most EAs. However, natural evolution's characteristic prolific creativity and accumulation of complexity may be natural byproducts of diversity and open-ended innovation instead of the struggle to optimize a particular metric (Gould, 1996; Lynch, 2007). That is, the driving abstraction behind EC may rest upon the wrong bedrock principle. However, alternative abstractions can easily be investigated while still preserving the main components of EC and GP algorithms by simply changing the selection criteria to be driven by something other than explicit objectives.

A narrow interpretation of this argument is that we might sometimes more effectively achieve our objectives by searching for something other than themselves. However, the implication of this body of work is actually more fundamental: There may be a trade-off in search that has to date received little attention yet that nevertheless explains why computational approaches seem so qualitatively different from processes in nature. In particular, it may be that search can either be prodded toward a specific yet not-too-ambitious objective (e.g., as with the traditional fitness function) *or* it can discover a multitude of interesting artifacts, none of which are anticipated a priori or even necessarily desired at all (e.g., as in nature). Thus, on the downside, perhaps it is not possible to *purposefully* drive search to our most ambitious objectives. However, on the upside, perhaps artificial processes *can* discover artifacts of unprecedented scope and complexity, yet only if we relinquish the insistence that we must define a priori what those discoveries should be. In effect, we might *search without objectives*. Who knows what we will find?

9. Conclusion

In conclusion, the reliance on objectives that pervades EC and GP may not capture the essential dynamics of natural evolution. Indeed, this prevalent paradigm may be preventing us from realizing computationally the profound creativity of natural evolution. That is, although natural evolution does not narrowly search for something in particular, that is how we as practitioners typically constrain evolution. Far from bearing a negative message, this paper highlights the opportunity to explore the yet untamed wilderness of non-objective search algorithms to create open-ended systems that yield a ratcheting proliferation of complex novelty.

10. Acknowledgements

This research was supported in part by DARPA grant HR0011-09-1-0045.

References

Barnett, Lionel (2001). Netcrawling - optimal evolutionary search with neutral networks. In *Proc. of the 2001 IEEE Intl. Conf. on Evol. Comp.*, pages 30–37. IEEE Press.

Brockhoff, Dimo, Friedrich, Tobias, Hebbinghaus, Nils, Klein, Christian, Neumann, Frank, and Zitzler, Eckart (2007). Do additional objectives make a problem harder? In *GECCO '07: Proc. of the 9th Annual Conf. on Genetic and Evol. Comp.*, pages 765–772, New York, NY, USA. ACM.

Cliff, Dave and Miller, Geoffrey (1995). Tracking the red queen: Measurements of adaptive progress in co-evolutionary simulations. *Advances in Artificial Life*, pages 200–218.

Deb, Kalyanmoy (1999). Multi-objective genetic algorithms: Problem difficulties and construction of test problems. *Evol. Comp.*, 7:205–230.

Doucette, John (2010). Novelty-based fitness measures in genetic programming. Master of science in computer science, Dalhouise University.

Drexler, K.E. and Minsky, M. (1986). *Engines of creation*. Anchor Press.

Ficici, Sevan and Pollack, Jordan B. (1998). Challenges in coevolutionary learning: Arms-race dynamics, open-endedness, and mediocre stable states. In *Proc. of the Sixth Intl. Conf. on Art. Life*, pages 238–247. MIT Press.

Goldberg, David E. (1987). Simple genetic algorithms and the minimal deceptive problem. In Davis, L. D., editor, *Genetic Algorithms and Simulated Annealing, Re- search Notes in Artificial Intelligence*. Morgan Kaufmann.

Goldsby, H.J. and Cheng, B.H.C. (2010). Automatically Discovering Properties that Specify the Latent Behavior of UML Models. In *Proceedings of MODELS 2010*.

Gomez, Faustino and Miikkulainen, Risto (1997). Incremental evolution of complex general behavior. *Adaptive Behavior*, 5:317–342.

Gould, Steven Jay (1996). *Full House: The Spread of Excellence from Plato to Darwin*. Harmony Books.

Holland, John H. (1975). *Adaptation in Natural and Artificial Systems: An Introductory Analysis with Applications to Biology, Control and Artificial Intelligence*. University of Michigan Press, Ann Arbor, MI.

Kelly, K. (2010). *What technology wants*. Viking Press.

Koza, John R., Keane, Martin A., Streeter, Matthew J., Mydlowec, William, Yu, Jessen, and Lanza, Guido (2003). *Genetic Programming IV: Routine Human-Competitive Machine Intelligence*. Kluwer Academic Publishers.

Lehman, Joel and Stanley, Kenneth O. (2008). Exploiting open-endedness to solve problems through the search for novelty. In *Proc. of the Eleventh Intl. Conf. on Artificial Life (ALIFE XI)*, Cambridge, MA. MIT Press.

Lehman, Joel and Stanley, Kenneth O. (2010a). Efficiently evolving programs through the search for novelty. In *Proceedings of the Genetic and Evolutionary Computation Conference (GECCO-2010)*. ACM.

Lehman, Joel and Stanley, Kenneth O. (2010b). Revising the evolutionary computation abstraction: Minimal criteria novelty search. In *Proceedings of the Genetic and Evolutionary Computation Conference (GECCO-2010)*. ACM.

Lehman, Joel and Stanley, Kenneth O. (2011). Abandoning objectives: Evolution through the search for novelty alone. *Evol. Comp.*, 19(2):189–223.

Lynch, Michael (2007). The frailty of adaptive hypotheses for the origins of organismal complexity. In *Proc Natl Acad Sci USA*, volume 104, pages 8597–8604.

Mahfoud, Samir W. (1995). *Niching methods for genetic algorithms*. PhD thesis, University of Illinois at Urbana-Champaign, Champaign, IL, USA.

Mill, John Stuart (1846). *A System of Logic, Ratiocinative and Inductive*. John W. Parker and Son.

Mouret, Jean-Baptiste (2009). Novelty-based multiobjectivization. In *Proc. of the Workshop on Exploring New Horizons in Evol. Design of Robots,2009 IEEE/RSJ Intl. Conf. on Intelligent Robots and Systems*.

Pelikan, Martin, Pelikan, Martin, Goldberg, David E., and Goldberg, David E. (2001). Escaping hierarchical traps with competent genetic algorithms. In *Proc. of the Genetic and Evolutionary Computation Conference (GECCO-2001)*, pages 511–518. Morgan Kaufmann.

Reil, Torsten and Husbands, Phil (2002). Evolution of central pattern generators for bipedal walking in a real-time physics environment. *IEEE Transactions on Evolutionary Computation*, 6(2):159–168.

Reynolds, AM (2010). Maze-solving by chemotaxis. *Physical Review E*, 81(6).

Risi, S., Hughes, C.E., and Stanley, K.O. (2010). Evolving plastic neural networks with novelty search. *Adaptive Behavior*.

Schmidhuber, J. (2006). Developmental robotics, optimal artificial curiosity, creativity, music, and the fine arts. *Connection Science*, 18(2):173–187.

Secretan, J., Beato, N., D'Ambrosio, D.B., Rodriguez, A., Campbell, A., Folsom-Kovarik, J.T., and Stanley, K.O. (2011). Picbreeder: A case study in collaborative evolutionary exploration of design space. *Evol. Comp.* To appear.

Spector, Lee, Barnum, Howard, Bernstein, Herbert J., and Swamy, Nikhil (1999). Quantum computing applications of genetic programming. In Spector, Lee, Langdon, William B., O'Reilly, Una-May, and Angeline, Peter J., editors, *Advances in Genetic Programming 3*, chapter 7, pages 135–160. MIT Press, Cambridge, MA, USA.

Stanley, Kenneth O. and Miikkulainen, Risto (2002). Evolving neural networks through augmenting topologies. *Evolutionary Computation*, 10:99–127.

Stewart, T. C. (2001). Extrema selection: Accelerated evolution on neutral networks. In *Proc. of the 2001 IEEE Intl. Conf. on Evol. Comp.* IEEE Press.

Veldhuizen, David A. Van and Lamont, Gary B. (2000). Multiobjective evolutionary algorithms: Analyzing the state-of-the-art. *Evolutionary Computation*, 8(2):125–147.

Weinberger, Edward (1990). Correlated and uncorrelated fitness landscapes and how to tell the difference. *Biological Cybernetics*, 63(5):325–336.

Wolpert, David H. and Macready, William (1995). No free lunch theorems for search. Technical Report SFI-TR-95-01-010, The Santa Fe Institute, Santa Fe, NM.

Woolley, Brian G. and Stanley, Kenneth O. (2011). On the deleterious effects of a priori objectives on evolution and representation. In *Proceedings of the Genetic and Evolutionary Computation Conference (GECCO-2011)*. ACM.

Yao, Xin (1999). Evolving artificial neural networks. *Proceedings of the IEEE*, 87(9):1423–1447.

Zaera, N., Cliff, D., and Bruten, J. (1996). (Not) evolving collective behaviours in synthetic fish. In *From Animals to Animats 4: Proc. of the Fourth Intl. Conf. on Simulation of Adaptive Behavior*. MIT Press Bradford Books.

Chapter 4

A FINE-GRAINED VIEW OF PHENOTYPES AND LOCALITY IN GENETIC PROGRAMMING

James McDermott[1], Edgar Galván-Lopéz[2] and Michael O'Neill[3]

[1]*Evolutionary Design and Optimization, CSAIL, MIT, USA;* [2]*School of Computer Science and Statistics at Trinity College University, Ireland;* [3]*Natural Computing Research and Applications, University College Dublin, Ireland.*

Abstract

The *locality* of the mapping from genotype to phenotype is an important issue in the study of landscapes and problem difficulty in evolutionary computation. In tree-structured Genetic Programming (GP), the locality approach is not generally applied because no explicit genotype-phenotype mapping exists, in contrast to some other GP encodings. In this paper we define GP phenotypes in terms of semantics or behaviour. For a given problem, a model of one or more phenotypes and mappings between them may be appropriate e.g. $g \rightarrow p_0 \rightarrow \ldots \rightarrow p_n \rightarrow f$, where g is the genotype, p_i are distinct types of phenotypes, and f is fitness. Thus, the behaviour of each component mapping can be studied separately. The locality of the genotype-phenotype mapping can also be decomposed into the effects of the encoding and those of the operator's genotypic step-size. Two standard benchmark problem classes—Boolean and artificial ant—are studied in a principled way using this *fine-grained view of locality*. The method of studying locality with phenotypes seems useful in the case of the artificial ant, but Boolean problems provide a counter-example.

Keywords: Evolutionary computation, genetic programming, fitness landscape, problem difficulty, phenotype, locality, artificial ant, Boolean problems

1.   Introduction

The *locality* of the mappings from genotype to phenotype and to fitness is an important issue in the study of landscapes and problem difficulty in evolutionary computation. The information provided to the selection operator by fitness evaluations is more reliable in the presence of well-behaved (highly local) mappings, compared to poorly-behaved (non-local) ones.

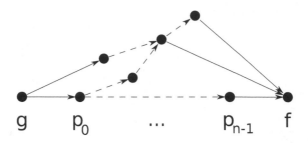

Figure 4-1. Each individual has a single genotype g and fitness value f, but there may be many parts of the phenotype $p_0 \ldots p_{n-1}$. In practice the $g \to p_0 \to f$ model is the most common.

In tree-structured Genetic Programming (GP), the locality approach (Roth-lauf, 2006) is not generally applied because no explicit genotype-phenotype mapping exists, in contrast to some other GP encodings such as Cartesian GP (Miller and Thomson, 2000), grammatical evolution (O'Neill et al., 2003), linear GP (Brameier and Banzhaf, 2007), and others. Some authors resort to measuring the locality of the GP genotype-fitness mapping (Langdon and Poli, 1998; Galvan-Lopez et al., 2010), but this does not tell the whole story. In particular, identifying a badly-behaved genotype-fitness mapping does not give us any clue about whether and how the mapping might be improved. Using phenotypes may help to identify the components of the algorithm responsible for the overall bad behaviour, or to conclude that no improvement is possible. In GP, it is possible to see program semantics or behaviour as a phenotype (Beadle and Johnson, 2009; Jackson, 2010), and this is the approach taken here. Phenotypes have not previously been used to study GP locality.

For a given problem, a model of one or more phenotypes p_i and mappings between them may be appropriate (see Figure 4-1). (It would be equivalent to talk about a single phenotype composed of multiple parts.) In general, the phenotypes are not equal in representational power: a reverse mapping may not be possible, or if possible may be one-to-many. The behaviour of each component mapping can be studied separately. The behaviour of the $g \to p_0$ mapping can also be decomposed into the effects of the encoding and those of the operator's genotypic step-size. For each representation, these components can be studied:

- The operators' genotypic step-size;

- The behaviour of the genotype-phenotype mapping;

- The behaviour of each phenotype-phenotype mapping, if multiple phenotypes exist;

- The behaviour of the final phenotype-fitness mapping.

In this paper, two standard benchmark problem classes are studied in a principled way using this *fine-grained view of locality*:

Artificial ant The model is $g \rightarrow p_0 \rightarrow p_1 \rightarrow f$, where p_0 is a behavioural phenotype based on the idea of binary decision diagrams, and p_1 a concrete phenotype based on the ant's path. The poor performance of all GP representations on this benchmark can not be regarded as an open problem (Langdon and Poli, 1998), but is here explained in a new way: the $p_0 \rightarrow p_1$ mapping, which is independent of the genetic representation, is badly-behaved.

Boolean problems The model is $g \rightarrow p_0 \rightarrow f$. The phenotype consists of the individual's truth table. A comparison between several distinct Boolean problems provides a counter-example to locality, i.e. a situation in which identical mapping behaviour does not lead to identical performance. This counter-example demonstrates the necessity of measures other than locality in predicting performance.

2. Previous Work on Problem Difficulty

Several methods have been used to measure and predict problem difficulty in GP and Evolutionary Computation (EC) in general. Common ones include fitness, distance correlation (FDC) (Jones, 1995), FDC extensions including fitness, clouds and negative slope coefficient (Vanneschi et al., 2007; Poli and Vanneschi, 2007), epistasis or linkage (Altenberg, 1997b), landscape autocorrelation (Weinberger, 1990; Kinnear, Jr., 1994), locality and distance, distortion (Rothlauf, 2006; Galvan-Lopez et al., 2010). Each is intended to measure the presence or absence of some representational feature suspected of making problems easier or more difficult. In many of these cases, a proposed measure of difficulty (e.g. (Jones, 1995)) is followed by a counter-example (e.g. (Altenberg, 1997a; Quick et al., 1998)): a problem which is easy to solve but is predicted to be difficult, or vice versa. In some cases the measure is then repaired or improved in some way (e.g. (Poli and Vanneschi, 2007)), to be followed by new counter-examples (e.g. (Vanneschi et al., 2009)). In addition to false predictions, there are problems of practicality including a requirement for large sample sizes. Jansen (Jansen, 2001) summarises the situation.

Despite this, research continues into methods of classifying problem difficulty. We take the attitude that although no measure can predict performance perfectly, there are known results which can be explained in terms of problem difficulty. Such explanations contribute to an understanding of what makes EC work.

We seek to understand the behaviour of the mapping from genotype to fitness in terms of its individual components. The behaviour of each component will be studied using the idea of *locality*, which was shown by Rothlauf to be a useful indicator of difficulty in genetic algorithms (Rothlauf, 2006). In the abstract sense, a mapping has locality if neighbourhood is preserved under that mapping. Genotype-phenotype locality has not been directly studied in the context of standard GP. Although Rothlauf and Oetzel (Rothlauf and Oetzel, 2006) compared the locality of grammatical evolution (GE) (O'Neill et al., 2003) and of standard GP, the GP genetic operators were in this case specially modified to make all genotypic neighbours correspond to phenotypic neighbours.

One practical shortcoming of existing work is that no absolute numerical threshold has been given which separates acceptable locality from unacceptable. In practice, it is possible only to make relative comparisons between values for different encodings (Rothlauf, 2006), or to examine the overall distribution of divergences (Rothlauf and Oetzel, 2006). The latter is our approach.

3.   Distance and Neighbourhood

In order to study the locality of a mapping from any space to any other, it is necessary to define neighbourhood in the first space, and distance in the second. In our experiments, neighbourhood in the genotype space is defined by mutation. Neighbourhood and distance over phenotypes are defined in Section 4. Distance in the fitness space is simply the absolute value of the difference between two values.

A topic closely related to locality is *genotypic step-size*. We define an operator's genotypic step-size as *the mean genotypic distance between a randomly-generated parent individual and an offspring created by applying the operator once to the parent*. Genotype-phenotype locality is influenced by the operator, and genotypic step-size provides a partial explanation of this influence.

The genotypic distance between a pair of individuals can be measured in several ways. When studying genotypic step-size, one is concerned with *dissimilarity* as opposed to *remoteness* (McDermott et al., 2011). Note that using distances with the property of *operator-distance coherence* (O'Reilly, 1997; Tomassini et al., 2005) is the *wrong* choice in this context, as follows.

We are attempting to break down the behaviour of the overall genotype-fitness mapping into its component parts: this includes comparing different operators' genotypic step-sizes and looking at phenotypic distances separately from genotypic distances. Using a new distance measure specialised to each operator will not allow such study. To see this, imagine two operators m_1 and m_2 each aligned with its own distance measure (d_1 and d_2). A single application of either mutation will produce a new individual whose distance from the original is represented by a number (d_1^* and d_2^*). We will want to know which of the operators is taking larger steps, on average, but no comparison of the numbers d_1^* and d_2^* will tell us that, since they are not necessarily on the same scale (for example one might be integer-valued and the other in the range

[0, 1]). We may choose to renormalise them, for example scaling both so that the average mutation gives a distance value in $[0, 1]$, but then both operators will be taking the same step-size by definition.

A second example concerns phenotypic distance measures. If a phenotypic distance measure is aligned with the action of a genetic operator, then again there will be a simple relationship between distances observed in the genotype and phenotype spaces, so we will learn nothing new by looking at phenotypic distances. All genotypic neighbours will be phenotypic neighbours by definition. In both cases, therefore, we use general-purpose distance measures which are not deliberately aligned with (or "coherent with") any particular operators. The FDC and related measures of difficulty, by contrast, require genetic similarity to reflect the likelihood of transforming one individual to another. In such contexts, a genetic distance measure aligned with genetic operators is indeed needed.

Instead, we use a general-purpose measure of genotypic dissimilarity, *structural distance*, extensively used in previous GP work (Tomassini et al., 2005; Vanneschi, 2004). Structural distance, also known as *tree-alignment distance*, is a continuous-valued measure which reflects the fact that the roots of syntactic trees tend to be more important than their lower levels. There are three steps to calculate the structural distance between two trees T_1 and T_2:

- T_1 and T_2 are left-aligned from the root (see Figure 4-2);

- For each pair of nodes at matching positions, the difference of their codes c (typically c is the index of a node-type within the primitive set) is calculated;

- The differences calculated in the previous step are combined into a weighted sum.

Formally, the distance between trees T_1 and T_2 with roots R_1 and R_2, respectively, is defined as follows:

$$dist(T_1, T_2, k) = d(R_1, R_2) + k \sum_{i=1}^{m} dist(child_i(R_1), child_i(R_2), \frac{k}{2}) \quad (4.1)$$

where: $d(R_1, R_2) = (|c(R_1) - c(R_2)|)^z$ and $child_i(Y)$ is the ith of the m possible children of a node Y, if $i < m$, or the empty tree otherwise. Note that c evaluated on the root of an empty tree is 0 by convention. The parameter k is used to give different weights to nodes belonging to different levels in the tree and $z \in \mathbb{N}$ is a parameter of the distance. The depth-weighting is well-motivated, in that GP trees' roots tend to be more important than their lowest levels. In our work, $k = 1/2$ and $z = 2$.

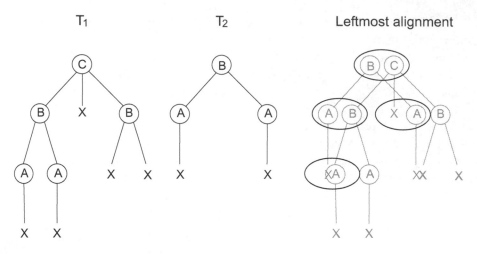

Figure 4-2. T_1 and T_2 are two trees. The figure at the right shows left-alignment.

4.   Phenotypes in GP

Some GP encodings feature explicit genotype-phenotype mappings, and in this are distinct from tree-structured GP. Examples include Cartesian GP (Miller and Thomson, 2000), grammatical evolution (O'Neill et al., 2003), linear GP (Brameier and Banzhaf, 2007), and others.

However, several authors have used aspects of program semantics or behaviour to perform, in tree-structured GP, roles performed by the phenotype in other forms of EC. Often semantics are defined as the values of a GP program on a set of fitness cases. Distance between phenotypes is then just Euclidean distance. Such methods have been used to enforce behavioural or semantic diversity (Beadle and Johnson, 2009; Jackson, 2010), and to modify operator behaviour (Krawiec and Lichocki, 2009; Quang et al., 2009).

We claim that for a given problem, multiple phenotypes can exist, of distinct types. In evolutionary biology, the idea that a phenotype need not be a single physical object, but may include behavioural aspects also, is called the "extended phenotype" (Dawkins, 1982). This informs our very broad definition, as follows. *Any data structure which is created during calculation of fitness, or which depends in some way on the genotype, or which affects in some way the value of fitness, may be a phenotype.* The most general situation is illustrated in Figure 4-1, in which multiple phenotypes each depend on the genotype, and/or on other, earlier phenotypes, and each may affect fitness.

In this paper we consider two standard benchmark problem classes: the artificial ant and boolean problems. We next define appropriate phenotypes for each and ways of measuring the difference between a pair of phenotypes in each case.

Artificial Ant

We present *two* definitions of ant phenotypes. First is p_0, a phenotype based on binary decision diagrams, which represents the ant's *behaviour* in an encoding-independent way. Next is p_1, a cell-sequence phenotype, which represents the ant's *path* concretely. This leads to the overall model $g \rightarrow p_0 \rightarrow p_1 \rightarrow f$.

Binary Decision Diagram Phenotypes. An ant's behaviour can be represented (Beadle and Johnson, 2009) in an abstract form, inspired by the idea of stateful binary decision diagrams (BDDs) (Bryant, 1992). BDDs are a formalism for representing Boolean functions. Any Boolean function composed of variables X_0, X_1, etc. and functions AND, OR, and NOT, for example, can be alternatively represented using a BDD. Initially, a BDD may be thought of as a tree. At the root is X_0. It has two outgoing edges, corresponding to two possible values of X_0, leading to two nodes for X_1. At layer n are 2^n nodes for variable X_n. At the very bottom layer are nodes labelled 0 and 1. The essential idea is similar to that of a finite state machine. To evaluate a BDD, one traverses from the root, at each node choosing which of its two outgoing edges to follow, depending on the value of the node's corresponding variable. The connectivity (i.e. the edges) ensures that the node one reaches at the bottom is the value of the Boolean function for the given variable values. In practice, it is common to use *reduced* BDDs, in which redundancies are eliminated: the BDD then no longer has a tree structure, since two divergent paths may re-join at a lower level.

Our definition of BDD-based ant phenotypes is similar but not identical to that of Beadle and Johnson (Beadle and Johnson, 2009). Each node contains a sequence of zero or more action commands (left, right, and move) and each branch represents an if-statement. Branches rejoin after execution of an if-statement. In the ant problem there is only one "variable", the result of the `iffoodahead` predicate. This variable is *stateful*: it varies during an ant's run, so it is necessary to use multiple layers of nodes to represent behaviour. Since the ant's behaviour depends on the order in which it perceives cells, it is not possible to re-order the BDD (as for BDDs in other contexts) without altering behaviour. The mapping from genotype to BDD-phenotype is thus unambiguous. The algorithm for performing the mapping is given in Algorithm 1. Code is available at `http://skynet.ie/~jmmcd/representations.html`. BDD-phenotypes are illustrated in Figure 4-3.

We can write BDD-phenotypes as strings. L, R, and M represent left, right, and move commands. A branch is represented by an `<X,Y>` construct. The positive branch is written first. Conversion from genotype to phenotype is not a simple matter of altering symbols. The sequencing implied by the `prog2` and

---

Algorithm 1 BDDMAP: Convert an artificial ant genotype to a BDD-based phenotype.

Require: Genotype g in s-expression form.

  1: $p \leftarrow g$
  2: {Convert}
  3: **while** replacements are possible **do**
  4:    replace in p: (if X Y) $\leftarrow$ <X,Y>
  5:    replace in p: (prog2 X Y) $\leftarrow$ XY
  6:    replace in p: (prog3 X Y Z) $\leftarrow$ XYZ
  7: **end while**
  8: {Canonicalise}
  9: **while** replacements are possible **do**
10:    replace in p: <<X,Y>W,Z> $\leftarrow$ <XW,Z>
11:    replace in p: <X,<Y,Z>W> $\leftarrow$ <X,ZW>
12:    replace in p: <XY,ZY> $\leftarrow$ <X,Z>Y
13:    remove in p: <,>
14: **end while**
15: return p

---

prog3 functions is abstracted away, and this allows some distinct genotypes to map to identical phenotypes. Several types of simplification are also required to obtain an abstract, canonical representation of ant behaviour:

- When one if-statement is nested directly inside another, one or the other branch of the inner one will never be executed. That is, we replace <<X,Y>W,Z> with <XW,Z>, and <X,<Y,Z>W> with <X,ZW> (here W, X, Y and Z are sequences of actions).

- When the two branches of an if-statement end with the same action, it is brought outside the branch. That is, we replace <XY,ZY> with <X,Z>Y.

- As a result of the above simplifications, it may happen that an if-statement has two empty branches: <,> can be removed.

A distinct but related canonicalisation process is applied by Looks (Looks, 2007).

An ant BDD can be run inside a suitable interpreter, and it will give the same ant path and fitness as the original GP genotype. The representation is sufficiently abstract that it could also be used as a phenotype for several other types of GP in which the ant problem might be run, including GE, Cartesian GP, evolutionary programming (i.e. a finite state machine encoding), and others.

We measure distance between BDD-phenotypes using the well-known string-edit distance. We acknowledge that it is likely imperfect, but we know of no

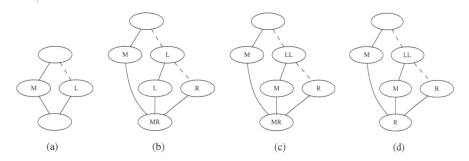

(a)   (b)   (c)   (d)

Figure 4-3. BDD phenotypes. The positive and negative branches of an if-statement are drawn with solid and dashed lines respectively. Edges from non-branching nodes are drawn with solid lines. In (a) a simple example: the genotype is (iffoodahead move left) and the phenotype <M,L>. In (b) the genotype is (prog3 (iffoodahead move (prog2 left (iffoodahead left (iffoodahead move right)))) move right). This translates to the phenotype <M,L<L,<M,R>>>MR. After removal of a redundant branch, we get <M,L<L,R>>MR, as shown. Phenotypic neighbours can have divergent fitness values: individual (c) has fitness 89, but its neighbour (d), created by a single phenotypic mutation, has fitness 1.

better distance for these structures. We define BDD-phenotypic neighbourhood via "minimal edits" or mutations on phenotypes, which consist of insertion, deletion, or editing of any of the action commands L, R and M. Figure 4-3 shows that phenotypic neighbours thus defined can have divergent fitness values. Our reasoning in considering only insertion, deletion and editing of the action commands is that non-minimal, structure-altering phenotypic edits will also lead *a fortiori* to divergent fitness values.

Examples of ant BDDs and canonicalisation are shown in Figure 4-3. Figures 4.3(c) and 4.3(d) show that the mapping from BDD to fitness is highly non-local. The large change in fitness between the two individuals occurs because behaviour at each step depends on position and orientation after previous steps, and is repeated multiple times. Small changes in behaviour are thus multiplied.

Cell-Sequence Phenotypes. Another definition for an ant's phenotype is *the time-indexed sequence of cells it visits*, as illustrated in Figure 4-4. This leads immediately to a natural definition of phenotypic distance: $d(a,b) = \sum_{t=0}^{T} d_c(a_t, b_t)$, where a_t and b_t are the position of ants a and b at time t, T is the maximum time, and d_c is a distance metric between cell positions, such as the toroidal taxi-driver's distance. The mapping from cell phenotype to fitness is highly local by definition.

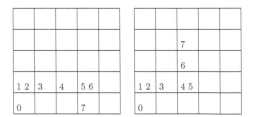

Figure 4-4. Two ants' cell-sequence phenotypes. An integer t in a cell indicates that the ant was in that cell at time t. The food pellets are not shown. The distance d between these two ants is calculated as the sum of toroidal taxi-driver distances between corresponding points in the paths. Where the ants coincide (as for $t < 5$) the distance is 0. For $t = 5$ the distance is 1, for $t = 6$ it is 2, and for $t = 7$ it is 3 (take a shortcut through the bottom, emerging at the top), so the total distance is $0 + 0 + 0 + 0 + 0 + 1 + 2 + 3 = 6$.

Boolean Problems

For Boolean problems, the phenotype p_0 is defined as the values of the genotype program at the set of fitness cases. Here the fitness cases are all 2^n possible combinations of Boolean values for the n inputs. We can then write the phenotype as a truth table, omitting the inputs since the order is implicit. The distance between phenotypes is simply the Hamming distance. This leads to the model $g \rightarrow p_0 \rightarrow f$. The $p_0 \rightarrow f$ mapping is well-behaved by definition.

BDDs have been used as phenotypes for Boolean problems in previous work (Beadle and Johnson, 2009). However, a key propery of BDDs is that reordering the variables can lead to a very different BDD which nevertheless has the same semantics. Therefore, measuring the distance between BDD phenotypes for Boolean problems would give misleading results, and so they are not used as phenotypes for this problem.

5.   Experiments and Results

In this section, for each benchmark problem, we relate the results of a study of locality with those of a set of evolutionary runs.

Boolean Problems

Here, we consider the standard GP tree structure together with its function and terminal sets to be an encoding, and our aim is to compare alternative encodings. We will examine the locality of the genotype-phenotype map for four encodings corresponding to the function sets {AND, OR, and NOT}, {AND, OR, NAND, NOR}, {AND, OR, NOT, IF}, and {NAND}. We abbreviate them as AON, AONN, AONI, and N, respectively. Each function set is sufficient to represent any Boolean function. We also consider four standard problems: True, Majority, Multiplexer, and Even Parity. We fix the problem size, i.e. number of inputs,

Table 4-1. Structural step-size (mean μ, standard deviation σ, and neutral ratio n).

Encoding	AON			AONI			AONN			N		
	μ	σ	n	μ	σ	n	μ	σ	n	μ	σ	n
True	5.9	12.7	0.1	9.4	24.5	0.1	7.4	18.9	0.1	3.1	7.5	0.1
Majority	5.8	12.5	0.1	9.5	25.0	0.1	7.3	18.7	0.1	3.0	7.4	0.1
Multiplexer	5.8	12.6	0.1	9.6	25.0	0.1	7.3	18.6	0.1	3.0	7.4	0.1
EvenParity	5.8	12.5	0.1	9.5	24.8	0.1	7.2	18.6	0.1	3.1	7.5	0.1
NoSelection	7.3	13.4	0.1	11.8	25.4	0.1	7.1	17.4	0.1	3.5	7.3	0.1

Table 4-2. Phenotypic step-size (mean μ, standard deviation σ, and neutral ratio n).

Encoding	AON			AONI			AONN			N		
	μ	σ	n	μ	σ	n	μ	σ	n	μ	σ	n
True	6.7	10.3	0.4	4.9	8.2	0.5	4.3	8.7	0.6	5.2	7.6	0.4
Majority	6.5	10.2	0.4	4.8	8.2	0.5	4.2	8.7	0.6	5.2	7.7	0.4
Multiplexer	6.5	10.2	0.4	4.8	8.2	0.5	4.1	8.6	0.6	5.2	7.6	0.4
EvenParity	6.6	10.2	0.4	4.9	8.3	0.5	4.2	8.7	0.6	5.3	7.7	0.4
NoSelection	12.2	13.2	0.3	10.2	11.8	0.3	8.5	11.6	0.4	8.3	9.0	0.3

Table 4-3. Fitness step-size (mean μ, standard deviation σ, and neutral ratio n).

Encoding	AON			AONI			AONN			N		
	μ	σ	n	μ	σ	n	μ	σ	n	μ	σ	n
True	4.5	8.2	0.5	2.9	5.6	0.5	3.0	6.9	0.6	2.5	3.6	0.4
Majority	2.4	4.3	0.6	1.7	3.3	0.6	1.6	3.5	0.7	1.7	3.2	0.5
Multiplexer	1.7	2.8	0.6	1.4	2.4	0.6	1.1	2.3	0.7	1.6	2.4	0.5
EvenParity	0.1	0.3	0.9	0.1	0.4	0.9	0.1	0.3	0.9	0.2	0.5	0.8
NoSelection	6.2	9.5	0.5	4.8	7.6	0.5	4.9	9.1	0.6	3.4	5.0	0.4

at 6, since this size is large enough to be difficult for some problems and the next possible size for Multiplexer (11) would impose a much greater burden of CPU time.

Sampling was conducted using the Metropolis-Hastings (MH) algorithm, as adapted for GP (Vanneschi, 2004). It works to bias the sample towards the higher-quality individuals most relevant to real runs. For each problem and each encoding, 100,000 individuals were sampled using MH and each was then mutated once using subtree mutation. A further 100,000 individuals were sampled not using MH but randomly, i.e. without selection bias. The distance between original and mutated offspring was then measured in the genotype, phenotype, and fitness spaces.

Evolutionary runs used mutation only. 100 runs were carried out, with a population of 500 and 50 generations. Ramped half-and-half initialisation was used with initial depth 1 and final depth 7. The maximum depth and length during the run were 7 and 1250, respectively. Tournament selection with tournament size 7 was used.

Tables 4-1 to 4-3 show the results of locality analysis. In each table, the columns represent the four encodings. Within each column, we show the mean step-size, the standard deviation, and the proportion of mutations which led

Table 4-4. Performance on Boolean problems measured over 100 runs (mean μ, standard deviation σ, and hits h). Higher is better.

Encoding	AON			AONI			AONN			N		
	μ	σ	h	μ	σ	h	μ	σ	h	μ	σ	h
True	64.0	0.0	100	64.0	0.0	100	64.0	0.0	100	64.0	0.0	100
Majority	59.5	2.4	3	61.5	2.3	24	60.9	2.8	19	64.0	0.0	100
Multiplexer	60.3	3.9	38	62.6	3.1	79	62.7	2.4	72	62.5	2.0	63
EvenParity	43.1	2.4	0	54.6	3.4	0	46.9	2.7	0	42.1	0.5	0

to zero step-size. The rows represent the method of sampling. For genotypic and phenotypic step-sizes, when MH sampling is used, the differences between problems are very slight. However, using random sampling changes things considerably, generally making genotypic, phenotypic, and fitness step-sizes larger. In the following we consider only MH sampling results, on the assumption that this method produces samples more relevant to real runs.

There are interesting effects in step-size among encodings. In genotypic step-size, $N < AON < AONN < AONI$. In phenotypic step-size, the results are very different: $AONN < AONI < N < AON$. In fitness step-size, AON gives the largest results with the others roughly equal. Therefore, although the phenotype-fitness mapping is perfectly local, the best-behaved genotype-phenotype mapping does not correspond to the best-behaved genotype-fitness mapping. Roughly the same results appear when step-sizes are rescaled, dividing by the mean distance between unrelated pairs of individuals (again sampled randomly, or by MH).

Next we relate these results with those of evolutionary runs shown in Table 4-4. Again, columns correspond to encodings (showing mean best fitness, standard deviation, and the number of hits, i.e. perfect solutions, out of 100 runs). Rows correspond to problems. As expected, AONI achieves the best score on the difficult Even Parity problem, because the if-statement is an important component of the solution. Overall performance can be characterised as $AON < N < AONN < AONI$. This ordering does not correspond to the results found in locality analysis above and can not be explained in terms of locality.

We turn next to the relative difficulty of the four problems. Table 4-4 shows very clearly that as expected, True is the easiest problem, and Even Parity the most difficult. Majority and Multiplexer appear roughly equal. Genotypic step-size (Table 4-1) is roughly equal across problems, and indeed is *a priori* identical if sampling is random (hence the "No Selection" results are not differentiated by problem). Similar remarks apply to the genotype-phenotype mapping (Table 4-2). Therefore analysis of the genotype-phenotype mapping can not explain the disparity in problem difficulty.

Similarly, the phenotype-fitness mapping is perfectly local in all cases: a single bit-flip in phenotype gives an increment or decrement of 1 in fitness. Again, the behaviour of this mapping can not explain the disparity in problem difficulty. Looking finally at fitness step-size (Table 4-3), it seems that larger step-sizes correspond to better performance. However, neutrality must be taken into account: the ratio of fitness-neutral mutations is much higher for Even Parity, leading to a smaller mean step-size. Therefore, the statistic with the best predictive power is the neutral ratio: fewer fitness-neutral mutations leads to better performance.

Summing up, locality analysis fails to correlate with performance across encodings or across problems in these results. The difference in performance across problems can be partly explained by the neutral ratio, and partly by larger ratios of perfect and good solutions in random samples of individuals for the easier problems, especially True. However it is easy to construct problems in which these indicators also fail to explain performance.

Artificial Ant

Although the relatively poor performance of various GP techniques on the artificial ant benchmark cannot be regarded as an open problem (Langdon and Poli, 1998; Langdon and Poli, 2002), the study of locality can still teach us something new. Again, we aim to relate the results of a study of locality (sampling, mutating, and measuring distances) with the results of evolutionary runs. We consider locality first. In Figure 4-5 we show: genotypic step-size, i.e. the size of the jumps in genotype space taken by two operators; the effect of the genotype-to-BDD-phenotype mapping on pairs of genotypic neighbours; the effect of the genotype-to-fitness mapping on genotypic neighbours; and the effect of the BDD-phenotype-to-fitness mapping on *phenotypic* neighbours.

Figure 4.5(a) shows that different operators define different genotypic neighbours. Figure 4.5(b) shows that genotypic neighbours map to similar phenotypes when neighbourhood is defined by one-point mutation, but often do not when it is defined by subtree mutation. Figure 4.5(c) (left and centre) shows that genotypic neighbours can have highly divergent fitness values when genotypic neighbourhood is defined by either mutation operator. Finally, 4.5(c) (right) shows that BDD-phenotypic neighbours can have highly divergent fitness values also.

The definition of non-trivial phenotypes allows us a fine-grained view of mapping behaviour. Recall that our model of the mapping is $g \to p_0 \to p_1 \to f$, where p_0 is the BDD-phenotype and p_1 is the cell-sequence. We already know that the overall map $g \to f$ is badly-behaved (confirmed by Figure 4.5(c), left and centre): we can now seek to explain which of its components are responsible. The $p_1 \to f$ mapping has high locality by definition and so is not to blame. However, $p_0 \to f$ has been shown to be badly-behaved (see Figure 4.5(c), right, and recall Figure 4.3(d)). Taking these results together shows that it is $p_0 \to p_1$, the mapping from the ant's abstract behaviour to its

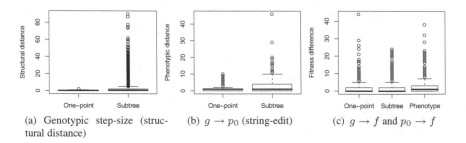

Figure 4-5. Artificial ant problem. Different operators have different step-sizes (a). The genotype-to-BDD-phenotype mapping (b) can therefore be well- or badly-behaved, depending on the operator used to define neighbourhood. The genotype-to-fitness mapping ((c), left and centre) is badly-behaved for both, as is the BDD-phenotype-to-fitness mapping ((c), right).

Table 4-5. Artificial Ant performance measured over 100 runs (mean μ, standard deviation σ, and hits h). Higher is better.

Algorithm/Setup	μ	σ	h
GP: no xover; subtree mut	60.54	9.98	6/100
GP: no xover; onepoint mut	51.24	7.22	0/100
GP: 9010 xover; subtree mut	61.27	10.10	5/100
GP: 9010 xover; onepoint mut	50.97	7.92	0/100
Random search:	60.86	13.93	1/100

cell-sequence, which is badly behaved and at least partly responsible for the behaviour of the overall $g \rightarrow f$ mapping. Note, however, that subtree mutation can also cause bad behaviour in the $g \rightarrow p_0$ mapping (see Figure 4.5(b)).

In Table 4-5 we show the results of evolutionary runs using standard GP. The aim is to confirm that GP techniques perform poorly on the ant problem. 100 runs were performed with each setup, with population 500 and 50 generations. Typical parameters were used: 90/10 crossover probability 0.7, mutation probability 0.01 (but 1.0 for mutation-only GP), and maximum tree depth 7. A random search (implemented as a GP run of population 25,000 and 1 generation, with ramped half-and-half initialisation) is also reported for comparison. The only "knowledge" input to the random search was to avoid tree depths less than 4.

An ANOVA and pairwise t-tests were performed on the 100 best fitness values from each setup. Three set-ups (subtree mutation, crossover/subtree, and random search) each performed significantly better than the other two (one-point and crossover/one-point) ($p < 0.01$, Bonferroni correction for 10 pairwise t-tests). But the overall result is that GP performs poorly. There is little novelty in this: it reinforces the conclusion of (Langdon and Poli, 1998), that the ant problem is difficult for many representations. Other representations including

Cartesian GP and GE have since produced largely similar results (Miller and Thomson, 2000; O'Neill et al., 2003).

It is noteworthy that subtree mutation does well relative to one-point, despite being more "randomising". It tends to take larger jumps in the search space. When a search space is badly-behaved, as here, highly local methods such as minimum-change operators lose any advantage they would have on smooth, well-behaved spaces. For difficult problems, then, random search tends to perform surprisingly well compared to more sophisticated algorithms.

6. Conclusions

In this paper we have reviewed previous GP work which uses program semantics or behaviour in the role played, in other forms of EC, by the phenotype. We have defined phenotypes for each of two benchmark problem classes— Boolean problems and the artificial ant. We have studied these problems using a *fine-grained view of locality*, in which the overall genotype-fitness mapping is separated out into (1) genotypic step-size, (2) the genotype-phenotype mapping, (3) phenotype-phenotype mapping, and (4) the phenotype-fitness mapping.

For (1) and (2), we have measured the extent to which neighbouring genotypes map to neighbouring phenotypes—i.e. the traditional view of locality. We have seen that a single mutation can lead to a large change in genotype and in phenotype in **Boolean** problems. None of the four Boolean encodings studied led to reliably well-behaved genotype-phenotype mappings.

When we wish to study what might be called the "inherent difficulty" of a problem—that is, the difficulty which cannot be removed by improved encodings or operators—then the mappings of interest are (3) and (4), from phenotype to fitness, where the phenotype is defined in a problem-specific but encoding-independent way. The fine-grained model of locality allows us to identify the component—the map from abstract behaviour to concrete path, i.e. (3)— responsible for the overall poor behaviour in the **artificial ant** problem. We have performed various evolutionary runs and as expected we have added to Langdon and Poli's list of poor results (Langdon and Poli, 1998) on this problem. Our conclusion is an attempt to explain these poor results: in the ant problem, the mapping from BDD-phenotypes to fitness is inherently poorly-behaved. Since these BDD-phenotypes can function as abstract behavioural phenotypes for many GP approaches to the problem, this result goes some way to explaining their universally poor performance. Thus, poor performance is not due to inadequate representations.

We note that another standard GP benchmark problem class—real-valued symbolic regression—can be treated in the same way as Boolean problems have been treated here. The natural model is again $g \to p_0 \to f$, where p_0 is a phenotype reflecting the semantics of the program. It could be a vector of the values of the program at the fitness cases (Krawiec and Lichocki, 2009). Again, the mapping from genotype to phenotype will depend on the encoding, but be independent of the fitness function, while the mapping from phenotype to fitness will be local by definition. Locality results for the genotype–phenotype mapping in real-valued symbolic regression, omitted due to space constraints, tell quite a similar story to that for Boolean problems, as expected. It is expected that symbolic regression will therefore provide another example in which the fine-grained view of locality fails to explain performance across differing fitness functions and differing encodings.

Identification of Phenotypes

Our definition of phenotypes is very broad, including any data structure created during fitness evaluation, any data structure which depends on the genotype, and any data structure on which fitness depends. However not every phenotype, so defined, will necessarily turn out to be useful.

In general, a phenotype may be particularly useful in breaking the genotype-fitness mapping into components if it can function equally well for different encodings (the BDD phenotype could function for many different GP encodings for the ant problem). A useful behavioural phenotype may not necessarily be closely tied to fitness: for example, an ant trained on the Santa Fe trail can be run on a different trail, such as the Los Altos trail. Its concrete behaviour and fitness will likely be very different. But its abstract behaviour, as encoded in its BDD phenotype, will be the same.

For a given problem, the multiple phenotypes will not necessarily be equal in representational power: a reverse mapping may not be possible, or if possible may be one-to-many. One example might be a phenotype composed of statistical measurements of ant behaviour in a large variety of test situations (e.g. the proportion of times an ant re-visits an already-visited cell); such a phenotype would not be sufficient to calculate either a fitness or a corresponding genotype.

When there is a clear ordering of chosen phenotypes, as in the ant problem (the cell-sequence phenotype can not be backward-mapped to the BDD-phenotype or genotype), extra phenotypes can be introduced without fear of introducing a dubious ordering.

A phenotype which is closely related to fitness calculation may often be useful (for example the cell-sequence ant phenotype, and the Boolean truth-table phenotype are very close to fitness). One could add an extra phenotype in the ant case: the set of cells visited (without time-indexing) is sufficient to calculate fitness and can be calculated directly from the time-indexed cell-sequence. It would fit naturally as a third phenotype, after the time-indexed cell-sequence and before fitness.

However, a general and principled method of identifying all useful phenotypes and discarding uninformative ones is beyond the scope of this paper.

Weaknesses of Locality

Although we have considered only issues relating to locality, we believe that any approach to the study of GP landscapes might benefit from a way to think about GP phenotypes and to separate the genotype-fitness mapping into components. However, locality analysis has weaknesses, demonstrated clearly by the study of Boolean problems. It does not take into account the size of the search space, or the relative size of the solution set. A small search space, or a search space rich in good solutions, will correspond to an easy problem regardless of locality. Any locality measure based purely on step-size can also be misled by neutrality, which can have either harmful or beneficial effects (Galvan, 2009). Finally, locality fails to consider the prevalence of local optima in the search space. As with other indicators of problem difficulty, locality seems to provide some insight but not a complete account. This conclusion agrees with that of Krawiec (Krawiec, 2011), who claims that "high locality of representation space cannot guarantee good search performance". Locality is a low-level characterisation of mapping behaviour, and it is possible to construct mappings of high locality which are nevertheless deceptive and difficult to solve.

Acknowledgements

Special thanks are due to Colin Johnson for discussion of BDDs, to Alberto Moraglio for discussion of locality, and to all in the NCRA for discussion of landscape topics. JMcD receives funding from the Irish Research Council for Science, Engineering and Technology, co-funded by Marie Curie Actions under FP7. EG-L and MO'N thank the support of Science Foundation Ireland under Grant No. 08/IN.1/I1868.

References

Altenberg, Lee (1997a). Fitness distance correlation analysis: An instructive counterexample. In *Proceedings of the Seventh International Conference on Genetic Algorithms*, pages 57–64.

Altenberg, Lee (1997b). NK fitness landscapes. In Bäck, Thomas, Fogel, David B., and Michalewicz, Zbigniew, editors, *Handbook of Evolutionary Computation*. IOP Publishing Ltd. and Oxford University Press.

Beadle, Lawrence and Johnson, Colin G. (2009). Semantic analysis of program initialisation in genetic programming. *Genetic Programming and Evolvable Machines*, 10(3):307–337.

Brameier, Markus and Banzhaf, Wolfgang (2007). *Linear Genetic Programming*. Number XVI in Genetic and Evolutionary Computation. Springer.

Bryant, R.E. (1992). Symbolic Boolean manipulation with ordered binary-decision diagrams. *ACM Computing Surveys (CSUR)*, 24(3):318.

Dawkins, Richard (1982). *The Extended Phenotype*. Oxford University Press.

Galvan, Edgar (2009). *An Analysis of the Effects of Neutrality on Problem Hardness for Evolutionary Algorithms*. PhD thesis, School of Computer Science and Electronic Engineering, University of Essex, United Kingdom.

Galvan-Lopez, Edgar, McDermott, James, O'Neill, Michael, and Brabazon, Anthony (2010). Defining locality in genetic programming to predict performance. In *2010 IEEE World Congress on Computational Intelligence*, pages 1828–1835, Barcelona, Spain. IEEE Computational Intelligence Society, IEEE Press.

Jackson, David (2010). Phenotypic diversity in initial genetic programming populations. In Esparcia-Alcazar, Anna Isabel et al., editors, *Proceedings of the 13th European Conference on Genetic Programming, EuroGP 2010*, volume 6021 of *LNCS*, pages 98–109, Istanbul. Springer.

Jansen, Thomas (2001). On classifications of fitness functions. In *Theoretical aspects of evolutionary computing*, pages 371–386. Springer.

Jones, Terry (1995). *Evolutionary Algorithms, Fitness Landscapes and Search*. PhD thesis, University of New Mexico, Albuquerque.

Kinnear, Jr., Kenneth E. (1994). Fitness landscapes and difficulty in genetic programming. In *Proceedings of the 1994 IEEE World Conference on Computational Intelligence*, volume 1, pages 142–147, Orlando, Florida, USA. IEEE Press.

Krawiec, Krzysztof (2011). Learnable embeddings of program spaces. In *Proceedings of EuroGP*, pages 166–177. Springer.

Krawiec, Krzysztof and Lichocki, Pawel (2009). Approximating geometric crossover in semantic space. In Raidl, Guenther et al., editors, *GECCO '09: Proceedings of the 11th Annual conference on Genetic and evolutionary computation*, pages 987–994, Montreal. ACM.

Langdon, W. B. and Poli, R. (1998). Why ants are hard. In Koza, John R. et al., editors, *Genetic Programming 1998: Proceedings of the Third Annual Conference*, pages 193–201, University of Wisconsin, Madison, Wisconsin, USA. Morgan Kaufmann.

Langdon, W. B. and Poli, Riccardo (2002). *Foundations of Genetic Programming*. Springer-Verlag.

Looks, Moshe (2007). Program evolution for general intelligence. In *Proceedings of the AGI workshop 2006: Advances in Artificial General Intelligence: Concepts, Architectures and Algorithms*, pages 125–143. IOS Press.

McDermott, James, O'Reilly, Una-May, Vanneschi, Leonardo, and Veeramachaneni, Kalyan (2011). How far is it from here to there? A distance that is coherent with GP operators. In *Proceedings of EuroGP*, Torino, Italy. Springer.

Miller, Julian F. and Thomson, Peter (2000). Cartesian genetic programming. In Poli, Riccardo et al., editors, *Genetic Programming, Proceedings of EuroGP'2000*, volume 1802 of *LNCS*, pages 121–132, Edinburgh. Springer-Verlag.

O'Neill, Michael, Ryan, Conor, Keijzer, Maarten, and Cattolico, Mike (2003). Crossover in grammatical evolution. *Genetic Programming and Evolvable Machines*, 4(1):67–93.

O'Reilly, Una-May (1997). Using a distance metric on genetic programs to understand genetic operators. In *IEEE International Conference on Systems, Man, and Cybernetics, Computational Cybernetics and Simulation*, volume 5, pages 4092–4097, Orlando, Florida, USA.

Poli, Riccardo and Vanneschi, Leonardo (2007). Fitness-proportional negative slope coefficient as a hardness measure for genetic algorithms. In *Proceedings of GECCO '07*, pages 1335–1342, London, UK.

Quang, Uy Nguyen, Nguyen, Xuan Hoai, and O'Neill, Michael (2009). Semantic aware crossover for genetic programming: the case for real-valued function regression. In Vanneschi, Leonardo et al., editors, *Proceedings of the 12th European Conference on Genetic Programming, EuroGP 2009*, volume 5481 of *LNCS*, pages 292–302, Tuebingen. Springer.

Quick, R. J., Rayward-Smith, Victor J., and Smith, G. D. (1998). Fitness distance correlation and ridge functions. In *Proceedings of the 5th International Conference on Parallel Problem Solving from Nature*, pages 77–86, London, UK. Springer-Verlag.

Rothlauf, Franz (2006). *Representations for Genetic and Evolutionary Algorithms*. Physica-Verlag, 2nd edition.

Rothlauf, Franz and Oetzel, Marie (2006). On the locality of grammatical evolution. In Collet, Pierre et al., editors, *Proceedings of the 9th European Conference on Genetic Programming*, volume 3905 of *Lecture Notes in Computer Science*, pages 320–330, Budapest, Hungary. Springer.

Tomassini, Marco, Vanneschi, Leonardo, Collard, Philippe, and Clergue, Manuel (2005). A study of fitness distance correlation as a difficulty measure in genetic programming. *Evolutionary Computation*, 13(2):213–239.

Vanneschi, Leonardo (2004). *Theory and Practice for Efficient Genetic Programming*. PhD thesis, Faculty of Sciences, University of Lausanne, Switzerland.

Vanneschi, Leonardo, Tomassini, Marco, Collard, Philippe, Verel, Sébastien, Pirola, Yuri, and Mauri, Giancarlo (2007). A comprehensive view of fitness landscapes with neutrality and fitness clouds. In Ebner, Marc et al., editors, *Proceedings of the 10th European Conference on Genetic Programming*, volume 4445 of *Lecture Notes in Computer Science*, pages 241–250, Valencia, Spain. Springer.

Vanneschi, Leonardo, Valsecchi, Andrea, and Poli, Riccardo (2009). Limitations of the fitness-proportional negative slope coefficient as a difficulty measure. In *Proceedings of the 11th Annual conference on genetic and evolutionary computation*, pages 1877–1878. ACM.

Weinberger, E. (1990). Correlated and uncorrelated fitness landscapes and how to tell the difference. *Biological Cybernetics*, 63(5):325–336.

Chapter 5

EVOLUTION OF AN EFFECTIVE BRAIN-COMPUTER INTERFACE MOUSE VIA GENETIC PROGRAMMING WITH ADAPTIVE TARPEIAN BLOAT CONTROL

Riccardo Poli[1], Mathew Salvaris[1], and Caterina Cinel[1]

[1] *School of Computer Science and Electronic Engineering, University of Essex, Wivenhoe Park, CO4 3SQ, UK*

Abstract   The Tarpeian method for bloat control has been shown to be a robust technique to control bloat. The covariant Tarpeian method introduced last year, solves the problem of optimally setting the parameters of the method so as to achieve full control over the dynamics of mean program size. However, the theory supporting such a technique is applicable only in the case of fitness proportional selection and for a generational system with crossover only. In this paper, we propose an adaptive variant of the Tarpeian method, which does not suffer from this limitation. The method automatically adjusts the rate of application of Tarpeian bloat control so as to achieve a desired program size dynamics. We test the method in a variety of standard benchmark problems as well as in a real-world application in the field of Brain Computer Interfaces, obtaining excellent results.

Keywords: Brain Computer Interfaces, Adaptive Tarpeian method, Bloat control

1.   Introduction

Many techniques to control bloat have been proposed in the last two decades (for recent reviews see (Poli et al., 2008; Luke and Panait, 2006; Silva and Costa, 2009; Alfaro-Cid et al., 2010)). One of these is the Tarpeian method introduced in (Poli, 2003). The method is extremely simple in its implementation. All that is needed is a wrapper for the fitness function like the following:

if size(program) > average_program_size **and** random() < p_t **then**
   return(f_{bad});
else
   return(fitness(program));

were p_t is a real number between 0 and 1, random() is a function which returns uniformly distributed random numbers in the range $[0, 1)$ and f_{bad} is a constant which represents an extremely low (or high, if minimising) fitness value such that individuals with such fitness are almost guaranteed not to be selected.

The Tarpeian method has been used in a variety of studies and applications. For example, in (Mahler et al., 2005) its performance and generalisation capabilities were studied, while it was compared with other bloat-control techniques in (Luke and Panait, 2006; Wyns and Boullart, 2009; Alfaro-Cid et al., 2010). The method has been used with success in the evolution of bin packing heuristics (Burke et al., 2007; Allen et al., 2009), in the evolution of image analysis operators (Roberts and Claridge, 2004), in artificial financial markets based on GP (Martinez-Jaramillo and Tsang, 2009), just to mention a few.

In all cases the Tarpeian method has been a solid and efficient choice. A particularly nice feature of this method is that, because the wrapper *does not* evaluate the individuals being given a bad fitness, the higher the anti-bloat intensity, p_t, the faster the algorithm. All studies and applications, however, have had to determine by trial and error the value of the parameter p_t such that the size of programs would not exceed a given range of sizes. In other words, for a new application there was no way of saying *a priori* what values of p_t corresponded to what values of mean program size.

Recent research (Poli, 2010) has developed a technique, called *covariant Tarpeian method*, that allows one to dynamically and optimally set the rate of application of the Tarpeian method, p_t, in such a way as to completely control the evolution of the mean program size. The method has excellent properties but also some important drawbacks which we seek to overcome in this paper.

We, therefore, start the paper with a brief review of the covariant Tarpeian method (Section 2). This is followed by our proposed adaptive technique in Section 3. We test the algorithm on a variety of benchmark problems in Section 4. We propose our real-world application in the domain of Brain Computer Interfaces (BCI) in Section 5. We provide our conclusions in Section 6.

2.   Covariant Tarpeian Method

The covariant Tarpeian method was inspired by the size evolution equation developed in (Poli, 2003; Poli and McPhee, 2003). As shown in (Poli and McPhee, 2008), this can be rewritten as follows

$$E[\Delta\mu] \;=\; \frac{\mathrm{Cov}(\ell, f)}{\bar{f}} \tag{5.1}$$

where E is the expectation operator, $\Delta\mu$ is the change in average program size from this generation to the next, ℓ is program size, f is fitness and $\bar{f}$ is the average fitness in the current generation. This equation applies if fitness proportionate selection is used in a generational system with independent selection and symmetric sub-tree crossover.

To model the effects on program size of the Tarpeian method in a GP system (Poli, 2010) specialised this equation and derived the following approximation:

$$E[\Delta\mu_t] \cong \frac{\mathrm{Cov}(\ell, f) - p_t\phi_> \left[\mathrm{Cov}_>(\ell, f) + (\mu_> - \mu)(\bar{f}_> - f_{bad})\right]}{\bar{f} - p_t\phi_>(\bar{f}_> - f_{bad})} \quad (5.2)$$

where $\Delta\mu_t$ is the change in average program size from one generation to the next *in the presence of Tarpeian bloat control*, $\phi_>$ is the proportion of above-average-size programs, $\bar{f}_>$ is the average fitness of such programs, $\mu_>$ is the average size of such programs, and $\mathrm{Cov}_>(\ell, f)$ is the covariance between program size and fitness within such programs.[1]

With this explicit formulation of the expected size changes, we can find out for what value of p_t we get $E[\Delta\mu_t] = 0$. By setting the l.h.s. of Equation (5.2) to 0 and solving for p_t, we obtain:

$$p_t \cong \frac{\mathrm{Cov}(\ell, f)}{\phi_> \left[\mathrm{Cov}_>(\ell, f) + (\mu_> - \mu)(\bar{f}_> - f_{bad})\right]}. \quad (5.3)$$

This equation allows one to determine how often the Tarpeian method should be applied to modify the fitness of above-average-size programs as a function of a small set of descriptors of the current state of the population and of the parameter f_{bad}.

An important limitation of these results is that they can be applied only to *generational* systems with *fitness proportionate selection*. Also, they are applicable only to systems with symmetric crossover and *no mutation*.

While there are many GP systems that fit this particular specification, many more, perhaps most, do not. In particular, the preferred selection strategy in GP is tournament selection (particularly when large populations are used, since it requires a computation load which is linear in the population size, while fitness proportionate selection is quadratic). Also, steady state systems are very frequently used in GP, since they avoid the overhead of storing two generations. For all these systems, we need a different recipe to adapt p_t.

---

[1]Note that because size distributions are typically skewed, the proportion of above-average-size programs, $\phi_>$, is not necessarily 0.5. For example, in a population containing 5 programs of size 1, 4 of size 2, 3 of size 3, 2 of size 4 and 1 of size 5, $\phi_> = \frac{2}{5}$.

3.   Adaptive Tarpeian Algorithm

The recipe we propose to set p_t to achieve this is very simple. We initially set $p_t = 0$. Then, at each generation, if the mean (or median) size of the individuals in the population is bigger than a user-settable threshold T, we increment p_t by an amount α, otherwise we decrement p_t by an amount α, where α is a constant ≤ 1. In these operations, p_t is clipped within the interval $[0, 1]$. As we will show later, the threshold T can be modified from generation to generation to follow a particular function of time, resulting in the size of the programs in the population approximately tracking the same function. However, in most cases $T = \text{constant}$.

Let us try to understand the rationale for this algorithm. We will do this by considering a generational system with fitness proportionate selection and we will apply the method to mean program sizes so as to be able to refer to the equations presented in the previous section for explanations. However, similar processes happen also in steady state algorithms, in systems which use forms of selection other than fitness proportionate and for median program sizes.

Since initially $p_t = 0$, if the user sets T to be bigger than the initial mean program size, for as long as the mean program size is below the threshold T, p_t remains zero. So, there is no Tarpeian bloat control and size can evolve freely. In a generational system using fitness proportionate selection mean program size will, therefore, obey Equation (5.2) with $p_t = 0$, i.e., Equation (5.1).

In the presence of bloat, at some point $\text{Cov}(\ell, f)$ will be sufficiently high for sufficiently long to cause the mean program size to surpass the threshold T. At this point the algorithm start increasing p_t thereby initially partially and then completely compensating this positive covariance (see numerator of Equation (5.2)). Normally it will take some generations to reach complete compensation, i.e., for $E[\Delta \mu_t]$ to become zero. By this time the mean program size will have exceeded T and therefore the algorithm continues to increase p_t, thereby overcompensating for the covariance and causing the mean program size to start dropping. Since p_t continues to be incremented until the mean program size is below T, eventually the mean program size will become less than T and in fact will continue to decrease for a while, until p_t is sufficiently small not to compensate for the covariance any more. At this point, in the presence of a positive covariance, the cycle will repeat (typically dampened). Naturally, the frequency of these oscillations will depend on the choice of α with the bigger its value the quicker the cycles.

Other than for the aforementioned effect, as we will see, the behaviour of the algorithm is little influenced by α. However, we still have one degree of freedom to fix: the parameter T. This is not different from other (non-covariant) bloat control methods. In the parsimony pressure method, for example, one needs to fix the parsimony coefficient, while in the original Tarpeian method one had to

Table 5-1. Primitive set used in our tests with polynomial regression problems.

Primitive	Arity	Functionality
x	0	Independent variable
$-1.0, -0.8, \ldots, 1.0$	0	Numerical constants
sin, cos	1	Sine and cosine functions
*, +, −	2	Standard arithmetic operators
%	2	Protected division. It returns 1 if the denominator is 0; $\min(\max(\frac{num}{den}, 10^{-5}), 10^5)$ otherwise.
if	3	If function. If the first argument is non-zero it returns its second argument, otherwise the third.

fix the rate of application of the operator. The difference between such methods and the adaptive Tarpeian method is that with the latter it is possible to precisely prescribe what size programs should have on average at each generations, while for the former the mapping from parameters to sizes is application-dependent and generally unknown.

4. Results on Benchmark Problems

GP Setup and Benchmark Problems

In order to extensively test the adaptive Tarpeian method we considered four symbolic regression problems. In three of the problems — the quartic, quintic and sextic polynomial problems — the objective was to evolve a function which fits a polynomial of the form $x + x^2 + \cdots + x^d$, where $d = 4, 5, 6$ is the degree of the polynomial, for x in the range $[-1, 1]$. In the fourth problem — the unequal-coefficients quartic polynomial problem — the objective was to fit the polynomial $x + 2x^2 + 3x^3 + 4x^4$. Fitness cases for all problems were obtained by sampling the corresponding polynomials at the 21 equally spaced points $x \in \{-1, -0.9, \ldots, 0.9, 1.0\}$.

We used a tree-based GP system implemented in Python with all numerical calculations done using the Numpy library (which is implemented in C). The system uses a steady-state update policy. It evolved a population of either 100 or 1,000 individuals with tournament selection with a tournament size of 5, the grow method with a maximum initial depth of 4, sub-tree crossover applied with a rate of 0.9 and sub-tree mutation with a rate of 0.1. Both used a uniform selection of crossover/mutation points. Runs lasted 50 generations unless otherwise stated. The system used the primitive set shown in Table 5-1.

We tested the system with and without adaptive Tarpeian bloat control. When the method was used, we tested it for $\alpha \in \{0.05, 0.1, 0.25, 0.5, 1.0\}$ and for a threshold $T = 30$. In each configuration we performed 30 independent runs. The threshold $T = 30$ was chosen based on previous experience with polynomial regression.

Polynomial Regression Results

In Figure 5-1 we show the evolution of the median (across 30 independent runs) of the best-of-generation fitness and of the median program size in runs with the Quartic polynomial problem for different values of the adaptive Tarpeian method parameter α and for populations of 1,000 individuals. In Figure 5-2 we show the corresponding results for the Sextic polynomial. For space limitations we do not report the results for the Quintic polynomial and the Quartic with unequal coefficients, but we note that results were qualitatively similar. Results with smaller populations of 100 individuals (not reported) were also similar in terms of program size dynamics, although best fitnesses were naturally significantly worse.

As we can see from Figures 5-1 and 5-2 there are no significant differences in the best-of-generation fitness dynamics between the case where no bloat control is exerted and in the case of adaptive Tarpeian bloat control. This is also confirmed by the success rate figures reported in Table 5-2.[2]

However, looking at the median size dynamics in Figures 5-1 and 5-2 we see that at all values of α tested the method keeps the median size of the individuals in the population under tight control, while in the absence of bloat control we see significant bloat. As a result runs lasted between 10 (for the Quartic polynomial) and 20 (for the Quartic polynomial with unequal coefficients) times more without bloat control. What differs as α is varied is the duration of the transient which takes place when the threshold $T = 30$ is first hit, with the smallest values of α being affected by the largest overshoots in program size.

As an example of the ability of the adaptive Tarpeian method to dynamically control the dynamics of program sizes, in Figure 5-3 we show the median of the median program size recorded in 10 independent runs with the Quintic polynomial problem with adaptive Tarpeian control with $T(t) = 50 + 25 \times \sin(\pi t/50)$. Runs lasted 200 generations. Population size was 1000. Tournament size was 2. All other parameters were the same as in the other polynomial regression problems.

---

[2]While the results reported in Table 5-2 provide a useful indication of relative performance differences, they were obtained for one particular definition of success: that the fitness is no greater than 1. Naturally, different definitions of success may produce different results.

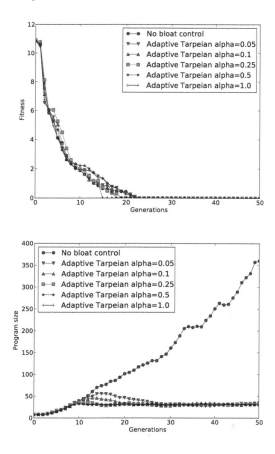

Figure 5-1. Evolution of the best-of-generation fitness and the median program size in the Quartic polynomial problem with different values of α and for a population of 1,000 individuals. Data points are medians across 30 independent runs.

5.   Results on a BCI Mouse Problem

The problem

Brain-computer interfaces convert signals generated from the brain into control commands for devices such as computers. Such systems are often based on the analysis of brain electrical activity obtained via electroencephalography (EEG). Within EEG-based BCIs, the analysis of event related potentials (ERPs) has been particularly effective. ERPs are electrical components of brain activity produced in response to external stimuli. Some such ERPs can be used to determine user intentions in BCIs by relating their presence to specific external stimuli.

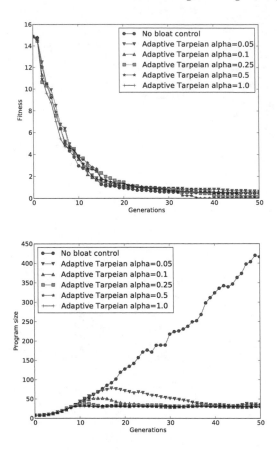

Figure 5-2. Evolution of the best-of-generation fitness and the median program size in the Sextic polynomial problem with different values of α and for a population of 1,000 individuals. Data points are medians across 30 independent runs.

Given the point-and-click nature of most modern user interfaces, an important application of BCI is controlling 2–D pointer movements. Some initial success in developing an ERP-based mouse has been reported in (Citi et al., 2008) and a variety of alternatives to this scheme were explored in (Salvaris et al., 2010). However, in both cases only semi-linear transformations were used to transform EEG signals into mouse movements. These have obvious limitations, particularly in relation to noise and artefact rejection. So, we wondered if GP, with its ability to explore the huge space of computer programs, could produce even more powerful transformations while also performing feature selection and artefact handling at the same time.

Our BCI mouse uses visual displays showing 8 circles arranged around a circle at the centre of the display as in Figure 5-4(far left). Each circle represents

Table 5-2. Success rates for different population sizes, benchmark problems in the presence and in the absence of adaptive Tarpeian bloat control with different values of α. Success was defined as a fitness no greater than 1. Success rate figures are percentages.

Population size	Problem polynomial	No bloat control	Adaptive Tarpeian with α				
			0.05	0.1	0.25	0.5	1.0
100	Quartic	50.0	33.3	56.7	**60.0**	43.3	43.3
100	Quintic	36.7	26.7	23.3	33.3	**40.0**	23.3
100	Sextic	**46.7**	10.0	26.7	30.0	30.0	43.3
100	Quartic Uneq.	**20.0**	3.3	0.0	3.3	6.7	10.0
1000	Quartic	96.7	96.7	96.7	**100.0**	96.7	96.7
1000	Quintic	93.3	86.7	96.7	**100.0**	**100.0**	96.7
1000	Sextic	90.0	76.7	**100.0**	90.0	90.0	**100.0**
1000	Quartic Uneq.	**66.7**	50.0	43.3	60.0	50.0	60.0

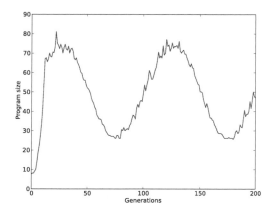

Figure 5-3. Median of median program sizes with adaptive Tarpeian bloat control with a threshold T following a sinusoidal time schedule.

a direction of movement for the mouse cursor. Circles temporarily changed colour – from grey to either red or green – for a fraction of a second. We will call this a *flash*. The aim was to obtain mouse control by mentally focusing on the flashes of the stimulus representing the desired direction and mentally naming the colour of the flash. Flashes lasted for 100 ms and the inter-stimulus interval was 0 ms. Stimuli flashed in clockwise order. This meant that the interval between two target events for the protocol was 800 ms. We used a black background, grey neutral stimuli and either red or green flashing stimuli.

Data from 8 participants with an average age of 33 were used. They all had normal or corrected normal vision except for subject 5 who had strabismus. Each session was divided into runs, which we will call *direction epochs*.

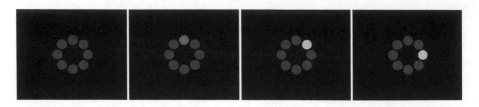

Figure 5-4. Stimuli used in our BCI experiments: initial display and three sequentially flashed stimuli.

Each participant carried out 16 direction epochs, this resulted in the 8 possible directions being carried out twice.

Each direction epoch started with a blank screen and after 2 seconds the eight circles appeared near the centre of the screen. A red arrow then appeared for 1 second pointing to the target (representing the direction for that epoch). Subjects were instructed to mentally name the colour of the flashes for that target. After 2 seconds the flashing of the stimuli started. This stopped after 20 to 24 trials, with a trial consisting of the sequential activation of each of the 8 circles. In other words each direction epoch involves between $20 \times 8 = 160$ and $24 \times 8 = 192$ flashes. After the direction epoch had been completed, subjects were requested to verbally communicate the colour of the last target flash.

Data were sampled at 2048 Hz from 64 electrode sites using a BioSemi ActiveTwo EEG system. The EEG channels were referenced to the mean of the electrodes placed on either earlobe.

The data from each subject were used to train an ensemble of 2 hard-margin linear Support-Vector Machines (SVMs) for that subject. No channel selection was performed, and, so, all 64 channels were used. The data were filtered between 0.15 and 30 Hz and downsampled to 128 Hz. Then, from each channel an 800 ms epoch was extracted which was further decimated to 32 Hz.

The SVM classification results were estimated using 16 fold cross-validations, with each direction epoch being a cross-validation fold. After training, the output of each SVM can be interpreted as a degree of targetness of a stimulus as inferred from the feature vector associated with the stimulus.

The data produced by the SVM can be used to control the mouse. If θ is the angle corresponding to the last flashed stimulus (0° for the North direction, 45° for the North-East direction, etc.) and S is the corresponding score produced by the SVM, it is sufficient to apply a displacement $S \times (\sin \theta, \cos \theta)$ to the mouse cursor to obtain a reasonable trajectory. This is because the SVM tends to produce positive scores for epochs that represent targets and negative values for epochs that represent non-targets. However, the trajectories of the mouse thus produced are very convoluted and suffer enormously from the artifacts produced by swallowing, eye blinks and neck tension (which can easily generate voltages which are one or two orders of magnitude bigger than ordinary EEG signals).

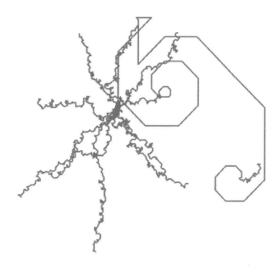

Figure 5-5. Example of normal and artifactual trajectories produced by the raw SVM output of one of our subjects. In all direction epochs shown the pointer starts in the middle of the screen and, ideally, is expected to move away from it at an angle of $0°$, $45°$, etc. and with a straight-line trajectory.

Examples of normal and artefactual trajectories produced by the raw SVM output are shown in Figure 5-5.

While the acquisition of data to train the SVMs of a subject and the training itself require only five minutes or so, making an SVM approach rather interesting, the particularly convoluted nature of the trajectories and the sensitivity of the SVMs to artifacts make the direct control of SVM raw output problematic. We, therefore, thought about using a program evolved by GP to post-process the output produced by the SVMs and to integrate this with the raw information available from the 64 EEG channels so as to straighten the trajectories produced by the raw SVM output and to make them insensitive to artifacts.

Naturally, GP cannot compete with the speed of SVMs and we cannot imagine subjects waiting for hours while GP finds a solution which suits their particular brain signals. So, the solution evolved by GP has to be general and reusable across subjects and across experiments.

GP Setup

For these experiments we used the same GP system as before, but in this case we switched on its strongly-typed features. Also, since fitness evaluation in this domain of application is extremely computationally intensive, we also switched on its parallel feature which allows one to perform fitness evaluations across multiple CPU cores (via farming).

Table 5-3. Primitive set used in our BCI mouse application.

Primitive	Output Type	Input Type(s)	Functionality
±0.5, ±1, ±2, ±5, ±10, 0, ···, 25	Float	None	Floating point constants used for numeric calculations and array indexing
Fp1, AF7, AF3, F1, ... (60 more channels)	Array	None	Returns an array of 26 samples following a flash from one of the channels. The samples are of type Float.
SVM	Float	None	Raw output of SVM ensemble.
targetQ1, targetMed, targetQ3, ... (6 more for non-targets and near-targets)	Float	None	First quartile, median and third quartile of the SVM scores for targets, near-targets and non-targets for a subject.
+, -, *, min, max	Float	(Float, Float)	Standard arithmetic operations plus maximum and minimum on floats.
>, <	Bool	(Float, Float)	Standard relational operations on floats
if	Float	(Bool, Float, Float)	If-then-else function. If the first argument evaluates to True, then the result of evaluating its second argument is returned. Otherwise the result of evaluating the third argument is returned.
abs	Float	Float	Returns the absolute value of a Float.
mean, median, std, Amin, Amax	Float	(Float, Float, Array)	Given a 26-sample array and two floats, treat the floats as indices for the array by casting them to integer and applying a modulus 26 operation. Then compute the mean, median, standard deviation, minimum or maximum, respectively, of the samples in the array falling between such indices (inclusive).

As before the system uses a steady-state update policy. It evolves a population of 1,000 individuals with tournament selection with a tournament size of 5, a strongly-typed version of the grow method with a maximum initial depth of 4, and strongly-typed versions of sub-tree crossover and sub-tree mutation. Both operators are applied with a 50% rate and use a uniform selection of crossover/mutation points. The system uses the primitive set shown in Table 5-3. Program trees were required to have a Float return type.

With this setup we performed runs of 50 generations. For Tarpeian we used a threshold $T = 20$ and $\alpha = 0.1$. The threshold was chosen based on the available computational resources and on the need to produce a reasonably analysable result. We did several runs with this system. However, because of the extreme computational load required by our fitness evaluation and the

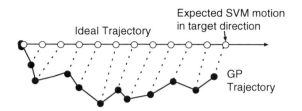

Figure 5-6. Ideal and actual trajectories used in the fitness calculation. Dashed lines indicate pairs of matching points. Fitness is the average distance between such points across trajectories.

complexity of the problem, here we only report the results of our best run. The run took approximately 6 *CPU days* to complete.

The fitness function we used measures the dissimilarity between the ideal trajectory and the actual trajectory produced by a program averaged over the direction epochs in our training set. The training set was formed by 80 direction epochs, obtained by taking the 39 most noisy direction epochs out of the 128 available from our subjects and mixing them with 41 less noisy direction epochs. Since each direction epoch consisted in an average of 176 trials and there were 80 such epochs, measuring the fitness of a program required executing the program for over 14,000 times. Being an error measure, fitness is, naturally, minimised in our system. We describe its elements below.

The actual trajectory produced by a program on a training epoch is obtained by iteratively evaluating the program, each time feeding the samples relating to a new flash into the Fp1, AF7, etc. terminals (which effectively act as a sliding window on the EEG) as well as the raw output produced on that epoch by the SVM ensemble. The output of the program, which, as noted above, is of type Float, is multiplied by a unit vector representing the direction corresponding to the stimulus that flashed on the screen. This produces a result of the form $(\Delta x, \Delta y)$ which is used as a displacement to be applied to the current mouse position.

As illustrated in Figure 5-6, the ideal trajectory for each direction epoch is obtained by sampling at regular intervals the line segment connecting the origin to a point along the desired direction. The point is chosen by computing the expected distance reached by the linear SVM trained on the data for subject. The ideal trajectory is sampled in such a way to have the same number of samples as the actual trajectory. The comparison between actual and ideal trajectory is then a matter of measuring the Euclidean distance between pairs of corresponding points in the two trajectories and taking an average. Notice that any detours from the ideal line and any slow-downs in the march along it in the actual trajectory are strongly penalised with our fitness measure.

In order to test the generality of evolved solutions we used a further 80 direction epochs obtained from a separate set of 5 subjects.

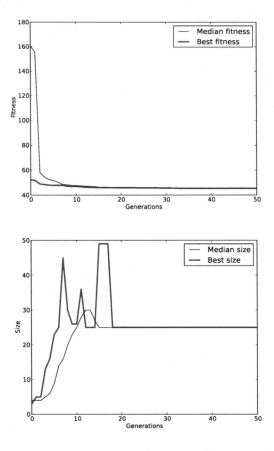

Figure 5-7. Plots of the median and best fitness and median and best program size vs generation number in our runs.

BCI Mouse Results

Figure 5-7 shows the dynamics of median and best program's fitness as well as of median and best program's size in our runs. As one can immediately see, essentially there is no bloat, while fitness continues to improve, albeit quite slowly, for the 50 generations of the run.

The best evolved program is presented in tree form in Figure 5-8. To evaluate its performance we will compare its output to the output produced by the raw SVM data on our independent test set of 5 subjects.

Let us start from a *qualitative* analysis of the behaviour of this program. Figure 5-9(top) shows the output produced by the SVM ensemble for each of the direction epochs in the test set of 5 subjects (after the transformation of the scores into $(\Delta x, \Delta y)$ displacements). Note how convoluted trajectories are.

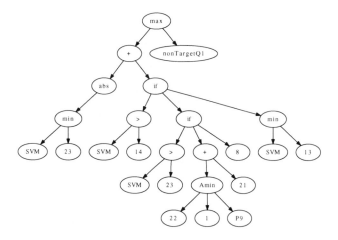

Figure 5-8. Best program evolved in our runs.

Table 5-4. Statistical comparison between SVM and the evolved solution for the BCI mouse problem.

Program	Mean	Median	Standard Deviation	Standard Error
GP	44.3389	41.5974	18.1760	2.0450
SVM	51.5003	50.9928	21.6596	2.4369

Clearly while the SVMs get a good portion of the job done, namely turning the EEG signals into trajectories that are in *approximately* the right direction, they leave much to desire in terms of usability. Figure 5-9(bottom) shows the corresponding trajectories produced by our best evolved programs. Qualitatively it is clear that these trajectories are far less convoluted. Also, their end points appear to cluster more precisely near the desired directions of motion.

To *quantitatively* verify these observations, Table 5-4 shows a statistical comparison between the trajectories produced by GP and those produced by the SVMs in terms of mean, median, standard deviation and standard error of the mean of the distances between the ideal trajectory and the actual trajectory recorded in each of the 80 direction trials in our test set of 5 subjects. As we can see the evolved program produces trajectories which are on average closer to the ideal line than the corresponding trajectories produced by the SVMs. The differences are highly statistically significant as shown by a one-sided Wilcoxon signed rank test for paired data (p-value $= 0.0009$).

6.   Conclusions

In this paper we have presented a variation of the Tarpeian method's for bloat control that allows the adaptation of the method main parameter — its rate of

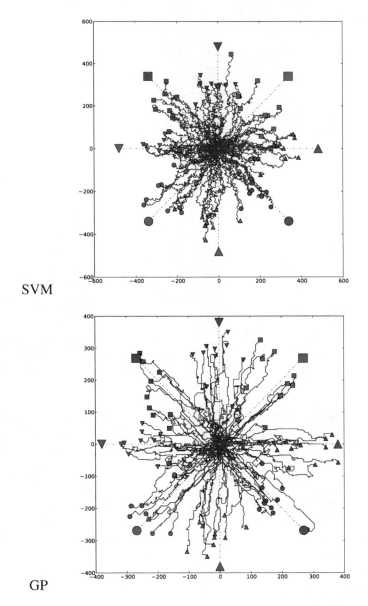

SVM

GP

Figure 5-9. Graphical representation of the 80 sequences of SVM scores and the evolved-program scores for our 5 test subjects. The larger symbols connected via dotted lines to the origin represent the 8 desired directions of motion. The smaller symbols demarcate the end points of the corresponding pointer trajectories.

application p_t — in such a way to guarantee that programs don't grow bigger than a given threshold. While this threshold is usually a constant, it can also be dynamically varied during evolution resulting in program sizes approximately tracking it.

An earlier method — the covariant Tarpeian method introduced last year (Poli, 2010) — can solve the problem of optimally setting p_t analytically. However, the method is only applicable to generational systems using fitness proportionate selection and relying only on crossover as their genetic operator. While the adaptive Tarpeian method is algorithmic and control of program size is asymptotic, it does not suffer from such limitations as we have demonstrated testing it with a steady state GP system with tournament selection and using a mix of sub-tree crossover (which is size-unbiased) and sub-tree mutation (which is size-biased).

We tested the method on a variety of standard benchmark problems as well as in a real-world application — the evolution of a Brain Computer Interfaces mouse controller. Results with benchmark problems indicate that the method is very effective at keeping the size of programs under control without incurring any particular penalty in terms of end-of-run fitness achieved. Runs, however, lasted only a fraction of the time required without bloat control.[3] The results in the BCI mouse problem were very good, the system being able to evolve a controller which is significantly better than a solution based on support vector machines. The solution also generalised very well to unseen data.

In this paper we did not directly compare the adaptive Tarpeian method with the non-adaptive version of the method. This is because our main objective was not to show that the former does better than the latter at controlling the growth of program sizes: we believe the original Tarpeian method will also work well when appropriately tuned. Instead, our aim was explore the possibility of automatically adjusting the rate of application of the Tarpeian method, p_t, so that one would have a *direct* (thought T) rather than *indirect* (through p_t) control over program sizes.

Why is this important? The work presented in this paper was originally motivated by the needs for bloat control in a real-world problem — the BCI mouse problem. In a domain such as this, where one cannot afford to perform production runs with different values of p_t until satisfactory control over program sizes is achieved, having a method where on can directly set the maximum program size is essential. We believe many other real-world problems may benefit from this feature of the adaptive Tarpeian method.

---

[3] In fact, preliminary attempts at solving the BCI problem showed that we could not even perform full scale runs without bloat control.

Acknowledgements

We would like to thank Luca Citi and the Engineering and Physical Sciences Research Council (grant EP/F033818/1).

References

Alfaro-Cid, Eva, Merelo, J. J., Fernandez de Vega, Francisco, Esparcia-Alcazar, Anna I., , and Sharman, Ken (2010). Bloat control operators and diversity in genetic programming: A comparative study. *Evolutionary Computation*, 18(2):305–332.

Allen, Sam, Burke, Edmund K., Hyde, Matthew R., and Kendall, Graham (2009). Evolving reusable 3D packing heuristics with genetic programming. In Raidl, Guenther et al., editors, *GECCO '09: Proceedings of the 11th Annual conference on Genetic and evolutionary computation*, pages 931–938, Montreal. ACM.

Burke, Edmund K., Hyde, Matthew R., Kendall, Graham, and Woodward, John (2007). Automatic heuristic generation with genetic programming: evolving a jack-of-all-trades or a master of one. In Thierens, Dirk et al., editors, *GECCO '07: Proceedings of the 9th annual conference on Genetic and evolutionary computation*, volume 2, pages 1559–1565, London. ACM Press.

Citi, L., Poli, R., Cinel, C., and Sepulveda, F. (2008). P300-based BCI mouse with genetically-optimized analogue control. *IEEE transactions on neural systems and rehabilitation engineering*, 16(1):51–61.

Luke, Sean and Panait, Liviu (2006). A comparison of bloat control methods for genetic programming. *Evolutionary Computation*, 14(3):309–344.

Mahler, Sébastien, Robilliard, Denis, and Fonlupt, Cyril (2005). Tarpeian bloat control and generalization accuracy. In Keijzer, Maarten et al., editors, *Proceedings of the 8th European Conference on Genetic Programming*, volume 3447 of *Lecture Notes in Computer Science*, pages 203–214, Lausanne, Switzerland. Springer.

Martinez-Jaramillo, Serafin and Tsang, Edward P. K. (2009). An heterogeneous, endogenous and coevolutionary GP-based financial market. *IEEE Transactions on Evolutionary Computation*, 13(1):33–55.

Poli, Riccardo (2003). A simple but theoretically-motivated method to control bloat in genetic programming. In Ryan, Conor et al., editors, *Genetic Programming, Proceedings of EuroGP'2003*, volume 2610 of *LNCS*, pages 204–217, Essex. Springer-Verlag.

Poli, Riccardo (2010). Covariant tarpeian method for bloat control in genetic programming. In Riolo, Rick, McConaghy, Trent, and Vladislavleva, Ekaterina, editors, *Genetic Programming Theory and Practice VIII*, volume 8 of *Genetic and Evolutionary Computation*, chapter 5, pages 71–90. Springer, Ann Arbor, USA.

Poli, Riccardo, Langdon, William B., and McPhee, Nicholas Freitag (2008). *A field guide to genetic programming*. Published via `http://lulu.com` and freely available at `http://www.gp-field-guide.org.uk`. (With contributions by J. R. Koza).

Poli, Riccardo and McPhee, Nicholas (2008). Parsimony pressure made easy. In Keijzer, Maarten et al., editors, *GECCO '08: Proceedings of the 10th annual conference on Genetic and evolutionary computation*, pages 1267–1274, Atlanta, GA, USA. ACM.

Poli, Riccardo and McPhee, Nicholas Freitag (2003). General schema theory for genetic programming with subtree-swapping crossover: Part II. *Evolutionary Computation*, 11(2):169–206.

Roberts, Mark E. and Claridge, Ela (2004). Cooperative coevolution of image feature construction and object detection. In Yao, Xin et al., editors, *Parallel Problem Solving from Nature - PPSN VIII*, volume 3242 of *LNCS*, pages 902–911, Birmingham, UK. Springer-Verlag.

Salvaris, Mathew, Cinel, Caterina, Poli, Riccardo, Citi, Luca, and Sepulveda, Francisco (2010). Exploring multiple protocols for a brain-computer interface mouse. In *Proceedings of 32nd IEEE EMBS Conference*, pages 4189–4192, Buenos Aires.

Silva, Sara and Costa, Ernesto (2009). Dynamic limits for bloat control in genetic programming and a review of past and current bloat theories. *Genetic Programming and Evolvable Machines*, 10(2):141–179.

Wyns, Bart and Boullart, Luc (2009). Efficient tree traversal to reduce code growth in tree-based genetic programming. *Journal of Heuristics*, 15(1):77–104.

Chapter 6

IMPROVED TIME SERIES PREDICTION AND SYMBOLIC REGRESSION WITH AFFINE ARITHMETIC

Cassio Pennachin[1], Moshe Looks[2] and J. A. de Vasconcelos[1]

[1]*Universidade Federal de Minas Gerais, Belo Horizonte, MG Brazil;*
[2]*Google Inc., Mountain View, CA 94043 USA.*

Abstract   We show how affine arithmetic can be used to improve both the performance and the robustness of genetic programming for problems such as symbolic regression and time series prediction. Affine arithmetic is used to estimate conservative bounds on the output range of expressions during evolution, which allows us to discard trees with potentially infinite bounds, as well as those whose output range lies outside the desired range implied by the training dataset. Benchmark experiments are performed on 15 symbolic regression problems as well as 2 well-known time series problems. Comparison with a baseline genetic programming system shows a reduced number of fitness evaluations during training and improved generalization on test data, completely eliminating extreme errors. We also apply this technique to the problem of forecasting wind speed on a real world dataset, and the use of affine arithmetic compares favorably with baseline genetic programming, feedforward neural networks and support vector machines.

Keywords: Symbolic regression, time series prediction, wind forecasting, affine arithmetic, robustness

1.   Introduction

Symbolic regression is an early and important application of Genetic Programming (GP). However, its practical applicability depends on avoiding overfitting to training data. While completely eliminating overfitting isn't feasible in most scenarios, we should at least minimize its probability and extent. A particularly damaging kind of overfitting is the error introduced when GP induces expressions containing asymptotes on points in parameter space that are not part of the training data. Out-of-sample evaluation of points lying near an asymptote can result in extremely high errors, which makes prevention of this form of overfitting especially important.

Numerous techniques have been proposed to make symbolic regression more reliable, including the use of ensembles, scaling program tree outputs (Keijzer, 2004), penalty functions or multi-objective optimization to reduce complexity and bloat (Smits and Kotanchek, 2004), interval methods (Keijzer, 2003), and combinations of multiple techniques (Kotanchek et al., 2007; Korns, 2009). We focus on the application of affine arithmetic, an interval method, to eliminate potentially harmful trees from the population during evolution.

Interval methods, also known as self-validated numerics, are techniques for numerical computation in which approximate results are produced with guaranteed ranges, or error bounds. They can be used to analyze expressions, such as the ones defined by program trees in a symbolic regression evolution run, and will produce output bounds for those expressions. If a program tree includes asymptotes, interval methods will detect them. This process of static analysis is used in (Keijzer, 2003) and in (Kotanchek et al., 2007) to significantly improve the generalization performance of symbolic regression, by assigning infinite error to program trees with potential asymptotes.

Since interval methods provide guaranteed bounds on the output range of a program tree, another potential use is the detection of well-formed trees which, despite having finite bounds, are guaranteed to have bad fitness. A desirable output range can be estimated from the training data, and trees whose output falls outside the desirable range can be eliminated without complete fitness evaluation. Because GP applied to symbolic regression problems typically generates many trees with very bad fitness (Langdon and Poli, 2002), this kind of elimination can significantly boost performance. Unfortunately, the intervals output by interval arithmetic, the simplest interval method and the one used in (Keijzer, 2003), tend to be too wide to be useful for this purpose.

In (Pennachin et al., 2010), we proposed a system similar to Keijzer's, but based on affine arithmetic, a more refined interval method that generates tighter, although still conservative, bounds for expressions. Our technique uses the affine arithmetic bounds to detect and discard program trees whose outputs lie outside a desirable range. Benchmark results for symbolic regression show that we managed to completely avoid extreme errors on previously unseen test data, and obtained much improved generalization when compared with baseline GP or an interval arithmetic-based system such as Keijzer's.

This paper is an extended version of our work in (Pennachin et al., 2010), and we apply the same system to time series prediction problems. We begin with a summary review of affine arithmetic in the next section. Section 3 outlines our system that incorporates affine arithmetic in GP evolution for fitness estimation and asymptote detection. We review results for 15 symbolic regression benchmark problems in Section 4, and present new results for time series prediction, covering 2 well-known benchmark datasets and a real world wind speed forecasting problem in Section 5, where we compare our system with well-known machine learning algorithms as well as baseline GP.

2. Interval Methods and Affine Arithmetic

The simplest and most widely adopted interval method is interval, arithmetic (IA) (Moore, 1966). In IA, a quantity x is represented by an *interval* $\bar{x} = [\bar{x}_L, \bar{x}_U]$, where $\bar{x}_L, \bar{x}_U \in \Re$ are the interval bounds, and $\bar{x}_L \leq \bar{x}_U$. Arithmetic operations are then based on the interval bounds. For instance:

$$\bar{x} + \bar{y} = [\bar{x}_L + \bar{y}_L, \bar{x}_U + \bar{y}_U]$$
$$\bar{x} - \bar{y} = [\bar{x}_L - \bar{y}_U, \bar{x}_U - \bar{y}_L]$$
$$\bar{x} \times \bar{y} = [min(\bar{x}_L\bar{y}_L, \bar{x}_L\bar{y}_U, \bar{x}_U\bar{y}_L, \bar{x}_U\bar{y}_U),$$
$$max(\bar{x}_L\bar{y}_L, \bar{x}_L\bar{y}_U, \bar{x}_U\bar{y}_L, \bar{x}_U\bar{y}_U)]$$
$$e^{\bar{x}} = [e^{\bar{x}_L}, e^{\bar{x}_U}]$$

The major downside of IA is that sequences of operations tend to accumulate and magnify errors. Since IA interval ranges are guaranteed to contain the actual value of an expression over the given input ranges, they can never be too narrow. As they ignore dependencies between variables, they often tend to be too wide. As a simple, but pathological case, consider $\bar{x} - \bar{x}$, where $\bar{x} = [-1, 1]$. The resulting interval is $[-2, 2]$, while clearly the correct value is $[0, 0]$. Repeated application of error-inducing operations during expression analysis tends to result in error propagation and magnification.

Several extensions and improvements to interval arithmetic have been proposed. Affine arithmetic (AA) is an interval method originally developed for computer graphics (Comba and Stolfi, 1993), which has found diverse applications, including robust optimization (de Figueiredo and Stolfi, 1997; de Figueiredo and Stolfi, 2004). Affine arithmetic keeps track of correlations between quantities, in addition to the ranges of each quantity. These correlations lead to significantly reduced approximation errors, especially over long computation chains that would lead to error explosion under IA. We now provide a brief overview of affine arithmetic, recommending the above references for further details.

In AA, a quantity x is represented by an *affine form* $\hat{x}$, which is a first-degree polynomial:

$$\hat{x} = x_0 + x_1\varepsilon_1 + \cdots + x_n\varepsilon_n$$

where x_0 is called the central value of $\hat{x}$, the x_i are finite numbers, called partial deviations, and the ε_i are called *noise symbols*, whose values are unknown but assuredly lie in the interval $\mathbb{U} = [-1, 1]$. Each noise symbol corresponds to one component of the overall uncertainty as to the actual value of x. This uncertainty may be intrinsic to the original data, or introduced by approximations in the computation of $\hat{x}$.

The fundamental invariant of affine arithmetic ensures that there is always a single assignment of values to each ε_i that makes the value of every affine form $\hat{x}$ equal to the true value of the corresponding x. All of these values assigned to ε_is are of course constrained to lie in the interval $\mathbb{U}$.

Correlation is accounted for in AA by the fact that the same symbol ε_i can be part of multiple affine forms created by the evaluation of an expression. Shared noise symbols indicate dependencies between the underlying quantities. The presence of such shared symbols allows one to determine joint ranges for affine forms that are tighter than the corresponding intervals of interval arithmetic.

Computations with AA involve defining, for each operation, a corresponding procedure that operates on affine forms and produces a resulting affine form. Therefore, an elementary function $z \leftarrow f(x, y)$ is implemented by a procedure $\hat{z} \leftarrow \hat{f}(\hat{x}, \hat{y})$, such that given

$$\hat{x} = x_0 + x_1\varepsilon_1 + \cdots + x_n\varepsilon_n$$
$$\hat{y} = y_0 + y_1\varepsilon_1 + \cdots + y_n\varepsilon_n$$

$\hat{f}$ produces some

$$\hat{z} = z_0 + z_1\varepsilon_1 + \cdots + z_m\varepsilon_m$$

for $m \geq n$, preserving as much information as possible about the constraints embedded in the noise symbols that have non-zero coefficients.

When f is itself an affine function of its arguments, $\hat{z}$ can be obtained by simple rearrangement of the noise symbols. This gives us addition, subtraction, and negation. Formally, for any given $\alpha, \beta, \zeta \in \Re$, $z \leftarrow \alpha x + \beta y + \zeta$:

$$\hat{z} = (\alpha x_0 + \beta y_0 + \zeta) + (\alpha x_1 + \beta y_1)\varepsilon_1 + \cdots + (\alpha x_n + \beta y_n)\varepsilon_n$$

With the exception of rounding errors, the above formula captures all the information available about x, y, and z, so it will introduce almost no error in the uncertainty estimates. Accordingly, the above formula will produce tight bounds for operations such as $\hat{x} - \hat{x}$, and identities such as $(\hat{x} + \hat{y}) - \hat{y}$ hold according to this formula, unlike in interval arithmetic. This rule of combination can be trivially extended to any number of inputs.

In the case of $z \leftarrow f(x, y)$ when f is not an affine function, z is given by $f^*(\varepsilon_1, \ldots, \varepsilon_n)$, where f^* is a non-affine function from $\mathbb{U}^n$ to $\Re$. This is the case for important functions such as multiplication, division, exponentiation, logarithm, and others.

In this case, z cannot be expressed exactly as an affine combination of the noise symbols. Instead, we need to find some affine function

$$f^a(\varepsilon_1, \ldots, \varepsilon_n) = z_0 + z_1\varepsilon_1 + \cdots + z_n\varepsilon_n$$

which is a reasonable approximation of f^* over $\mathbb{U}^n$, and then introduce an extra term $z_k \varepsilon_k$ that represents the approximation error incurred when using f^a. The noise symbol ε_k has to be exclusive to this operation; it cannot be shared with other affine forms. The magnitude of its coefficient z_k must be an upper bound on the approximation error, i.e.,

$$|z_k| \geq max\{|f^*(\varepsilon_1, \ldots, \varepsilon_n) - f^a(\varepsilon_1, \ldots, \varepsilon_n)|, \varepsilon_1, \ldots, \varepsilon_n \in \mathbb{U}\}$$

The choice of the affine approximation f^a is an implementation decision, and there are many possibilities. For purposes of simplicity and efficiency, one can consider approximations that are affine combinations of the inputs $\hat{x}$ and $\hat{y}$, so $f^a(\varepsilon_1, \ldots, \varepsilon_n) = \alpha \hat{x} + \beta \hat{y} + \zeta$. Using affine approximations gives us only $k + 1$ parameters to estimate for functions of k inputs.

These parameters have to be chosen in order to minimize the approximation error term $|z_k|$. The best choice, therefore, is arguably the one that minimizes the maximum value of $|\alpha \hat{x} + \beta \hat{y} + \zeta - f(x, y)|$ over the joint range $\langle \hat{x}, \hat{y} \rangle$. This is called the *Chebychev or minmax affine approximation* of f over $\langle \hat{x}, \hat{y} \rangle$; it guarantees that the volume of the joint range is minimized. This, however, does not always minimize the range for $\hat{z}$ alone. A minimum range approximation will do that. Also, the Chebychev approximation may introduce undesirable values in the range of $\hat{z}$, such as negative values for the exponential function, which are avoided by the minimum range approximation. The choice between the Chebychev approximation and the minimum range approximation is application-dependent, although the latter is usually easier to compute.

One does not necessarily have or want to use the best affine approximation, however. A well-known example is the case of multiplication, for which computing the best approximation is expensive, but a simple and efficient heuristic is often used in its place, with an error at most four times greater than the best affine approximation. Detailed presentations of the approximations for a number of non-affine operations are provided in (de Figueiredo and Stolfi, 1997), including pseudo-code and implementation discussions.

Affine arithmetic typically gives tighter bounds than interval arithmetic, in some cases dramatically so, as we have shown by example. However, it can also sometimes lead to *worse* bounds. For example, the product of two non-negative forms, when computed with the usual heuristic, may need to have a negative lower bound in order to preserve the (linear) dependency information while respecting the constrained (i.e., center-symmetric and convex) affine form representation. To see how this can be problematic for our GP application, consider an expression such as $log(x * y)$; we need to be able to accept such expression as valid when x and y are known to be strictly positive.

In order to handle these cases, our implementation of AA is hybridized with standard IA, as suggested in (de Figueiredo and Stolfi, 1997). Affine forms are extended by the presence of independent minimal and maximal values, which by default are set to their AA minima and maxima. When a non-affine operation is computed, its minima and maxima according to IA are computed as well, and the tightest possible bounds are kept and exploited by AA to allow expressions that would otherwise be disallowed. This is achieved by maintaining a residual error term, which is adjusted after each operation to be the smallest needed to cover the combined (minimal) interval - see (Pennachin et al., 2010) for full details. The hybrid model produces tighter bounds than either AA or IA could attain independently, and is not significantly costlier than plain AA to compute.

Extensions to standard affine arithmetic have been proposed to make it even less conservative (Messine, 2002; Shou et al., 2003), including the use of quadratic or matricial forms to supplement the original affine forms and provide non-linear approximations for functions such as multiplication. However, these extensions introduce significant computational overhead and implementation complexity in return for incremental improvements on accuracy, and have not been explored in our work.

3.   Genetic Programming with Affine Arithmetic

Static Analysis of Program Trees

When a program tree is generated, it can be analyzed by recursively applying the elementary operations of affine arithmetic, given interval representations of its inputs. For symbolic regression and time series prediction, these intervals are estimated from the training data, and this analysis will generate conservative bounds for the program output over the region of the input space covered by the training data. These bounds can be infinite, in the case of trees containing possible asymptotes. Such trees are then eliminated from the population. This is the approach used in (Keijzer, 2003), in combination with linear scaling of program tree outputs, to reduce generalization error in symbolic regression. The same technique was subsequently applied to the estimation of phytoplankton concentration in oceans from satellite spectrometer measurements (Valigiani et al., 2004).

Note, however, that due to the conservative nature of IA, some harmless expressions that do not compute functions with asymptotes may nonetheless be eliminated. For example, given $\bar{x} = [-2, 2]$, IA gives an infinite interval for the harmless expression $1/(1 + x^2)$ because the interval computed for the denominator straddles zero. Affine arithmetic is less conservative, and correctly handles the above example and many others.

Proposed System Overview

We utilize a simple, generational GP system in our experiments, based on Koza's classic configuration (Koza, 1992). This baseline GP system has protected operators for division and logarithm, as well as random ephemeral constants. Parents are chosen for reproduction via tournament selection. New expressions are created via subtree crossover (probability 0.9) and mutation (probability 0.1). Elitism preserves the top 10% of each generation without modification. The initial population is created via the ramped half-and-half method with a maximal depth of 6.

This baseline system can be extended by the integration of a number of enhancements:

Interval Arithmetic As in (Keijzer, 2003), we perform static analysis of expressions through interval arithmetic to detected and reject trees containing asymptotes.

Affine Arithmetic for Asymptote Rejection Same as above, but substituting affine arithmetic for interval arithmetic.

Affine Arithmetic for Output Bounds Rejection We determine bounds for each expression, rejecting those that are outside the desirable range, defined as $r(Y^T) = [min(Y^T) - \alpha r, \ max(Y^T) + \alpha r]$, where Y^T are the target outputs for all training cases, $r = (max(Y^T) - min(Y^T))/2$, and α is a parameter.

Linear Scaling As in (Keijzer, 2003). Given an expression producing outputs Y for n training cases X, and with Y^T being the target output values, a linear regression can be performed as:

$$b = \frac{\sum_{i=1}^{n}(y_i^T - \tilde{Y}^T)(y_i - \tilde{Y})}{\sum_{i=1}^{n}(y_i - \tilde{Y})}$$
$$a = \tilde{Y}^T - b\tilde{Y}$$

where $\tilde{Y}$ and $\tilde{Y}^T$ denote the average output and average desired output, respectively. Replacing outputs by $a + bY$ minimizes mean squared error with respect to Y^T. Trees whose output variance is greater than 10^7 or lower than 10^{-7} are discarded.

We purposefully avoid introducing common improvements, such as measures to penalize bloat, to more easily observe the impact of our proposed improvements. We believe a complexity penalty would benefit both the baseline system and our extensions to an equal or similar extent.

We implement the baseline system as well as the enhancements in Common Lisp, as part of the PLOP open source project (Looks, 2010).

4.   Symbolic Regression Experiments

We test our system on the same set of 15 benchmark problems used in (Keijzer, 2003), summarized in Table 6-1. Parameters are chosen to enable direct comparison with (Keijzer, 2003), and were not tuned. See (Pennachin et al., 2010) for more details on experimental setup and results. We summarize results for the following combinations of enhancements described above:

Base Baseline GP system with protected operators.

IA Linear scaling and interval arithmetic for asymptote rejection as in (Keijzer, 2003).

AA Linear scaling and affine arithmetic for asymptote rejection.

AA+ Linear scaling and affine arithmetic for asymptote rejection, plus output bounds rejection.

In terms of wall clock time, the baseline system is fastest, as expected, while **IA** introduces a modest penalty. **AA** and **AA+** are significantly more expensive, which suggests that their application is best suited for hard problems that the other systems can't solve effectively, as well as problems for which the fitness function is expensive to compute, thus justifying the overhead imposed by static analysis.

In terms of generalization ability, we use the Normalized Root Mean Square Error (NRMS) as a performance measure:

$$NRMS = \frac{\sqrt{\frac{n}{n-1}MSE}}{\sigma_{YT}}$$

where n is the number of training (or test) cases, σ_{YT} is the standard deviation of desired outputs for those cases, and MSE is the mean squared error. An expression that always produces the mean desired output will have an NRMS of 1, while a perfect expression will have an NRMS of 0.

We measure the NRMS of the best evolved expression in each run over the test set and compare these values with the training NRMS values. Figure 6-1 shows the ratio between test and train NRMS[1] for each problem, as an indication of generalization quality. The baseline system has the worst generalization performance, followed by **IA**, while **AA+** outperforms all other configurations, especially on the last five problems, which are harder.

We also look at absolute test error. As an NRMS value of 1 over the test set implies performance no better than constantly outputting the mean desired value, we use this value as a threshold for overfitting. The baseline configuration

---

[1] Test NRMS was capped at 1000 to minimize disruption caused by ill-formed exceptions in the baseline system.

Table 6-1. Symbolic Regression benchmarks. The last two columns describe how training and test data are generated. Datasets can be uniformly spaced (notation *[lower:step:upper]*) or a random sample of n uniformly distributed points (notation $r_n(lower, upper)$). For multidimensional problems, the *[lower:step:upper]* notation denotes an n-dimensional mesh, and hence $((upper - lower)/step)^n$ total data points.

Prob.	Equation	Train	Test
1		$[-1:0.1:1]$	$[-1:0.001:1]$
2	$f(x) = 0.3x sin(2\pi x)$	$[-2:0.1:2]$	$[-2:0.001:2]$
3		$[-3:0.1:3]$	$[-3:0.001:3]$
4	$f(x) = x^3 e^{-x} cos(x) sin(x)(sin^2(x)cos(x) - 1)$	$[0:0.05:10]$	$[0.05:0.05:10.05]$
5	$f(x, y, z) = \dfrac{30xz}{(x-10)y^2}$	$x, z = r_{10^3}(-1, 1)$ $y = r_{10^3}(1, 2)$	$x, z = r_{10^4}(-1, 1)$ $y = r_{10^4}(1, 2)$
6	$f(x) = \sum_i^x 1/i$	$[1:1:50]$	$[1:1:120]$
7	$f(x) = log x$	$[1:1:100]$	$[1:0.1:100]$
8	$f(x) = \sqrt{x}$	$[0:1:100]$	$[0:0.1:100]$
9	$f(x) = arcsinh(x)$	$[0:1:100]$	$[0:0.1:100]$
10	$f(x, y) = x^y$	$x, y = r_{100}(0, 1)$	$[0:0.1:1]$
11	$f(x, y) = xy + sin((x-1)(y-1))$		
12	$f(x, y) = x^4 - x^3 + y^2/2 - y$		
13	$f(x, y) = 6sin(x)cos(y)$	$x, y = r_{20}(-3, 3)$	$[-3:0.01:3]$
14	$f(x, y) = 8/(2 + x^2 + y^2)$		
15	$f(x, y) = x^3/5 + y^3/2 - y - x$		

produces overfit expressions in 13 problems, while **IA** and **AA** suffer from overfitting in 5 and 4 problems, respectively. **AA+** outperforms all alternatives, producing overfit trees in 1% of the runs for problem 15 and 4% of the runs for problem 13, for which the baseline system is overfit in 98% of the runs - again, see (Pennachin et al., 2010) for full details.

5.   Time Series Prediction

Benchmark Problems

Our initial experiments with time series prediction use 2 well-known datasets. The sunspots time series (Weigend et al., 1992) measures the yearly count of sunspots since 1700. It is typically split into a training set covering the period from 1700 to 1920, and 2 separate test sets, the first one from 1921 to 1955, and the second one from 1956 to 1979. We repeat this split. The time series is linearly normalized to fit in the interval $[0, 1]$ before learning. The Mackey-Glass dataset (Glass and Mackey, 2010) is derived from a time-delay ordinary differential equation, and one typically discards the first 3500 points in the time

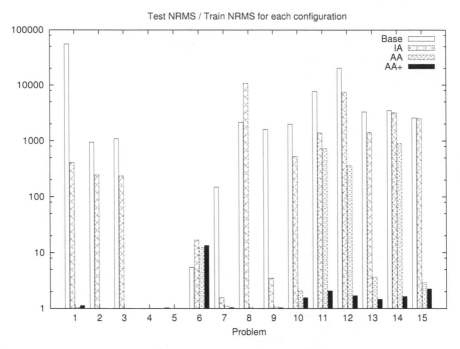

Figure 6-1. Test NRMS divided by train NRMS for each problem (log scale).

series, using the following 1000 points for training and the final 500 points for testing. No normalization is performed.

In our experiments we use a population size of 2000 individuals, allow up to 500,000 fitness evaluations, set the maximal program depth at 12, and use the following function vocabulary, with protected operators where appropriate: $+, -, \times, \div, exp, log, sin, cos, sqrt, 1/x, -x$. Inputs include the past L values of the time series up to x_t, where the desired output is the one-step lookahead value x_{t+1} and L is a lookback parameter, set to 5 for the sunspot series and to 8 for the Mackey-Glass series, according to existing literature. Other parameters are as described in Section 3.

Results are averaged over 50 runs and we compare the baseline GP system with a configuration that uses linear scaling and affine arithmetic for asymptote rejection, plus output bounds rejection (the equivalent of **AA+** in the previous Section). Results using only linear scaling (not shown) are not statistically significant.

Table 6-2 presents results for the sunspot series. We show the typical performance measure often reported for this time series, defined as $E = MSE/\sigma^2$, where MSE is the mean squared error and $\sigma^2 \sim 0.041$ is the variance over the entire dataset. Typically, generalization is easy in the first test set of the sunspot series, while it is hard on the second set. We see that in our results, where the baseline system does well in the first subset, but is outperformed in the second one, while also presenting much higher variance which is a consequence of the strong overfitting observed in some runs. The **AA+** configuration, while displaying a modest degree of overfitting, is much more robust. Also, this configuration rejects approximately 13% of expressions created during each run.

Table 6-3 presents results for the Mackey-Glass series. We show RMS (root mean squared error) and NRMS (as defined in the previous Section), as well as p-values for a two sample Kolmogorov-Smirnov test over the test set. While both configurations show little evidence of overfitting, the **AA+** version has much better performance on both training and test data, and much lower variance (of results); it also rejects approximately 17.5% of the expressions generated during each run (around 7.3% being rejected for containing potential asymptotes, and the remaining 10.2% for output bounds outside the desirable range). Figure 6-2 shows error over the test set for both configurations.

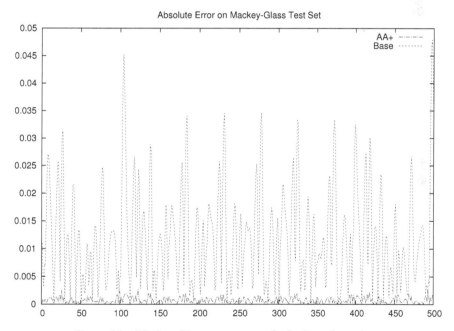

Figure 6-2. Mackey-Glass test set error for both configurations.

Table 6-2. Sunspot prediction results and Kolmogorov-Smirnov two sample test p-values.

Cfg	Train	Test 1	Test 2
Base	0.102 ± 0.014	0.115 ± 0.020	1.011 ± 1.483
AA+	0.097 ± 0.008	0.113 ± 0.013	0.427 ± 0.144
p-value		0.095	**0.001**

Table 6-3. Mackey-Glass prediction results and Kolmogorov-Smirnov two sample test *p*-values.

Cfg	Train		Test	
	RMS	NRMS	RMS	NRMS
Base	0.016 ± 0.013	0.068 ± 0.053	0.016 ± 0.013	0.070 ± 0.055
AA+	0.002 ± 0.001	0.012 ± 0.005	0.002 ± 0.001	0.012 ± 0.005
p-value			$\mathbf{1.087 \times 10^{-13}}$	

Wind Speed Forecasting

Wind provides a non-polluting renewable energy source, and it has been growing in importance over the past several years as countries attempt to minimize their dependency on fossil fuels and reduce their emissions. However, wind power production is highly volatile, as it depends on wind speed, which is determined by a number of weather factors. Therefore, wind speed prediction is an important problem in the clean energy world, and it also has applications for the wider energy production and market sectors (Lei et al., 2009).

One can perform wind speed forecasts on multiple time scales, with different application purposes (Soman et al., 2010). Long-term prediction can be used as an aid in wind turbine location decisions. Short term prediction on daily data can be used to estimate wind power generation over the next 24 to 48 hours, and those estimates are used to determine how much power will be needed from traditional sources. Finally, very short term prediction, over minutes up to a couple of hours, is useful for energy auctions as well as electrical grid operation, as wind speed is a major factor in overhead transmission line ampacity,[2] and forecasts can be used to guide dynamic rating systems (Michiorri and Taylor, 2009). A number of statistical and machine learning techniques have been applied to this problem, such as neural networks and autoregressive integrated moving average (ARIMA) models.

Herein we focus on short term, daily prediction. We run experiments on two wind speed time series, corresponding to the weather stations in the southern Brazilian cities of Curitiba (station code 838400) and Florianopolis (station code 838990), respectively.[3] We use data from the years 2008 and 2009 for training, and test on data covering the first 11 months of 2010. Both series contain missing entries, and we handle that by replicating the previous observation.

We note that wind speed forecasting is a very complex problem, and one shouldn't hope to build accurate models using only past wind speed as inputs. Several climatological factors have as much or more influence on one-step looka-

---

[2]Ampacity is the maximal current a transmission line can carry without being damaged.
[3]These time series were obtained from the US National Climatic Data Center (NCDC), and are part of the Global Surface Summary of Day Data (GSOD) base, avaliable via http://www.ncdc.noaa.gov/cgi-bin/res40.pl?page=gsod.html

head wind speed, such as temperature, pressure, humidity, as well as seasonal factors and other climate phenomena. In fact, using only past wind speed data can be actively misleading, and lead to very poor out of sample performance. Our goal, therefore, is to provide acceptable out of sample performance, determined as beating a zero-intelligence model that always outputs the mean value of the past data. Such model would have a test set NRMS very close to 1, so the same overfitting test we devised for symbolic regression in Section 4 can be used here. We note that the zero intelligence benchmark is frequently used in the wind forecasting literature (Soman et al., 2010; Lei et al., 2009).

The system configuration is the same as used in the benchmarks presented above. No normalization is performed on the data (preliminary experiments with both linear and zero-mean unit-variance normalization showed no improvements). We also present results from feed-forward neural networks trained via backpropagation and support vector machines using the Gaussian kernel for regression. Parameters for neural nets and SVMs are tuned via cross-validation on the training set. We use code from the WEKA open source project (Hall et al., 2009). We execute 10 runs for each configuration on each dataset.

Table 6-4 presents summary results for both time series. For each series, we show test RMS, as well as the percentage of runs with good generalization (defined as a test NRMS below 1). Given the difficulty of the problem, the higher RMS values are not unexpected. We see that the baseline system is competitive with SVMs, while neural networks have the worst performance. The **AA+** configuration is the only one to achieve good generalization on all runs.

Table 6-4. Wind speed prediction results on 2010 data (test set).

Cfg	St. 838400		St. 838990	
	RMS	$\% NRMS < 1$	RMS	$\% NRMS < 1$
Base	2.001	60	2.165	20
AA+	1.972	100	2.125	100
SVM	2.070	40	2.203	30
NN	4.023	0	5.149	0

Figure 6-3 shows the actual time series and predicted values on the test set for one of the **AA+** runs.

6.   Conclusion

We have developed a GP system that utilizes affine arithmetic to detect and discard program trees that might include asymptotes, and also to estimate the output bounds of these trees and discard those that lie outside a desirable range, determined from training data. Our system greatly improves out of sample performance for symbolic regression problems, when compared with a baseline

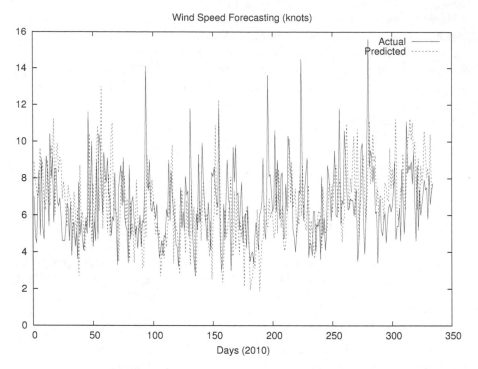

Figure 6-3. Actual and predicted wind speed values over 2010 for the Curitiba weather station.

GP system as well as a similar system that relies on interval arithmetic, a simpler but less accurate estimation method.

We have applied the same system to time series prediction problems. Experiments on the Mackey-Glass dataset show much higher accuracy and lower variance than the ones obtained with baseline GP. Similarly, experiments on the sunspot time series show better generalization and lower variance. Experiments on the much harder wind speed forecasting problem also show improved generalization in comparison with standard GP as well as leading machine learning method such as SVMs and neural networks.

We should note that our improved generalization comes at a price in runtime, as the **AA+** configuration is more computing intensive than the baseline GP system, by a factor of 3-5 on the time series experiments presented here. The extra cost of affine arithmetic evaluation can, however, be vastly reduced by caching the estimated output ranges of subtrees, so only a small fraction of each program tree needs to be re-estimated after crossover or mutation. Another alternative to reduce the computational overhead would be performing static analysis only on a subset of the population, such as individuals selected for recombination.

Future research opportunities include the incorporation of other improvements over standard GP, such as ensembles and complexity penalties, as done in (Kotanchek et al., 2007); devising improved mutation and crossover operators that take into consideration the estimated output ranges of subtrees; pruning operators that eliminate constant or low-variance subtrees, replacing them with new constant input nodes; automated building block identification and preservation through analysis of shared affine arithmetic noise symbols in subtrees; exploring potential limitations of linear scaling (such as scaling-deceptive search spaces) as well as alternative ways to scale program output; and, finally, application to other problem domains such as ranking and supervised classification.

References

Comba, J. and Stolfi, J. (1993). Affine arithmetic and its applications to computer graphics. In *Anais do VI SIBGRAPI*.

de Figueiredo, L. H. and Stolfi, J. (1997). *Self-Validated Numerical Methods and Applications*. Brazilian Mathematics Colloquium monographs. IMPA, Rio de Janeiro, Brazil.

de Figueiredo, L. H. and Stolfi, J. (2004). Affine arithmetic: Concepts and applications. *Numerical Algoritms*, 37:147–158.

Glass, L. and Mackey, M. (2010). Mackey-glass equation. *Scholarpedia*.

Hall, Mark, Frank, Eibe, Holmes, Geoffrey, Pfahringer, Bernhard, Reutemann, Peter, and Witten, Ian H. (2009). The weka data mining software: an update. *SIGKDD Explor. Newsl.*, 11:10–18.

Keijzer, Maarten (2003). Improving symbolic regression with interval arithmetic and linear scaling. In Ryan, Conor et al., editors, *Genetic Programming, Proceedings of EuroGP'2003*, volume 2610 of *LNCS*, pages 70–82, Essex. Springer-Verlag.

Keijzer, Maarten (2004). Scaled symbolic regression. *Genetic Programming and Evolvable Machines*, 5(3):259–269.

Korns, Michael F. (2009). Symbolic regression of conditional target expressions. In Riolo, Rick L., O'Reilly, Una-May, and McConaghy, Trent, editors, *Genetic Programming Theory and Practice VII*, Genetic and Evolutionary Computation, chapter 13, pages 211–228. Springer, Ann Arbor.

Kotanchek, Mark, Smits, Guido, and Vladislavleva, Ekaterina (2007). Trustable symbolic regression models: using ensembles, interval arithmetic and pareto fronts to develop robust and trust-aware models. In Riolo, Rick L., Soule, Terence, and Worzel, Bill, editors, *Genetic Programming Theory and Practice V*, Genetic and Evolutionary Computation, chapter 12, pages 201–220. Springer, Ann Arbor.

Koza, John R. (1992). *Genetic Programming: On the Programming of Computers by Means of Natural Selection*. MIT Press, Cambridge, MA, USA.

Langdon, W. B. and Poli, Riccardo (2002). *Foundations of Genetic Programming*. Springer-Verlag.

Lei, Ma, Shiyan, Luan, Chuanwen, Jiang, Hongling, Liu, and Yan, Zhang (2009). A review on the forecasting of wind speed and generated power. *Renewable and Sustainable Energy Reviews*, 13(4):915 – 920.

Looks, M. (2010). PLOP: Probabilistic learning of programs. http://code.google.com/p/plop.

Messine, F. (2002). Extentions of affine arithmetic: Application to unconstrained global optimization. *Journal of Universal Computer Science*, 8(11):992–1015.

Michiorri, A. and Taylor, P.C. (2009). Forecasting real-time ratings for electricity distribution networks using weather forecast data. In *20th International Conference and Exhibition on Electricity Distribution (CIRED)*, pages 854–854.

Moore, R. (1966). *Interval Analysis*. Prentice Hall.

Pennachin, Cassio L., Looks, Moshe, and de Vasconcelos, Joao A. (2010). Robust symbolic regression with affine arithmetic. In Branke, Juergen et al., editors, *GECCO '10: Proceedings of the 12th annual conference on Genetic and evolutionary computation*, pages 917–924, Portland, Oregon, USA. ACM.

Shou, Huahao, Lin, Hongwei, Martin, Ralph, and Wang, Guojin (2003). Modified affine arithmetic is more accurate than centered interval arithmetic or affine arithmetic. In Wilson, Michael J. and Martin, Ralph R., editors, *10th IMA International Conference on the Mathematics of Surfaces*, volume 2768 of *Lecture Notes in Computer Science*, pages 355–365. Springer.

Smits, Guido and Kotanchek, Mark (2004). Pareto-front exploitation in symbolic regression. In O'Reilly, Una-May, Yu, Tina, Riolo, Rick L., and Worzel, Bill, editors, *Genetic Programming Theory and Practice II*, chapter 17, pages 283–299. Springer, Ann Arbor.

Soman, S.S., Zareipour, H., Malik, O., and Mandal, P. (2010). A review of wind power and wind speed forecasting methods with different time horizons. In *North American Power Symposium (NAPS)*.

Valigiani, Gregory, Fonlupt, Cyril, and Collet, Pierre (2004). Analysis of GP improvement techniques over the real-world inverse problem of ocean color. In Keijzer, Maarten et al., editors, *Genetic Programming 7th European Conference, EuroGP 2004, Proceedings*, volume 3003 of *LNCS*, pages 174–186, Coimbra, Portugal. Springer-Verlag.

Weigend, A. S., Huberman, B. A., and Rumelhart, D. E. (1992). Predicting sunspots and exchange rates with connectionist networks. In Casdagli, M. and Eubank, S., editors, *Nonlinear Modeling and Forecasting*. Addison-Wesley.

Chapter 7

COMPUTATIONAL COMPLEXITY ANALYSIS OF GENETIC PROGRAMMING - INITIAL RESULTS AND FUTURE DIRECTIONS

Frank Neumann[1], Una-May O'Reilly[2] and Markus Wagner[1]

[1] *School of Computer Science, University of Adelaide, Australia;* [2] *CSAIL, MIT, Cambridge, USA.*

Abstract   The computational complexity analysis of evolutionary algorithms working on binary strings has significantly increased the rigorous understanding on how these types of algorithm work. Similar results on the computational complexity of genetic programming would fill an important theoretic gap. They would significantly increase the theoretical understanding on how and why genetic programming algorithms work and indicate, in a rigorous manner, how design choices of algorithm components impact its success. We summarize initial computational complexity results for simple tree-based genetic programming and point out directions for future research.

Keywords: genetic programming, computational complexity analysis, theory

1.   Introduction

Genetic programming (GP) (Koza, 1992) is a type of evolutionary algorithm that has proven to be very successful in various fields including modeling, financial trading, medical diagnosis, design and bioinformatics (Poli et al., 2008). It differs from other types of evolutionary algorithms by searching for solutions which are *executable*, i.e. that are program-like functions, which can be interpreted or execute when their input variables and formal parameters are bound. To apply variation operators that transform one candidate solution (or program) into another, conventional GP first converts an executable function into its parse tree (a.k.a. abstract syntax tree) representation then randomly modifies the tree in a way that preserves syntactic correctness but varies its size and/or structure. GP contrasts with other evolutionary algorithms, such as genetic algorithms and evolution strategies, because, rather than optimizing a given objective function, the goal in genetic programming is to search and identify one or more programs that exhibit a set of desired functionality. Usually this functionality is described in terms of desired input-output behaviour.

In contrast to numerous successful applications of genetic programming, the theoretical understanding of GP lags far behind its practical success (see (Poli et al., 2010) for an excellent appraisal of state of the art). While a number of theoretical approaches have been pursued and are active (e. g. schema theory, building block analysis, Markov chains, search space, bloat and problem difficulty analysis), a new direction which can provide proofs of convergence and time and space complexity analysis is most welcome. Our aim is to build up such a theory to gain new theoretical insights into the working principles of GP.

Computational complexity of evolutionary algorithms with binary representations

In the field of evolutionary algorithms that operate on binary solution representations, numerous theoretical insights have been gained in the last 15 years by computational complexity analyses. Initial results were obtained on simple pseudo-Boolean functions which point out basic working principles of simple evolutionary algorithms using binary representations (Droste et al., 2002). Results have been derived for a wide range of classical combinatorial optimization problems such as minimum spanning tress, shortest path and different cutting and covering problems (see e. g. (Neumann and Witt, 2010) for an overview). Problem specific algorithms for some of the classical problems enable them to be solved in polynomial time. We can not and do not expect that evolutionary algorithms to outperform such algorithms. However, studying the same problems and deriving run time bounds for evolutionary algorithms that solve them, allows us to gain a rigorous theoretical understanding of how these evolutionary algorithms work. Further, it yields insights as to how evolutionary algorithms are useful for tackling NP-hard variants of these problems.

To explain the type of results that might arise from computation complexity analysis of GP algorithms, it is helpful to review complexity analysis results for binary evolutionary algorithms. A good counterpart example is the classical minimum spanning tree problem which is one of the first problems where computational complexity results have been obtained for evolutionary algorithms working with binary representation. Runtime in these studies is always measured as the number of constructed solutions until an optimal solution has been found. In GP we would think of this as the number of fitness evaluations. The runtime bound for a simple evolutionary algorithms called (1+1) EA is $O(m^2(\log n + \log w_{\max}))$, where m is the number of edges, n is the number of vertices, and $w_{\max}$ is the largest weight of an edge in the given graph (Neumann and Wegener, 2007). Given evolutionary algorithms do not use global information, it is remarkable that they can provably solve classical combinatorial optimization problems in such a small amount of time. The analysis carried out in (Neumann and Wegener, 2007) shows rigorously that the result arises because several advantageous mutations can often be carried out in each iteration. This, and related, results have later been used to obtain a runtime bound for the NP-hard multi-objective minimum spanning tree problem (Neumann, 2007). In this case, it is shown that multi-objective evolutionary algorithms obtain a 2-approximation for this NP-hard problem in expected polynomial time if the size of the Pareto front is polynomially bounded. Note that this subsequent analysis considers a more complex evolutionary algorithm—one that is population based and using optimizing more than one objective.

Computational Complexity Analysis of GP

Our long term ambition is to develop, from the present simple state of art, an extended suite of computational complexity analyses for a range of GP algorithms solving model problems which represent important and commons aspects of real world GP counterparts. We intend to describe GP algorithms in a strict mathematical sense which will help lead to a rigorous understanding of GP algorithm convergence and time complexity which, in turn, will reveal the complexity implications of a variety of algorithm features (and specific choices) such as selection, variation and even bloat control. GP complexity analysis will appear similar to binary evolutionary algorithm analysis with respect to analyzing each algorithms in the context of solving a specific problem. In progressive analyses, along a daunting path, the sophistication of the algorithm, can optimistically ratchet upwards, likely in modest steps, from a simple hill climbing algorithm (e.g. (1+1) EA) with simplified operators towards population based versions with more realistic operators. The analysis, in general, however, will be distinct and contrasting primarily because GP algorithms work with executable candidate solutions. For example, conventional, a.k.a. Koza or tree-style, GP's variation operators modify a tree by changing its size and or structure. The variable size and tree-shape representations will challenge current complexity analysis techniques because the tree size changes over time and genetic material that can be added or deleted anywhere in any amount implies complicated consequences on the likelihood of fitness improvement from parent to child. The variation operators, particularly crossover, are more complicated, than their counterparts in evolutionary algorithms working with binary representations because of they are frequently designed to be quite unconstrained in terms of where and how much material is exchanged. New methods will be needed to analyze them.

We would aim to develop these methods and achieve computational complexity results for a wide range of algorithmic design choices and model problems so that practitioners will gain new insights into their working principles. Theoretical insights would ideally be used to develop even more powerful genetic programming techniques. We believe there can be a close relationship between theoretical work which offers rigorous proofs and substantial applied work that leads to new effective GP algorithms. Additionally, insights gained by the computational complexity analysis will help to teach this growing field of research in a much clearer way to undergraduate and postgraduate students.

In the rest of this chapter, we give an overview on some initial results we have derived and point different areas of research that we think are interesting to work on. We start by defining simplified GP algorithms that have been used to start the computational complexity analysis of genetic programming in Section 2. Afterwards, we present some initial results that have been obtained recently. The first results are on two problem modeling isolated program semantics called ORDER and MAJORITY. We present computational complexity results for these functions in Section 3. In Section 4, we investigate results for fitness functions motivated by the classical SORTING problem. For this problem the different variables in a GP program depend on each other which imposes other difficulties than for ORDER and MAJORITY. After having giving some insights into recent results we outline possible topics for future work which are often motivated by successful research projects on the computational complexity analysis for binary search spaces.

2.   Simple Algorithms

To use tree-based genetic programming (Koza, 1992), one must first choose a set of primitives A, which contains a set F of functions and a set L of terminals. Each primitive has explicitly defined semantics; for example, a primitive might represent a Boolean condition, a branching statement such as an IF-THEN-ELSE conditional, the value bound to an input variable, or an arithmetic operation. Functions are parameterized. Terminals are either functions with no parameters, i.e. arity equal to zero, or input variables to the program that serve as actual parameters to the formal parameters of functions.

In our derivations, we assume that a GP program is initialized by its parse tree construction. In general, we start with a root node randomly drawn from A and recursively populate the parameters of each function in the tree with subsequent random samples from A, until the leaves of the tree are all terminals. Functions constitute the internal nodes of the parse tree, and terminals occupy the leaf nodes. The exact properties of the tree generated by this procedure will not figure into the analysis of the algorithm, so we do not discuss them in depth.

HVL-Prime

The HVL-Prime operator is an update of O'Reilly's HVL mutation operator (O'Reilly, 1995; O'Reilly and Oppacher, 1994) and motivated by minimality rather than inspired from a tree-edit distance metric. HVL first selects a node at random in a copy of the current parse tree. Let us term this the `currentNode`. It then, with equiprobability, applies one of three sub-operations: insertion, substitution, or deletion. Insertion takes place above `currentNode`: a randomly drawn function from F becomes the parent of `currentNode` and its additional parameters are set by drawing randomly from L. Substitution changes `currentNode` to a randomly drawn function of F with the same arity. Deletion replaces `currentNode` with its largest child subtree, which often admits large deletion sub-operations.

The operator we consider here, HVL-Prime, functions slightly differently, since we restrict it to operate on trees where all functions take two parameters. Rather than choosing a node followed by an operation, we first choose one of the three sub-operations to perform. The operations then proceed as shown in Figure 7-1. Insertion and substitution are exactly as in HVL; however, deletion only deletes a leaf and its parent to avoid the potentially macroscopic deletion change of HVL that is not in the spirit of bit-flip mutation. This change makes the algorithm more amenable to complexity analysis and specifies an operator that is only as general as our simplified problems require, contrasting with the generality of HVL, where all sub-operations handle primitives of any arity. Nevertheless, both operators respect the nature of GP's search among variable-length candidate solutions because each generates another candidate of potentially different size, structure, and composition.

In our analysis on these particular problems, we make one further simplification of HVL-Prime: substitution only takes place at the leaves. This is because our two problems only have one generic "join" function specified, so performing a substitution anywhere above the leaves is a vacuous mutation. Such operations only constitute one-sixth of all operations, so this change has no impact on any of the runtime bounds we derive.

Algorithms

We define two genetic programming variants called $(1+1)$ GP and $(1+1)$ GP*. Both algorithms work with a population of size one and produce in each iteration one single offspring.

$(1+1)$ GP is defined as follows and accepts an offspring if it is as least as fit as its parent.

1. Choose an initial solution X.

2. Set $X' := X$.

3. Mutate X' by applying HVL-Prime k times. For each application, randomly choose to either substitute, insert, or delete.

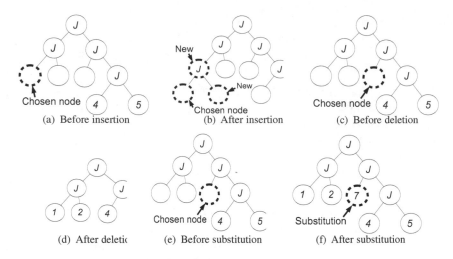

(a) Before insertion   (b) After insertion   (c) Before deletion

(d) After deletic   (e) Before substitution   (f) After substitution

Figure 7-1. Example of the operators from HVL-Prime.

- If substitute, replace a randomly chosen leaf of X' with a new leaf $u \in L$ selected uniformly at random.

- If insert, randomly choose a node v in X' and select $u \in L$ uniformly at random. Replace v with a join node whose children are u and v, with the order of the children chosen randomly.

- If delete, randomly choose a leaf node v of X', with parent p and sibling u. Replace p with u and delete p and v.

4. Acceptance for (1+1) GP:
     If $f(X') \geq f(X)$, set $X := X'$.

5. Go to 2.

(1+1) GP* is the same as above, with an alternative for step 4:

4'. Acceptance for (1+1) GP*:
     If $f(X') > f(X)$, set $X := X'$.

That is, (1+1) GP* differs from (1+1) GP by accepting only solutions that are strict improvements.

For each of (1+1) GP and (1+1) GP* we consider two further variants which differ in using one application of HVL-Prime ("single") or in using more than one ("multi"). For (1+1) GP-single and (1+1) GP*-single, we set $k = 1$, so that we perform one mutation at a time according to the HVL-Prime framework. For (1+1) GP-multi and (1+1) GP*-multi, we choose $k = 1 + \text{Pois}(1)$, so that the number of mutations at a time varies randomly according to the Poisson distribution.

We will analyze these four algorithms in terms of the expected number of fitness evaluations to produce an optimal solution for the first time. This is called the expected optimization time of the algorithm.

3.   ORDER and MAJORITY

We consider two separable problems called ORDER and MAJORITY that have an independent, additive fitness structure. They both have multiple solutions, which we feel is a key property of a model GP problem because it holds generally for all real GP problems. They also both use the same primitive set, where $\bar{x}_i$ is the complement of x_i:

- $F := \{J\}$, J has arity 2.

- $L := \{x_1, \bar{x}_1, \ldots, x_n, \bar{x}_n\}$

The ORDER Problem

ORDER represents problems where the primitive sets include conditional functions, which gives rise to conditional execution paths. GP classification problems, for example, often employ a numerical comparison function (e.g. greater than X, less than X, or equal to X). This sort of function has two arguments (subtrees), one branch which will be executed only when the comparison returns true, the other only when it returns false (Koza, 1992). Thus, a conditional function results in a branching or conditional execution path, so the GP algorithm must identify and appropriately position the conditional functions to achieve the correct conditional execution behavior for all inputs.

ORDER is an abstracted simplification of this challenge: the conditional execution paths of a program are determined by tree inspection rather than execution. Instead of evaluating a condition test and then executing the appropriate condition body explicitly, an ORDER program's conditional execution path is determined by simply inspecting whether a primitive or its complement occurs first in an in-order leaf parse. Correct programs for the ORDER problem must express each positive primitive x_i before its corresponding complement $\bar{x}_i$. This correctness requirement is intended to reflect a property commonly found in the GP solutions to problems where conditional functions are used: there exist multiple solutions, each with a set of different conditional paths.

The $f(X)$ for the ORDER problem is:

1. Derive conditional execution path P of X:

   Init: l an empty leaf list, P an empty conditional execution path

   1.1 Parse X in order and insert each leaf at the rear of l as it is visited.

1.2 Generate P by parsing l front to rear and adding ("expressing") a leaf to P only if it or its complement are not yet in P (i.e. have not yet been expressed).

2. $f(X) = |\{x_i \in P\}|$.

For example, for a tree X, with (after the inorder parse)

$$l = (x_1, \bar{x}_4, x_2, \bar{x}_1, x_3, \bar{x}_6), P = (x_1, \bar{x}_4, x_2, x_3, \bar{x}_6) \text{ and } f(X) = 3.$$

ORDER has the characteristic that whenever a solutions is non-optimal many successful mutation operators are possible to achieve an improvement in fitness. More precisely, let k be the fitness of a solution then there are $\Omega((n - k)^2)$ different mutation operators that lead to an improvement. Taking into a account the maximal tree size $T_{\max}$ during the run of the algorithm, one can show that the probability of an improvement is lower bounded by $\Omega\left(\frac{(n-k)^2}{nT_{\max}}\right)$ in this situation. As the fitness is not decreasing during the run of the algorithm, we can use the method of fitness-based partitions (see Chapter 4.2 in (Neumann and Witt, 2010) for an explanation of this method) to bound the runtime of our GP algorithms. This leads to the following results on the expected optimization time.

THEOREM 7.1 *The expected optimization time of the single-operation and multi-operation cases of (1+1) GP and (1+1) GP* on ORDER is $O(nT_{\max})$ in the worst case, where n is the number of x_i and $T_{\max}$ denotes the maximal tree size at any stage during the evolution of the algorithm.*

The MAJORITY problem

MAJORITY reflects a general (and thus weak) property required of GP solutions: a solution must have correct functionality and no incorrect functionality. Like ORDER, MAJORITY is a simplification that uses tree inspection rather than program execution. A correct program in MAJORITY must exhibit at least as many occurrences of a primitive as of its complement and it must exhibit all the positive primitives of its terminal (leaf) set. Both the independent sub-solution fitness structure and inspection property of MAJORITY are necessary to make our analysis tractable.

The $f(X)$ for the MAJORITY problem is:

1. Derive the combined execution statements S of X:

   Init: l an empty leaf list, S is an empty statement list.

   1.1 Parse X inorder and insert each leaf at the rear of l as it is visited.

   1.2 For $i \leq n$: if count$(x_i \in l) \geq$ count$(\bar{x}_i \in l)$ and count$(x_i \in l) \geq 1$, add x_i to S

2. $f(X) = |S|$.

For example, for a tree X, with (after the inorder parse)

$$l = (x_1, \bar{x}_4, x_2, \bar{x}_1, \bar{x}_3, \bar{x}_6, x_1, x_4), S = (x_1, x_2, x_4) \text{ and } f(X) = 3.$$

To solve the MAJORITY problem, a GP algorithm has to achieve for each i at least as many x_i as $\bar{x}_i$ variables. Therefore, it is crucial to analyze how to reduce the deficit of each variable according to the following definition.

DEFINITION 7.2 *For a given GP tree, let $c(x_i)$ be the number of x_i variables and $c(\bar{x}_i)$ be the number of negated x_i variables present in the tree. For a GP tree representing a solution to the MAJORITY problem, we define the deficit in the ith variable by*

$$D_i = c(\bar{x}_i) - c(x_i).$$

DEFINITION 7.3 *In a GP tree for MAJORITY, we say that x_i is expressed when $D_i \leq 0$ and $c(x_i) > 0$.*

The analysis considers the evolution of the deficits D_i over the course of the algorithm as n parallel random walks. It is shown that each positive D_i reaches zero at least as quickly as a balanced random walk, which is the condition for the corresponding x_i to be expressed; this, then, gives us the expected number of operations that we are required to perform on a particular variable before it is expressed.

These arguments lead to the following result for (1+1) GP-single.

THEOREM 7.4 *Let $D = \max_i D_i$ for an instance of MAJORITY initialized with T terminals drawn from a set of size 2n (i.e. terminals $x_1, ..., x_n, \bar{x}_1, ..., \bar{x}_n$). Then the expected optimization time of (1+1) GP-single is*

$$O(n \log n + DT_{\max} n \log \log n)$$

in the worst case.

Further results for ORDER and MAJORITY can be found in (Durrett et al., 2011). This, in particular, includes an average-case analysis for MAJORITY which shows that simple GP algorithms find solutions for this problem very quickly when the initial tree is chosen uniformly at random among all trees having a linear number of leaves.

4. The SORTING Problem

The problems ORDER and MAJORITY are in a sense easy as they have isolated problem semantics, and thus allow one to treat subproblems independently. The next step then is to consider problems that have dependent problem semantics, and we will do this in the following based on the SORTING problem. Sorting is one of the most basic problems in computer science. It is also the first combinatorial optimization problem for which computational complexity results have been obtained in the area of discrete evolutionary algorithms (Scharnow et al., 2004; Doerr and Happ, 2008). In (Scharnow et al., 2004), sorting is treated as an optimization problem where the task is to minimize the unsortness of a given permutation of the input elements. To measure unsortness, different fitness functions have been introduced and studied with respect to the difficulty of being optimized by permutation-based evolutionary algorithms.

In general, given a set of n elements from a totally ordered set, sorting is the problem of ordering these elements. We will identify the given elements by $1, \ldots, n$.

The goal is to find a permutation π_{opt} of $1, \ldots, n$ such that

$$\pi_{opt}(1) < \pi_{opt}(2) < \ldots < \pi_{opt}(n)$$

holds, where $<$ is the order on the totally ordered set. W. l. o. g. we assume $\pi_{opt} = id$, i.e. $\pi_{opt}(i) = i$ for all i.

The set of all permutations π of $1, \ldots, n$ forms a search space that has already been investigated in (Scharnow et al., 2004) for the analysis of permutation-based evolutionary algorithms. The authors of this paper, investigate sorting as an optimization problem whose goal is to maximize the sortedness of a given permutation. We consider the following two fitness functions measuring the sortedness of a given permutation π.

- $INV(\pi)$, measuring the number of pairs in correct order,[1] which is the number of pairs (i, j), $1 \le i < j \le n$, such that $\pi(i) < \pi(j)$,

- $HAM(\pi)$, measuring the number of elements at correct position, which is the number indices i such that $\pi(i) = i$.

Considering tree-based genetic programming, we have to deal with the fact that certain elements are not present in a current tree. We extend our notation of permutation to incompletely defined permutations. Therefore, we use π to denote a list of elements, where each element of the input set occurs at most once. This is a permutation of the elements that occur in the tree. Furthermore, we use $\pi(x) = p$ to get the position p that the element x has within π. In the case that $x \notin \pi$, $\pi(x) = \perp$ holds. We adjust the definition of π to later accommodate the use of trees as the underlying data structure. For example, $\pi = (1, 2, 4, 6, 3)$ leads to $\pi(1) = 1$, $\pi(2) = 2$, $\pi(3) = 5$, $\pi(4) = 3$, $\pi(6) = 4$, and $\pi(5) = \perp$.

---

[1]Originally, INV measures the numbers of pairs in wrong order. Our interpretation has the advantage that we need no special treatment of incompletely defined permutations.

The derivation of $f(X)$ for the SORTING problem is as follows:

1. Derive a possibly incompletely defined permutation P of X:

   Init: l an empty leaf list, P an empty list representing a possibly incompletely defined permutation

   1.1 Parse X in order and insert each leaf at the rear of l as it is visited.

   1.2 Generate P by parsing l front to rear and adding ("expressing") a leaf to P only if it is not yet in P, i.e. it has not yet been expressed.

2. Compute $f(X)$ based on P and the chosen fitness function.

The basic idea behind showing a runtime bound on INV is the following. It is always possible to increase the fitness by inserting a specific leaf at its correct position in order to achieve a fitness increment of at least 1. Therefore, the probability for such an improvement for each of our algorithms is $\Omega\left(\frac{1}{nT_{\max}}\right)$. Again $T_{\max}$ denotes the maximal size of a tree during the run of the algorithm. Using the method of fitness-based partitions, and based on the observation that $n \cdot (n-1)/2 + 1$ fitness values are possible, the optimization time is upper bounded by $\sum_{k=0}^{n(n-1)/2} O\left(nT_{\max}\right)$ which leads to the following result.

THEOREM 7.5 *The expected optimization time of the single- and multi-operation cases of (1+1) GP* with INV is $O(n^3 T_{\max})$.*

For the sortedness measure HAM, we present a worst case example to demonstrate that the single- and multi-operation cases of (1+1) GP* can get stuck during the optimization process. Assuming that we initialize the algorithms with the following initial solution called T_w

$$\underbrace{n, n, \ldots, n}_{n+1 \text{ of these}}, 2, 3, \ldots, n-1, 1, n$$

it is easy to see that it is hard to achieve an improvement. It is clear that with a single HVL-Prime application, only one of the leftmost n can be removed. For an improvement in the sortedness, all $n+1$ leftmost leaves have to be removed in order for the rightmost n to become expressed. Additionally, a leaf labeled 1 has to be inserted at the beginning, or alternatively, one of the $n+1$ leaves labeled n has to be replaced by a 1. This cannot be done by the (1+1) GP*-single, resulting in an infinite runtime. However, (1+1) GP*-multi can improve the fitness, but at least $n+1$ sub-operations have to be performed, assuming that we, in each case, delete one of the leftmost ns. Because the number of sub-operations per mutation is distributed as $1 + Pois(1)$, the Poisson random variable has to take a value of at least n. This implies that the probability for such a step is $e^{-\Omega(n)}$ and the expected waiting time for such a step is therefore $e^{\Omega(n)}$.

THEOREM 7.6 *Let T_w be the initial solution to SORTING. Then the expected optimization time of (1+1) GP*-single and (1+1) GP*-multi is infinite respectively $e^{\Omega(n)}$ for the sortedness measure HAM.*

The proofs and further computational complexity results for genetic programming on the SORTING problem can be found in (Wagner and Neumann, 2011).

5.   Future Directions

To conclude this chapter, we want to point out topics for future research. The results mentioned in the previous sections are initial ones and there are different ways to extend these studies. In the following, we point out which are the most interesting directions for future research from our point of view.

Problems of Different Fitness Structure

The functions ORDER and MAJORITY can be seen as variants of the One-Max problem for binary strings. The characteristic of this problem is that each possible variable has the same weight and contributes independently to fitness. It would be interesting to analyze simplified GP algorithm on a much broader class where each variable contributes a different weight. A special case is linear scaling and exponential scaling of independent weights which has been studied experimentally in (Goldberg and O'Reilly, 1998). The general model we are thinking of matches the class of linear, functions in the case of binary representations. The analysis of evolutionary algorithms working with binary representations carried out in (Droste et al., 2002) was a major breakthrough for the binary case and we expect that such results and the therefore developed methods will significantly pushed forward the theoretical understand of GP algorithms and set basis analysis of more complex problems.

Complexity versus accuracy

GP algorithms face the problem that the tree gets too large during the learning and optimization process. In the case of learning, it can often be observed that there is a trade-off between the accuracy of the learned function and the size of the tree (Gustafson et al., 2004). On the other hand, GP algorithms allow to express patterns several times in the tree although this does not increase the performs. Parsimony GP algorithms prefer trees of a smaller size if they have equal good performance. It would be interesting to study the impact of dealing with the complexity of the tree size in different ways. First, it would be interesting to study the impact of the parsimony approach and point out the impact on the runtime behaviour. Accepting only trees of lower complexity gives a clear search direction on plateaus, i. e. regions in the search space where solutions have equal good fitness. The aim would be to understand how this influences the run of a GP algorithm. One could point out the benefits and drawbacks of this approach in a rigorous way by computational complexity analyses.

The parsimony approach favours solutions of low complexity. Often users of genetic programming algorithms are interested in the trade-off between complexity and accuracy and want to obtain a set of solutions that gives them possible options according to these two objectives. Therefore, it would be interesting to analyze the trade-off between complexity and accuracy that genetic programming algorithms observe when optimizing these two objective in a multi-objective approach. Our goal is understand how multi-objective genetic programming algorithms construct this set of trade-off solutions. For evolutionary algorithms working with binary representations it has been shown that the multi-objective model gives an additional search direction which allows to compute optimal solutions or good approximations much quicker than in the single-objective model (Neumann and Wegener, 2006; Friedrich et al., 2010). Therefore, it is interesting to study situations where the multi-objective formulation (complexity vs accuracy) is beneficial for the success of GP algorithms.

Populations, Crossover, and Diversity

One crucial parameter in a GP algorithm is the choice of the population size. Theoretical studies on the impact of the population size for evolutionary algorithms working on binary strings have shown that the choice of the population size can have a drastic impact on the runtime behaviour (Witt, 2006; Storch, 2008). Working with a population size of 1 leads to a hill-climbing behaviour that has the disadvantage of getting stuck in local optima. Therefore, often a larger population size is chosen to cope with this issue. The goal is to keep a diverse set of solutions during the run of the algorithm which allows to explore different regions of the search space. Closely connected to the choice of the population size, is the application of diversity mechanisms that ensure that a population consists of a diverse set of solutions. Such diversity mechanisms play a crucial role for the success of these algorithms (Burke et al., 2004). Therefore, our studies will concentrate on the impact of the population size in conjunction with commonly used diversity mechanisms. Diversity can be maintained by different mechanisms. One possibility is to compare the structure of the trees that constitute the population. Another possibility is to introduce a distance measure that is based on the number of subtrees that two solutions in the population share. Furthermore, diversity can be obtained by maintaining trees of different fitness. This allows to keep solutions of lower fitness which usually have a different structure than the best solutions in the population. It would be interesting to figure out the differences of these approaches by computational complexity analyses and show where they lead to significant different runtime results of such algorithms. Having solutions of different structure in the population is also crucial for successful crossover operators. Therefore, another topic of research is to study the impact of crossover in conjunction with the population size and appropriate diversity mechanisms.

6.   Conclusions

The computational complexity analysis of genetic programming can provide new rigorous insight into the working principles of simplified genetic programming algorithms. In this chapter, we have pointed out the results of some initial studies. These studies show how to obtain computational complexity bounds for GP algorithms on problems with different characteristics. We outlined some topics for future research which would help to gain further rigorous insights into the behavior of genetic programming. We are optimistic that such computational complexity results can be obtained in the near future and that they will provide valuable new insights into this type of algorithms.

References

Burke, Edmund K., Gustafson, Steven, and Kendall, Graham (2004). Diversity in genetic programming: An analysis of measures and correlation with fitness. *IEEE Transactions on Evolutionary Computation*, 8(1):47–62.

Doerr, Benjamin and Happ, Edda (2008). Directed trees: A powerful representation for sorting and ordering problems. In *2008 IEEE World Congress on Computational Intelligence*, pages 3606–3613. IEEE Computational Intelligence Society, IEEE Press.

Droste, Stefan, Jansen, Thomas, and Wegener, Ingo (2002). On the analysis of the (1+1) evolutionary algorithm. *Theor. Comput. Sci.*, 276:51–81.

Durrett, Greg, Neumann, Frank, and O'Reilly, Una-May (2011). Computational complexity analysis of simple genetic programming on two problems modeling isolated program semantics. In *FOGA '11: Proceedings of the 11th ACM SIGEVO workshop on Foundations of Genetic Algorithms*. ACM. (to appear).

Friedrich, Tobias, He, Jun, Hebbinghaus, Nils, Neumann, Frank, and Witt, Carsten (2010). Approximating covering problems by randomized search heuristics using multi-objective models. *Evolutionary Computation*, 18(4):617–633.

Goldberg, David E. and O'Reilly, Una-May (1998). Where does the good stuff go, and why? how contextual semantics influence program structure in simple genetic programming. In Banzhaf, Wolfgang, Poli, Riccardo, Schoenauer, Marc, and Fogarty, Terence C., editors, *Proceedings of the First European Workshop on Genetic Programming*, volume 1391 of *LNCS*, pages 16–36, Paris. Springer-Verlag.

Gustafson, Steven, Ekart, Aniko, Burke, Edmund, and Kendall, Graham (2004). Problem difficulty and code growth in genetic programming. *Genetic Programming and Evolvable Machines*, 5(3):271–290.

Koza, John R. (1992). *Genetic Programming: On the Programming of Computers by Means of Natural Selection.* MIT Press, Cambridge, MA, USA.

Neumann, Frank (2007). Expected runtimes of a simple evolutionary algorithm for the multi-objective minimum spanning tree problem. *European Journal of Operational Research*, 181(3):1620–1629.

Neumann, Frank and Wegener, Ingo (2006). Minimum spanning trees made easier via multi-objective optimization. *Natural Computing*, 5(3):305–319.

Neumann, Frank and Wegener, Ingo (2007). Randomized local search, evolutionary algorithms, and the minimum spanning tree problem. *Theor. Comput. Sci.*, 378(1):32–40.

Neumann, Frank and Witt, Carsten (2010). *Bioinspired Computation in Combinatorial Optimization – Algorithms and Their Computational Complexity.* Springer.

O'Reilly, Una-May (1995). *An Analysis of Genetic Programming.* PhD thesis, Carleton University, Ottawa-Carleton Institute for Computer Science, Ottawa, Ontario, Canada.

O'Reilly, Una-May and Oppacher, Franz (1994). Program search with a hierarchical variable length representation: Genetic programming, simulated annealing and hill climbing. In Davidor, Yuval, Schwefel, Hans-Paul, and Manner, Reinhard, editors, *Parallel Problem Solving from Nature – PPSN III*, number 866 in Lecture Notes in Computer Science, pages 397–406, Jerusalem. Springer-Verlag.

Poli, Riccardo, Langdon, William B., and McPhee, Nicholas Freitag (2008). *A field guide to genetic programming.* Published via http://lulu.com and freely available at http://www.gp-field-guide.org.uk. (With contributions by J. R. Koza).

Poli, Riccardo, Vanneschi, Leonardo, Langdon, William B., and McPhee, Nicholas Freitag (2010). Theoretical results in genetic programming: the next ten years? *Genetic Programming and Evolvable Machines*, 11(3-4):285–320.

Scharnow, Jens, Tinnefeld, Karsten, and Wegener, Ingo (2004). The analysis of evolutionary algorithms on sorting and shortest paths problems. *Journal of Mathematical Modelling and Algorithms*, 3:349–366.

Storch, Tobias (2008). On the choice of the parent population size. *Evolutionary Computation*, 16(4):557–578.

Wagner, Markus and Neumann, Frank (2011). Computational complexity results for genetic programming and the sorting problem. *CoRR*, abs/1103.5797.

Witt, Carsten (2006). Runtime analysis of the (mu + 1) EA on simple pseudo-boolean functions. *Evolutionary Computation*, 14(1):65–86.

Chapter 8

ACCURACY IN SYMBOLIC REGRESSION

Michael F. Korns

Korns Associates, 98 Perea Street, Makati 1229, Manila Philippines

Abstract

This chapter asserts that, in current state-of-the-art symbolic regression engines, accuracy is poor. That is to say that state-of-the-art symbolic regression engines return a champion with good fitness; however, obtaining a champion with the correct formula is not forthcoming even in cases of only one basis function with minimally complex grammar depth.

Ideally, users expect that for test problems created with no noise, using only functions in the specified grammar, with only one basis function and some minimal grammar depth, that state-of-the-art symbolic regression systems should return the exact formula (or at least an isomorph) used to create the test data. Unfortunately, this expectation cannot currently be achieved using published state-of-the-art symbolic regression techniques.

Several classes of test formulas, which prove intractable, are examined and an understanding of why they are intractable is developed. Techniques in Abstract Expression Grammars are employed to render these problems tractable, including manipulation of the epigenome during the evolutionary process, together with breeding of multiple targeted epigenomes in separate population islands.

A selected set of currently intractable problems are shown to be solvable, using these techniques, and a proposal is put forward for a discipline-wide program of improving accuracy in state-of-the-art symbolic regression systems.

Keywords: Abstract Expression Grammars, Differential Evolution, Grammar Template Genetic Programming, Genetic Algorithms, Particle Swarm, Symbolic Regression.

1. Introduction

The discipline of Symbolic Regression (SR) has matured significantly in the last few years. There is at least one commercial package on the market for several years *http://www.rmltech.com/*. There is now at least one well documented commercial symbolic regression package available for

Mathmatica *www.evolved-analytics.com*. There is at least one very well done open source symbolic regression package available for free download *http://ccsl.mae.cornell.edu/eureqa*. In addition to our own ARC system (Korns, 2010), currently used internally for massive (million row) financial data nonlinear regressions, there are a number of other mature symbolic regression packages currently used in industry including (Smits et al., 2010) and (Castillo et al., 2010). Plus there is an interesting work in progress by (McConaghy et al., 2009).

During the process of enhancing our ARC system with the latest thinking in published symbolic regression papers, we ran across several test problems for which our system failed to return the correct formula. Normally this is not surprising in large scale regression with much noise; however, these test problems were generated with no noise and were fairly simplistic formulas of only one basis function with minimally complex grammar depth.

After further study it is now apparent that there are very large numbers of simple test formulas against which current state-of-the-art symbolic regression systems suffer poor accuracy. For these intractable problems state-of-the-art symbolic regression engines fail to return a champion with the correct formula.

This is a serious issue for several reasons. First, users expect to receive a correct formula when inputting a simple test case. When a correct formula is not forthcoming, user interest and trust in the symbolic regression system wanes. Second, if symbolic regression cannot return a correct formula in even simplistic test cases then symbolic regression loses its differentiation from other black box machine learning techniques such as support vector regression or neural nets. Third, from its very inception (Koza, 1992) symbolic regression has been represented as a technique for returning, not just coefficients, but a correct formula. If this claim cannot be fulfilled by independent scientific review, a serious reputational issue will develop and research money will flow in other directions.

This chapter begins by outlining the accuracy issue. A simple symbolic regression grammar of fifteen obvious mathematical functions is established. All test cases are limited to a single basis function of no more than three grammar nodes deep. For all test cases the data is limited to ten thousand sample points, of five features each, and absolutely no noise. Even with these very severe limitations, large numbers of simple formulas are shown to be intractable.

The chapter continues with an examination of techniques which allow ARC to solve these previously intractable problems. The chapter closes with a proposal for a discipline wide approach to solving our symbolic regression accuracy issues.

Testing Regimen

Our testing regimen uses only statistical best practices out-of-sample testing techniques. We test each of the test cases on matrices of 10000 sample points and five features with absolutely no noise. Each sample point $x = <x_1,x_2,x_3,x_4,x_5>$ is associated with a dependent variable y. The data is constructed so that there is an exact functional relationship between each sample point and each associated dependent variable: $F(x) = y$.

For each test, a training matrix is filled with pseudo random numbers between -50 and +50 (*each test is random but reproducible on demand*). The test case target functions, F, are limited to one basis function whose maximum depth is three grammar nodes. The target function for the test case is applied to the training matrix to compute the dependent variable. The symbolic regression system is trained on the training matrix to produce the regression champion. Following training, a testing matrix is filled with random numbers between -50 and +50. The target function for the test case is applied to the testing matrix to compute the dependent variable. The regression champion is evaluated on the testing matrix for all scoring (i.e. out of sample testing).

Our fitness measure is normalized least squared error (NLSE) as defined in (Korns, 2009). Normalized least squared error is the least squared error value divided by the standard deviation of Y. A returned regression champion formula is considered *accurate* if the normalized least squared error (NLSE) on the testing run is .0001 or below. This approach allows isomorphs, such as (x1+x3) and (x3+x1), to be included in the accurate category. It also allows formulas to be considered accurate if they are not isomorphic but are so statistically close as to be approximately identical.

All results in this paper were achieved on a workstation computer, specifically an Intel® Core™ 2 Duo Processor T7200 (2.00GHz/667MHz/4MB), running our Analytic Information Server software generating Lisp agents that compile native code using the on-board Intel registers and on-chip vector processing capabilities so as to maximize execution speed. Details can be found at *http://www.korns.com/Document Lisp Language Guide.html*. Furthermore, our Analytic Information Server is available in an open source software project at *aiserver.sourceforge.net*.

All tables have omitted run timings in favor of numbers of candidate Well Formed Formulas (WFFs) examined. This allows the comparison of results across disparate computer systems and between disparate symbolic regression packages as well as cloud computing systems. Furthermore, numbers of individuals (WFFs) examined is often proposed as a fundamental measure of the actual work involved in a symbolic regression search, and is closely related to Koza's concepts of computational effort (Koza, 1992).

A Tutorial on Abstract Expression Grammars

In standard Koza-style tree-based Genetic Programming (Koza, 1992) the genome and the individual are the same Lisp s-expression which is usually illustrated as a tree. Of course the tree-view of an s-expression is a visual aid, since a Lisp s-expression is normally a **list** which is a special Lisp data structure. Without altering or restricting standard tree-based GP in any way, we can view the individuals not as trees but instead as s-expressions.

- (*S1*) **depth 0 binary tree s-exp**: 3.45
- (*S2*) **depth 1 binary tree s-exp**: (+ x2 3.45)
- (*S3*) **depth 2 binary tree s-exp**: (/ (+ x2 3.45) (* x0 x2))
- (*S3*) **depth 2 irregular tree s-exp**: (/ (+ x2 3.45) 2.0)

In standard GP, applied to symbolic regression, the non-terminal nodes are all operators (*implemented as Lisp function calls*), and the terminal nodes are always either real number constants or features. An important point to remember is that we are not making a substantive change in standard GP. We are simply refocusing our view of the individuals as s-expressions.

The maximum depth of a GP individual is limited by the available computational resources; but, it is standard practice to limit the maximum depth of a GP individual to some managable limit at the start of a symbolic regression run.

Given any selected maximum depth k, it is an easy process to construct a maximal binary tree s-espression U_k, which can be produced by the GP system without violating the selected maximum depth limit. As long as we are reminded that each **f** represents a function node while each **t** represents a terminal node, the construction algorithm is simple and recursive as follows.

- U_0: t
- U_1: (f t t)
- U_2: (f (f t t) (f t t))
- U_3: (f (f (f t t) (f t t)) (f (f t t) (f t t)))
- U_k: (f $U_{k-1}U_{k-1}$)

Any individual produced by the standard GP system may be smaller than, may be irregular, but will not be larger than U_k.

For the purposes of this tutorial section, we shall select the maximum depth limit to be $k = 3$. We will only allow two features **x0 x1** and the IEEE double real number constants in each terminal node. Our set of valid functions will be the binary operators: **+ - *** and **/**. Furthermore, to make node identification easier, we shall enumerate each node in U_3, and revert to more easily read functional notation as follows.

- U_3: f0(f1(f2(t0,t1),f3(t2,t3)),f4(f5(t4,t5),f6(t6,t7)))

An example of a individual, which fits the form of U_3 is as follows:

- (*I1*): (* (/ (- x0 3.45) (+ x0 x1)) (/ (- x1 1.31) (* x0 x1)))

Up until this point we have not altered or restricted standard GP in any way; but, now we are about to make a slight alteration.

It is a little difficult, in (I1), to tell which * operator is associated with which function node in U_3, so we are going to add an *annotation* to the individual (I1). We are going to restore the enumerated function nodes in U_3, and we are going to add a function chromosome vector to (I1). The individual (I1) will now have two components: an s-expression and a function chromosome as follows.

- (*I1$_d$*,**s-exp**): (**f0** (**f1** (**f2** x0 3.45) (**f3** x0 x1)) (**f4** (**f5** x1 1.31) (**f6** x0 x1)))
- (*I1$_d$*,**f-chrome**): (* / - + / - *)

In order to make (I1) evaluate as it used to, we will need to make one additional slight alteration in the definition of the enumerated function nodes. From now on the function notation **fn** will be evaluated as: call the *nth* function found in the function chromosome vector. Hence, in (I1), **f0** will call *, **f1** will call /, **f2** will call -, etc. We still have not restricted standard GP in any way. The same population operators work in the same way they always worked. However, we have added a new annotation to each individual and added a level of indirection to each function evaluation.

In the same vein we will add a constant chromosome vector for each constant reference in U_3, so that the individual (I1) now has a new *annotation*, and each abstract constant reference **cn** evaluates to: return the *nth* constant found in the constant chromosome vector. The individual (I1) will now have three components: an s-expression, a function chromosome, and a constant chromosome as follows.

- (*I1$_c$*,**s-exp**): (f0 (f1 (f2 x0 **c1**) (f3 x0 x1)) (f4 (f5 x1 **c5**) (f6 x0 x1)))
- (*I1$_c$*,**f-chrome**): (* / - + / - *)
- (*I1$_c$*,**c-chrome**): (0 3.45 0 0 1.31 0 0)

Also in the same vein we will add a variable chromosome vector for each feature reference in U_3, so that the individual (I1) now has a new *annotation*, and each abstract feature reference **vn** evaluates to: return the *nth* feature found in the feature chromosome vector. The individual (I1) will now have four components: an s-expression, a function chromosome, a constant chromosome, and a variable chromosome as follows.

- (*I1$_b$*,**s-exp**): (f0 (f1 (f2 **v0** c1) (f3 **v2 v3**)) (f4 (f5 **v4** c5) (f6 **v6 v7**)))
- (*I1$_b$*,**f-chrome**): (* / - + / - *)
- (*I1$_b$*,**c-chrome**): (0 3.45 0 0 1.31 0 0 0)

- ($I1_b$,**v-chrome**): (x0 x0 x0 x1 x1 x0 x0 x1)

Finally in the same vein we will add a term chromosome vector for each term reference in U_3, so that the individual (I1) now has yet another a new *annotation*, and each abstract term reference **tn** evaluates to: examine the *nth* value found in the term chromosome vector. If the term value is 0, then return the *nth* value in the variable chromosome; otherwise, return the *nth* value in the constant chromosome. The individual (I1) will now have four chromosomes: a function chromosome, a constant chromosome, a variable chromosome and a term chromosome; and a standard abstract functional-expression. Plus the original concrete s-expression will be retained as follows.

- ($I1_a$,**f-exp**): f0(f1(f2(**t0,t1**),f3(**t2,t3**)),f4(f5(**t4,t5**),f6(**t6,t7**)))
- ($I1_a$,**f-chrome**): (* / - + / - *)
- ($I1_b$,**c-chrome**): (0 3.45 0 0 1.31 0 0 0)
- ($I1_b$,**v-chrome**): (x0 x0 x0 x1 x1 x0 x0 x1)
- ($I1_a$,**t-chrome**): (0 1 0 0 0 1 0 0)
- ($I1_a$,**concrete**): (* (/ (- x0 3.45) (+ x0 x1)) (/ (- x1 1.31) (* x0 x1)))

At this point in the tutorial take a brief pause. Examine the final abstract annotated version ($I1_a$) above and compare it to the original concrete version (I1). Walk through the evaluation process for each version. Satisfy yourself that the concrete s-expression (I1) and the abstract annotated ($I1_a$) both evaluate to exactly the same interim and final values.

We have made no restrictive nor destructive changes in the orginal individual (I1). Slightly altered to handle the new indirect references and the new chromosome annotations, any standard GP system will behave as it did before. Prove it to yourself this way. Take the annotated individual ($I1_a$), and replace each indirect reference with the proper value from the proper chromosome. This converts the abstract annotated ($I1_a$) back into the concrete s-expression (I1). Let your standard GP system operate on (I1) any way it wishes to produce a new individual (I2). Now convert (I2) back into an abstract annotated ($I2_a$) with the same process we used to annotate (I1).

We make three more slight alterations and enhancements in order to complete this tutorial on Abstract Expression Grammars (*AEGs*). First, we slightly alter the evaluation process for any unary functions (*such as* **cos log** *etc.*) such that any excess arguments are simply ignored. Second, we add a special unary operator (**lpass**) which simply returns its first argument (leftmost) and, of course, ignores any excess arguments. Our valid functions are now: **+ - * /** and **lpass**. Third, we no longer think of evaluating ($I1_a$) the way we evaluate (I1). Instead we borrow important grammar template concepts from (O'Neill and Ryan, 2003) (McKay et al., 2010) and refocus our view of ($I1_a$) as an abstract expression grammar wherein the f-expression and chromosomes are evaluated as grammar rules and used to produced the concrete annotation (II_a,**concrete**). Any changes in the chromosomes cause the individual to produced a new appropriate concrete annotation matching the new chromosome contents.

In summary we have simply added extra information as annotations and we've even kept the original s-expression. The standard GP system has not been restricted or limited in any way and may continue to operate much as it did before - albeit with these extra annotations. We've added an abstract functional-expression containing indirect: function references *fn*, constant references *cn*, variable references *vn*, and term references *tn*. We've also added annotations for four chromosomes for: functions, constants, variables, and terms.

Furthermore, given a selected maximum depth limit k, our **lpass** grammar rule allows the maximal binary tree s-expression U_k to generate ANY s-epression which the original GP system can generate *up to the selected depth limit*. Clearly the ($I1_a$) individual, shown above, can express any maximal 3-deep s-expression with appropriate changes to its chromosomes. But, what about smaller and irregular s-expressions which are not the same maximal shape as U_k? The **lpass** grammar rule allows all smaller and irregular s-expressions to be generated as in the examples below.

- ($I2_a$,**f-exp**): f0(f1(f2(t0,t1),f3(t2,t3)),f4(f5(t4,t5),f6(t6,t7)))
- ($I2_a$,**f-chrome**): (lpass lpass lpass lpass lpass lpass lpass)
- ($I2_b$,**c-chrome**): (0 0 0 0 0 0 0 0)
- ($I2_b$,**v-chrome**): (x0 x0 x0 x0 x0 x0 x0 x0)
- ($I2_a$,**t-chrome**): (0 0 0 0 0 0 0 0)
- ($I2_a$,**concrete**): x0

- ($I3_a$,**f-exp**): f0(f1(f2(t0,t1),f3(t2,t3)),f4(f5(t4,t5),f6(t6,t7)))
- ($I3_a$,**f-chrome**): (lpass / * lpass lpass lpass lpass)
- ($I3_b$,**c-chrome**): (0 4.2 0 0 0 0 0 0)
- ($I3_b$,**v-chrome**): (x0 x0 x1 x0 x0 x0 x0 x0)
- ($I3_a$,**t-chrome**): (0 1 0 0 0 0 0 0)
- ($I3_a$,**concrete**): (/ (* x0 4.2) x1)

Because of this property we speak of U_k as a *universal* Abstract Expression to depth k.

Space restrictions prevent us from expanding on this brief tutorial. The basics of Abstract Expression Grammars and Universal Abstract Expressions are described in (Korns, 2010). Reviewing Abstract Expression Grammars is strongly advised before continuing with this chapter.

With all this new information, we have a number of new options. We can keep our GP system operating as it did before; or, now that we have all the constants in one vector, we can apply swarm operators to the constants for better constant mangement. Similarly we can apply genetic algorithm operations to the function, variable, and term vectors. If we decide to upgrade to a more complicated context sensitive grammar, many standard GP population operators become much easier with extra annotations. Finally when users ask for constraints on the search output and search process, user constraints become much easier with added annotations.

A Simple Symbolic Regression Grammar

In our symbolic regression research with financial data we set our maximum depth limit quite high. We allow many basis functions, and we allow many data features. However, for this chapter, we will set our maximum depth limit to only three and will allow only one basis function. Our purpose is to demonstrate that absolute accuracy issues arise quite quickly with current published symbolic regression techniques - even with simple problems. One would never dream of attacking an industrial regression problem with maximum depth set to three and only one basis function; but, that makes the appearance of absolute accuracy problems even more disappointing.

In this chapter we will create a series of simple test cases - all of which have absolute solutions within a maximum s-expression depth of three, only five features, and all with only one basis function. Theoretically each of our test cases should be easily solved by any GP symbolic regression system - even when set to these low depth and basis function limits. Unfortunately, we discovered that our ARC symbolic regression system could not solve ALL of these simple test cases.

Our simple symbolic regression grammar has the following basic elements.

- **Real Numbers**: 3.45, -.0982, 100.389, and *all other real constants.*
- **Features**: x0, x1, x2, x3, and x4 *a maximum of five features.*
- **Binary Operators**: +, -, *, /
- **Unary Operators**: sqrt, square, cube, cos, sin, tan, tanh, log, exp
- **lpass Operator**: lpass(expr,expr) *returns the left expression unaltered*
- **rpass Operator**: rpass(expr,expr) *expr returns the right expression unaltered*

Our concrete numeric expressions are C-like expressions containing the elements shown above and ready for compilation. All test cases are solved with univariate regression because, in this chapter, we limit our study to one basis function intractable problems. Our **lpass** and **rpass** operators are idempotents which allow our grammar to be used with AEG universal abstract expressions (*also all unary operators, should they receive two arguments, operate on the left expression and ignore the right expression*). Our basic expression grammar is functional in nature, therefore all operators are viewed grammatically as function calls. The final regression champion will be the compilation of a basic concrete expression such as:

- (*E1*): f = (log(x3)/sin(x2*45.3))

In order to be considered *accurate* the NLSE of the regression champion, on the testing data (see Testing Regimen), must be .0001 or below.

The *universal* abstract expression U_3, used for all test cases, consists of one basis function with a maximum depth of three function applications, as follows.

- (*E2*): f0(f1(f2(t0,t1),f3(t2,t3)),f4(f5(t4,t5),f6(t6,t7)))

By way of a review example if, in the AEG (E2), we replace f0 with **cos**, f1 with **lpass**, f2 with *, t0 with **3.45**, and t1 with **x2**, then (E2) generates the following WFF candidate with the following concrete annotation *cos(3.45*x2)* ready for compilation.

- (*E3$_a$*,**f-exp**): f0(f1(f2(t0,t1),f3(t2,t3)),f4(f5(t4,t5),f6(t6,t7)))
- (*E3$_a$*,**f-chrome**): (cos lpass * lpass lpass lpass lpass)
- (*E3$_b$*,**c-chrome**): (3.45 0 0 0 0 0 0 0)
- (*E3$_b$*,**v-chrome**): (x0 x2 x0 x0 x0 x0 x0 x0)
- (*E3$_a$*,**t-chrome**): (1 0 0 0 0 0 0 0)
- (*E3$_a$*,**concrete**): **cos(3.45*x2)**

Even though our test cases are as limited as they are (*we have purposely limited them in this chapter so we can focus on absolute accuracy issues*), the size of the search space is quite large. This is one of the main issues faced by symbolic regression systems. Even simple test problems can have very large search spaces.

Our universal abstract expression U_3 has seven abstract function placeholders. Each abstract function placeholder may hold one of fifteen function values (*4 binary operators, 9 unary operators,* **lpass**, *and* **rpass**). Our universal abstract expression also has eight abstract term placeholders. Each term placeholder may hold one of 2^{64} IEEE double constant values or one of the five features. On test cases with five data features the size of the search space is 10^{162}. The presence of constants does make the search space much larger; however, even if we do not allow constants, thus limiting each term to features only, the size of the search space is still 10^{14}.

By way of comparison, the number of quarks in our universe is estimated to be roughly in the neighborhood of 10^{80}. The age of our universe in nanoseconds is estimated to be roughly in the neighborhood of 10^{23}, and the age of our universe in seconds is estimated to be roughly in the neighborhood of 10^{14}. So theoretically, if we could evaluate each individual in a second, we might be able to exhaustively search the restricted space (*with no constants allowed*); but, it would require approximately the age of the universe to complete the exhaustive search.

ARC System Architecture

The ARC system is now restructured into three nested collections (*pools*). The first collection is the pool of islands. There may be more than one population island and the number of population islands may grow or wane during an evolutionary run (the search). Inside each island is the second collection: a survivor pool. In each population island there may be more than one surviving individual (WFF) and, in each island, the number of individuals may grow or wane during the search. Finally, inside each individual is the third collection: a swarm constant pool. The number of constants in each swarm constant pool, inside each individual, may grow or wane during the search.

By way of further explanation, let me point out that it is often the case that several individuals, in an island population, will be identical in every way except the values of their real number constants as shown below with (E4) and (E6). Notice how the survivor pool is over-supplied with two individuals (which are essentially the same WFF - except for constant values); and, it tends to get much worse with entire survivor pools exclusively dominated by essentially the same WFF forms differing only in constant values.

- (*E4*): cos(3.45*x2)
- (*E5*): sin(x3)/exp(x1*4.5)
- (*E6*): cos(-5.1*x2)
- (*E7*): sqrt(x4/x3)-exp(-log(x2))

ARC thinks of individuals (E4) and (E6) as *constant homeomorphs* and automatically combines them into an *abstract constant homeomorph*. All concrete real number constant references are replaced with abstract constant references, and the appropriate constant vectors are stored in a constant pool inside the individual as shown below.

- (*E8*): cos(**c0***x2), **constant pool** = *(3.45, -5.1)*
- (*E5*): sin(x3)/exp(x1*4.5)
- (*E7*): sqrt(x4/x3)-exp(-log(x2))

The ARC system supports operations on each of its nested collections. The swarm operators, such as particle swarm (Eberhart et al., 2001) and differential evolution (Price et al., 2005), act upon the constant pools inside each individual. The population operators, such as mutation and crossover (Man et al., 1999), act upon the individuals within each island population. The island operators act upon the islands themselves.

By way of further explanation, the ARC island operators (*breeders*) are algorithms, such as *Age Layered Population Structures* (Hornby 2006) and *Age-Fitness Pareto* (Schmidt and Lipson, 2010), which govern the sorting, pruning, and synchronizing of fitness and survival within each island population plus any migration between islands. ARC currently supports several island operators. The *epoch* breeder initially fills its empty island with a large number of random individuals then does nothing unless the population grows stagnant at which time it kills off every individual and begins again. The *age-fitness* breeder implements a version of the age-fitness pareto algorithm explained in (Schmidt and Lipson, 2010). The *alps* breeder implements a version of the Age-Layered Population Structure algorithm explained in (Hornby, 2006) altered to operate inside a single island. The *weed* breeder initially fills its empty island with a large number of random individuals then does nothing unless the population grows stagnant at which time it kills off every individual *over a specified age*. All of these island operators introduce a small number of random individuals at the start of each generation. Additionally, there is a special *national* island which records the best (most fit) individuals ever seen at any time during the search. The individuals collected in the national island are the answers which ARC provides the user at the termination of the search.

Finally, there is a specification language which guides the search process, states the goal formula, sets up disparate islands for breeding individuals, and specifies the island operators and search constraints.

In summary a bullet point list of the main architectural components of ARC is as follows

- *islands*: a flexible number of islands for breeding individuals
- *survivors*: a flexible number of individuals in each island
- *swarm*: a flexible number of constants inside each individual
- *swarm operators*: act on the constant pools inside each individual
- *population operators*: act on the individuals in each island
- *island operators*: act on the islands themselves
- *specification language*: guides the entire search process

Search Specification Language

In (Korns, 2010) a number of important concepts are developed including: abstract expression grammars (AEG), universal abstract expressions, a new prototype search specification language inspired by the SQL/database-search relationship, and the concept of epigenome constraints to focus the search process in specific island populations. In this chapter, we will employ these concepts to help solve previously intractable problems.

Our universal abstract expression (E2), can be further constrained with where clauses. Each where clause sets up an independent island population, with a possibly further constrained epigenome, as follows.

- (*E9*): f0(f1(f2(t0,t1),f3(t2,t3)),f4(f5(t4,t5),f6(t6,t7)))
- (*E9.1*): island(alps,256,50)
- (*E9.2*): where island(alps,500,50)
- (*E9.3*): where f0(cos,sin,tan) v0(x1,x4) c1(1.0)
- (*E9.4*): where et() ec()

Each where clause is important both because of the choice of breeder and island population size, but also because the increased search focus and reduced search space size possible. For example, (E9.1) sets the default size of all islands to 256 individuals, 50 constants, and the breeder to Age-Layered Population Structure. Where clause (E9.2) overrides the defaults so that island one has 500 individuals, 50 constants, and the breeder to Age-Layered Population Structure and no constraints. The search space size is 10^{162}. Where clause (E9.3) constrains island two with f0 to the three trig functions, v0 to x1 and x4, and c1 to 1.0. All individuals in island two will be constrained as specified, and the search space size is reduced to 10^{159}. Where clause (E9.4) constrains island three to have no constants - effectively limiting search to features only. All individuals in island three will be constrained as specified, and the search space size is reduced to 10^{14}.

In this chapter, our approach to solving intractable problems will employ intelligent choices of multiple islands, breeders, and epigenome constraints.

Example Test Problems

In this chapter we list the example test problems which we will address. All of these test problems are no more than three grammar nodes deep (Note: in problem P10, $quart(x) = x^4$). All test problems reference no more than five input features. Some are easily solved with current Symbolic Regression techniques. Others are not so easily solved.

- (*P1*): y = 1.57 + (24.3*x3)
- (*P2*): y = 0.23 + (14.2*((x3+x1)/(3.0*x4)))
- (*P3*): y = -5.41 + (4.9*(((x3-x0)+(x1/x4))/(3*x4)))
- (*P4*): y = -2.3 + (0.13*sin(x2))

- (*P5*): y = 3.0 + (2.13*log(x4))
- (*P6*): y = 1.3 + (0.13*sqrt(x0))
- (*P7*): y = 213.80940889 - (213.80940889*exp(-0.54723748542*x0))
- (*P8*): y = 6.87 + (11*sqrt(7.23*x0*x3*x4))
- (*P9*): y = ((sqrt(x0)/log(x1))*(exp(x2)/square(x3)))
- (*P10*): y = 0.81 + (24.3*(((2.0*x1)+(3.0 * square(x2)))/((4.0*cube(x3))+(5.0*quart(x4)))))
- (*P11*): y = 6.87 + (11*cos(7.23*x0*x0*x0))
- (*P12*): y = 2.0 - (2.1*(cos(9.8*x0)*sin(1.3*x4)))
- (*P13*): y = 32.0 - (3.0*((tan(x0)/tan(x1))*(tan(x2)/tan(x3))))
- (*P14*): y = 22.0 - (4.2*((cos(x0)-tan(x1))*(tanh(x2)/sin(x3))))
- (*P15*): y = 12.0 - (6.0*((tan(x0)/exp(x1))*(log(x2)-tan(x3))))

As a discipline, our goal is to demonstrate that *all* of the 10^{162} possible test problems can be solved after a reasonable number of individuals have been evaluated. This is especially true since we have limited these 10^{162} possible test problems to target functions which are univariate, reference no more than five input features, and which are no more than three grammar nodes deep. On the hopeful side, if the Symbolic Regression community can achieve a demonstration of absolute accuracy, then the same rigorous statistical inferences can follow a Symbolic Regression as now follow a Linear Regression, which would be a significant advancement in scientific technique.

As a base line for current state-of-the-art symbolic regression technique, we use aged layered population structure (ALPS) with an island population size of 256. If ARC runs all the test problems with a single ALPS island, we see that, at least with ARC, we are far from our accuracy goal. In fact we quickly demonstrate that there are large sets of test problems which are intractable with current state-of-the-art ALPS symbolic regression.

The base line search specification is as follows, and the search results are shown in Table 1.

- (*E10*): f0(f1(f2(t0,t1),f3(t2,t3)),f4(f5(t4,t5),f6(t6,t7)))
- (*E10.1*): where island(alps,256,50)

A number of our test cases are solved very quickly with current state-of-the-art ALPS symbolic regression. Unfortunately, a number are not solved. Furthermore, these unsolved example test cases are representative of larger sets of intractable test problems within the 10^{162} possible target functions.

Throughout the remainder of this chapter, we will try a number of enhanced techniques to improve our search results on the example problems. These enhanced techniques will include:

Table 8-1. Results with one ALPS island

Test	WFFs	Train-NLSE	Train-TCE	Test-NLSE	Test-TCE
P01	.14K	0.00	0.00	0.00	0.00
P02	.96K	0.00	0.00	0.00	0.00
P03	74.90K	0.00	0.00	0.00	0.00
P04	0.34K	0.00	0.00	0.00	0.00
P05	.94K	0.00	0.00	0.00	0.00
P06	.12K	0.00	0.00	0.00	0.00
P07	82.58K	0.00	0.00	0.00	0.00
P08	1.03K	0.00	0.00	0.00	0.00
P09	71.89K	0.01	0.00	0.97	0.37
P10	85.50K	0.83	0.39	1.00	0.49
P11	81.29K	0.99	0.46	1.00	0.49
P12	89.24	0.99	0.48	1.04	0.50
P13	85.98K	0.81	0.30	1.00	0.93
P14	83.49K	0.53	0.17	1.53	0.47
P15	1.27K	0.00	0.00	0.00	0.00

(*Note: the number of individuals evaluated before finding a solution is listed in the Well Formed Formulas (WFFs) column*)

- Employing a cloud of islands
- Employing an opening rule book
- Employing a closing rule book

Employing a Cloud Of Islands

Employing a cloud of islands is one obvious approach to solving more of our test problems. Of course, employing a cloud of islands will increase the total number of individuals evaluated; but, those additional individuals will be evaluated in parallel. With a cloud, we increase our computational effort by a factor of ten while making some progress on some previously intractable problems. Unfortunately we see that, at least with ARC, even with a cloud of islands, performance improves over the base line; but, we are still far from our accuracy goal. Furthermore we quickly demonstrate that, there remain large sets of intractable problems even with a cloud of ALPS islands.

The search specification is as follows, and the search results are shown in Table 2.

- (*E11*): f0(f1(f2(t0,t1),f3(t2,t3)),f4(f5(t4,t5),f6(t6,t7)))
- (*E11.1*): where island(alps,256,50)

Test	WFFs	Train-NLSE	Train-TCE	Test-NLSE	Test-TCE
P01	.15K	0.00	0.00	0.00	0.00
P02	3.26K	0.00	0.00	0.00	0.00
P03	804.49K	0.00	0.00	0.00	0.00
P04	.59K	0.00	0.00	0.00	0.00
P05	.25K	0.00	0.00	0.00	0.00
P06	.13K	0.00	0.00	0.00	0.00
P07	187.26K	0.00	0.00	0.00	0.00
P08	5.99K	0.00	0.00	0.00	0.00
P09	97.24K	0.00	0.00	0.00	0.00
P10	763.53K	0.01	0.02	0.99	0.29
P11	774.89K	0.99	0.47	1.00	0.48
P12	812.79K	0.99	0.47	1.04	0.51
P13	624.78K	0.00	0.00	0.00	0.00
P14	454.15K	0.00	0.00	0.00	0.00
P15	.045K	0.00	0.00	0.00	0.00

Table 8-2. Results with ten ALPS island

- (*E11.2*): where island(alps,256,50)
- (*E11.3*): where island(alps,256,50)
- (*E11.4*): where island(alps,256,50)
- (*E11.5*): where island(alps,256,50)
- (*E11.6*): where island(alps,256,50)
- (*E11.7*): where island(alps,256,50)
- (*E11.8*): where island(alps,256,50)
- (*E11.9*): where island(alps,256,50)
- (*E11.10*): where island(alps,256,50)

Employing an Opening Rule Book

Employing a cloud of islands with a well thought out opening book of search constraint rules is the next obvious approach to solving more of our test problems. Of course, employing an opening rule book will increase the total number of individuals evaluated; but, those additional individuals will be evaluated in parallel, and each island can be tailored, with constraint rules, to search its own limited area of expertise for difficult-to-learn patterns that are commonly encountered.

One very interesting aspect of our experimentation with opening books is that the resources in many of the islands were successfully concentrated. Notice that the default survivor population has been reduced from 256 to 10 and the default swarm pool size has been reduced from 50 to 25. Thus we use nine islands but our computational resources are much less than nine times those used by a single island general purpose ALPS approach.

Our **opening rule book** is as follows, and the search results, with our opening book, are shown in Table 3.

- (*E11*): f0(f1(f2(t0,t1),f3(t2,t3)),f4(f5(t4,t5),f6(t6,t7)))
- (*E11.1*): national(10,25)
- (*E11.2*): island(weed,10,25)
- // Opening Book
- (*E11.3*): where
- (*E11.4*): where ec() et()
- (*E11.5*): where f0(*) f1..6(lpass,*) ef(f1,f2,f3,f4,f5,f6) ec() et()
- (*E11.6*): where f0(*,square,sqrt,cube,cos,sin,tan,tanh,log,exp)
      f1..6(lpass,*)
- (*E11.7*): where op(lpass,rpass,*,/,cos,sin,tan,tanh)
      island(smart,gade,256,25,50)
- (*E11.8*): where f0(*,cos,sin,tan,tanh) f1..6(lpass,*)
- (*E11.9*): where f0(cos,sin,tan,tanh) ef(f0,f1,f2,f3) ev(v0,v1,v2,v3)
      ec(c0,c1,c2,c3) et(t0,t1,t2,t3)
- (*E11.10*): where f0,f2,f5(*) f1,f4(cos,sin,tan,tanh) ef(f1,f4)
      ev(v1,v5) ec(c0,c4) et() island(smart,256,25,10)
- (*E11.11*): where f0,f1,f4(+,-,*,/) f2,f3,f5,f6(cos,sin,tan,tanh)
      ev(v0,v2,v4,v6) ec() et() island(smart,256,25,10)

A brief explanation of the search constraint rules in our **Opening Book** is as follows. Rule (E11.1) tells ARC to apply population operators to the national island. Rule (E11.2) sets the default island using the **weed** breeder with 10 individual individuals and 25 constants in its swarm pool. Rule (E11.3) requests an unrestricted search island. Rule (E11.4) requests an unrestricted search island with no terms and no constants. Rule (E11.5) requests a search for all possible two, three, and four way cross correlations of features. Rule (E11.6) requests a search for all possible two, three, and four way cross correlations of features with a possible unary cap. Rule (E11.7) requests a search of only the restricted trigonometric operators specified. Rule (E11.8) requests a search for all possible two, three, and four way cross correlations of features with a possible trigonometric cap. Rule (E11.9) requests a search of only the restricted

Table 8-3. Results with an opening book

Test	WFFs	Train-NLSE	Train-TCE	Test-NLSE	Test-TCE
P01	.06K	0.00	0.00	0.00	0.00
P02	113K	0.00	0.00	0.00	0.00
P03	222.46K	0.00	0.00	0.00	0.00
P04	0.86K	0.00	0.00	0.00	0.00
P05	0.16K	0.00	0.00	0.00	0.00
P06	0.01K	0.00	0.00	0.00	0.00
P07	4.10K	0.00	0.00	0.00	0.00
P08	11.00K	0.00	0.00	0.00	0.00
P09	116.81K	0.00	0.00	0.00	0.00
P10	214.27K	0.83	0.45	1.00	0.46
P11	206.04K	0.99	0.47	1.00	0.49
P12	217.25K	0.99	0.47	1.00	0.49
P13	22.40K5	0.00	0.00	0.00	0.00
P14	9.54K	0.00	0.00	0.00	0.00
P15	1.99K	0.00	0.00	0.00	0.00

trigonometric operators. Rule (E11.10) requests a search of only the products of trigonometric operators. Rule (E11.11) requests a search of only the restricted operators specified.

We arrived at this opening book of search constraint rules experimentally. It has been tailored to the behavior of the ARC system plus the chosen operators. It has been designed to capture a large number of commonly occurring test problems without increasing computation resources excessively. Creating an opening rule book is time consuming; but, it need only be created once for each SR system and each operator set. Employing an opening book moves one forward in solving a broad range of test problems with fewer individuals searched.

Unfortunately we see that, at least with ARC, even with an opening book we have still not achieved our accuracy goal. In fact employing an opening book did not significantly improve accuracy over the cloud of ALPS islands; but, it did reduce the computational resources required to arrive at the same accuracy.

One polynomial and two of the more complicated trigonometric test problems continue to resist solution. Largely this is because the sine and cosine function produce a wavy response surface which makes it very difficult for ARC to distinguish the local from the global minima.

It has been our experience that attempting to provide more islands and a much longer search time does not improve the situation. We have run these problems thorough several months of elapsed time and millions and billions of individuals evaluated with no significant improvement. When the search space is 10^{162}, with a very choppy surface, throwing more brute force resources does not seem to be helpful.

Employing a Closing Rule Book

Employing a cloud of islands with a well thought out opening and closing book of search constraint rules is our next approach to solving more of our test problems. We create a so called **smart** breeder which initially implements the same opening book strategy as shown in the previous section. however, **smart** maintains a set of closing search constraint rules ready to be used when the opening book search is not progressing well.

Smart constantly monitors each one of the opening book islands it has allocated. When an island search is not progressing to its satisfaction, smart can employ a search constraint rule from its *closing rule book*. The island is then co-opted to perform the search specified in the selected closing book search constraint rule.

Employing a cloud of islands with a well thought out **closing rule book** is yet another approach to solving more of our intractable test problems. In the case of a closing book, smart does not employ the closing book until the opening book rules have failed. This allows ARC to focus the individuals searched, in each affected island, toward problem areas which we know *a priori* to be difficult. Adding a closing book will increase the individuals evaluated; but, each island can be tailored to search its own limited area of expertise for common difficult-to-learn patterns that are known to be problematic. Furthermore, without the closing book, even after billions of individuals searched there was no convergence on the intractable problems; however, with the closing book there was convergence on some of the problems after only millions of individuals searched.

The closing rule book is as follows, and the search results, with our closing book, are shown in Table 4.

- (*E12*): f0(f1(f2(t0,t1),f3(t2,t3)),f4(f5(t4,t5),f6(t6,t7)))
- (*E12.1*): national(10,25)
- (*E12.2*): island(smart,10,25)
- // Opening Book
- (*E12.3*): where
- (*E12.4*): where ec() et()
- (*E12.5*): where f0(*) f1..6(lpass,*) ef(f1,f2,f3,f4,f5,f6) ec() et()

- (*E12.6*): where f0(*,square,sqrt,cube,cos,sin,tan,tanh,log,exp)
  f1..6(lpass,*)
- (*E12.7*): where op(lpass,rpass,*,/,cos,sin,tan,tanh)
  island(smart,gade,256,25,50)
- (*E12.8*): where f0(*,cos,sin,tan,tanh) f1..6(lpass,*)
- (*E12.9*): where f0(cos,sin,tan,tanh) ef(f0,f1,f2,f3) ev(v0,v1,v2,v3)
  ec(c0,c1,c2,c3) et(t0,t1,t2,t3)
- (*E12.10*): where f0,f2,f5(*) f1,f4(cos,sin,tan,tanh) ef(f1,f4) ev(v1,v5)
  ec(c0,c4) et() island(smart,256,25,10)
- (*E12.11*): where f0,f1,f4(+,-,*,/) f2,f3,f5,f6(cos,sin,tan,tanh)
  ev(v0,v2,v4,v6) ec() et() island(smart,256,25,10)
- // Closing Book
- (*E12.12*): where f0(cos,sin,tan,tanh) f1(*) f2(*) f3(*) ef(f0) ev(v0,v2,v3)
  ec(c1) et() island(smart,gade,1000,100,50,1000)
- (*E12.13*): where f0(cos,sin,tan,tanh) f1(*) f2(*) f3(lpass,*) ef(f0) ec(c1)
  et() eb(b0) island(smart,gade,100,100,50,100)
- (*E12.14*): where f0(lpass,*,/) f1(cos,sin,tan,tanh) f2(*) f4(cos,sin,tan,tanh)
  f5(*) ef(f0,f1,f4) ev(v1,v5)ec(c0,c4) et()
  island(weed,gade,1000,100,50,1000)
- (*E12.15*): where f0(+,-,*,/) f1(+,-,*,/) f2(cos,sin,tan,tanh)
  f3(cos,sin,tan,tanh) f4(+,-,*,/) f5(cos,sin,tan,tanh)
  f6(cos,sin,tan,tanh) ev(v0,v2,v4,v6) ec() et()
  eb(b0) island(smart,gade,1000,100,100,1000)
- (*E12.16*): where f0(lpass,*,+,/) f1(lpass,+)
  f2(*,psqrt,psquare,pcube,pquart) f3(*,psqrt,psquare,pcube,pquart)
  f4(lpass,+) f5(*,psqrt,psquare,pcube,pquart)
  f6(*,psqrt,psquare,pcube,pquart) ec(c0,c2,c4,c6) ev(v1,v3,v5,v7)
  et() eb(b0) island(smart,gade,1000,100,100,100)
- (*E12.17*): where op(lpass,rpass,+,-,*,/)
  island(smart,gade,1000,256,200,1000)

A brief explanation of the search constraint rules in our **Closing Book** is as follows. Rule (E12.12) tells ARC to look for three way cross correlations capped with any of the trigonometric functions. Rule (E12.13) requests a search for all possible two way cross correlations capped with any of the trigonometric functions. Rule (E12.14) requests a search for all possible constants times variables capped with any of the trigonometric functions. Rule (E12.15) requests a search for all possible products, sums, ratios, and differences of trigonometric singleton products or ratios. Rule (E12.16) requests a search for all possible

Table 8-4. Results with a closing book

Test	WFFs	Train-NLSE	Train-TCE	Test-NLSE	Test-TCE
P01	.06K	0.00	0.00	0.00	0.00
P02	113K	0.00	0.00	0.00	0.00
P03	222.46K	0.00	0.00	0.00	0.00
P04	0.86K	0.00	0.00	0.00	0.00
P05	0.16K	0.00	0.00	0.00	0.00
P06	0.01K	0.00	0.00	0.00	0.00
P07	4.10K	0.00	0.00	0.00	0.00
P08	11.00K	0.00	0.00	0.00	0.00
P09	116.81K	0.00	0.00	0.00	0.00
P10	1.34M	0.00	0.00	0.00	0.00
P11	4.7M	0.00	0.00	0.00	0.00
P12	16.7M	0.99	0.47	1.00	0.49
P13	22.40K	0.00	0.00	0.00	0.00
P14	9.54K	0.00	0.00	0.00	0.00
P15	1.99K	0.00	0.00	0.00	0.00

products, sums, and ratios of polynomials. Rule (E12.17) requests a search for all possible arithmetic functions.

We arrived at this closing rule book experimentally. It has been tailored to the behavior of the ARC system plus the chosen operators. It has been designed to capture a large number of commonly occurring test problems without increasing computation resources excessively. Creating a closing book is time consuming; but, it need only be created once for each SR system and each operator set. Employing a closing book moves us one step forward toward solving a broader range of more difficult test problems.

We see that, at least with ARC, with a closing rule book we have achieved additional improvement with respect to these chosen test problems. Unfortunately, we are far from asserting that ARC is absolutely accurate on *ALL* possible test problems of one basis function and three grammar nodes in depth. In fact, from copious end user experimentation, we know that ARC, even with the current enhancements, cannot solve all of the possible 10^{162} test problems. The problem space is so large that end users routinely uncover problems which return incorrect answers or fail to find even an acceptable champion.

The next step is clearly to find credible answers to some of the current mysteries. Is it possible to identify the larger areas of more complicated intractable problems within the 10^{162} search space? Are these problems isolated all over the 10^{162} search space, or are they clustered together in sets amenable to closing book island search specifications? How many identifiable intractable problems clusters are there? What are the best approaches for solving each identified problems set? Will each vendor be required to develop opening and closing books specific to each of their systems and chosen grammars, or will some, as of now unknown, automated method be discovered such as in (Ryan et al., 2005) or as in (Spector, 2010)?

Once we have found answers to the many current mysteries, verification will be the next serious challenge. Is there some internationally acceptable way to declare victory given the fact that we cannot hope to test all possible 10^{162} problems? The best situation would be to have the independent scientific community supportive of SR claims. The worst situation would be to have the independent scientific community skeptical of SR claims. What are the necessary conditions for even hazarding an assertion that SR is absolutely accurate on *ALL* possible test problems of one basis function and three grammar nodes in depth?

2. Conclusion

The use of abstract grammars in symbolic regression provides the end user with fine tuned control of the search process. Joint projects with end users have pointed out that user control of both the search process and the fitness measure will be essential for many applications. The use of opening and closing books, and multiple island intelligent breeding with epigenome constraints, moves the entire discipline much closer to *industrial ready* for many applications.

Nevertheless, state-of-the-art Symbolic Regression techniques continue to suffer poor accuracy on very large categories of test problems even under the most favorable minimalist assumptions.

The opportunity is unprecedented. If the symbolic regression community is able to offer accuracy, even within the favorable minimalist assumptions of this chapter, and if that accuracy is vetted or confirmed by an independent body (distinct from the SR community), then symbolic regression will realize its true potential. SR could be yet another machine learning technique (such as linear regression, support vector machines, etc.) to offer a foundation from which hard statistical assertions can be launched. Furthermore, we would finally have realized the original dream of returning not just accurate coefficients but accurate formulas as well.

The challenge is significant. It is unlikey that any single research team, working alone, will be sufficient to meet the challenge. We will have to band together as a community, developing standardized test problems, and standardized grammars. More importantly we will have to reach out to the theoreticians in our GP discipline and in the mathematical and statistical communities to establish some body of conditions whereby independent communities will be willing to undertake the task of confirming SR accuracy. And, of course, first we, in the SR community, will have to work together to achieve such accuracy.

It is not clear that opening and closing books are the final solution to our accuracy problem. The most desirable situation would be to discover some automated self-adaptive method.

What is clear is that if we, in the symbolic regression community, wish to continue making the claim that we return *accurate formulas*; and, if we wish to win the respect of other academic disciplines, then we will have to solve our accuracy issues.

References

Castillo, Flor, Kordon, Arthur, and Villa, Carlos (2010). Genetic programming transforms in linear regression situations. In Riolo, Rick, McConaghy, Trent, and Vladislavleva, Ekaterina, editors, *Genetic Programming Theory and Practice VIII*, volume 8 of *Genetic and Evolutionary Computation*, chapter 11, pages 175–194. Springer, Ann Arbor, USA.

Eberhart, Russell, Shi, Yuhui, and Kennedy, James (2001). *Hidden Order: How Adaptation Builds Complexity*. Springer, New York.

Hornby, Gregory S. (2006). ALPS: the age-layered population structure for reducing the problem of premature convergence. In Keijzer, Maarten et al., editors, *GECCO 2006: Proceedings of the 8th annual conference on Genetic and evolutionary computation*, volume 1, pages 815–822, Seattle, Washington, USA. ACM Press.

Korns, Michael F. (2009). Symbolic regression of conditional target expressions. In Riolo, Rick L., O'Reilly, Una-May, and McConaghy, Trent, editors, *Genetic Programming Theory and Practice VII*, Genetic and Evolutionary Computation, chapter 13, pages 211–228. Springer, Ann Arbor.

Korns, Michael F. (2010). Abstract expression grammar symbolic regression. In Riolo, Rick, McConaghy, Trent, and Vladislavleva, Ekaterina, editors, *Genetic Programming Theory and Practice VIII*, volume 8 of *Genetic and Evolutionary Computation*, chapter 7, pages 109–128. Springer, Ann Arbor, USA.

Koza, John R. (1992). *Genetic Programming: On the Programming of Computers by Means of Natural Selection*. MIT Press, Cambridge, MA, USA.

Man, KimFung, Tang, KitSang, and Kwong, Sam (1999). *Genetic Algorithms*. Springer, New York.

McConaghy, Trent, Palmers, Pieter, Gao, Peng, Steyaert, Michiel, and Gielen, Georges (2009). *Variation-Aware Analog Structural Synthesis - A Computational Intelligence Approach*. Analog Circuits and Signal Processing. Springer, Netherlands.

McKay, Robert I., Hoai, Nguyen Xuan, Whigham, Peter Alexander, Shan, Yin, and O'Neill, Michael (2010). Grammar-based genetic programming: a survey. *Genetic Programming and Evolvable Machines*, 11(3/4):365–396. Tenth

Anniversary Issue: Progress in Genetic Programming and Evolvable Machines.

OŃeill, Michael and Ryan, Conor (2003). *Grammatical Evolution: Evolutionary Automatic Programming in an Arbitrary Language.* Kluwer Academic Publishers, Dordrecht Netherlands.

Price, Kenneth, Storn, Rainer, and Lampinen, Jouni (2005). *Differential Evolution: A Practical Approach to Global Optimization.* Springer, New York.

Ryan, Conor, Keijzer, Maarten, and Cattolico, Mike (2005). *Favourable Biasing of Function Sets using Run Transferable Libraries in Genetic Programming Theory and Practice II.* Springer, New York.

Schmidt, Michael and Lipson, Hod (2010). Age-fitness pareto optimization. In Riolo, Rick, McConaghy, Trent, and Vladislavleva, Ekaterina, editors, *Genetic Programming Theory and Practice VIII*, volume 8 of *Genetic and Evolutionary Computation*, chapter 8, pages 129–146. Springer, Ann Arbor, USA.

Smits, Guido F., Vladislavleva, Ekaterina, and Kotanchek, Mark E. (2010). Scalable symbolic regression by continuous evolution with very small populations. In Riolo, Rick, McConaghy, Trent, and Vladislavleva, Ekaterina, editors, *Genetic Programming Theory and Practice VIII*, volume 8 of *Genetic and Evolutionary Computation*, chapter 9, pages 147–160. Springer, Ann Arbor, USA.

Spector, Lee (2010). Towards practical autoconstructive evolution: Self-evolution of problem-solving genetic programming systems. In Riolo, Rick, McConaghy, Trent, and Vladislavleva, Ekaterina, editors, *Genetic Programming Theory and Practice VIII*, volume 8 of *Genetic and Evolutionary Computation*, chapter 2, pages 17–33. Springer, Ann Arbor, USA.

Chapter 9

HUMAN-COMPUTER INTERACTION IN A COMPUTATIONAL EVOLUTION SYSTEM FOR THE GENETIC ANALYSIS OF CANCER

Jason H. Moore, Douglas P. Hill, Jonathan M. Fisher, Nicole Lavender, and La Creis Kidd

Dartmouth Medical School, One Medical Center Drive, HB7937, Lebanon, NH 03756 USA

Abstract   The paradigm of identifying genetic risk factors for common human diseases by analyzing one DNA sequence variation at a time is quickly being replaced by research strategies that embrace the multivariate complexity of the genotype to phenotype mapping relationship that is likely due, in part, to nonlinear interactions among many genetic and environmental factors. Embracing the complexity of common diseases such as cancer requires powerful computational methods that are able to model nonlinear interactions in high-dimensional genetic data. Previously, we have addressed this challenge with the development of a computational evolution system (CES) that incorporates greater biological realism than traditional artificial evolution methods, such as genetic programming. Our results have demonstrated that CES is capable of efficiently navigating these large and rugged fitness landscapes toward the discovery of biologically meaningful genetic models of disease predisposition. Further, we have shown that the efficacy of CES is improved dramatically when the system is provided with statistical expert knowledge, derived from a family of machine learning techniques known as Relief, or biological expert knowledge, derived from sources such as protein-protein interaction databases. The goal of the present study was to apply CES to the genetic analysis of prostate cancer aggressiveness in a large sample of European Americans. We introduce here the use of 3D visualization methods to identify interesting patterns in CES results. Information extracted from the visualization through human-computer interaction are then provide as expert knowledge to new CES runs in a cascading framework. We present a CES-derived multivariate classifier and provide a statistical and biological interpretation in the context of prostate cancer prediction. The incorporation of human-computer interaction into CES provides a first step towards an interactive discovery system where the experts can be embedded in the computational discovery process. Our working hypothesis is that this type of human-computer interaction will provide

more useful results for complex problem solving than the traditional black box
machine learning approach.

Keywords: Computational Evolution, Genetic Epidemiology, epistasis, Prostate Cancer, Visualization

1.   Introduction

An important goal of human genetics and genetic epidemiology is to understand the mapping relationship between interindividual variation in DNA
sequences, variation in environmental exposure and variation in disease susceptibility. Stated another way, how do one or more changes in an individual's DNA
sequence increase or decrease their risk of developing disease through complex
networks of biomolecules that are hierarchically organized, highly interactive,
and dependent on environmental exposures? Understanding the role of genomic
variation and environmental context in disease susceptibility is likely to improve
diagnosis, prevention, and treatment. Success in this important public health
endeavor will depend critically on the amount of nonlinearity in the mapping of
genotype to phenotype and our ability to address it. Here, we define as nonlinear
an outcome that cannot be easily predicted by the sum of the individual genetic
markers. Nonlinearities can arise from phenomena such as locus heterogeneity
(i.e. different DNA sequence variations leading to the same phenotype), phe-
nocopy (i.e. environmentally determined phenotypes that don't have a genetic
basis), and the dependence of genotypic effects on environmental exposure (i.e.
gene-environment interactions or plastic reaction norms) and genotypes at other
loci (i.e. gene-gene interactions or epistasis). Each of these phenomena have
been recently reviewed and discussed by (Thornton-Wells et al., 2004) who call
for an analytical retooling to address these complexities.

The limitations of the linear model and other parametric statistical approaches
for modeling nonlinear interactions have motivated the development of data mining and machine learning methods e.g. (Mitchell, 1997; Hastie et al., 2001). The
advantage of these computational approaches is that they make fewer assumptions about the functional form of the model and the effects being modeled
(McKinney et al., 2006). In other words, data mining and machine learning
methods are much more consistent with the idea of letting the data tell us what
the model is rather than forcing the data to fit a preconceived notion of what
a good model is. Several recent reviews highlight the need for new methods
(Thornton-Wells et al., 2004; Moore and Williams, 2009; Moore et al., 2010)
and discuss and compare different strategies for detecting nonlinear gene-gene
interactions or epistasis (Motsinger et al., 2007; Cordell, 2009).

The goal of this study is to explore genetic programming (GP) as a model-
free computational approach to modeling complex genetic effects in studies

of human disease. Genetic programming is an automated computational discovery tool that is inspired by Darwinian evolution by natural selection (Koza, 1992; Banzhaf et al., 1998). The goal of GP is to 'evolve' computer programs to solve complex problems. This is accomplished by first generating or initializing a population of random computer programs that are composed of the basic building blocks needed to solve or approximate a solution to the problem. For genetic association studies this might be a list of single-nucleotide polymorphisms (SNPs) or single base changes, other important attributes such as age and gender along with a list of useful mathematical functions. Each randomly generated program is evaluated and the good programs are selected and recombined and mutated to form new computer programs. This process of selection based on fitness and recombination to generate variability is repeated until a best program or set of programs is identified. Genetic programming and its many variations have been applied successfully in a wide range of different problem domains including bioinformatics e.g. (Fogel and Corne, 2003) and genetic analysis (Moore et al., 2010). GP is an attractive approach to the genetic analysis problem because it is inherently flexible, stochastic and parallel. These features are necessary in a computational analysis strategy when the problem is complex and it isn't clear to the modeler what a valid solution looks like.

It has been suggested e.g. (Spector, 2003; Banzhaf et al., 2006) that the incorporation of greater biological realism into GP may offer further performance improvements. Specifically, (Banzhaf et al., 2006) have called for the development of open-ended computational evolution systems (CES) that attempt to emulate, rather than ignore, the complexities of biotic systems. With this in mind, we have recently developed a hierarchical, spatially-explicit CES that allows for the evolution of arbitrarily complex solutions and solution operators, and includes population memory via archives, feedback loops between archives and solutions, and environmental sensing (Moore et al., 2008; Greene et al., 2009b; Greene et al., 2009c; Greene et al., 2010; Moore and Williams, 2009; Payne et al., 2010). Analyses of this system have demonstrated its ability to identify complex disease-causing genetic architectures in simulated data, and to recognize and exploit useful sources of expert knowledge. Specifically, we have shown that statistical expert knowledge, in the form of ReliefF scores (Moore and White, 2007), can be incorporated via environmental sensing (Greene et al., 2010) and population initialization (Payne et al., 2010) to improve system performance. In addition, we recently showed that biological expert knowledge in the form of protein-protein interactions could be used to guide CES toward valid gene-gene interaction models (Pattin et al., 2011).

A Role for Human-Computer Interaction in Computational Discovery

Genetic programming is often presented as a black box that solves problems independently of the user. We propose here a working hypothesis that visualization of GP results will provide important information to the user that can then in turn be used as expert knowledge to help guide the GP toward a useful solution. If true, this would suggest that the ability of the users to interact with the GP in an intuitive visual manner will facilitate the discovery process. The close integration of computational analysis with visualization and human-computer interaction is an emerging discipline called visual analytics (Thomas and Cook, 2005). This is distinguished from scientific visualization that focuses on the mathematics and physics of visualizing 3D objects and information visualization that focuses on methods such as heat maps for showing high-dimensional research results. (Heer et al., 2010) provide a thorough review of information visualization methods. What makes visual analytics different is the integration of the visualization methods with data analysis. That is, the GP analysis can be launched directly from the visualization and the visualization, in turn, can be changed in a manner that is dependent on the data analysis results. This iterative and synergistic process of visualization and analysis is facilitated by computer hardware technology that makes it easy for the user to interact with the software. For example, new touch-based computer interfaces such as the Microsoft Surface Computer or the Apple iPad could replace the keyboard and mouse as the preferred interface for visual analytics. All of this combined with a 3D visualization screen or wall provides a modern visual analytics discovery environment that immerses the user in their data and research results. Our ultimate goal is to engineer a CES-based discovery environment for the genetic analysis of complex human disease that combines all of these features. The goal of the present study was to develop a 3D visualization method that could be used to interactively extract expert knowledge from CES results that could in turn improve CES modeling through cascading.

2.   Methods

In this section, we first present our computational evolution system for the genetic analysis of complex diseases. We then discuss our 3D visualization approach to information extraction. Lastly, we present our experimental design and the prostate cancer data that was analyzed.

Computational Evolution System

In Figure 9-1, we provide a graphical overview of CES, which is both hierarchically organized and spatially explicit. The bottom level of the hierarchy

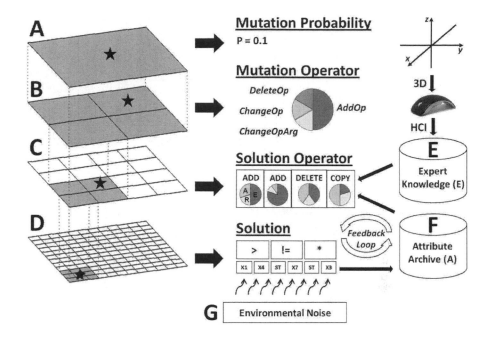

Figure 9-1. Visual overview of our computational evolution system for discovering symbolic discriminant functions that differentiate disease subjects from healthy subjects using information about single nucleotide polymorphisms (SNPs). The hierarchical structure is shown on the left while some specific examples at each level are shown in the middle. At the lowest level (D) is a grid of solutions. Each solution consists of a list of functions and their arguments (e.g. X1 is an attribute or SNP) that are evaluated using a stack (denoted by ST in the solution). The next level up (C) is a grid of solution operators that each consists of some combination of the ADD, DELETE and COPY functions each with their respective set of probabilities that define whether expert knowledge (E) based on 3D visualization and human-computer interaction (HCI) is used instead of a random generator (denoted by R in the probability pie). The attribute archive (F) is derived from the frequency with which each attribute occurs among solutions in the population. For this study use of the attribute archive was prohibited. Finally, environmental noise (G) perturbs the data in small ways to prevent over fitting. The top two levels of the hierarchy (A and B) exist to generate variability in the operators that modify the solutions. This system allows operators of arbitrary complexity to modify solutions. A 12×12 grid is shown here as an example. A 16×16 grid was used in the present study.

consists of a lattice of solutions (Fig. 9-1d), which compete with one another within spatially-localized, overlapping neighborhoods. The second layer of the hierarchy contains a lattice of arbitrarily complex solution operators (Fig. 9-1c), which operate on the solutions in the lower layer. The third layer of the hierarchy contains a lattice of mutation operators (Fig. 9-1b), which modify the solution operators in the second layer, and the highest layer of the hierarchy governs the rate at which the mutation operators are modified (Fig. 9-1a).

CES includes environmental noise (Fig. 9-1h), which perturbs the attribute values of the solutions with probability p_{noise}, as they are read from the input data. Intermediate values of p_{noise} allow for the escape of local optima, and improve classification power (Greene et al., 2009a). In this study we chose instead to use a fitness penalty for solution size. Both methods promote parsimony. CES also possesses an attribute archive (Fig. 9-1g), which stores the frequencies with which attributes are used. The solution operators can then exploit these data to bias the construction of solutions toward frequently utilized attributes. Here, we used the archive only in the first phase of the analysis. Expert knowledge was used in the subsequent phases.

Solution Representation, Fitness Evaluation, and Selection

Each solution represents a classifier, which takes a set of SNPs as input and produces an output that can be used to assign diseased or healthy status. These solutions are represented as stacks, where each element in the stack consists of a function and two operands (Fig. 9-1). The function set contains $+, -, *, \%, <, \leq, >, \geq, ==, \neq$, where $\%$ denotes protected modulus (i.e., $x \% 0 = x$. Operands are either SNPs, constants, or the output of another element in the stack (Fig. 9-1).

Each solution produces a discrete output S_i when applied to an individual i. Symbolic discriminant analysis (Moore et al., 2002) is then used to map this output to a classification rule, as follows. The solution is independently applied to the set of diseased and healthy individuals to obtain two separate distributions of outputs, $S^{diseased}$ and $S^{healthy}$, respectively. A classification threshold S_0 is then calculated as the arithmetic mean of the medians of these two distributions. The corresponding solution classifies individual i as diseased if $S_i > S_0$ and healthy otherwise.

Solution accuracy is assessed through a comparison of predicted and actual clinical endpoints. Specifically, the number of true positives (TP), false positives (FP), true negatives (TN), and false negatives (FN) are used to calculate accuracy as

$$A = \frac{1}{2} \left(\frac{TP}{TP + FN} + \frac{TN}{TN + FP} \right). \qquad (9.1)$$

Solution fitness is then given as a function of accuracy and solution length L

$$f = A + \frac{\alpha}{L}, \qquad (9.2)$$

where α is a tunable parameter used to encourage parsimony. For Phase I of the analysis, we set $\alpha = 0$ and added 0.001 for each node exceeding a threshold of 12 and for each attribute or SNP exceeding a threshold of six. For Phase II of the analysis, we set $\alpha = 0$ and added 0.002 for each node exceeding a threshold of 10 and for each attribute or SNP exceeding a threshold of five. For Phase III of the analysis, we set $\alpha = 0$ and added 0.003 for each node exceeding a threshold of eight and for each attribute or SNP exceeding a threshold of four.

The population is organized on a two-dimensional lattice with periodic boundary conditions. Each solution occupies a single lattice site, and competes with the solutions occupying the eight spatially adjacent sites. Selection is both synchronous and elitist, such that the solution of highest fitness within a given neighborhood is always selected to repopulate the focal site of that neighborhood. Reproduction is either sexual or asexual, as dictated by the evolvable solution operators that reside in the next layer of the hierarchy.

The population is initialized by randomly generating solutions with one to 15 elements subject to the constraint that they produce a valid output that is not constant for all input. While the functions are selected at random with uniform probability from the function set, the SNP attributes are selected using an enumerative scheme. Specifically, SNPs are drawn with uniform probability and without replacement until all SNPs are represented. The SNP pool is then regenerated and the process repeated, until the attribute requirements of all solutions are satisfied.

Solution Operators

CES allows for the evolution of arbitrarily complex variation operators used to modify solutions. This is achieved by initializing the solution operator lattice (Fig. 1c) with a set of basic building blocks which can be recombined in any way to form composite operators throughout the execution of the program. The action of some of these operators is influenced by any of several types of expert knowledge (EK) that CES recognizes. In this study we have used two types of EK, Attribute EK and Cluster EK. Attribute EK is used to help CES to more quickly find solutions using specific attributes or SNPs. Cluster EK is used to help CES find solutions with specific combinations (clusters) of coupled attributes. The following are the building blocks and the way they are influenced by EK.

- ADD: Inserts a randomly generated element into the solution at a randomly selected position.

    - Attribute EK: The selection of attributes in the new element is biased toward those favored in the Attribute EK file.

    - Cluster EK: The existing attribute just upstream of the new element is taken into account. The selection of new attributes is biased toward others in the same cluster.

- ALTER: Modifies either the function or an argument of a randomly selected element.

– Attribute EK: If an attribute argument is chosen, its selection is biased toward those favored in the Attribute EK file.

– Cluster EK: If an attribute argument is chosen, the nearest upstream attribute is taken into account as in the ADD operator.

- COPY: Within a randomly selected neighboring solution, randomly selects an element and inserts it into a randomly selected position in the focal solution.

  – Attribute EK: The element chosen to copy has an attribute among the most favored in the Attribute EK file.

  – Cluster EK: No effect.

- DELETE: Removes an element from a randomly selected position.

  – Attribute EK: The element chosen for deletion has an attribute among the least favored in the Attribute EK file.

  – Cluster EK: No effect.

- REPLACE: Within a randomly selected neighboring solution, randomly selects a source position. In the focal solution, randomly selects a destination position. Replaces everything between the destination position and the end (root) of the focal solution with everything between the source position and the end of the source solution.

  – Attribute EK: The source position is chosen to have an attribute among the most favored in the Attribute EK file.

  – Cluster EK: No Effect.

Solution operators possess evolvable probability vectors that determine the frequency with which functions and attributes are selected at random, from expert knowledge sources, or archives. Archives were used only in the first phase. In subsequent phases, to highlight the influence of expert knowledge on system performance, attribute selection was allowed to evolve among two EK sources and random selection. Function selection was always random.

The solution operators reside on a periodic, toroidal lattice of coarser granularity than the solution lattice (Fig. 1c). Each site is occupied by a single solution operator, which is assigned to operate on 3x3 sub-grid of solutions. These operators compete with one another in a manner similar to the competition among solutions, and their selection probability is determined by the fitness changes they evoke in the solutions they control

In this study we derived Attribute and Cluster EK from 3D visualization of the CES results and human-computer interaction or HCI (Fig. 1e). Our process for extracting expert knowledge is explained in more detail below.

Mutation Operators

The third level of the hierarchy (Fig. 9-1b) contains the mutation operators, which are used to modify the solution operators. These reside on a toroidal lattice of even coarser granularity, and are assigned to modify a subset of the solution operators below. The mutation operators are represented as three-element vectors, where each element corresponds to the probability with which a specific mutation operator is used. These three mutation operators work as follows. The first (DeleteOp) deletes an element of a solution operator; the second (AddOp) adds an element to a solution operator, and the third (ChangeOp) mutates an existing element in a solution operator. The probabilities with which these mutation operators are used undergo mutation at a rate specified in the highest level of the hierarchy (Figure 9-1a).

3D Visualization and Human-Computer Interaction

The goal of the visualization was to explore an initial set of CES results to identify information about SNPs found in best models that could be provided to future CES runs. Here, we utilized the 3D heat map application of (Moore et al., 2011) that harnesses the power of the Unity 3D video game engine for information visualization and visual analytics. The 3D heat map extends the traditional 2D heat map into a third dimension (z-axis) allowing the tops and sides of the resulting 3D bars to be colored thus permitting additional dimensions of information to be visualized. The video game platform allows interactive exploration of the 3D heat map. Here, we used the x-axis for SNPs, the y-axis for CES generations, the z-axis for SNP frequency across best models, the tops of the bars for whether that SNP appeared in the overall best model at a given generation and the sides of the bars for the accuracy of the best model that SNP appeared in.

The 3D visualization was used to select a subset of SNPs based on the five dimensions of information provided in the 3D heat map. In Phase I we ran CES 1000 times each for 1000 generations. We selected those SNPs that appeared in the final generations in overall best models. In addition, the visualization revealed other interesting patterns of SNPs that were selected. These are further discussed in the Results.

Prostate Cancer Data

This study population consists of nationally available genetic data from 2,286 men of European-descent (488 non-aggressive and 687 aggressive cases, 1,111 controls) collected through the Prostate, Lung, Colon, and Ovarian (PLCO) Cancer Screening Trial., a randomized, well-designed, multi-center investigation sponsored and coordinated by the National Cancer Institute (NCI) and their

Cancer Genetic Markers of Susceptibility (CGEMS) program. We focused here on prostate cancer aggressiveness as the endpoint. Between 1993 and 2001, the PLCO Trial recruited men ages 55-74 years to evaluate the effect of screening on disease specific mortality, relative to standard care. All participants signed informed consent documents approved by both the NCI and local institutional review boards. Access to clinical and background data collected through examinations and questionnaires was approved for use by the PLCO. Men were included in the current analysis if they had a baseline PSA measurement before October 1, 2003, completed a baseline questionnaire, returned at least one Annual Study Update (ASU), and had available SNP profile data through the CGEMS data portal (http://cgems.cancer.gov/). We used a biological filter to reduce the set of genes to just those involved in apoptosis (programmed cell death), DNA repair and antioxidation/carcinogen metabolism. These biological processes are hypothesized to play an important role in prostate cancer. A total of 219 SNPs in these genes were studied here.

Experimental Design

The goal of this study was to apply CES to the genetic analysis of prostate cancer. We first applied a biological filter to reduce the total number of SNPs to 219. We then ran CES 1000 times with 1000 generations each on this reduced data set. We applied a penalty of 0.001 to the fitness for each node over 12 and each attribute or SNP over six. This was implemented to put a selective pressure on smaller models. We called this part of the analysis Phase I. We then selected interesting SNPs from the visualization and provided those to new CES runs as expert knowledge. This new CES was also run 1000 times for 1000 generations each. A new penalty of 0.002 was applied to the fitness for each node over 10 and each attribute or SNP over five. We called this Phase II. We repeated the expert knowledge generation from the visualization and performed another 1000 runs of CES each with 1000 generations. Here, a new penalty of 0.003 was applied to the fitness for each node over eight and each attribute or SNP over four. We picked an overall best model at the end of this Phase III run.

3.   Results

Visualization Results

Figure 9-2 provides a visual summary of the CES results from all three phases of analysis in both 2D and 3D. The 2D visualization shows in white the SNPs at each generation that appeared in the overall best model at that generation. The 3D visualization adds information about how frequently each SNP appeared in all 1000 best models (z-axis, height) at each generation and the accuracy of the best model that SNP appeared in (side color). In both visualizations it was

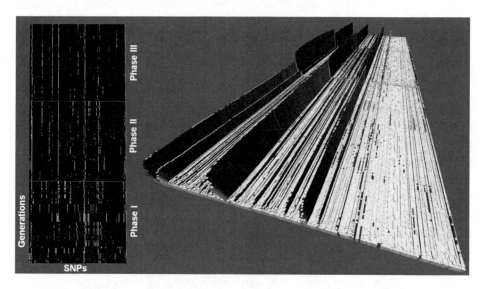

Figure 9-2. 2D (left) and 3D (right) visualization of CES results across the three phases. The left panel illustrates in white the SNPs (x-axis) that were present in the overall best model across 1000 independent runs at a particular generation (y-axis). Note that only every fifth generation is shown for clarity. The right panel illustrates the same results in 3D allowing for several extra dimensional of information to be visualized. Here, the x- and y-axes represent SNPs and generations as in the left panel. Here, we use blue as the top color to indicate a particular SNP is present in an overall best model at a particular generation. The z-axis is used to visualize the relative abundance of a particular SNP across all best models at a given generation. The side color of the 3D bars is used to represent the accuracy of the best model that SNPs was present in at a given generation. Note that most SNPs start (foreground) with a short bar height and a green or poor classifier accuracy (close to 0.500). The 3D visualization allows SNPs to be selected for subsequent CES runs using multiple dimensions of information not accessible in the 2D heat map.

clear that certain SNPs were consistently showing up over many generations. This was expected for those SNPs that have a relatively large effect on disease susceptibility. We selected at the end of Phase I and Phase II those SNPs that were consistently identified across multiple generations. These were then provided as expert knowledge to the next phase.

An unexpected finding revealed in both visualizations was the presence of SNPs that appeared to be coupled with other SNPs in the overall best model. For example, the middle generations of Phase I revealed a set of about 10 SNPs that all seemed to appear together over the span of multiple generations. Other groups of SNPs showed a similar coupled pattern over multiple generations. We selected many of these SNPs for inclusion as expert knowledge in Phase II and III runs. In addition to providing weight to these SNPs, we allowed the system to preferentially use coupled SNPs when one of the group was selected for inclusion in a model. Therefore, CES was able to exploit both commonly occurring SNPs and SNPs coupled with each other.

In addition to selecting SNPs based on their commonality across generations in overall best models, we also took into consideration other information such as the frequency that the SNPs occur across best models and the accuracy of the best model that SNP appeared in at that generations. These additional layers of information are combined in the 3D visualization with the other information to provide a richer context for the data used to select SNPs as expert knowledge. It is clear from the 3D visualization that a small subset of the SNPs appears very frequently across best models while many do not. Another trend that is visible is the slight decrease in the accuracy of best models that can be seen as darker red on the sides of the bars in later phases. This is due to the selective pressure on smaller models. In each subsequent phase CES is selecting more parsimonious models that are presumably doing less overfitting of the data. Note the overall decrease in 'noise' from Phase I to II to III in the 2D visualization. In other words, the results become more consistent in each subsequent phase.

Modeling Results

Figure 9-3 illustrates that overall best model selected at the end of Phase III. This model consisted of seven total SNPs, 10 total nodes and four constants. This model has a classification accuracy of 0.628. We have highlighted in Figure 9-3 the classification accuracy of each node in the tree thus making it possible to see where the information is coming from. First, it is interesting to note that the very top node (I-1) is a <= function with a constant that does not provide any additional information. This particular node, or others like it, appears often in best model across the phases and generations. This is because these nodes create a binary output that can be used as a convenient classifier. Thus, CES has learned to generate models with binary outputs.

Statistical Interpretation

It is clear that each node in the model is contributing differing amounts of information. Some, like IV-1, IV-2 and V-1, appear to contribute a lot of information while others, such as III-1, IV-3, V-2 and V-3, appear to contribute little. To clarify these contributions and the relationships between nodes we created a new dataset with the output of each node and case-control status. This new data set was analyzed using entropy-based measures of information gain as described by (Moore et al., 2006). Figure 9-4 illustrates the information gain for each single node and each pair of nodes from the best model in Figure 9-3. As expected, the tope nodes (I-1 and II-1) provide the most information about case-control status individually and appear to be redundant or highly correlated as indicated by the negative information gain for the joint effect.

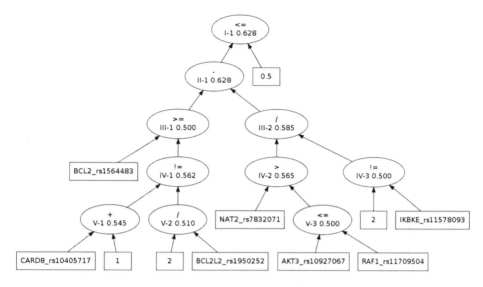

Figure 9-3. The overall best model discovered by CES at the end of Phase III. This model includes seven different attributes or SNPs (rectangles), four constants (squares) and 10 mathematical functions or nodes (ovals). Each node is labeled by depth and number in the tree from left to right. Next to each node label is the accuracy of the classifier at that point in the tree.

This trend continues down the tree. It is interesting to note that there is a moderate synergistic (nonadditive) effect of nodes III-1 and III-2. In fact, the synergistic effect of these two nodes in stronger than the primary effect of four of the 10 nodes. This partly explains why the accuracies jump from 0.500 and 0.585 for nodes III-1 and III-2, respectively, to 0.628 for node II-1. This is clearly a nonadditive effect and suggests that there may be interactions between subsets of SNPs.

It is important to note that the AKT3, IKBKE and CARD8 have all been previously identified as having statistically significant univariate effects on prostate cancer risk after adjusting for age, family history and multiple comparisons at the gene level in these same data (Lavender et al., in preparation). CES was able to recapitulate these effects in addition to some new discoveries.

Biological Interpretation

The final and most important step for this model is the biological interpretation. Of the seven genes identified in our overall best model, six (AKT3, BCL2, BCL2L2, CARD8, IKBKE, NAT2, RAF1) are involved in programmed cell death or apoptosis and the seventh (NAT2) is involved in drug and carcinogen metabolism. All have been associated with prostate cancer or the prostate more generally to varying degrees. For example, there are more than 100 published

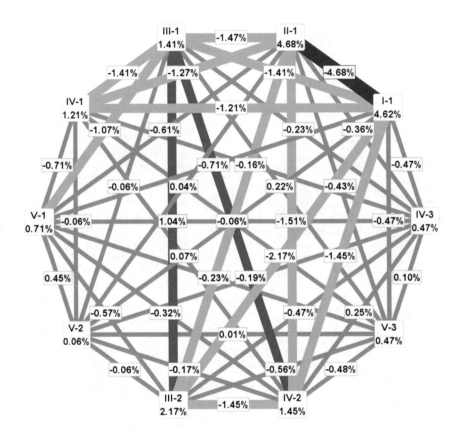

Figure 9-4. Entropy-based interpretation of the relationships between nodes in the overall best model. Numbers indicate the percentage of entropy or uncertainly about case-control status (i.e. class) that is removed by knowledge of that node or pairs of nodes. Orange lines indicate a synergistic nonadditive interaction between two nodes while a yellow line indicates independence. A green or blue line indicates redundancy or correlation that is expected when two nodes share much of the same information. Note the synergistic interaction between nodes III-1 and III-2 representing the two main branches of the tree. This results in an accuracy boost in node II-1.

papers reporting a direct or indirect role for BCL2 in prostate cancer. The IK-BKE and NAT2 genes had 18 and 38 publications, respectively, while the other each had two to five publications. Most of these published studies report the results of molecular, cellular or pharmacologic research. The fact that each of these genes has been previously implicated in prostate pathobiology adds some credibility to the findings.

The goal of a multivariate modeling approach such as CES is to identify combinations of genetic variations that are predictive of a clinical endpoint such as prostate cancer aggressiveness. The underlying assumption is that this relationship is complex and that powerful machine learning and computational intelligence methods are needed. As indicated above, the statistical interpretation indicated some synergistic effects among difference branches of the tree. We used the Pathway Studio (www.ariadnegenomics.com) database and software to determine whether there are known or predicted interactions among the protein products of the genes in our model. Figure 9-5 shows the results of this query. We find both predicted and experimentally confirmed interactions among all the proteins. Although not conclusive, these results suggest that there might be biomolecular interactions between all seven genes in our final model.

4.   Summary and Discussion

We have applied a computational evolution system (CES) to the genetic analysis of prostate cancer aggressiveness. We implemented here a CES analysis pipeline that includes a cascade of CES runs that each learns from the experience of its predecessors. Here, we used 3D visualization and human-computer interaction (HCI) to select interesting attributes or SNPs that are then provided to future CES runs in the form of expert knowledge. We showed that over time the variability of attributes selected in best models decreased and overall model size decreased as a result of increasing selective pressure for smaller models. We also showed that the visualization revealed interesting patterns of coupled SNPs that appeared to track together through best models. This new knowledge was in turn provided to the CES. A total of 9 million fitness evaluations over three phases generated an overall best model that correctly predicted prostate cancer aggressiveness approximately 63% of the time. This model consisted of seven SNPs from seven different genes. Several of the SNPs have been previously associated with prostate cancer in a univariate statistical analysis and an entropy-based analysis revealed evidence of synergy among the branches of the tree. Each of these genes is related to the prostate in previous publications and a subset has evidence for protein-protein interactions. Whether this computationally-derived model has biological underpinnings remains to be determined. However, CES moves the modeling from a one SNP at a time approach to an approach that embraces the complexity of the problem with few

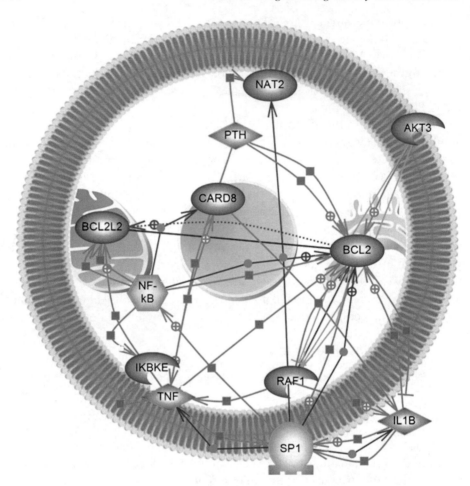

Figure 9-5. A cartoon of a cell showing the locations and interactions of the protein products (red ovals) from the seven genes in the overall best model. The outer yellow ring is the cell membrane while the inner blue circle is the nucleus. The left structure is the mitochondria while the right structure is the Golgi apparatus. The partial ovals (AKT3, IKBKE and RAF1) indicate proteins that have kinase activity. Also shown are other classes of molecules including ligands (diamonds), transcription factors (pink oval) NF-kB functional class (hexagon). A line connects two molecules if there is a known or predicted biomolecular interaction inferred from experiments, published papers or other sources such as protein-protein interaction databases. For example, the numerous lavender colored lines indicate that one protein influences the expression of another in the direction of the arrow. The purple line indicates there is a physical interaction between two proteins. The yellow lines indicate on protein changes the protein modification of the target molecule. The green lines indicate one protein binds to the promoter of another proteinÕs gene. The gray line indicates that one protein regulates another protein through physical interaction. Note that each of the seven proteins directly or indirectly interact with each other.

assumptions about the underlying model. This is an important step towards the use of computational intelligence for sifting through large volumes of human genetics data.

Our future work will focus enhancing the visualization and HCI components of the system. First and foremost, we would like to further develop CES as an integrated visual analytics strategy. The system described here is capable of visualizing CES results with HCI for interactive exploration and model visualization. What is missing is the ability to launch CES analyses directly from the visualization. This capability will complete the visual analytics loop and provide a comprehensive visual discovery environment. As (Langley, 2002) notes, biologists don't want automated computational discovery methods. Rather, they prefer computational assistance. Visualization and HCI methods put the biologist or the practitioner in the driver seat and make it possible to interactively explore results and analyses with a computational expert at their side. We hypothesize that this type of collaboration is needed to transform biomedical discovery in large, high dimensional data sets.

Acknowledgments

This work was supported by NIH grants LM009012, LM010098 and AI59694. We would like to thank the past and present participants of GPTP for their stimulating feedback and discussion that helped formulate some of the ideas in this paper.

References

Banzhaf, W., Beslon, G., Christensen, S., Foster, J.A., Képès, F., Lefort, V., Miller, J.F., Radman, M., and Ramsden, J.J. (2006). From artificial evolution to computational evolution: a research agenda. *Nature Reviews Genetics*, 7:729–735.

Banzhaf, W., Nordin, P., Keller, R.E., and Francone, F.D. (1998). *Genetic Programming Đ An Introduction; On the Automatic Evolutionof Computer Programs and its Applications*. Morgan Kaufmann, San Francisco, CA, USA.

Cordell, H.J. (2009). Detecting gene-gene interactions that underlie human diseases. *Nature Reviews Genetics*, 10:392–404.

Fogel, G.B. and Corne, D.W. (2003). *Evolutionary Computation in Bioinformatics*. Morgan Kaufmann Publishers.

Greene, C.S., Hill, D.P., and Moore, J.H. (2009a). Environmental noise improves epistasis models of genetic data discovered using a computational evolution system. In *Proceedings of the Genetic and Evolutionary Computation Conference*, pages 1785–1786.

Greene, C.S., Hill, D.P., and White, B.C. (2010). *Genetic Programming Theory and Practice VII*, chapter Environmental sensing using expert knowledge in a computational evolution system for complex problem solving in human genetics, pages 195–210. Springer, Ann Arbor.

Greene, C.S., White, B.C., and Moore, J.H. (2009b). An expert knowledge-guided mutation operator for genome-wide genetic analysis using genetic programming. In *Lecture Notes in Bioinformatics*, volume 4774, pages 30–40.

Greene, C.S., White, B.C., and Moore, J.H. (2009c). Sensible initialization using expert knowledge for genome-wide analysis of epistasis using genetic programming. In *Proceedings of the IEEE Congress on Evolutionary Computation*, pages 1289–1296.

Hastie, T., Tibshirani, R., and Friedman, J. (2001). *The Elements of Statistical Learning : Data Mining, Inference, and Prediction.* New York: Springer-Verlag.

Heer, J., Bostock, M., and Ogievetsky, V. (2010). A tour through the visualization zoo. *Comm ACM*, 53:59.

Koza, J.R. (1992). *Genetic Programming: On the Programming of Computers by Means of Natural Selection.* MIT Press, Cambridge, MA, USA.

Langley, P. (2002). Lessons for the computational discovery of scientific knowledge. In *Proceedings of First International Workshop on Data Mining Lessons Learned*, volume 1, pages 9–12.

McKinney, B.A., Reif, D.M, Ritchie, M.D., and Moore, J.H. (2006). Machine learning for detecting gene-gene interactions: a review. *Appl. Bioinformatics*, 5:77–88.

Mitchell, T.M. (1997). *Machine Learning.* MacGraw-Hill, Boston.

Moore, J.H., Andrews, P.C., Barney, N., and White, B.C. (2008). Development and evaluation of an open-ended computational evolution system for the genetic analysis of susceptibility to common human diseases. In *Lecture Notes in Computer Science*, volume 4973, pages 129–140.

Moore, J.H., Asselbergs, F.W., and Williams, S.M. (2010). Bioinformatics challenges for genome-wide association studies. *Bioinformatics*, 26(4):445–455.

Moore, J.H., Gilbert, J.C., Tsai, C.-T., Chiang, F.T., Holden, W., Barney, N., and White, B.C. (2006). A flexible computational framework for detecting, characterizing, and interpreting statistical patterns of epistasis in genetic studies of human disease susceptibility. *Journal of Theoretical Biology*, 241:252–61.

Moore, J.H., Lari, R.C., Hill, D., Hibberd, P.L., and Madan, J.C. (2011). Human microbiome visualization using 3d technology. In *Pac Symp Biocomput.*, pages 154–64.

Moore, J.H., Parker, J.S., Olsen, N.J., and Aune, T.M. (2002). Symbolic discriminant analysis of microarray data in autoimmune disease. *Genetic Epidemiology*, 23:57–69.

Moore, J.H. and White, B.C. (2007). Tuning relieff for genome-wide genetic analysis. *Lec. Notes Comp. Sci.*, 4447:166–175.

Moore, J.H. and Williams, S.M. (2009). Epistasis and its implications for personal genetics. *American Journal of Human Genetics*, 85:309–320.

Motsinger, A.A., Ritchie, M.D., and Reif, D.M (2007). Novel methods for detecting epistasis in pharmacogenomics studies. *Pharmacogenomics*, 8:1229–41.

Pattin, K.A., Payne, J.L., Hill, D.P., Caldwell, T., Fisher, J., and Moore, J.H. (2011). *Genetic Programming Theory and Practice VIII*, chapter Exploiting expert knowledge of protein-protein interactions in a computational evolution system for detecting epistasis in common human disease, pages 195–210. Springer.

Payne, J.L., Greene, C.S., Hill, D.P., and Moore, J.H. (2010). *Exploitation of Linkage Learning in Evolutionary Algorithms*, chapter 10: Sensible initialization of a computational evolution system using expert knowledge for epistasis analysis in human genetics, pages 215–226. Springer.

Spector, L. (2003). *Genetic Programming Theory and Practice*, chapter An essay concerning human understanding of genetic programming, pages 11–24. Springer.

Thomas, J. and Cook, K. (2005). *Illuminating the Path: Research and Development Agenda for Visual Analytics*. IEEE Press.

Thornton-Wells, T.A., Moore, J.H., and Haines, J.L. (2004). Genetics, statistics and human disease: analytical retooling for complexity. *Trends Genet.*, 20:640–7.

Chapter 10

BASELINE GENETIC PROGRAMMING: SYMBOLIC REGRESSION ON BENCHMARKS FOR SENSORY EVALUATION MODELING

Pierre-Luc Noel[1], Kalyan Veeramachaneni[2] and Una-May O'Reilly[2]

[1]*Swiss Federal Institute of Technology, Switz.* [2]*Massachusetts Institute of Technology, USA*

Abstract   We introduce hedonic, modeling benchmarks for the field of sensory science evaluation. Our benchmark framework provides a general means of defining a response surface which we call a "sensory map". A sensory map is described by a mathematical expression which rationalizes domain specific knowledge of the explanatory variables and their individual or higher order contribution to hedonic, response. The benchmark framework supports the sensory map's so-called *ground truth* to be controllably distorted to mimic the human and protocol factors that obscure it. To provide a baseline for future algorithm comparison, we evaluate a public research release of genetic programming symbolic regression algorithm on a sampling of the framework's benchmarks.

Keywords: symbolic regression, benchmarks, sensory evaluation, hedonic modeling

1.   Introduction

Benchmark problems (or simply "benchmarks") allow the evaluation of algorithms. The GP research community has a variety of useful, realistic general GP symbolic regression benchmarks including non-linear non-polynomials (Keijzer, 2003; Vladislavleva et al., 2009), publicly obtainable financial market data (Nikolaev and Iba, 2001; Becker et al., 2006; Becker et al., 2007; Becker and O'Reilly, 2009), the Mathematica-Wolfram data set (Kotanchek et al., 2009) and the accuracy problems of (Korns, 2011).

To systematically design a general benchmark for GP symbolic regression is straightforward. One creates a response surface which is a function of explanatory variables. The function is executed to obtain observational samples of the response surface. Samples are usually collected all at once and split into training and cross validation sets before the GP symbolic regression algorithm executes. When the algorithm completes and produces a predictive model of the response surface, this model can be queried with a set of unseen samples (i.e. the test set) and its predictive accuracy on the benchmark response surface can be ascertained.

We have developed a suite of GP symbolic regression and complementary algorithms (Veeramachaneni et al., 2010; Vladislavleva et al., 2010a; Vladislavleva et al., 2010b) to knowledge-mine hedonic preferences data collected when multiple assessors (also called panelists) are each asked how much he or she likes a set of food or highly aromatic stimuli. Figure 10-1 depicts the general sensory evaluation process. In a study (or experiment) each *assessor* is presented, in succession, with a limited quantity of randomly ordered, preselected, different products from a design space. On each presentation, the assessor must sense the product (by taste or smell) and respond to a query designed to elicit information as to how much s/he likes it. In the benchmarks we present here, the query to the assessor is "how much do you like X?" and the response structure (or format) is that the assessor must respond with one of nine discrete choices from the range bounded by *extremely dislike* through *neutral* to *extremely like*. An assessor's responses are collected for one experiment. These responses are observational samples of the assessor's (unknown) hedonic response surface. GP symbolic regression can be used to model an assessor's hedonic response to the product space by training with some (or all) of these numerically converted observations and knowledge of the design inputs (i.e. explanatory variables, ingredients of the food or the constituents of the aroma) in the product space (Vladislavleva et al., 2010a).

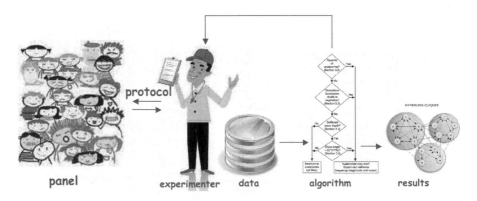

Figure 10-1. The sensory protocol and experimental analysis process which situates the context of the presented benchmark design and framework.

Validating this hedonic modeling of real data is virtually impossible because the number of queries is extremely low - around 10 for taste and around 40 for smell due to sensory fatigue. Using precious data samples for testing and cross validation is of little value because frequently the queries are determined by experimental design and are very distant from one another in the design space (i.e. they are at design corners). They are better exploited for training.

Other means of validation might be to use domain experts' experience, ask assessors to test optimized product designs derived using the predictive models or go back to the original assessors to confirm unseen sample predictions. These options turn out to be infeasible because assessors individually tend to not be consistent across days with their hedonic responses to a set of products (though as an aggregate there is stability), experts do not match with naive assessors, and, often neither are available. Thus, in the domain of sensory evaluation, there is no means of evaluating modeling methods.

Using a general symbolic regression benchmark is also insufficient. First, there is no rational basis for using any existing benchmark. They do not rationally express domain specific knowledge of how the ingredients, individually or in higher order combinations, contribute to hedonic response. Second, a benchmark should express one defining aspect of the sensory evaluation domain: a human is in the loop and introduces "noise" into the sampling for a number of different reasons. These range from human factors like fatigue, moodiness, inconsistency, perceptual confusion and memory loss to how humans deal with the protocol's response format, e.g. the 9 value hedonic range.

As a solution, we present a means of systematically designing, in a parameterized, controllable manner, domain-informed sensory evaluation benchmarks. To accomplish this, a benchmark expresses a sensory map **plus** what an assessor will report given this ground truth sensory map and the distortions arising from human judgment and protocol-driven response decision. The benchmark framework simulates the end to end process of sensory evaluation (see Figure 10-2): Queries, each accompanied by a sample, are formulated according the protocol. Each sample is presented the assessor, the latter sniffs or tastes it (which is a physical stimulus) and responds to the query. The benchmark framework assumes the physical stimulus generates a raw sensory interpretation in the brain which it represents via the sensory map. It assumes the way the assessor reports each response, which also depends on the protocol, is the combination of this raw information, and the distortions involved by the human judgment and reporting.

We proceed thus: Section 2 describes sensory map construction. Section 3 describes how we tunably model distortion. Section 4 uses the benchmark framework to evaluate the predictive accuracy of simple GP symbolic regression models trained on successively less training samples and on successively more distortion. Section 5 concludes.

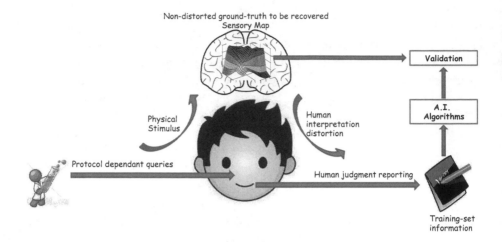

Figure 10-2. Simulation scope of the benchmark framework.

2.   Generation of a sensory map (Ground truth)

The benchmark framework assumes there exists a "ground-truth" definition of the non-distorted hedonic function, a so-called sensory map. It is convenient to think of the map as being in the assessor's brain. The sensory map describes the hedonic response of the assessor for each possible product in a design space. For example, in (Vladislavleva et al., 2010b), the design (or product) space is all possible combinations of seven flavoring ingredients, referred to as keys. Here, the sensory map is a function of seven variables (the volume of each key) and one output which is the hedonic score. Each key level is normalized to range continuously from 0 to 1, meaning respectively *ingredient not present* and *clearly too much of this ingredient*. For comparison, the range of a map is always $[-4, \ 4]$ where -4 means *extremely dislike*, 4 means *extremely like*, and a 0-value means neutrally like.

Naive sensory maps

A naive sensory map is a completely analytic function of explanatory variables (e.g. the key levels) with one output ranging from -4 to 4. It is not intended to represent a plausible human sensory response to flavors. Because of this drawback, we present only one example, Equation 10.1, (of 7 dimensions):

$$h_{naive}(\vec{k}) = sigmoid(sin(10k_1) + cos(10k_3) + sin(7k_2 + 3k_4) \\ + sin(3k_7 + k_5k_6), [-4, \ 4], 0.75)$$

$$(10.1)$$

where $\vec{k}$ is the sample i.e. the vector of the key levels k_i and sigmoid is:

$$sigmoid(x, [a, \ b], \beta) = (b - a)\frac{1}{1 + e^{-2\beta x}} + a \qquad (10.2)$$

where a and b respectively are the lower and upper asymptotes and β controls the steepness of the curve. This easily keeps the hedonic score within the range of $[-4, \ 4]$.

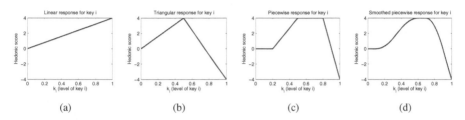

(a) (b) (c) (d)

Figure 10-3. Examples of sensory response to individual keys (a) Linear response (b) Roof response (c) Piecewise response and (c) smoothed piecewise response

Rational Sensory Maps

Rational sensory maps exploit domain specific knowledge expressing an assessor's hedonic response to a single ingredient (a.k.a. key). Founding our approach on this knowledge provides plausibility to the extent this knowledge is acquired or estimated. Our approach is to rationally combine the response function of each ingredient (domain knowledge) into a comprehensive one for multiple ingredients. We mathematically construct an n-dimensional sensory map which uses lower dimensional information which is known, or easily accessible. Two domain specific properties are integrated as design invariants:

Invariant #1 If all key levels are 0, meaning that only the base is present, the liking score has to be neutral, i.e. 0.

Invariant #2 For each key i, the single response for this specific key has to be continuously recovered when all other keys are at their zero levels.

Design Steps. Designing a rational sensory map involves 3 steps: **(1)** design 1-dimensional sensory responses **(2)** combine these single responses to form a multi-dimensional map, **(3)** design a merging function for the combination to preserve the two invariant properties. Use a post-merging coefficient γ to scale the merged map relative to the combined responses, then, if necessary, apply a sigmoid function to ensure responses are within the range $[-4, \ 4]$.

Step 1. 1-Dimensional Sensory Response Design. A 1D sensory response expresses how an assessor responds to an increasing level of one flavor ingredient. We describe a 1D response to key i as h_i, with one of four parameterized functions:

1. **Linear response**: A linear sensory response either increases or decreases linearly with the increase of an ingredient. The response is parameterized by the slope and intercept of the linear function given in the following equation.

$$h_i = a_i \times k_i + b_i \tag{10.3}$$

2. **Piecewise linear (2-piece)**: This map models the following hedonic response behavior: as the key level k_i increases, the assessor likes it more until a point of maximal preference. Then, when the key level further increases, the flavor is too strong and the assessor actually starts to dislike it. This is characterized by a *piecewise* linear function with 2-pieces. For any key k_i this function is parameterized by $\{l_i, a_i^{(1)}, b_i^{(1)}, a_i^{(2)}, b_i^{(2)}\}$.

$$h_i = \begin{cases} a_i^{(1)} \times k_i + b_i^{(1)} & \text{if } k_i \leq l_i \\ a_i^{(2)} \times k_i + b_i^{(2)} & \text{if } l_i < k_i < 1 \end{cases} \tag{10.4}$$

3. **Piecewise linear (n-piece)**: This map models hedonic response behavior in which an assessor changes from positive to negative or vice versa, or has a constant hedonic response at multiple volume intervals between the minimum and maximum of the key. In any volume interval the response is a linear function with a specific slope. This is thought to be more realistic for many ingredients and assessors. For any key k_i this function is parameterized by a set of interval extrema $\{l_i^{(1)}, ...l_i^{(n)}\}$ and the coefficients for the linear function that describes each segment. These are $a_1, \ldots a_n$ and, $b_1, \ldots b_n$.

$$h_i = \sum_{p=1}^{n-1} a_p \times k_i + b_p \text{ if } l_i^{(p)} \leq k_i \leq l_i^{(p+1)} \tag{10.5}$$

4. **Piecewise linear smooth**: Piecewise linear single responses are defined by their intervals and slopes within each interval. However, smoothed single responses are presumably even more plausible. To model this, we apply a smoothing mean filter, Equation 10.6), over a range controlled by a so-called smoothing coefficient s_c. The smoothed single response of Figure 10-3 (c) is Figure 10-3(d) when a smoothing coefficient of 0.1 is used.

$$h_{i_{smoothed}}(k) = \int_{k-s_c}^{k+s_c} h_i dk, \tag{10.6}$$

Examples of these single response models are shown in Figure 10-3-bottom. We can design a *homogeneous* set of 1D responses for the keys in which all the keys have similar sensory response functions but the parameters are varied. A *heterogeneous* alternative mixes multiple kinds of 1D response functions.

Step 2. Multi-dimensional Sensory Map Design. These sensory maps are a combination of the 1D response functions. We call the functional relationship linking the lower dimensional functions to the higher dimensional sensory map a *combining function*. Combining function outputs are scaled with λ, a scaling coefficient before merging. We defer explaining λ until the end of Step 3 where we also explain a second scaling coefficient, γ.

Three kinds of *combining functions* are:

1. **Additive**:

$$h_{1,\cdots,d} = \lambda \sum_{i=1}^{d} h_i, \tag{10.7}$$

2. **Multiplicative**

$$h_{1,\cdots,d} = \lambda * \Pi_{i=1}^{d} h_i \tag{10.8}$$

3. **Second order combining function** Pairs of keys may also generate second-order responses, on top of first order ones. This 2nd order combining function is:

$$h_{1,\cdots,d} = \lambda \Sigma \left((H^T H) * K \right), \tag{10.9}$$

where K is the coefficient matrix for the second order terms and $*$ the term-by-term multiplication of it with the single response functions in H. An example of a 7-dimensional function is given by

$$H = \begin{pmatrix} h_1 \\ h_2 \\ h_3 \\ h_4 \\ h_5 \\ h_6 \\ h_7 \end{pmatrix}, \text{ and } K = \begin{pmatrix} 0 & 2 & 0 & 1 & 3 & 1 & 0 \\ 0 & 0 & 1 & 0 & 1 & 0 & 2 \\ 0 & 0 & 0 & 3 & 0 & 0 & 0 \\ 0 & 0 & 0 & 0 & 1 & 2 & 1 \\ 0 & 0 & 0 & 0 & 0 & 1 & 0 \\ 0 & 0 & 0 & 0 & 0 & 0 & 0 \\ 0 & 0 & 0 & 0 & 0 & 0 & 0 \end{pmatrix},$$

Step 3. Merging to Preserve Map Invariants. In all but additive combining functions, *merging* is required to preserve design invariant #2. Recall that this invariant maintains that the 1D response to a key i is recoverable when all other key levels are 0. To understand a merging function, first consider a simpler case where there is only two ingredients. Then, the merging procedure can be formulated as follows:

$$
\begin{aligned}
h'_{1,2} &= m^{r_2}_{down}(k_2)h_1 \\
&+ m^{r_1}_{down}(k_1)h_2 \\
&+ (1 - m^{r_1}_{down}(k_1))(1 - m^{r_2}_{down}(k_2))h_{1,2}
\end{aligned} \tag{10.10}
$$

with $h_{1,2}$ as the combining function from Step 2 and $m^{r_i}_{down}$ the "merging-down" function defined by:

$$
m^{r_i}_{down}(k_i) = \begin{cases} 1 - (\frac{k_i}{r_i} - \frac{1}{2\pi}sin(2\pi\frac{k_i}{r_i})), & \text{if } 0 \le k_i \le r_i \\ 0, & \text{if } r_i < k_i \le 1 \end{cases} \tag{10.11}
$$

with r_i the *range* of the merging in the direction of k_i. Figure 10-4 depicts this merging down function with a range of 0.5.
Correspondingly, note that $1 - m^{r_i}_{down}(k_i)$ can be seen as a "merging-up" coefficient.

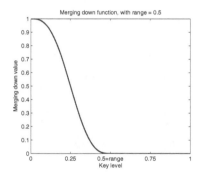

Figure 10-4. Merging down function with $r_i = 0.5$.

The idea of this merging procedure is that the 2d sensory map $h_{1,2}$ (which is the result of a combination of both single responses h_1 and h_2) is valid when both key levels k_1 and k_2 are sufficiently large. However, when a key level, say k_1, approaches zero, one wants to smoothly recover the 1d response h_2. This is implemented using the merging coefficient of equation (10.10). In the example, as k_1 approaches 0, the coefficient $m^{r_1}_{down}(k_1)$ approaches 1, emphasizing the influence of the single response h_2, while at the same time, the coefficient $(1 - m^{r_1}_{down}(k_1))$ approaches 0 diminishing the influence of $h_{1,2}$. The same logic applies when key level k_2 approaches zero. This approach can be generalized to the n-dimensional case as follows:

$$
\begin{aligned}
h'_{1,\cdots,d} &= \sum_{i=1}^{d} M_i(k_1, \cdots, k_{i-1}, k_{i+1}, \cdots, k_d)h_i \\
&+ \prod_{i=1}^{d}(1 - M_i)\, h_{1,\cdots,d}
\end{aligned} \tag{10.12}
$$

with $M_i(k_1, \cdots, k_{i-1}, k_{i+1}, \cdots, k_d) = \prod_{j \neq i} m_{down}^{r_j}(k_j)$.

Maintaining consistency of the 2-d hedonic response 'building blocks' (i.e. when other key levels approach 0), can be achieved with the following equation:

$$
\begin{aligned}
h'_{1, \cdots, d} = & \sum_{i=1}^{d} M_i h_i \\
+ & \prod_{i=1}^{d} (1 - M_i) \\
& [\sum_{(p,q) \in S} h_{pq} M_{pq} \\
& + \prod_{(p,q) \in S} (1 - M_{pq}) h_{1, \cdots, d, \cdots, p_1 q_1, \cdots, p_s, q_s}))]
\end{aligned}
\tag{10.13}
$$

with $M_{pq} = \prod_{j \neq p, j \neq q} m_{down}^{r_j}(k_j)$,

and S the set of the s pairs (p_i, q_i) whose 2-d responses are known and used to build the d dimensional sensory space.

A post-merging coefficient γ is used to scale the merging function. If responses are outside the range $[-4\ 4]$, a sigmoid function with parameter β is further applied:

$$
h''_{1, \cdots, d} = sigmoid(\gamma \times h'_{1, \cdots, d}, [-4\ 4], \beta)
\tag{10.14}
$$

Scaling Coefficients, λ, γ: We "tune" a map by choosing the λ and γ coefficients in a coupled manner. We aim for a factor of 2 between the entire range of the map, $h_{1, \ldots, d}$, and the sub-range when only a single key level is non-zero. The range of a combining function can be calculated in a straight-forward analytical manner for any heterogenous or homogeneous set of 1D responses. This allows us to pick one of λ or γ and set the other accordingly. For example, in map 1 of Table 10-2, the range of h before scaling with λ is $[-8\ 8]$ so, when we pick $\gamma = 1/2$, we set $\lambda = 1$. In map 2 of Table 10-2, the maximum of h happens to be 176 (occurring at key levels equaling $[0.5, 0.25, 0.75, 1.0, 0.5, 0.5, 0]$) so, picking $\gamma = 1/2$, implies we set $\lambda = 4/88 = 8/176$.

When using a second order combining function, the choice of coefficients is arbitrary. We proceed by identifying "interesting" 2D cuts of the multi-dimensional surface and use particle swarm optimization to find the range of h'. We loosely aim for a factor of 2 between this range and the range of the responses when only a single key level is non-zero when picking λ, γ and β.

3.   Sample Distortion

When reporting their judgment, humans are sources of error (Leibowitz and Post, 1982). These errors or distortions arise from: (1) assessors' intrinsic characteristics/abilities, and (2) protocol induced factors. The literature on psychological analysis of hedonics and hedonics protocols describes such errors and human characteristics. As well, experts who conduct many hedonic sensory evaluation protocols record many examples. Certain error sources are well understood and can be avoided very easily. For instance, expectation of the observer can be avoided by labeling samples in a neutral manner (Leibowitz and Post, 1982). This eliminates expectations and *a priori* biases in judgment. Table 10-1 mathematically describes our framework's distortions. We use h_j^t where h denotes the hedonic response (undistorted at first, later successively changed by each distortion), the superscript t indexes the position of the sample in the query sequence and subscript j indexes each successive distortion.

Human Induced Distortion

The first distortion factor is the *inconsistency* in the ratings from an assessor. For instance in (Costello et al., 2007), only roughly $1/3$ of assessors gave the exact same rating to actually identical flavors. The second factor is *mood*, which increases or decreases the hedonic response. The third factor is the *sensitivity* of an assessor to distinguishing among samples.

Protocol Induced Distortion

How a judgment is reported can lead to different information (Moskowitz, 1982). While this is not strictly "error", it implies that ground truth will be transformed in a protocol dependent way before it is reported. For instance, when using fixed 9-point category scaling (a.k.a. a hedonic scale), assessors must respond within this range. This causes *clipping* and *discretization* distortion. In addition, an assessor may use an extremum of the scale early on one sample then later like (or dislike) another sample more. Assessors "solve" this dilemma with truncation – i.e. re-using an extremum to express a more extreme response. For the forced response hedonic protocol we initially simulate, we model these distortions as *first query ignorance*.

Sensory judgment will be biased by previously tested samples. For instance, a given sample will tend to be judged saltier when presented in a set that includes many low salt concentration samples, while it will tend to be judged less salty when presented in a distribution including many high salt concentration samples (Riskey, 1982). We call this type of distortion *contextual exaggeration*.

Time Varying Fatigue Distortion

Sensory fatigue that increases over causes time varying error. We assume time to be discrete and corresponding to successive presentation of samples. The quality and accuracy of human input greatly degrades with repeated prompts for input (Schmidt and Lipson, 2006). Even though protocols are often designed to keep sample quantity low, fatigue will eventually alter assessors' capabilities. For instance, the average person can sample only up to seventy aromas before they become biased (Costello et al., 2007). In our framework, this is modelled by giving a temporal dimension to every source of

Table 10-1. Models for a variety of distortion sources

Distortion	Source	Model	Parameter
Inconsistency	Human	$h_1^t = h_0^t + \eta(0, \sigma_1(t))$	$\sigma_1(t)$
Sensitivity	Human	$h_2^t = s(t) \times h_1^t$	$0 \le s(t) \le 1$
Mood	Human	$h_3^t = h_2^t + m(t)$	$m(t)$
Ist Query Ignorance	Protocol	$h_4^1 = h_3^1 + \eta(0, \sigma_4)$	σ_4
Contextual Exaggeration	Protocol	$h_4^t = h_3^{t-1} + \alpha(\delta, t) \times \delta$ with $\delta = h_3^t - h_3^{(t-1)}$ and $\forall t > 1$	$\alpha(\delta, t)$

distortion. This means that the parameters described for different distortions in Table 10-1 change over time. $\sigma_1(t)$, $s(t)$ and $m(t)$ change using a temporal evolution function defined below. α is a function of t and δ. Its values with changing t for different δ's is shown in the figure 10-5(b).

Starting with an initial value of a distortion parameter r_i and a set final value r_f of this same parameter, the temporal evolution of the parameter corresponds to equation 10.15 and is depicted in figure 10-5. In this equation, τ is a time constant that can be interpreted in term of number of sample tested.

$$r(t) = r_i + (r_f - r_i)(1 - e^{-t/\tau}) \qquad (10.15)$$

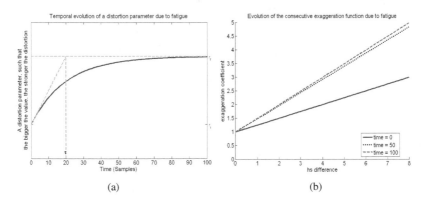

(a)   (b)

Figure 10-5. Temporal evolution of a distortion parameter due to (a) panelist fatigue, (b) contextual exaggeration.

4.   Baseline GP symbolic regression experiments

We now apply "standard" symbolic regression to sensory evaluation benchmarks of varied difficulty. We use the GPLAB toolbox (Silva and Almeida, 2003; Silva, 2011). We control modeling difficulty via sensory map choice, presence or absence of distortion, and, the number of samples recorded. We set the dimensionality of all maps to 7 and use the four sensory maps described in Table 10-2. We then set the initial and final levels for the distortion as detailed in Table 10-3 or choose not to have distortion. We use sample sizes of $[40, 100, 1000]$. Thus we have experiments pertaining to 36 datasets. A benchmark experiment proceeds per Figure 10-6.

Table 10-2. The 4 sensory maps used.

Sensory Map	Single Responses	Combining Function	Merging Range	Scaling Parameters
1	Linear with different coefficients	Additive	No merging needed	$\lambda = 1$ $\gamma = \frac{1}{2}$
2	2-piece-linear with different coefficients	2nd order, K per example in 2.0	$r_i = 0.5$	$\lambda = \frac{4}{88}$ $\gamma = \frac{1}{2}$
3	Diverse and more complex	Involving $+$, $\times$, cos, sin, $\sqrt{}$, and $\mid\mid$	$r_i = 0.3$	$\lambda = \frac{4}{5}$ $\gamma = 3.5$ $\beta = 0.1$
4	Naive Sensory Map, Equation 10.1			

Table 10-3. Parameter settings for distortion

	No Distortion	Strong Distortion With Fatigue ($\tau = 20$)	Strong Distortion Without Fatigue
Parameter	r	$\{r_i, r_f\}$	r
σ_1	0	$\{0.75, 2.25\}$	0.75
s	1	$\{0.5, 0.2\}$	0.5
m	0	$\{1, -1\}$	1
σ_4	0	2	2
$\alpha(\delta)$	1	$\{1 + \frac{1}{4}\delta, 1 + \frac{1}{2}\delta\}$	$1 + \frac{1}{4}\delta$
Rating range	$[-4, 4]$ Cont.	$[1, 9]$ Discrete	$[1, 9]$ Discrete

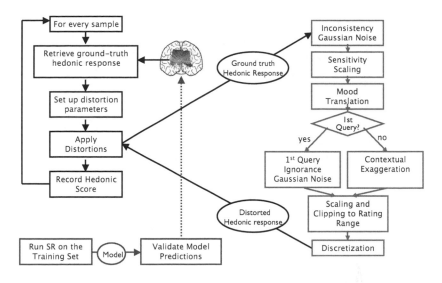

Figure 10-6. Flow of the benchmark framework.

Results

We perform 30 runs for each experiment and collect statistics on the GP symbolic regression performance. We evaluate model predictive accuracy. Predictive accuracy compares the predictions from the best evolved model to the hedonic response values (ground truth) in the sensory map (without distortion). Our definition of accuracy uses a tolerance of 1, meaning that if the predicted liking score of a testing sample is in the range of the actual ground-truth liking score plus or minus 1, the prediction is considered as being correct. Accuracy is defined as a ratio of quantity of correctly predicted samples to the total quantity of testing samples. We use 3000 samples that are generated using a uniform random distribution for testing. We run GP symbolic regression with a population of 500, for 39 generations after random population initialization. During each run we compute the predictive accuracy (using the testing dataset) of the best-so-far evolved model every second generation. At the experiment's end we compute the mean and variance of accuracy.

Figure 10-7 shows how well the 4 sensory maps can be predicted without any distortion. GP symbolic regression is able to very accurately predict map 1 which is an additive map of 7 1D linear response functions after approximately 20 generations with just 40 samples. For the map 2 which is a 2nd order map composed of 2-piece linear 1D responses, the more samples, the higher the prediction accuracy. That is, for 40 and 100 samples, prediction accuracy is above 0.9 and with 1000 samples accuracy hits 1.0. The 1000 sample experiment's accuracy is achieved by the end of 39 generations. For the two smaller sample sizes, it is possible that the accuracy could improve more if GP symbolic regression had been run for additional generations.

Maps 3 and 4, *'diverse and more complex'* and *naive* respectively, cannot be accurately modeled even with 1000 training samples. Their accuracy varies over sample size from 40 to 1000 between $(0.4 \dots 0.55)$ and $(0.3 \dots 0.4)$ respectively. However, more samples definitely improve their prediction performance. The reason for lower performance on these maps is the complexity of the underlying sensory map. E.g., the third map, whose features are presented in Table 10-2 is more complex and diverse due to the presence of *cos*, *sin*, *square* root and *absolute* functions. It doesn't appear that more evolutionary generations would substantially improve accuracy way for either map.

Consider the same 4 maps, but now with the strong distortion and fatigue we choose to model as arising from the protocol and human behavior. Modeling results are shown in Figure 10-8. There is a large drop in prediction accuracy compared to the distortion-free, fatigue-free experiment set. For map 1 and map 2, prediction accuracy, with distortion and fatigue present, drops from perfect (samples=1000) or near perfect (samples=100 or 40) to 0.2, 0.3, and 0.3 respectively. Map 3's modeled accuracy is similar to those of maps 1 and 2, but, compared to its distortion-free, fatigue free equivalent, this represents a drop from 0.4, 0.4 and 0.5 for sample sizes 40,100,1000 respectively to 2.5, 2.4 and 1.9.

This implies that protocol and human "noise" are the key contributors to inability to recover ground truth. Together, distortion and fatigue sufficiently reduce the information content of later samples in the query chain to make them not worth soliciting (under the distortion and fatigue levels modeled with the parameters of Table 10-3). When the samples increase from 40 to 100, the information content of the extra 60 samples is relatively neutral or slightly detrimental toward recovering the ground truth of the map. When the samples increase from 100 to 1000, there is always a decrease in model accuracy. The results call for further work to understand the sensitivity of sample size and map properties to fatigue and distortion levels.

Figure 10-9 shows the results of experiments that model only distortion. Let ss denote sample size. In the case of map 1, for $ss = 100$, predictive accuracy improves by about 0.15 (to 0.48 from 0.32) without fatigue. For $ss = 100$, the predictive accuracy of 0.3 does not change. For $ss = 1000$, predictive accuracy improves to 0.1 (from 0.2 to 0.3). Map 2 results are essentially similar to those of map 1. With map 3 there is a clearer distinction between $ss = 40$ and $ss = 100$, and the order based on predictive accuracy changes from 100 being better with fatigue to 40 being better without fatigue. The predictive accuracy ranking according to sample size of map 4 is $\{40, 100, 1000\}$ with distortion and fatigue. When fatigue was not modeled, the ordering changes to $ss = 100$ with highest predictive accuracy and no difference between $ss = 40$

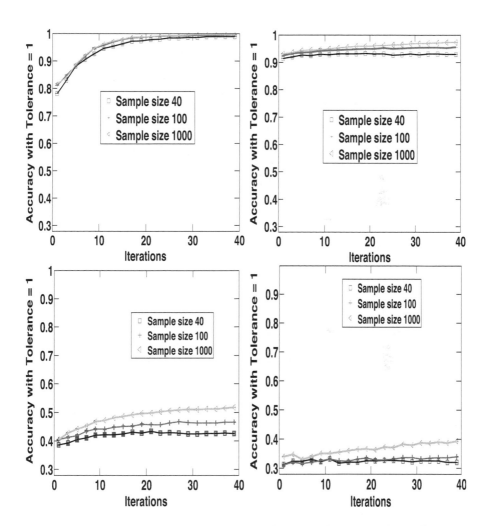

Figure 10-7. GP symbolic regression modeling performance without distortion or fatigue and three training sample sizes. Clockwise from top left: map 1, map 2, map 3, map 4.

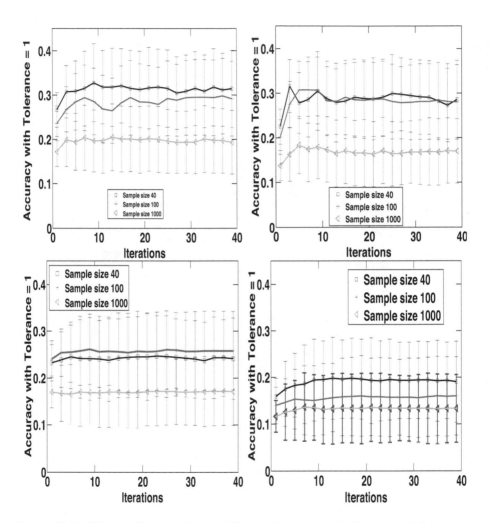

Figure 10-8. GP symbolic regression modeling performance with distortion and fatigue and three training sample sizes. Clockwise from top left: map 1, map 2, map 3, map 4.

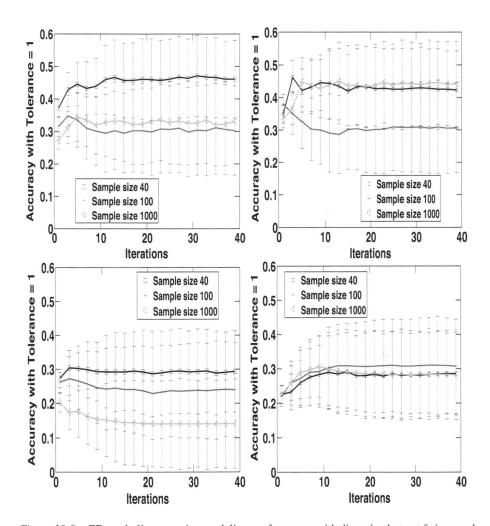

Figure 10-9. GP symbolic regression modeling performance with distortion but not fatigue and three training sample sizes. Clockwise from top left: map 1, map 2, map 3, map 4.

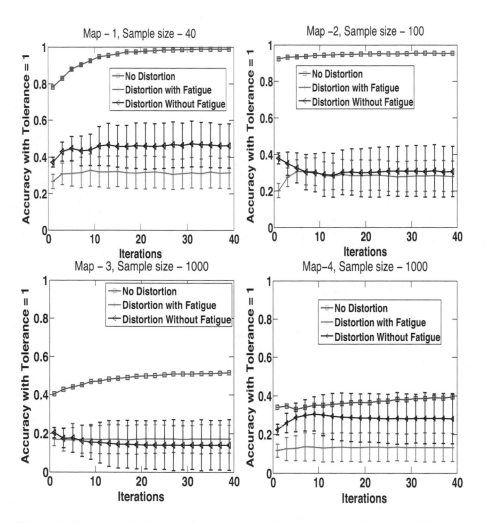

Figure 10-10. GP symbolic regression modeling performance comparing cases of distortion-noise-free, distortion only, distortion+noise.

or $ss = 1000$. Figure 10-10 cross-references data from each of Figures 10-7 to 10-9 to show the impact of fatigue and/or distortion on predictive accuracy for one sample size for each map.

5.   Summary, Discussion and Future Work

Our aims in designing this specialized benchmark framework for sensory evaluation are:

1. to rationally support the description of sensory maps which are hedonic response surfaces as a function of product design inputs

2. to rationally express, with mathematics, the distortions which arise when using a specific hedonic sensory evaluation protocol

3. to support the assessment of the performance of GP symbolic regression algorithms with respect to how predictive accuracy scales with:

   - sampling quantity for training
   - sensory maps with different degrees of ruggedness
   - different sources and levels of distortion which arise when using a specific hedonic sensory evaluation protocol

Our goal is a level of generality which:

- supports the modeling of different sources of human sensory distortion manifested when assessors are queried about hedonic response

- supports modeling how a protocol's query-response component contributes to distorting the ground truth of the sensory map, in addition to human sourced distortions

We have demonstrated the benchmark framework in a baseline evaluation of GP symbolic regression on sensory maps while controlling distortion and the simulation of human sensory fatigue. We have gained insights into predictive accuracy and determined in what cases more samples help in increasing predictive capability. When there is no distortion, additional samples always increase predictive capability. However, when distortion is present, this is not necessarily the case. With an additional factor of fatigue, the performance declines with additional number of samples, as the data becomes more and more noisy with each additional sample.

Experts with commercial interest in sensory evaluation have noted that the benchmark framework can also assist with the specialized co-design of algorithms and protocols for a given product design space. When these domain experts have evidence of assessor characteristics and feedback on how protocols are interpreted by assessors, or when they have deeper knowledge of the sensory map for the product design space, this knowledge can be expressed via the benchmark framework. This allows them to explore the limits of what they can learn if they use a protocol, with some limited number of samples, on a specific quality of assessor, given the product space and an algorithm for analyzing the data after the experiment. Interactively, they can gain insight into the impact of how assessor errors (which partially relate to the number of samples) makes some surveys impractical. They can also vary sensory maps under the same set of protocol and assessor conditions to see how a product design space may be suitable for a real experiment. Alternatively, for a design space they can describe, they can determine how many samples are needed by the algorithm to derive models that predict accurately.

We plan to extend the algorithm suite we can run on the benchmarks. As well, we will extend the benchmark framework with additional protocols.

Acknowledgments

We would like to thank Dr. Hansruedi Gygax and Dr. Guillaume Blancher of Givaudan Flavors Corporation plus our reviewers.

References

Becker, Ying, Fei, Peng, and Lester, Anna M. (2006). Stock selection : An innovative application of genetic programming methodology. In Riolo, Rick L., Soule, Terence, and Worzel, Bill, editors, *Genetic Programming Theory and Practice IV*, volume 5 of *Genetic and Evolutionary Computation*, chapter 12, pages 315–334. Springer, Ann Arbor.

Becker, Ying L., Fox, Harold, and Fei, Peng (2007). An empirical study of multi-objective algorithms for stock ranking. In Riolo, Rick L., Soule, Terence, and Worzel, Bill, editors, *Genetic Programming Theory and Practice V*, Genetic and Evolutionary Computation, chapter 14, pages 239–259. Springer, Ann Arbor.

Becker, Ying L. and O'Reilly, Una-May (2009). Genetic programming for quantitative stock selection. In Xu, Lihong et al., editors, *GEC '09: Proceedings of the first ACM/SIGEVO Summit on Genetic and Evolutionary Computation*, pages 9–16, Shanghai, China. ACM.

Costello, E., McGinty, L., Burland, M., and Smyth, B. (2007). The role of recommendation for flavor innovation and discovery. In *IC-AI*, pages 463–469.

Keijzer, Maarten (2003). Improving symbolic regression with interval arithmetic and linear scaling. In Ryan, Conor et al., editors, *Genetic Programming, Proceedings of EuroGP'2003*, volume 2610 of *LNCS*, pages 70–82, Essex. Springer-Verlag.

Korns, Michael (2011). Accuracy in symbolic regression. Genetic and Evolutionary Computation, chapter 8. Springer, Ann Arbor.

Kotanchek, Mark E., Vladislavleva, Ekaterina Y., and Smits, Guido F. (2009). Symbolic regression via GP as a discovery engine: Insights on outliers and prototypes. In Riolo, Rick L., O'Reilly, Una-May, and McConaghy, Trent, editors, *Genetic Programming Theory and Practice VII*, Genetic and Evolutionary Computation, chapter 4, pages 55–72. Springer, Ann Arbor.

Leibowitz, HW and Post, RB (1982). Capabilities and limitations of the human being as a sensor. *Selected sensory methods: problems and approaches tomeasuringhedonics*, page 2.

Moskowitz, HR (1982). Utilitarian benefits of magnitude estimation scaling for testing product acceptability. In *Selected sensory methods: problems and approaches to measuring hedonics: a symposium*, page 11. ASTM International.

Nikolaev, Nikolay and Iba, Hitoshi (2001). Genetic programming using chebishev polynomials. In Spector, Lee et al., editors, *Proceedings of the Genetic and Evolutionary Computation Conference (GECCO-2001)*, pages 89–96, San Francisco, California, USA. Morgan Kaufmann.

Riskey, DR (1982). Effects of context and interstimulus procedures in judgments of saltiness and pleasantness. In *Selected sensory methods: problems and approaches to measuring hedonics: a symposium*, page 71. ASTM International.

Schmidt, Michael D. and Lipson, Hod (2006). Actively probing and modeling users in interactive coevolution. In *Proceedings of the 8th annual conference on Genetic and evolutionary computation*, GECCO '06, pages 385–386, New York, NY, USA. ACM.

Silva, S. (2011). http://gplab.sourceforge.net/index.html. GPLab v.3 April 2007.

Silva, S. and Almeida, J. (2003). GPLAB-a genetic programming toolbox for MATLAB. In *Proceedings of the Nordic MATLAB Conference*, pages 273–278.

Veeramachaneni, Kalyan, Vladislavleva, Katya, Burland, Matt, Parcon, Jason, and O'Reilly, Una-May (2010). Evolutionary optimization of flavors. In Branke, Juergen et al., editors, *GECCO '10: Proceedings of the 12th annual conference on Genetic and evolutionary computation*, pages 1291–1298, Portland, Oregon, USA. ACM.

Vladislavleva, Ekaterina J., Smits, Guido F., and den Hertog, Dick (2009). Order of nonlinearity as a complexity measure for models generated by symbolic regression via pareto genetic programming. *IEEE Transactions on Evolutionary Computation*, 13(2):333–349.

Vladislavleva, Katya, Veeramachaneni, Kalyan, Burland, Matt, Parcon, Jason, and O'Reilly, Una-May (2010a). Knowledge mining with genetic programming methods for variable selection in flavor design. In Branke, Juergen et al., editors, *GECCO '10: Proceedings of the 12th annual conference on Genetic and evolutionary computation*, pages 941–948, Portland, Oregon, USA. ACM.

Vladislavleva, Katya, Veeramachaneni, Kalyan, and O'Reilly, Una-May (2010b). Learning a lot from only a little: Genetic programming for panel segmentation on sparse sensory evaluation data. In Esparcia-Alcazar, Anna Isabel et al., editors, *Proceedings of the 13th European Conference on Genetic Programming, EuroGP 2010*, volume 6021 of *LNCS*, pages 244–255, Istanbul. Springer.

Chapter 11

DETECTING SHADOW ECONOMY SIZES WITH SYMBOLIC REGRESSION

Philip D.Truscott[1] and Michael F. Korns[2]

[1]*Department of Information Systems and Computer Science, Ateneo de Manila University, Loyola Hts, Quezon City, Philippines.* [2]*Korns Associates, Shang Grand Tower, Unit 17E, 98 Perea Street, Makati 1229, Philippines.*

Abstract

This chapter examines the use of symbolic regression to tackle a real world problem taken from economics: the estimation of the size a country's 'shadow' economy. For the purposes of this chapter this is defined as a country's total monetary economic activity after subtracting the official Gross Domestic Product. A wide variety of methodologies are now used to estimate this. Some have been criticized for an excessive reliance on subjective predictive variables. Others use predictive data that are not available for many developing countries. This chapter explores the feasibility of developing a general-purpose regression formula using objective development indicators. The dependent variables were 260 shadow economy measurements for various countries from the period 1990-2006. Using 16 independent variables, seven basis functions, and a depth of one grammar level a search space of 10^{13} was created. This chapter focuses on the power conferred by an abstract expression grammar allowing the specification of a universal goal formula with grammar depth control, and the customization of the scoring process that defines the champion formula that 'survives' the evolutionary process. Initial searching based purely on R-Squared failed to produce plausible shadow economy estimates. Later searches employed a customized scoring methodology. This produced a good fit based on four variables: GDP, energy consumption squared, this size of the urban population, and the square of this figure. *The same formula produced plausible estimates for an out of sample set of 510 countries for the years 2003-2005 and 2007.* Though shadow economy prediction will be controversial for some time to come, this methodology may be the most powerful estimation formula currently available for purposes that require *verifiable data* and a single global formula.

Keywords: abstract expression grammars, customized scoring, grammar template genetic programming, genetic algorithms, universal form goal search

1.   Introduction

This chapter describes the use of symbolic regression to tackle a research problem from economics: the estimation of shadow economy sizes.

Social scientists have long been aware of various model construction tools to select the best-fitting combination of variables using software packages like SPSS (Nurusis, 1996) and SAS (Muller, 2002). Compared to these tools, Symbolic Regression (Korns, 2010) involves a process that adds many orders of magnitude to the size of the search space typically attempted by social scientists. Korns has developed an Abstract Expression Grammar. His software for performing the search will be referred to by the acronym ARC (for Abstract Regression Classification).

Two concepts in particular add to search space size:

- *Abstract functions* Abstract Expression Grammar Symbolic Regression allows a variable to be modified by mathematical functions not defined explicitly. For example, an 'abstract' function might include the square root, square, cube, log, exponent or be left unmodified. All of these functions might be applied to the independent variables during the model fitting process.

- *Grammar Level Depth* Abstract Expression Grammar Symbolic Regression defines a generic form for the specification of models that use variables in combinations of varying complexity. To illustrate this concept consider a model that predicts economic activity from energy consumption and population. At a grammar depth of 0 each of these will be considered as separate variables within the goal formula. At a grammar depth of 1 the goal formula might include the term "energy consumption * population". At a grammar depth of 2, two functions might be applied such as "cube(energy consumption * population)".

With five basis functions and three grammar levels, the search space of potential models rises to 10^{852}.

2.   Shadow Economy Estimation Methods

There is currently no general agreement among economists on the correct procedure for measuring the size of a country's 'shadow' or 'informal' economy. For the purposes of this paper *it will be defined as a country's total monetary economic activity after subtracting the official GDP statistic* (hence referred to as the IDP - Informal Domestic Product and it includes all black market and other illegal activities including the gray activities in between).

Directly measuring the shadow economy is difficult; critical data is missing or because available data cannot be verified. Some researchers have attempted to measure the IDP through the 'currency demand' method(Schneider, 1994; Schneider, 1998). This examines the ratio of cash holdings to bank deposits, on the assumption that informal businesses will want to evade the reporting procedures of financial institutions. Macroeconomists have built models that simulate the IDP size in relation to tax rate changes and changes in currency demand. Unfortunately this process gives no procedure for measuring the IDP size in the base year, which has lead some model builders to assume a zero IDP as their starting point which has been criticized as an unrealistically heroic assumption.

One technique called the "Physical Input" method (Kaufmann and Kaliberda, 1996) estimates the size of various post-Soviet economies by assuming that they grew in proportion to electricity consumption in the years after 1989. As with the currency demand approach they could not use the same methodology for their base year and had to use initial estimates from the European Bank of Reconstruction and Development. A similar set of electricity-based estimates has been produced by a group based at the World Bank(Johnson et al., 1998b; Johnson et al., 1998a).

There is also more complex electricity-based approach based on household usage (Lackó, 1997b; Lackó, 1997a; Lackó, 1998; Lackó, 2000). This takes into account such things as the country's average temperature and the cost per unit of electricity.

Another approach (Yoo and Hyun, 1998) uses expenditure surveys to measure the true level of economic activity by multiplying household micro-level data up to the national level. This is one of the most objective approaches in that it uses hard data and few assumptions. However its applicability is limited by the small number of countries where such survey data is available and by the difficulty of verifying the survey data.

The most extensive set of country statistics (Schneider et al., 2010) show IDP estimates for 162 countries. This approach uses independent variables that include subjective freedom indices from the Heritage Foundation (for example a 'Business Freedom Index' defines zero as the least business freedom and 100 as the most). Their dependent variables include a measurement of currency demand, growth rate of GDP per capita and labor force participation rate. Their methodology is described by the acronym MIMIC (Multiple Indicators Multiple Causes). The MIMIC model approach is considerably more complex than a multiple regression formula (Schneider et al., 2010). For micro-economists who favor hard data, this approach suffers from the defect that the quantities that are 'predicted' have not, in themselves, been proven to be measurements of the shadow economy. However the MIMIC enthusiasts can derive some comfort from the fact their IDP estimates for developed countries are often similar to the numbers produced by other methods.

Table 11-1. Sources of Shadow Economy Estimates.

Estimation Method	Author	Number of Country Estimates
Electricity Consumption	Lackó (1996, 1997a, 1997b, 1999)	19
Currency Demand	Schneider (1994, 1998)	30
Electricity Consumption	Johnson, Kaufmann, and Zoido-Lobatón (1998a, 1998b)	18
Electricity Consumption	Schneider using data from Lackó (1996)	25
Electricity Consumption	Johnson, S., Kaufmann, D., and Zoido-Lobatón, P. (1998)	52
Electricity Consumption	Lackó, M (1999)	53
Survey Micro-data	Hyun and Yoo (1998)	5
MIMIC Model	Schneider, Buehn & Montenegro (12)	61
Various Single Country Studies	Hartzenburg, G.M., and Leimann, A. (1992) Bagachwa, M.S.D. and A. Naho (1995) Pozo, Susan (ed.) (1996)	5

In addition to these multi-country estimations, a few single-state shadow economy estimates have also been used(Bagachwa and Naho, 1995; Bhattacharyya, 1999; Hartzenburg and Leimann, 1992; Pozo, 1996; Madzarevic and Mikulic, 1997).

These descriptions are intended to give a brief overview to show that the current estimation methodologies are both diverse and controversial. A much fuller review of shadow economy estimations is given by the MIMIC model estimators (Schneider et al., 2010) (who tend to downplay the value of direct measurement techniques using micro-simulation). There is also a lengthy research review (Lackó, 2000) which is less sanguine about the MIMIC technique (referring to it as the 'soft model' approach).

This paper examines the following question. Can a single global regression equation 'predict' the results of these diverse shadow economy estimates using objective data on development indicators? Currently the most extensive prediction set uses three separate estimation formulae for three groups of countries: OECD (developed) countries, former Soviet and allied states, and other (mainly developing) countries. The development of a single predictive formula would enable policy research to compare developed and developing countries more easily.

3.   The Dependent Variable

The dependent variables used in this analysis are estimates of the size of the shadow economy for various countries from the years 1989-2006 using different methodologies as shown in Table 11-1. One of the goals of this research was to facilitate analysis of taxation policies. Therefore the country estimates taken from the MIMIC research were limited to those that do not use tax burden variables as predictors.

The various measurements in Table 11-1 may include the same country's IDP for the same year using different methodologies. The approach of collecting different estimations is similar to the technique of taking a "polls of polls" or taking the average of the forecasts of different economists. The IDPs estimated by the research in Table 11-1 express the shadow economy as a proportion of the official GDP. These proportions are then used to calculate the Comprehensive Domestic Product (CDP) for each country in each year.   This is defined as the official GDP plus the IDP. It is the CDP and not the IDP that is the dependent variable of the regression equations shown below.

Table 11-2. Average, Minimum and Maximum Shadow Economy Sizes.

IDP (Shadow Economy) as % of Official GDP					
Region	Mean	Minimum		Maximum	
1 (OECD)	14.8	5.1	(Austria 1990)	50.5	(Spain 1990)
2 (Mainly Ex-Soviet)	29.0	6.4	(Czech Rep. 1990)	74.9	(Russia 1995)
3 (Mainly Developing)	34.9	9.0	(South Africa 1990)	76.0	(Nigeria 1990)

Table 11-2 gives a general impression of the range of shadow economy sizes that have been estimated by the different techniques listed in Table 11-1.

4.   The Independent Variables

The independent variables are various development indicators that to try to predict the size of the CDP objectively.   Not only electricity but total energy usage increases as economies grow. More developed economies also tend to be more urban and the birth rate tends to decline. More developed economies are less agricultural and more densely populated. This methodology does not seek to predict economic evasiveness directly. This contrasts with approaches like the currency demand method which measures the amount of cash kept out of banks. The current technique tries to measure total economic activity. The IDP is estimated afterwards by subtracting the official GDP. For certain countries and years the development indicator data in Table 11-2 were missing. After deleting these data, 260 country estimates remained with all the corresponding development indicators for the years concerned.

Among the development indicators in Table 11-3 the power consumption variables (per capita electricity, total electricity, and total energy) are particularly interesting to researchers because the 1990s showed them to be powerful predictors of both economic growth and contraction; the former soviet states showed absolute declines in electricity consumption and GDP. Western Europe and North America showed increases in both. The telecommunications vari-

ables covering mobile phones and broadband Internet subscriptions have been
combined with landline phones to create two composite variables:

- *COMSTWO* includes two types of telephone (fixed line and Mobile)

- *COMSTHREE* includes both types of phone and broadband Internet subscriptions

Table 11-3. Average,Minimum and Maximum Shadow Economy Sizes.

URBAN_PER	Proportion of population that is urban
URBAN_POP	Number of urban persons
LABOR_PARTICIPATION	Labor participation rate, total (% of total population ages 15+)
BIRTH_RATE	Birth rate, crude (per 1,000 people)
ELEC_PER_CAP	Electric power consumption (kWh per capita)
TOTELEC	Total Electric power consumption (kWh)
ENERGY	Indicator: Energy use (kilotons of oil equivalent)
C02	CO2 emissions (kilotons)
PHONES	Telephone lines
IMPORTS	Imports of goods and services (current US$)
POPULATION	Population
POPDENS	Population density (people per sq. km)
ARABLE_PER_AG	Arable Land as a % of Agricultural Land
AGLAND_PER	Agricultural land (% of land area)
ARABLE_PER	Arable land (% of land area)
AREA	Surface area (sq. km)
COMSTWO	Telephone (landlines) and Mobile Phone subscriptions
COMSTHREE	Telephones (landlines), Mobiles + Broadband Subscriptions
GDP_PPP	GDP, PPP (current international $)

Combining the newer communication methods with landline phones avoids
a dataset with many missing values for the 1990s. The ability to predict shadow
economy sizes with objective development indicators has important policy research implications. Global banking institutions might wish to assess if particular types of tax increase the size of the IDP. Are direct taxes more damaging
than sales taxes? Are taxes on starting a business or employing workers more
negative in their effect on tax revenues? Since the MIMIC approach uses tax
variables to predict the IDP, it is impossible to make such analyses with their
data. Such analyses would involve making tax data both the independent and
dependent variables. For developing countries tax collection is often extremely
inefficient in turn leading to poor quality education, health care and environmental protection. The inability of developing country governments to maintain law
and order, and impose their will generally led them to be termed 'soft states'
by the Nobel Prize winning economist Myrdal (1968). A fuller understanding
of the causes and cures of large shadow economies is essential to address this
problem.

5.   Model Optimization with Standard Scoring

Initial testing of Abstract Expression Grammar Symbolic Regression showed that the usual method of assigning a score to potential champion formulae was unsuitable for the task at hand. Previous papers using this approach have based the scoring on a combination of Normalized Least Square Error (NLSE) and Tail Classification Error (TCE) which measures how well the regression champion classifies the bottom 10% and the top 10% of the data set (Korns, 2010).

Using five variables and one grammar level of depth the champion formula estimated the Comprehensive Domestic Products with an R-squared of over 96%. However when the official GDP figures where subtracted from the CDP figures, some countries had negative values. Common sense indicates that no populations are so honest that they have zero-sized informal economies. Negative IDPs are also unreasonable.

6.   Customized Scoring

One of the more powerful features of ARC is the ability to fine tune the scoring that determines which formulae will survive the evolutionary process. In the case of IDP estimation a scoring methodology was required to penalize potential champions with negative IDPs as well as those with excessively high IDPs.

The approach adopted was to calculate the IDP for each of the 260 country measurements for each potential champion formula. The official GDP was stored in a global array for each country and measurement year. The official GDP was then subtracted from the predicted Comprehensive Domestic Product for that country/year for the regression formula being scored. The result was the 'predicted' Informal Domestic Product. In order to penalize implausible predictions, a given formula's fitness score was multiplied by 1.25 if:

- One country's estimated IDP% was lower than 3%

- One country's estimated IDP% was higher than 140%

In theory the scoring process would have penalized any formula that produced an IDP estimate higher than 100%. The largest IDP% estimate in Table 11-2 is 76% for Nigeria in 1990. Philosophically there is no reason to discount the possibility of very large shadow economies. An IDP percentage above 100% simply means that the shadow economy is larger than the official GDP estimate. For countries recently emerging from communism with sharply contracting economies (like some central Asian states in the 1990s) such large shadow economies seem entirely plausible.

Initial tests of this procedure found that the scoring penalties prevented the search algorithm from finding any strong champions at all. This problem was solved by allowing the NLSE-based scoring to proceed in the normal way until an NLSE value lower than 0.2 was discovered. Only at that point was the scoring modified according to the minimum and maximum shadow economy size. The customized scoring function could he adapted and reprogrammed outside the main calculation engine using a version of LISP. The programming required would seem reasonably familiar to any researcher with familiarity with a fourth generation language, though the use of pre-fix operators takes some getting used to for those more accustomed to in-fix operators.

7.   The Universal Goal Formula

The Abstract Expression Grammar allows the user to define the general form of the desired regression equation with a LISP statement illustrated by the following example:

(E1): universal(2,4,v)

This example specifies that the desired formula should be "universal" in form. The three parameters following the keyword universal constrain the formula as follows:

- *Grammar Level Depth*: 1st parameter is the permitted grammar level depth to be searched (the example shown in E1 above searches to a depth of two grammar levels). A zero in this position would produce the simplest formulae. Since the independent variables are unmodified the zero grammar level makes the process resemble model testing in SAS and SPSS. Increasing this value greatly adds to the size of the search space.

- *Number of Terms*: The 2nd parameter specifies the number of terms that will be used as independent variables. Since the example in E1 above limits the predictors to four terms and the final parameter is set to 'V' this means the goal formula will have exactly four independent variables.

- *Term Format*: The 3rd parameter specifies whether the terms should be in the form of a variable or an abstract term. In E1 above the letter 'V' has been specified indicating the use of variables. If the letter 'T' had been used an abstract term could be entered (which means that a variable could be replaced by a constant)

In the interests of methodological rigor the coefficients of each ARC champion formula were recalculated in SPSS version 15. The coefficients shown in the tables below are those produced by SPSS. The significance scores are those produced by SPSS using the Student's T procedure.

Table 11-4. Champion Formula at Grammar Depth 0

Region	Mean	Smallest Shadow Economy		Largest Shadow Economy	
1 OECD	16.6%	9.7%	(USA 1990)	35.0%	(Australia 1990)
2 Ex-Soviet	27.4%	9.5%	(Ukraine 1990)	96.6%	(Georgia 1995)
3 Developing	37.7%	-3.1%	(Trinidad 2006)	230.3%	(Mongolia 2006)

Variable	Beta	t	Significance
GDP_PPP	1.113	91.643	0
URBAN_POP	3007.583	9.506	0
CO2	-122862.124	-8.398	0
AREA	9329.823	6.395	0
POPULATION	-577.44	-6.28	0

8.   Baseline Test: Searching at Grammar Depth Zero

A baseline test was conducted which forced ARC to search in a way that imitated the model testing procedures available in traditional statistical packages like SAS and SPSS. At a grammar depth of zero using variable terms (rather than abstract terms) ARC tests different combinations of variables unmodified by each other or by mathematical functions.

(E2): universal (0,5,v)

Equation E2 above specifies that the desired goal formula should have five unmodified variable terms.

The resulting shadow economy estimates immediately show the need for customized scoring. Even though all of the terms were significant at the 1% level and an R-Squared of 0.95 was reached some shadow economies were implausibly high or low. As can be seen from Table 11-4 Trinidad was estimated to have a negative shadow economy, while Mongolia had one of 230%.

9.   A Search using Grammar Depth 1

Searching at a grammar depth of 1 allowed ARC to use mathematical functions and operators. Where the operators take two operands this caused ARC to use some very complex composite terms. The first term below uses the addition operator to combine the official GDP with the urban population. Those who express skepticism about elaborate model searching procedures would immediately raise the problem of 'over-fitting'. Why should the sum of the official GDP and the urban population be an indicator of the Comprehensive

Domestic Product? Re-running the champion formula in SPSS gives some credence to the over-fitting objection in this case because one of the five terms was removed as it failed a built-in test for co-linearity. So SPSS constructed a regression formula without the last term which was the sum of Energy consumption and COMSTWO (Landline Phones + Mobile Phones). As with the previous champion formula, high significance levels and a high R-Square values did not guarantee plausible estimates (see Table 11-5). It should be pointed out that many academic papers publish regression formulae using two variables in combination (such as GDP per capita). The champion shown in Table 11-5 was found after only 6.24 thousand Well Formed Formulas (WFFs). If a larger number of WFFs had been searched, ARC might have discovered a better fit using more complex (and more plausible) binary terms. For the purposes of this paper, more parsimonious model selection was attempted rather than a longer search process.

Table 11-5. Champion Formula at Grammar Depth 1

REGION	Mean	Smallest Shadow Economy		Largest Shadow Economy	
1 OECD	25.1%	10.5%	(USA 1990)	57.2%	(Ireland 1990)
2 Ex-Soviet	38.1%	11.9%	(Russia 1995)	89.7%	(Estonia 1995)
3 Developing	49.5%	0.2%	(Vietnam 2006)	141.4%	(Togo 2006)

Variable	Beta	t	Significance
GDP + URBAN_POP	1.16	95.966	0
SQRT NET_IMPORTS	139026.804	6.125	0
PHONES + COMSTWO	-5196.454	-8.088	0
COMSTWO + ENERGY	7074.87	8.393	0

Note : The term (GDP_PPP + COMSTWO) was removed from this champion because it failed a built-in SPSS co linearity check.

10.   Searching with Function Limitations

Four of the five terms in Table 11-5 use the plus operator to construct complex terms involving two variables. The resulting complex formula illustrates a common criticism of regression formulae emerging from genetic programming - the so-called 'bloated' nature of the winners. Luckily ARC provides several effective ways to limit bloat. One of them is to apply a restriction to the function that can be selected during model evolution.

(E3): universal(2,5,v) where op(noop,sqrt,square,cube,log,exp,abs);

Equation E3 applies a "where" clause to the goal search formula that restricts the search to unary mathematical operators. At the same time the first parameter has been set to "2" which raises the grammar depth by one level. This allows a variable to be modified by two functions in combination. The first term shown in Table 11-6 used two operators that cancelled each other out (the square root of GDP squared). Four of the five other terms used the ABS function which would have removed the minus sign from any negative variable values. Since there were no negatives, this function had no effect. In a sense the search algorithm appears to be using the ABS function as a "No Operator" function. This was equivalent to ARC choosing keyword "noop" in equation E3.

Table 11-6. Champion Formula at Grammar Depth 2 with only unary operators

REGION	Mean	Smallest Shadow Economy		Largest Shadow Economy	
1 OECD	21.8%	9.4%	(USA 1990)	31.3%	(Ireland 1990)
2 Ex-Soviet	42.1%	14.7%	(Ukraine 1990)	133.8%	(Kyrgyz Rep. 1995)
3 Developing	34.5%	9.9%	(China 2006)	123.6%	(Togo 2006)

Variable	Beta	t	Significance
$SQRT\_GDP^2$	1.188	123.642	0
$ABS\ ENERGY^2$	-0.289	-5.177	0
$ABS\ AREA^3$	6.04E-11	9.474	0
$ENERGY^6$	9.22E-27	2.819	0.005
$ABS\ LOG\ GDP$	232909816.1	1.472	0.142

The third term (AREA to the power of 6) is the equivalent of repeating the "cube" function for area: "cube(cube(AREA))". In natural language one could express this as "the cube of area cubed".

As with Table 11-5, the champion formula at grammar depth two might have been improved by allowing more search time. Also some of the individual country estimates were implausible (such as the Irish estimate of over 31%). The final term (the Log of GDP) was not significant at the 10% level.

11.   Function Restriction at Grammar Depth 1

In the interests of parsimony the function-restricted goal formula was further restricted to 1 grammar level of depth. This only required a small change to the goal formula. The first parameter was reduced to 1, resulting in this goal:

(E4): universal(1,5,v) where op(noop,sqrt,square,cube,log,exp,abs);

This search was allowed to run for 30.73K WFFs but ARC found the eventual champion after only 5.78K WFFs. Using both customized scoring and a relatively parsimonious goal formula ARC produced the first of a series of plausible estimation sets.

Table 11-7. Champion Formula at Grammar Depth 1 with only unary operators

Region	Mean	Smallest Shadow Economy	Largest Shadow Economy
1 OECD	14.9%	9.5% (USA 1993)	19.1% (Korea 1996)
2 Ex-Soviet	38.3%	14.7% (Slovenia 1995)	95.1% (Georgia 1995)
3 Developing	35.7%	7.6% (Trinidad 2006)	113.8% (Togo 2006)

Variable	Beta	t	Significance
PHONES^3	-1.4E-13	-7.701	0
COMSTHREE^2	0.00000943	7.537	0
POPULATION^3	-4.95E-16	-10.012	0
URBAN_POP	2135.92	13.397	0
GDP	1.063	135.62	0

The countries that commonly have the smallest shadow economies in the existing research (Switzerland, Austria and the USA) have similarly low estimates using the formula in Table 11-7. Togo is the only country estimate above 100%. The next highest was Georgia with an estimate of 95%. Trinidad's score might seem to be unduly low, but a similar low estimate is given by Schneider (2010). If one defines 'free' business registration as a process requiring less 1.5% of per capita incomes then Trinidad is virtually the only non-OECD country in the free registration category, which lends plausibility to the idea that it might have a small shadow economy (since its government makes it so easy for entrepreneurs to be honest reporters). A regression champion was found similar to the formula at the bottom of Table 11-7 that used total energy consumption in place of the communications variables. This is shown in Table 11-8 below.

12.   An Out of Sample Check

One of the most commonly suggested solutions to over-fitting is to calculate regression estimates for a set of cases separate from the original data. The results of an out of sample check are shown in Table 11-9 below. The GDP, energy consumption and urbanization values for the years 2003-2005 and 2007 were applied to the four term regression formula shown in Table 11-8.

In Table 11-9 the Democratic Republic of Congo is a notable outlier with an IDP of 305%. However this was one of only four countries with estimates

Table 11-8. 'Energy' Champion with only Unary Operators and Grammar Depth 1

Region	Mean	Smallest Shadow Economy		Largest Shadow Economy	
1 (OECD)	15.6%	9.8%	(USA 1993)	19.3%	(Korea 1996)
2 (Ex-Soviet)	40.3%	15.9%	(Slovenia 1995)	100.5%	(Georgia 1993)
3 (Developing)	30.0%	8.3%	(Trinidad 2006)	120.2%	(Togo 2006)

Variable	Beta	t	Significance
ENERGY^3	-1.94E-08	-2.469	0.014
GDP_PPP	1.071	88.924	0
URBAN_POP	2255.715	11.57	0
URBAN_POP^2	-2.72E-06	-7.839	0

Table 11-9. Out of Sample Prediction 510 country estimates for 2003-05 and 2007

Region	Average	Smallest Shadow Economy		Largest Shadow Economy	
1 (OECD)	12.3%	8.1%	(USA 2007)	15.6%	(Korea 2003)
2 (Ex-Soviet)	27.6%	11.2%	(Slovenia 2007)	62.8%	(Moldova 2003)
3 (Developing)	41.2%	8.3%	(Trinidad 2007)	305.8%	(Congo, D.R. 2003)

510 shadow economy predictions for various countries in 2003-05 & 2007 based on official GDP, Urban Population, Urban Population Squared, and Energy Consumption cubed as shown in table 8 above (2006 data was "in-sample" and so has been omitted).

higher than 100%. The others were Mozambique (Highest 140%), Togo (127%), Ghana (107%) and Haiti (101%). Given the political pressures on the GDP estimation procedure in developing countries it seems entirely plausible that a broadly accurate estimation formula will produce such outliers in a given year. In the developing world a government economist may be pressured to show unduly high economic growth to secure government loans from global financial institutions. If tax revenues are low in relation to official GDP the opposite pressure might apply. Tanzania was once penalized by a sharp reduction in foreign aid due to 'under-taxation.' (Gould, 2005).

An accurate estimation formula based heavily on urbanization may correctly predict the CDP while economies are growing but not when there are sharp economic contractions. Populations that move to the cities will not flood back to the countryside in a recession. The three largest IDPs mentioned above were all in countries that experienced significant economic contractions between 1960 and 2007 (see Figure 11-1). Togo's per capita income stayed about the same over this period while the per capita incomes in the rest of the world increased from $4,200 USD to $13,600 (Heston et al., 2006). The Democratic Republic of the Congo actually experienced a sharp decline. A predictive

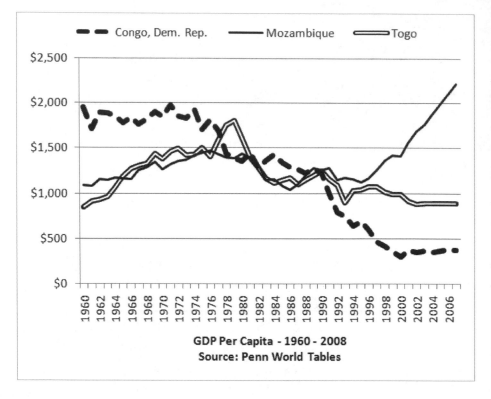

Figure 11-1. GDP Per Capita in Togo, Mozambique and Congo Democratic Rep.

formula relying more heavily on energy data might capture such declines, but it seems unlikely that a global formula solely based on energy could have a high level of explanatory power with the data currently available. Given the intense war and civil disturbances in the countries shown in Figure 11-1, the high IDP estimates shown may in fact be true values even though they exceed those in previously published research. As (Schneider et al., 2010) points out this type of research involves a scientific passion for "knowing the unknown."

Researchers who want to make detailed year-to-year predictions of IDP will not be satisfied with these estimations. It is not claimed that the predictor variables shown can track both downward and upward movements in the size of the CDP in a given year, however over a 5-10 year period the estimates shown may be the more accurate than the MIMIC estimates. For researchers who prefer predictions based on 'harder' quantitative data than the MIMIC approach, the regression formulae in Tables 11-7, 11-8 may currently provide the most accurate procedure for the countries covered by the formula shown in Table 11-8 (126 countries with known energy, GDP and urbanization data).

13.   Assessing ARC's Abstract Expression Grammar

ARC revealed some missing analytical tools during the conduct of this research. It would be useful to use Student's T statistics and co-linearity values calculated inside ARC. Given ARC's main strengths, we recommend adding these additional statistical tools as soon as possible. ARC was able to find useful regression champions within a gigantic search space, while supporting the very high degree of user control necessary in real world applications. Even with function restriction, four variables, and a grammar depth of 1 a search space of 100 trillion combinations was created. This is such a large area that traditional statistical packages would have been entirely impractical for these estimations. The Abstract Expression Grammar shown in equations E1-E4 allowed the parsimony of the goal formula to be adjusted quickly with a trivial amount of effort. The regression formulae shown above are a useful gain in knowledge that would have been difficult to achieve without a genetic programming approach to regression analysis.

References

Bagachwa, M.S.S. and Naho, A. (1995). *Estimating the Second Economy in Tanzania*. World Development, Vol. 23:8, pp 1387-1399.

Bhattacharyya, Dilip K. (1999). *On the Economic Rationale of Estimating the Hidden Economy*. The Economic Journal, Vol. 109:456, pp 348-359.

Gould, J. (2005). *The New Conditionality: the politics of poverty reduction strategies*. Zed Books, London UK.

Hartzenburg, G.M. and Leimann, A. (1992). The informal economy and its growth potential. In E.Adebian and Standis, B., editors, *Economic Growth in South Africa*, pages 187–214. Oxford University Press, Oxford UK.

Heston, A., Summers, R., and Aten, B. (2006). Penn world table version 6.2. Technical report, Center for International Comparisons of Production, Income and Prices at the University of Pennsylvania.

Johnson, Simon, Kaufmann, Daniel, and Zoido-Lobatón, Pablo (1998a). *Corruption, Public Finances and the Unofficial Economy - Discussion Paper*. The World Bank, Washington DC.

Johnson, Simon, Kaufmann, Daniel, and Zoido-Lobatón, Pablo (1998b). *Regulatory Discretion and the Unofficial Economy*. American Economic Review Vol. = 88:2 pp 387-392.

Kaufmann, D. and Kaliberda, A. (1996). Integrating the unofficial economy into the dynamics of post socialist economies: A framework of analyses and evidence. In Kaminski, B., editor, *Economic Transition in Russia and the New States of Eurasia*, pages 81–120. M.E.Sharpe, London UK.

Korns, Michael F. (2010). Abstract expression grammar symbolic regression. In Rick Riolo, Una-May O'Reilly and McConaghy, Trent, editors, *Genetic Programming Theory and Practice VIII*. Springer, Ann Arbor MI.

Lackó, Maria (1997a). *Do Power Consumption Data Tell the Story? (Electricity Intensity and the Hidden Economy in Post-Socialist Countries) - Working Paper*. International Institute for Applied Systems Analysis, Laxenberg Austria.

Lackó, Maria (1997b). *The Hidden Economies of Visegrád Countries in International Comparison: A Household Electricity Approach - Working Paper*. Institute of Economics - Hungary.

Lackó, Maria (1998). The hidden economies of visegrad countries in international comparison: A household electricity approach. In Wyplosz, Charles, editor, *Hungary: Towards a Market Economy*, pages 128–152. Cambridge University Press, Cambridge MA.

Lackó, Maria (2000). Hidden economy - an unknown quantity? comparative analysis of hidden economies in transition countries, 1989-95. In *The Economies of Transition*, volume 8, pages 117–149. Wiley-Blackwell.

Madzarevic, Sanja and Mikulic, Davor (1997). *Measuring the unofficial economy by the system of national accounts - Working Paper*. Zagreb Institute of Public Finance.

Muller, K.E. (2002). *Regression and ANOVA: an integrated approach using SAS software*. SAS Publications Cary NC.

Nurusis, M.J. (1996). *SPSS regression models 10.0*. SPSS Inc., Chicago IL.

Pozo, Susan (1996). *Exploring the Underground Economy: Studies of Illegal and Unreported Activity*. W.E.Upjohn, Institute for Employment Research, Kalamazoo MI.

Schneider, F., Buehn, A., and Montenegro, C. (2010). *Shadow Economies All over the World - New Estimates for 162 Countries from 1999 to 2007*. The World Bank Development Research Group, Washington DC.

Schneider, Friedrich (1994). Measuring the size and development of the shadow economy: Can the causes be found and the obstacles be overcome? In H.Brandstaetter and Güth, W., editors, *Essays on Economic Psychology*, pages 193–212. Springer, Berlin.

Schneider, Friedrich (1998). *Further Empirical Results of the Size of the Shadow Economy of 17 OECD-Countries over Time*. Paper presented at the 54th Congress of the IIPF Cordoba, Argentina.

Yoo, I. and Hyun, J.K. (1998). *International Comparison of the Black Economy: Empirical Evidence Using Micro-level Data. Working Paper 98-04*. Korea Institute of Public Finance.

Chapter 12

THE IMPORTANCE OF BEING FLAT – STUDYING THE PROGRAM LENGTH DISTRIBUTIONS OF OPERATOR EQUALISATION

Sara Silva[1,2] and Leonardo Vanneschi[3,1]

[1] *KDBIO group, INESC-ID Lisboa, Portugal;* [2] *ECOS group, Center for Informatics and Systems of the University of Coimbra, Portugal;* [3] *D.I.S.Co., University of Milano-Bicocca, Italy.*

Abstract

The recent Crossover Bias theory has shown that bloat in Genetic Programming can be caused by the proliferation of small unfit individuals in the population. Inspired by this theory, Operator Equalisation is the most recent and successful bloat control method available. In a recent work there has been an attempt to replicate the evolutionary dynamics of Operator Equalisation by joining two key ingredients found in older and newer bloat control methods. However, the obtained dynamics was very different from expected, which prompted a further investigation into the reasons that make Operator Equalisation so successful. It was revealed that, at least for complex symbolic regression problems, the distribution of program lengths enforced by Operator Equalisation is nearly flat, contrasting with the peaky and well delimited distributions of the other approaches. In this work we study the importance of having flat program length distributions for bloat control. We measure the flatness of the distributions found in previous and new Operator Equalisation variants and we correlate it with the amount of search performed by each approach. We also analyze where this search occurs and how bloat correlates to these properties. We conclude presenting a possible explanation for the unique behavior of Operator Equalisation.

Keywords: Genetic Programming, Bloat, Operator Equalisation, Crossover Bias, Program Length Distributions

1.   Introduction

The most recent theory concerning bloat in Genetic Programming (GP) is the Crossover Bias theory (Poli et al., 2007; Dignum and Poli, 2007; Dignum and Poli, 2008a). It explains code growth in tree based GP by the effect that standard subtree crossover has on the distribution of tree sizes, or program lengths, in the population. Whenever subtree crossover is applied, the amount of genetic material removed from the first parent is the exact same amount inserted in the second parent, and vice versa. The mean tree size, or mean program length, remains unchanged. However, as the population undergoes repeated crossover operations, it approaches a particular distribution of tree sizes, specifically a Lagrange distribution of the second kind. It has been observed that, in this distribution, small individuals are much more frequent than the larger ones (Dignum and Poli, 2008a). For example, crossover generates a high amount of single-node individuals. Because very small individuals are generally unfit, selection tends to reject them in favor of the larger individuals, causing an increase in mean tree size. According to the theory, it is the proliferation of these small unfit individuals, perpetuated by crossover, that ultimately causes bloat. Strong theoretical and empirical evidence supports the Crossover Bias theory. It has been shown that the bias towards smaller individuals is more intense when the population mean tree size is low, and that when the population is initialized using a Lagrange length distribution, it bloats more easily than if initialized with traditional methods (Poli et al., 2007). It was also found that the usage of size limits may actually speed code growth in the early stages of the run, as it promotes the proliferation of the smaller individuals (Dignum and Poli, 2008a). Along with further theoretical developments, it has also been shown that smaller populations bloat more slowly (Poli et al., 2008b), and that elitism reduces bloat (Poli et al., 2008c; Poli et al., 2008a).

Inspired by the Crossover Bias theory, Operator Equalisation (Dignum and Poli, 2008b; Silva and Dignum, 2009), from now on generically referred to as OpEq, is the most recent and successful bloat control method available today. It can bias the population towards a desired program length distribution by accepting or rejecting each newly created individual into the population. OpEq can easily avoid the small unfit individuals resulting from the crossover bias, as well as the excessively large individuals that are no better than the smaller ones already found. Preventing the larger individuals from entering the population is a common bloat control practice; preventing the smaller ones is not. A recent attempt has been made to replicate the behavior of OpEq by coupling a standard GP system with two key ingredients taken from older and newer bloat control methods (Silva, 2011). However, the obtained evolutionary dynamics was very different from that of OpEq, which prompted a further investigation into the reasons that make OpEq so successful. It was revealed that the distribution of program lengths enforced by OpEq is nearly flat, contrasting with the peaky and well-delimited distributions of the other approaches.

In this work we study the importance of having flat program length distributions for OpEq bloat control. In the next section we describe OpEq with some detail, while Section 3 summarizes the experiments that revealed the nearly flat program length distributions of OpEq, and Section 4 travels back in time to investigate flatness in early published OpEq work. Section 5 introduces new variants of OpEq and presents a measure of flatness of length distributions. It studies the correlation between this measure and the amount of search performed, also analyzing where this search occurs and how bloat correlates to these properties. Section 6 draws the main conclusions from this work.

2. Operator Equalisation

Developed alongside the Crossover Bias theory (see Section 1), OpEq is a recent technique to control bloat that allows an accurate control of the program length distribution inside a population during a GP run. Already used a number of times in benchmark and real world problems (e.g. (Silva and Vanneschi, 2012; Vanneschi and Silva, 2009; Silva et al., 2010)), it is however still a fairly new approach. Here we provide a detailed explanation of how it works, and a description of the two main variants used so far, DynOpEq and MutOpEq.

Distribution of program lengths

We use the concept of a histogram. Each bar of the histogram can be imagined as a bin containing those programs (individuals, solutions) whose length is within a certain interval. The width of the bar determines the range of lengths that fall into this bin, and the height specifies the number of programs allowed within. We call the former *bin-width* and the latter *bin-capacity*. All bins are the same width, placed adjacently with no overlapping. Each length value l, belongs to one and only one bin b, identified as follows:

$$b = \left\lfloor \frac{l-1}{bin\_width} \right\rfloor + 1 \tag{12.1}$$

For instance, if $bin\_width = 5$, bin 1 will hold programs of lengths 1,...,5, bin 2 will hold programs of lengths 6,...,10, etc. The set of bins represents the distribution of program lengths in the population.

OpEq biases the population towards a desired target distribution by accepting or rejecting each newly created individual into the population (and into its corresponding bin). The original idea of OpEq (Dignum and Poli, 2008b), where the user was required to specify the target distribution and maximum program length, rapidly evolved to a self adapting implementation (Silva and Dignum, 2009) that was designated as DynOpEq, where both these elements are automatically set and dynamically updated to provide the best setting for each stage of the evolutionary process.

There are two tasks involved in DynOpEq: calculating the target (in practical terms, defining the capacity of each bin) and making the population follow it (making sure the individuals in the population fill the set of bins).

Calculating the Target Distribution

In DynOpEq, the dynamic target length distribution simply follows fitness. For each bin, the average fitness of the individuals within is calculated, and the target is proportional to these values. Bins with better average fitness will have higher capacity, because that is where search is proving to be more successful. Formalizing, the capacity, or target number of individuals, for each bin b, is calculated as:

$$bin\_capacity_b = round(n \times (\bar{f}_b / \sum_i \bar{f}_i)) \qquad (12.2)$$

where $\bar{f}_i$ is the average fitness in the bin with index i, $\bar{f}_b$ is the average fitness of the individuals in b, and n is the number of individuals in the population. Equation 12.2 is used for maximization problems where higher fitness is better (so the fitness values must undergo a transformation for minimization problems, for example a sign inversion and mapping back to positive values).

Initially based on the first randomly created population, the target is updated at each generation, always based on the fitness measurements of the current population. This creates a fast moving bias towards the areas of the search space where the fittest programs are, avoiding the small unfit individuals resulting from the crossover bias, as well as the excessively large individuals that are no better than the smaller ones already found. Thus the dynamic target is capable of self adapting to any problem and any stage of the run.

Following the Target Distribution

In DynOpEq, every newly-created individual must be validated before eventually entering the population and the ones who do not fit the target are rejected. Each offspring is created by genetic operators as in any other GP system. After that, its length is measured and its corresponding bin is identified using Equation 12.1. If this bin already exists and is not full (meaning that its capacity is higher than the number of individuals already there), the new individual is immediately accepted. If the bin still does not exist (meaning it lies outside the current target boundaries) the fitness of the individual is measured and, in case we are in the presence of the new best-of-run (the individual with best fitness found so far), the bin is created to accept the new individual, becoming immediately full. Any other non-existing bins between the new bin and the target boundaries also become available with capacity for only one individual each. The dynamic creation of new bins frees DynOpEq from the fixed maximum program length that was present in the original OpEq idea. The criterion of creating new bins whenever needed to accommodate the new best-of-run individual is inspired by the Dynamic Limits bloat control technique (Silva and Costa, 2009).

In DynOpEq, when the intended bin exists but is already at its full capacity, or when the intended bin does not exist and the new individual is not the best-of-run, the individual is evaluated and, if we are in the presence of the new best-of-bin (meaning the individual has better fitness than any other already in that bin), the bin is forced to increase its capacity and accept the individual. Otherwise, the individual is rejected. Permitting the addition of individuals beyond the bin capacity allows the target distribution to be overridden where necessary, by further biasing the population towards the lengths where the search is having a higher degree of success. In the second case, when the bin does not exist and the individual is not the best-of-run, rejection always occurs.

A different variant of OpEq was introduced shortly after DynOpEq, and designated as MutOpEq (Silva and Vanneschi, 2009). Unlike DynOpEq, it never rejects individuals. So in both the cases mentioned above (when the intended bin exists but is already at its full capacity, or when the intended bin does not exist and the new individual is not the best-of-run), MutOpEq performs the same action: it searches for the closest existing non-full bin, and then mutates the new individual until its length fits this bin. The mutations used are "weak" mutations in the sense that they modify the least possible amount of code each time they are applied. Loosely based on the shrink and grow mutations defined in (Vanneschi et al., 2003; Vanneschi, 2004), these weak mutations can be informally described as follows:

Shrink Chooses a terminal branch (a minimum-depth branch containing only one function whose arguments are all terminals) and replaces it with one of its terminal nodes (one of the arguments of the function);

Grow Chooses a terminal node and replaces it with a terminal branch where one of the arguments is the replaced terminal.

One or the other is used, depending on whether the individual is to be reduced or enlarged. Whenever there is a tie (there are two existing non-full bins at the same distance), the preferred option is to reduce. The same individual will undergo several mutations until it reaches the desired length. It is expected that, by iteratively inserting or removing only terminal elements, instead of inserting or removing a larger branch in a single operation, the impact on the fitness of the individual is minimized (Igel and Chellapilla, 1999; Luke, 2003).

3.   Flatness Revealed

In a recent work (Silva, 2011) there has been an attempt to replicate the
evolutionary dynamics of OpEq by coupling a standard GP system with two
key ingredients taken from older and newer bloat control methods, namely
Brood Recombination and Dynamic Limits. Here we summarize the main
experiments and findings of this work.

Brood Recombination and Dynamic Limits

Brood Recombination was popularized by Tackett in 1994 (Tackett, 1994)
as a new recombination operator to serve as a substitute for the standard subtree
crossover. Instead of recombining two parents once to produce one pair of
offspring, Brood Recombination recombines two parents n times, each time
selecting different crossover points, to produce n pairs of offspring, where n
is called the *brood size*. Then only two offspring are selected, the best of the
brood, and the rest discarded. According to the Crossover Bias theory, Brood
Recombination should help control bloat. In practical terms, creating several
pairs of offspring and then choosing only the best may reduce the crossover bias
to create many small individuals. If it is verified that the smaller offspring are
indeed the most unfit, they will not be selected from among the brood members,
and not introduced into the population. The larger the brood, the larger the
reduction of bias. Brood Recombination was therefore the first key element
used on the attempt to recreate the successful behavior of Operator Equalisation.
A variant of Brood Recombination was also introduced, designated as Batch
Recombination. The only difference is that, instead of repeatedly selecting two
offspring from the $2n$ brood members produced by each single couple, all the
offspring needed to form a new generation are now selected only once from
among the several broods produced by all the couples. This should reduce the
crossover bias even further.

Tree-based GP traditionally uses a static depth limit to avoid the excessive
growth of its individuals. When an individual is created that violates this limit,
one of its parents is chosen for the new generation instead (Koza, 1992). The
Dynamic Limits approach (Silva and Costa, 2009) also imposes a depth limit on
the individuals accepted into the population, but this one is dynamic, meaning
that it can be changed during the run. The dynamic limit is initially set with a
low value, usually the same as the maximum depth of the initial random trees.
Any new individual who breaks this limit is rejected and replaced by one of its
parents (as with the traditional static limit), unless it is the best individual found
so far. In this case, the dynamic limit is raised to match the depth of the new
best-of-run and allow it into the population. Dynamic Limits can coexist with
the traditional depth limit. Originally introduced in (Silva and Almeida, 2003),
the Dynamic Limits idea was later extended to include two variants (Silva and

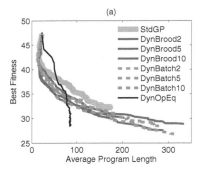
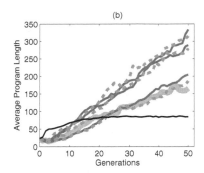

Figure 12-1. Summary of results obtained in (Silva, 2011) with StdGP, all the combined techniques, and DynOpEq. (a) Best fitness versus average program length; (b) Average program length versus generations. The two lines closer to StdGP are DynBrood2 and DynBatch2.

Costa, 2004): a heavy dynamic limit, called heavy because it falls back to lower values whenever allowed, and a dynamic limit on size instead of depth. Since Operator Equalisation itself was inspired by the Dynamic Limits for the decision on when to open new bins (see Section 2.0), it was only natural to assume that this would be the second key element for its success.

Experiments and Findings

Starting from a standard GP system (StdGP), Dynamic Limits (Dyn) were coupled with Brood Recombination (Brood), alternatively Batch Recombination (Batch), using different brood/batch sizes (2,5,10). These combined techniques were all compared to each other and to StdGP and DynOpEq with bin width 1, to check how much they push the evolutionary behavior away from StdGP and closer to DynOpEq.

The behavior of these combined techniques was tested in the first real world problem ever tackled by OpEq, the prediction of the human oral bioavailability of a set of candidate drug compounds on the basis of their molecular structure. The dataset[1] is the same used in (Silva and Vanneschi, 2009; Silva and Vanneschi, 2012). This is a hard regression problem involving 241 variables and a dataset with 359 samples. The function set was composed of only the four binary operators $+$, $-$, $\times$ and $/$. For more details on the problem, dataset and settings see (Archetti et al., 2006; Archetti et al., 2007; Silva and Vanneschi, 2012)

Figures 12-1 and 12-2 show a summary of the results obtained in (Silva, 2011). The plots do not discriminate between the different brood/batch sizes

[1]Freely available at http://personal.disco.unimib.it/Vanneschi/bioavailability.txt

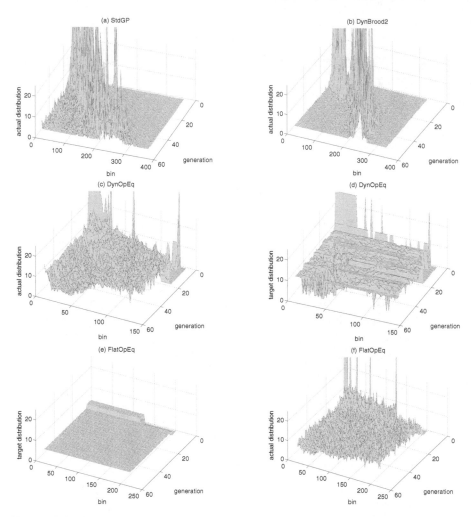

Figure 12-2. Summary of results obtained in (Silva, 2011). Examples of actual and target length distributions. (a) Typical length distribution of StdGP; (b) Typical length distribution of DynBrood2; (c) Typical length distribution of DynOpEq; (d) Target length distribution that originated the distribution in plot c; (e) Typical target length distribution of DynOpEq with flat target; (f) Length distribution originated by the target in plot e. All frequencies above 25 are not shown.

because the differences are not important. Figure 12-1a shows the evolution of fitness against average program length, completely disregarding generations, evaluations, or time spent in the search process, which in the real world is not always that important. For more information on this type of (still unconventional) plot see (Silva and Dignum, 2009). In the same line of thought, Figure 12-1b shows the evolution of average program length along the generations, ignoring the fact that different techniques require very different amounts of computation to complete one generation. Figure 12-1 clearly shows that none of the combined techniques produced the expected OpEq-like behavior. Eliminating the smaller individuals (with Brood Recombination) and dynamically controlling the maximum allowed program length (with Dynamic Limits) does not produce a bloating behavior even remotely similar to the one of DynOpEq. By design, the combined approaches should emulate the decisions of DynOpEq on whether to accept or reject the individuals (large or small) that fall outside the limits of the target, so the next step was to analyze the target itself.

Figure 12-2 shows examples of different target and actual program length distributions obtained with different techniques. For visualization purposes the bins containing even lengths are not shown, since the function set does not allow the creation of even length individuals. The effect of a combined technique on the actual length distribution can be observed by comparing Figures 12-2a and 12-2b. While the Dynamic Limits do not seem to produce any visible effect, Brood Recombination is able to "clean" the smaller individuals from the population, strongly suggesting that these are indeed the most unfit. According to the Crossover Bias theory (see Section 1) this should act against bloat, but these results show only a minimal effect, at least when compared to DynOpEq (Figure 12-1). The actual length distribution of DynOpEq (plot 12-2c) is completely different from the non-equalizing ones, and its flatness was attributed to the nearly flat target that it uses (plot 12-2d). Had the target been faithfully followed, the actual distribution would be even flatter, but the several overrides gave it a less artificial look. A variant of OpEq that uses an artificially created flat target (FlatOpEq, described in Section 5.0 ahead) was also tested, with its target and actual length distributions shown in Figures 12-2e and 12-2f. Further results of FlatOpEq, compared to other OpEq techniques, will be presented in Section 5.

The surprising flatness of the DynOpEq target was attributed to the diversity and amplitude of fitness values that occurs in the problem of bioavailability prediction, as well as other complex symbolic regression problems, which almost guarantees the presence of very unfit outliers in the population, practically every generation. These fitness values are so much worse than the others that, compared to them, all the rest looks the same, and all the bins end up getting the same capacity according to Equation 12.2.

The results presented in (Silva, 2011), including the FlatOpEq technique, suggest that the flatter the target, the most success is achieved in bloat control. Instead of avoiding small unfit individuals, the flat target actually prevents the search from moving away from the shorter lengths, even long after better and larger solutions have been found. It simply spreads individuals across all the previously visited lengths, ensuring that search does not abandon any of them. In the conclusions of this work it was suggested that we look back at the early successes of OpEq and check if they were also the result of an unintended flat distribution target, remarking that a flat target may appear as a consequence of, not only extremely high, but also extremely low, phenotypic diversity. Investigating flatness in early OpEq work is the theme of the next section.

4.   Investigating Flatness in Early OpEq Work

When the idea of OpEq was first introduced (Dignum and Poli, 2008b), even before DynOpEq or MutOpEq were proposed, different fixed length targets were used to compare OpEq to a simple non-equalizing length limit. These targets were *"a triangular distribution which has a linearly increasing bias towards sampling larger programs, a 'reverse' triangle where smaller programs are sampled more often and a reverse exponential distribution where we sample larger programs exponentially more frequently than shorter ones"* and also *"a uniform distribution where each length is sampled with the same frequency"* (Dignum and Poli, 2008b) which is basically a flat target. Even-10 Parity and Poly-10 Regression were the problems chosen, the maximum program length was 100, and the bin width was 2 to avoid empty bins, since in both problems only binary functions were used. In all the tests the target length distribution was reached quickly, and the average program length stabilized after a few generations. That is not surprising, since the target was fixed and no new bins could be created. Regarding the evolution of fitness, for the parity problem the effects of following a given target greatly depended on its shape; for the regression problem, the simple length limit was better than any of the fixed targets. The flat target did not stand out from the other targets.

When OpEq evolved to become DynOpEq (Silva and Dignum, 2009), four different benchmark problems were used to assess the performance of the new approach. These were Symbolic Regression of the quartic polynomial, Artificial Ant on the Santa Fe trail, Even-5 Parity, and 11-Bit Multiplexer. In this work, some target and actual length distributions of the regression and parity problems were shown. They were averages of 30 runs, accompanied by a note stating that "there is considerable variance between Regression runs, but not much in the Parity case" so their flatness remained unnoticed, also because there was no direct comparison with the length distributions of the standard non-equalizing approach (StdGP). We go back to that work and visualize the length distributions obtained in the four benchmark problems, not in average but for a single typical run, and perform a direct visual comparison between StdGP and DynOpEq, in Figure 12-3. We only look at DynOpEq runs with bin width 1. For the parity problem, which only uses binary functions, the bins supposedly containing the individuals of even length were removed for visualization purposes, since they are all empty. Some of the DynOpEq distributions are indeed very flat, like the one of Multiplexer, while others do not look flat at all, like the one of

Parity. However, for all these problems the DynOpEq distributions look much flatter than their StdGP counterparts, something that had not been given proper emphasis before.

5.   Experiments and Results

Here we introduce new variants of OpEq and compare them to the previous ones, using StdGP as the non-equalizing representative. We introduce a simple measure of flatness and correlate it with the amount of search performed during the evolutionary process, also analyzing where that search occurs. We also measure bloat and correlate it with the other measures. The only problem we use from now on is the same bioavailability problem used in (Silva and Vanneschi, 2009; Silva and Vanneschi, 2012) and mentioned in Section 3.0. Details about this application are not relevant for the aim of this study, except the knowledge that this is indeed a hard real-world problem, and that the function set used does not allow the creation of individuals of even length. The tridimensional distribution plots presented here never include the even length bins. We also use the same settings and parameters as in (Silva and Vanneschi, 2009; Silva and Vanneschi, 2012), but with 20 runs per experiments. For visualization purposes, the boxplots use shortened names for the OpEq techniques. When describing the boxplots, whenever we refer to a 'significant' difference between techniques this means statistical significance determined by ANOVA with $p = 0.05$.

Comparing previous and new variants

As described in Section 2, the first two variants of OpEq were DynOpEq and MutOpEq. DynOpEq has so far been much more used and studied than MutOpEq. The targets of both are built in the same way, and the main difference between them is that MutOpEq does not reject individuals, and instead mutates them until they fit the nearest non-full bin.

Section 3.0 mentions FlatOpEq as a variant that uses an artificially created flat target. FlatOpEq does not calculate the capacity of the bins with Equation 12.2, but instead gives the same capacity to all of them. All the rest, in particular the decisions on whether to accept or reject an individual and when to create new bins, are exactly like in DynOpEq. Note that for most problems, the actual length distribution is never exactly equal to the target, because when bins get full the target begins to be overridden. In our particular bioavailability problem, this is aggravated by the fact that there are no individuals of even length. This means that half of the bins of the perfectly flat target are never filled, and half of the individuals of the population are guaranteed to override the target. To avoid this we have implemented a slight variation of FlatOpEq, which we call FlatOpEq2, that doubles the capacity of the bins containing individuals of odd

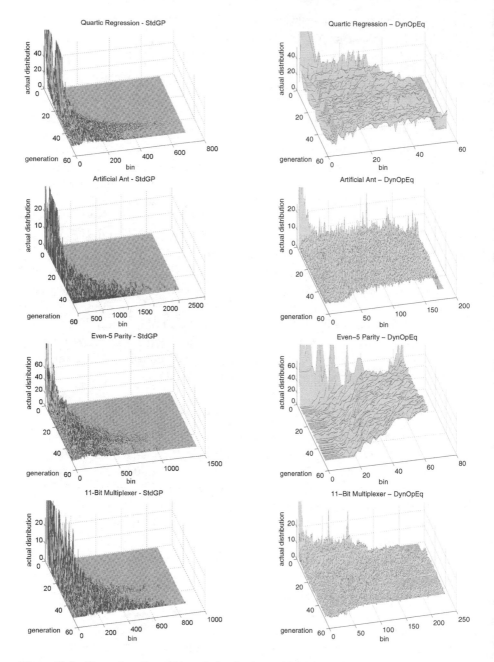

Figure 12-3. Examples of actual length distributions of StdGP and DynOpEq on the four bench-mark problems used in (Silva and Dignum, 2009).

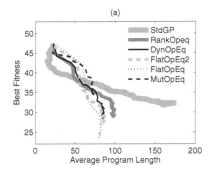
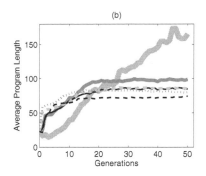

Figure 12-4. Plots of (a) best fitness versus average program length and (b) average program length versus generations, for StdGP and previous and new variants of OpEq.

size, while giving null capacity to the bins of even length. In practical terms this is the same as having FlatOpEq with bin width 2.

Finally, we also implemented another variant of OpEq, called RankOpEq, that calculates the target distribution based on the ranking of the individuals inside the population (the lower the better), instead of their fitness. Everything else is equal to DynOpEq.

Figure 12-4 shows the results of all these techniques, in two plots similar to the ones previously seen in Figure 12-1. Figure 12-4a shows the best fitness against the average program length while Figure 12-4b shows the evolution of average program length along the generations. RankOpEq has the worst behavior of all OpEq techniques. Despite its clear OpEq-like behavior, it leads the average program length to higher values. From the remaining OpEq techniques, FlatOpEq stands out for reaching better fitness, while MutOpEq appears to keep the average program length in lower values than the others. Looking at Figure 12-4a it looks like MutOpEq would need longer runs (more generations) to completely define its behavior, however Figure 12-4b suggests that MutOpEq has stabilized the average program length just like the other OpEq techniques. The reason why MutOpEq does not reach fitness values as good as the others is hypothetically the same that allows FlatOpEq to reach the best values, already stated in (Silva, 2011): more rejections means more search, hence more learning. As we will see in Section 5.0, the flatness of the length distributions is directly related to the amount of search performed.

Measuring flatness

We have seen examples of target and actual length distributions obtained by different techniques on benchmarks (Figure 12-2) and on the bioavailability problem (Figure 12-3), and commented on their amount or lack of flatness. In many cases it is easy to say which distribution is flatter than the other, espe-

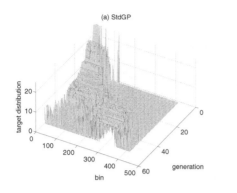
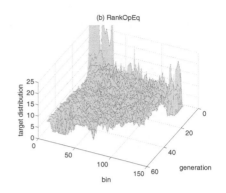

Figure 12-5. Examples of target length distributions of StdGP and RankOpEq. In StdGP the target can be calculated, but is never followed.

cially when comparing OpEq to non-OpEq techniques, and when comparing flat targets with rugged actual distributions. Other examples are not so obvious, like the ones in Figure 12-5. These are the target distributions of StdGP and RankOpEq. Of course the target is not to be followed in StdGP, but it can still be calculated in the same way used for other OpEq techniques like DynOpEq and MutOpEq. As mentioned in Section 12-5, RankOpEq uses rank instead of fitness to calculate the target, while FlatOpEq and FlatOpEq2 simply give the same capacity to all the existent bins. Figure 12-5 is interesting in itself, for showing that even the StdGP target has a flat quality that the RankOpEq target lacks, which is consistent with the explanation given in Section 3.0 for the origin of the flat target. The figure is also interesting because it shows an example of the difficulty in deciding which target is flatter. If we want to treat flatness quantitatively, and correlate it with other quantities, we have to measure it.

We propose measuring the flatness of a length distribution in a very simple way: we use the variance of the frequencies as a measure of "non-flatness". The values used to draw each of the tridimensional plots (like the ones in Figure 12-5) are aligned in a bidimensional vector; the zeros are discarded to ignore all the empty / nonexistent bins; the variance is calculated on this vector. Some of the empty bins appear for reasons other than the impossibility of creating individuals of that length, and as such should not be discarded, but we do not consider this a serious inaccuracy that would prevent us from drawing valid conclusions. In summary, variance now means lack of flatness, and flatness now means lack of variance. From now on, we will use these terms interchangeably.

Figure 12-6 shows boxplots of the variance of the length distributions for all the techniques. Following from the last paragraph, it is worth noting that, according to the variance, the target of StdGP is significantly flatter than the one of RankOpEq. All other differences are also significant, the most interesting

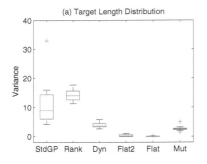 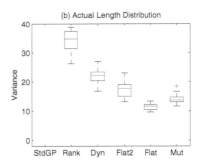

Figure 12-6. Boxplots of the variance of (a) the target length distributions and (b) the actual length distributions. The variance of StdGP is outside the boxplot for the actual distribution, with a median value of 151.9.

ones being that FlatOpEq has a flatter target than FlatOpEq2, and MutOpEq has a flatter target than DynOpEq. In both cases no significant difference would be expected, however we pinpoint that the target for each generation is based on the fitness of the individuals of the previous generation. Therefore, unless both techniques act upon the population in the exact same way, the targets tend to diverge after only a few generations (we go back to this subject in Section 6). In both the abovementioned cases, the main cause for obtaining significantly different flatness may simply be a different number of new bins created during the run, supposedly more bins created by FlatOpEq2/DynOpEq than by FlatOpEq/MutOpEq. Regarding the actual length distributions, as expected StdGP has the highest variance since it does not follow the target. There are significant differences among all the techniques, and all the OpEq techniques maintain their relative ranking in terms of flatness, except MutOpEq that is now flatter than FlatOpEq2. This results from MutOpEq being faithful to the target (except for creating new bins) while FlatOpEq2 overrides it, thus adding ruggedness to the actual distribution.

Flatness and Search

To understand how the flatness of the length distributions affects the evolutionary dynamics, we begin by correlating it with the number of rejections, i.e. the number of individuals that are not accepted in the population because they do not gather the necessary conditions to fit or override the target. In all OpEq techniques except MutOpEq (that never rejects individuals), for each individual rejected another one is created and evaluated, so we can safely say that the number of rejections is a measure of the amount of search performed. Figure 12-7a shows a boxplot of the number of individuals rejected by each technique. Discarding StdGP and MutOpEq, RankOpEq is the technique with a significantly lower number of rejections, followed by DynOpEq and FlatOpEq2 (no significant difference between them) and finally FlatOpEq with an extremely high number of rejections.

Using the values of flatness and rejections of the 20 runs of all the OpEq techniques except MutOpEq, we have measured the correlation between the variance of the target distribution and the number of rejections, as well as the correlation between the number of rejections and the flatness of the actual length distribution. The values obtained were -0.41 and -0.53, respectively. This means that the higher the variance of the target, the lower the number of rejections (conversely, the flatter the target, the more rejections) and the higher the number of rejections, the lower the variance of the actual distribution (the more rejections, the flatter the actual distribution). If we do not consider RankOpEq (for its non-flat nature) the correlations get stronger, respectively -0.46 and -0.60. The most interesting conclusion we gather from these results is that flatness is positively correlated with the amount of search performed.

Another step towards the understanding of how flatness affects evolution is to know where the search is concentrated in terms of program length. By summing the actual length distributions with the rejections, we obtain the joint search distribution regardless of acceptances or rejections. Figure 12-7b shows a boxplot of this joint distribution, revealing an already expected but interesting fact: despite the flatness of targets and actual distributions, the search performed is not flat (except for MutOpEq). All the differences are significant (MutOpEq is significantly lower than StdGP, although not perceptible in the plot) and the variance of FlatOpEq is so high that we left it outside the plot. Figure 12-8 shows specific examples of these joint distributions, for all the techniques. The tridimensional distributions are a clear picture of where the search is performed, and the thick bidimensional lines indicate where the best individual is found in each generation. In all except MutOpEq, there is a moving peak of concentrated search and, not surprisingly, the best individual is found within that peak. It is interesting to realize that in these plots StdGP exhibits a behavior similar to the OpEq techniques (except MutOpEq). But some questions remain to be answered. Does the peak move to chase the best individual, or is the best individual simply being found where the bulk of the search is being performed? And what makes the peak of StdGP move to higher lengths so fast, instead of stabilizing like the OpEq peaks?

Flatness and Bloat

After measuring and studying the flatness of targets, acceptances and rejections, we now measure bloat and analyze how it correlates to these. To measure bloat we use the formula introduced in (Vanneschi et al., 2010), to our knowl-

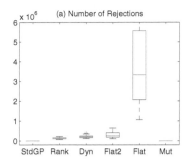
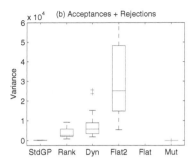

Figure 12-7. Boxplots of (a) the number of rejections and (b) the variance of the joint search distribution represented as acceptances + rejections. The variance of FlatOpEq is outside the boxplot, with a median value higher than 10^6.

edge the only formal quantification of bloat ever proposed:

$$bloat(g) = \frac{(\bar{\delta}(g) - \bar{\delta}(0))/\bar{\delta}(0)}{(\bar{f}(0) - \bar{f}(g))/\bar{f}(0)} \qquad (12.3)$$

where $\bar{\delta}(g)$ is the average program length at generation g and $\bar{f}(g)$ is the average fitness in the population at generation g.

Figure 12-9a shows a boxplot of the amount of bloat for all the techniques, while Figure 12-9b zooms on the OpEq techniques, ignoring StdGP and leaving several outliers out. All the differences are significant except between DynOpEq and FlatOpEq2, and between FlatOpEq and MutOpEq. Since not all the techniques are allowed the same amount of search (based on the number of rejections, previous section), it is tempting to normalize the value of bloat somehow, for example dividing it by the number of rejections. This would follow the intuition that the more search is allowed, the more bloat may occur. However, we already know that OpEq contradicts this intuition, since some of the techniques with the highest amount of rejections (like FlatOpEq) exhibit a much better behavior than other techniques with much fewer rejections (like StdGP) in the plots of Figure 12-4. If we normalized bloat in this manner, FlatOpEq would appear to be even better and MutOpEq would seem to be the highest bloating technique. Therefore, we use the bloat values without normalization.

Using the values of the 20 runs of all the techniques (including StdGP), we have measured the correlation between bloat and the number of rejections, as well as the correlation between bloat and the flatness of the actual length distributions (when including StdGP it makes no sense to use the target distribution). The values obtained were -0.21 and 0.64, respectively. This means that bloat is negatively correlated to the number of rejections, confirming that more rejections means less bloat (previous paragraph), although the correlation is not strong; it also means, now strongly, that bloat is positively correlated to the

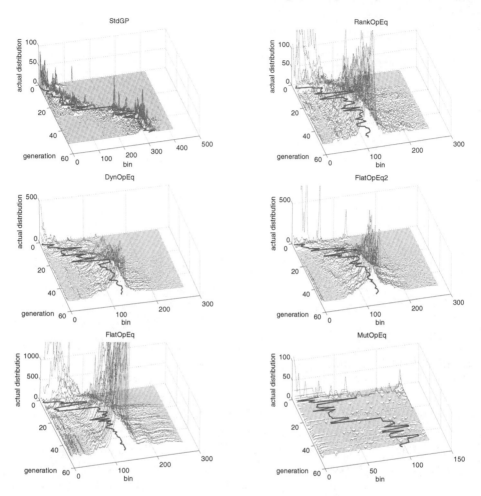

Figure 12-8. Examples of the joint acceptance and rejection distributions, representing where the search is performed. The thick line indicates where the best individual is found in each generation.

variance in the actual length distributions, which in practical terms means that flatter distributions result in less bloat. This supports the hypothesis advanced in (Silva, 2011) that, as far as bloat control is concerned, the flatter the better. If we do not consider StdGP and calculate the correlations only for the OpEq techniques we obtain the values of -0.20 and 0.30 (0.29 for the target instead of the actual distribution), respectively. Although not as strong as previously, the correlation is still there. If we measure the correlation between bloat and the flatness of the search as presented in Figure 12-7b we obtain the values -0.16 and -0.19 with and without StdGP, respectively. We conclude that bloat is

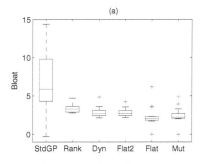 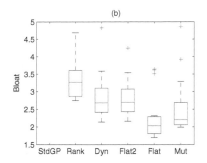

Figure 12-9. Boxplots of bloat (a) for all the techniques and (b) zooming on the OpEq techniques only, leaving several outliers out.

positively correlated with the flatness of the length distributions but not with the flatness of the search.

6. Summary and Conclusions

In the light of the new findings regarding OpEq (Silva, 2011) we have studied the importance of having flat program length distributions for successful bloat control. We have measured the flatness of the distributions found in previous and new OpEq variants and have correlated it with the amount of search performed by each approach. We have also analyzed where this search occurs and how bloat correlates to each of these properties. The discussion regarding the role of flatness on the unique behavior of OpEq allowed us to draw some conclusions, although some questions remain unanswered.

The main global question we want to answer is: Why does OpEq work so well? We have found that the actual length distributions of all OpEq techniques are significantly flatter than the ones of StdGP. However, we also realized that the search performed by OpEq is not more uniformly distributed across the different lengths than the search performed by StdGP. All the techniques except MutOpEq exhibit a similar search behavior, with the only difference that StdGP moves this search to higher lengths while the OpEq techniques keep it concentrated in smaller individuals. Bloat was found to be positively correlated with the flatness of the length distributions, not with the flatness of the search. So how do the flat length distributions allow OpEq to maintain the non-flat search concentrated on lower lengths? The constraints applied to OpEq do not prevent its search from following the same path as StdGP, so why do they follow different paths? The reason may be the same that explains why the targets of DynOpEq and MutOpEq are different, as described in Section 5.0. In the first generation, they are expected to be the same, but as the target for each generation always depends on the population of the previous generation, small differences propagate during the evolution and may result in highly diverging paths.

The small difference between StdGP and OpEq is that, through a high number of rejections on the most "popular" lengths, OpEq increases the chances of creating less common individuals, the ones with lengths farther away from the search peaks shown in Section 5.0. From these, the smaller ones are promptly accepted while the larger ones are usually rejected unless they prove to be the best. Therefore, OpEq promotes the acceptance of smaller-than-best individuals. The simple presence of these individuals in the population increases the probability that they become parents to the next generation. Smaller parents generate on average smaller offspring, thus biasing the search to lower lengths. StdGP cannot use these smaller-than-best individuals as parents because they are not even given the chance of being created from the previous generation. We may question if the fitness of these smaller-than-best individuals is important, or if they simply need to be part of the population to create the bias towards smaller offspring. By definition they are less fit than the best, but we cannot compare them to their StdGP counterparts because in StdGP they do not exist. So we can only hypothesize that OpEq may be simply decreasing the selective pressure by choosing worse individuals to become parents, something that is well known to reduce bloat.

Assuming that the last paragraph provides a reasonable explanation for the OpEq bias to search smaller lengths, another question arises: Why does the average program length stabilize after only a few generations? Different OpEq variants have length distributions with different values of flatness, either in benchmarks or in real-world problems, and yet they all reach this stabilization, while StdGP keeps increasing the average program length as long as the evolution continues (see Figures 12-1 and 12-4 and also (Vanneschi and Silva, 2009; Silva et al., 2010)). Even MutOpEq, the exceptional variant that produces OpEq-like behavior without rejections or a search peak (see Figure 12-8, bottom right plot), stabilizes the average program length very rapidly. Would longer runs result in additional, albeit slow, code growth, or does OpEq effectively find the "right" lengths to search? These questions remain open and finding their answers is one of the main goals of our current research.

We finalize by remarking once again the exceptional results that MutOpEq obtains at the expense of only minimal search effort. To perform fair comparisons among the different OpEq variants it is important to allow them the same amount of effort. For MutOpEq this is even more important, as only with longer runs we will be able to know its true potential.

Acknowledgments. This work was partially supported by FCT (INESC-ID multiannual funding) through the PIDDAC Program funds. The authors also acknowledge project PTDC/EIA-CCO/103363/2008 from FCT, Portugal.

References

Archetti, Francesco, Lanzeni, Stefano, Messina, Enza, and Vanneschi, Leonardo (2006). Genetic programming for human oral bioavailability of drugs. In Keijzer, Maarten et al., editors, *GECCO 2006: Proceedings of the 8th annual conference on Genetic and evolutionary computation*, volume 1, pages 255–262, Seattle, Washington, USA. ACM Press.

Archetti, Francesco, Lanzeni, Stefano, Messina, Enza, and Vanneschi, Leonardo (2007). Genetic programming for computational pharmacokinetics in drug discovery and development. *Genetic Programming and Evolvable Machines*, 8(4):413–432. special issue on medical applications of Genetic and Evolutionary Computation.

Dignum, Stephen and Poli, Riccardo (2007). Generalisation of the limiting distribution of program sizes in tree-based genetic programming and analysis of its effects on bloat. In Thierens, Dirk et al., editors, *GECCO '07: Proceedings of the 9th annual conference on Genetic and evolutionary computation*, volume 2, pages 1588–1595, London. ACM Press.

Dignum, Stephen and Poli, Riccardo (2008a). Crossover, sampling, bloat and the harmful effects of size limits. In O'Neill, Michael et al., editors, *Proceedings of the 11th European Conference on Genetic Programming, EuroGP 2008*, volume 4971 of *Lecture Notes in Computer Science*, pages 158–169, Naples. Springer.

Dignum, Stephen and Poli, Riccardo (2008b). Operator equalisation and bloat free GP. In O'Neill, Michael et al., editors, *Proceedings of the 11th European Conference on Genetic Programming, EuroGP 2008*, volume 4971 of *Lecture Notes in Computer Science*, pages 110–121, Naples. Springer.

Igel, Christian and Chellapilla, Kumar (1999). Investigating the influence of depth and degree of genotypic change on fitness in genetic programming. In Banzhaf, Wolfgang et al., editors, *Proceedings of the Genetic and Evolutionary Computation Conference*, volume 2, pages 1061–1068, Orlando, Florida, USA. Morgan Kaufmann.

Koza, John R. (1992). *Genetic Programming: On the Programming of Computers by Means of Natural Selection*. MIT Press, Cambridge, MA, USA.

Luke, Sean (2003). Modification point depth and genome growth in genetic programming. *Evolutionary Computation*, 11(1):67–106.

Poli, Riccardo, Langdon, William B., and Dignum, Stephen (2007). On the limiting distribution of program sizes in tree-based genetic programming. In Ebner, Marc et al., editors, *Proceedings of the 10th European Conference on Genetic Programming*, volume 4445 of *Lecture Notes in Computer Science*, pages 193–204, Valencia, Spain. Springer.

Poli, Riccardo, McPhee, Nicholas F., and Vanneschi, Leonardo (2008a). Analysis of the effects of elitism on bloat in linear and tree-based genetic programming. In Riolo, Rick L., Soule, Terence, and Worzel, Bill, editors, *Genetic Programming Theory and Practice VI*, Genetic and Evolutionary Computation, chapter 7, pages 91–111. Springer, Ann Arbor.

Poli, Riccardo, McPhee, Nicholas F., and Vanneschi, Leonardo (2008b). The impact of population size on code growth in GP: analysis and empirical validation. In Keijzer, Maarten et al., editors, *GECCO '08: Proceedings of the 10th annual conference on Genetic and evolutionary computation*, pages 1275–1282, Atlanta, GA, USA. ACM.

Poli, Riccardo, McPhee, Nicholas Freitag, and Vanneschi, Leonardo (2008c). Elitism reduces bloat in genetic programming. In Keijzer, Maarten et al., editors, *GECCO '08: Proceedings of the 10th annual conference on Genetic and evolutionary computation*, pages 1343–1344, Atlanta, GA, USA. ACM.

Silva, Sara (2011). Reassembling operator equalisation - a secret revealed. In *Genetic and Evolutionary Computation Conference (GECCO-2011)*. ACM Press.

Silva, Sara and Almeida, Jonas (2003). Dynamic maximum tree depth. In Cantú-Paz, E. et al., editors, *Genetic and Evolutionary Computation – GECCO-2003*, volume 2724 of *LNCS*, pages 1776–1787, Chicago. Springer-Verlag.

Silva, Sara and Costa, Ernesto (2004). Dynamic limits for bloat control: Variations on size and depth. In Deb, Kalyanmoy et al., editors, *Genetic and Evolutionary Computation – GECCO-2004, Part II*, volume 3103 of *Lecture Notes in Computer Science*, pages 666–677, Seattle, WA, USA. Springer-Verlag.

Silva, Sara and Costa, Ernesto (2009). Dynamic limits for bloat control in genetic programming and a review of past and current bloat theories. *Genetic Programming and Evolvable Machines*, 10(2):141–179.

Silva, Sara and Dignum, Stephen (2009). Extending operator equalisation: Fitness based self adaptive length distribution for bloat free GP. In Vanneschi, Leonardo et al., editors, *Proceedings of the 12th European Conference on Genetic Programming, EuroGP 2009*, volume 5481 of *LNCS*, pages 159–170, Tuebingen. Springer.

Silva, Sara and Vanneschi, Leonardo (2009). Operator equalisation, bloat and overfitting: a study on human oral bioavailability prediction. In Raidl, Guenther et al., editors, *GECCO '09: Proceedings of the 11th Annual conference on Genetic and evolutionary computation*, pages 1115–1122, Montreal. ACM.

Silva, Sara and Vanneschi, Leonardo (2012). Bloat free genetic programming: Application to human oral bioavailability prediction. *International Journal of Data Mining and Bioinformatics*. to appear.

Silva, Sara, Vasconcelos, Maria, and Melo, Joana (2010). Bloat free genetic programming versus classification trees for identification of burned areas in satellite imagery. In Di Chio, Cecilia et al., editors, *EvoIASP*, volume 6024 of *LNCS*, Istanbul. Springer.

Tackett, Walter Alden (1994). *Recombination, Selection, and the Genetic Construction of Computer Programs*. PhD thesis, University of Southern California, Department of Electrical Engineering Systems, USA.

Vanneschi, Leonardo (2004). *Theory and Practice for Efficient Genetic Programming*. PhD thesis, Faculty of Sciences, University of Lausanne, Switzerland.

Vanneschi, Leonardo, Castelli, Mauro, and Silva, Sara (2010). Measuring bloat, overfitting and functional complexity in genetic programming. In Branke, Juergen et al., editors, *GECCO '10: Proceedings of the 12th annual conference on Genetic and evolutionary computation*, pages 877–884, Portland, Oregon, USA. ACM.

Vanneschi, Leonardo and Silva, Sara (2009). Using operator equalisation for prediction of drug toxicity with genetic programming. In Lopes, Luis Seabra, Lau, Nuno, Mariano, Pedro, and Rocha, Luis Mateus, editors, *Progress in Artificial Intelligence, 14th Portuguese Conference on Artificial Intelligence, EPIA 2009*, volume 5816 of *LNAI*, pages 65–76, Aveiro, Portugal. Springer.

Vanneschi, Leonardo, Tomassini, Marco, Collard, Philippe, and Clergue, Manuel (2003). Fitness distance correlation in structural mutation genetic programming. In Ryan, Conor et al., editors, *Genetic Programming, Proceedings of EuroGP'2003*, volume 2610 of *LNCS*, pages 455–464, Essex. Springer-Verlag.

Chapter 13

FFX: FAST, SCALABLE, DETERMINISTIC SYMBOLIC REGRESSION TECHNOLOGY

Trent McConaghy[1]

[1] *Solido Design Automation Inc., Canada*

Abstract

Symbolic regression is a common application for genetic programming (GP). This paper presents a new non-evolutionary technique for symbolic regression that, compared to competent GP approaches on real-world problems, is orders of magnitude faster (taking just seconds), returns simpler models, has comparable or better prediction on unseen data, and converges reliably and deterministically. I dub the approach FFX, for Fast Function Extraction. FFX uses a recently-developed machine learning technique, pathwise regularized learning, to rapidly prune a huge set of candidate basis functions down to compact models. FFX is verified on a broad set of real-world problems having 13 to 1468 input variables, outperforming GP as well as several state-of-the-art regression techniques.

Keywords: technology, symbolic regression, genetic programming, pathwise, regularization, real-world problems, machine learning, lasso, ridge regression, elastic net, integrated circuits

1. Introduction

Consider when we type "A/B" into a math package. This is a least-squares (LS) linear regression problem. The software simply returns an answer. We do not need to consider the intricacies of the theory, algorithms, and implementations of LS regression because others have already done it. LS regression is fast, scalable, and deterministic. *It just works.*

This gets to the concept of "technology" as used by Boyd: "We can say that solving least-squares problems is a (mature) technology, that can be reliably used by many people who do not know, and do not need to know, the details" (Boyd and Vandenberghe, 2004). Boyd cites LS and linear programming as representative examples, and convex optimization getting close. Other examples might include linear algebra, classical statistics, Monte Carlo methods, software compilers, SAT solvers[1], and CLP solvers[2].

(McConaghy et al., 2010) asked: "What does it take to make genetic programming (GP) a technology? ... to be adopted into broader use beyond that of expert practitioners? ... so that it becomes another standard, off-the-shelf method in the 'toolboxes' of scientists and engineers around the world?"

This paper asks what it takes to make symbolic regression (SR) a technology. SR is the automated extraction of whitebox models that map input variables to output variables. GP (Koza, 1992) is a popular approach to do SR, with successful applications to real-world problems such as industrial processing (Smits et al., 2010; Castillo et al., 2010), finance (Korns, 2010; Kim et al., 2008), robotics (Schmidt and Lipson, 2006), and integrated circuit design (McConaghy and Gielen, 2009).

Outside the GP literature, SR is rare; there are only scattered references such as (Langley et al., 1987). In contrast, the GP literature has dozens of papers on SR every year; even the previous GPTP workshops had seven papers involving SR (Riolo et al., 2010). In a sense, the home field of SR is GP. This means, of course, that when authors aim at SR, they start with GP, and look to modify GP to improve speed, scalability, reliability, interpretability, etc. The improvements are typically 2x to 10x, but fall short of performance that would make SR a "technology" the way LS or linear programming is.

We are aiming for SR as a technology. What if we did not constrain ourselves to using GP? To GP researchers, this may seem heretical at first glance. But if the aim is truly to improve SR, then this should pose no issue. And in fact, we argue that the GP literature is still an appropriate home for such work, because (a) GP authors doing SR deeply care about SR problems, and (b) as already mentioned, GP is where all the SR publications are. Of course, we can draw inspiration from GP literature, but also many other potentially-useful fields.

This paper presents a new technique for SR, called FFX – Fast Function Extraction. Because of its speed, scalability, and deterministic behavior, FFX has behavior approaching that of a technology. FFX's steps are:

- Enumerate to generate a massive set of linear and nonlinear basis functions.

- Use pathwise regularized learning to find coefficient values for the basis functions in mapping to y. Pathwise learning actually returns a *set* of coefficient vectors; with each successive vector explaining the training data better but with greater risk of overfitting. This has the computational cost of a single LS regression, thanks to recent developments in machine learning (Friedman et al., 2010; Zou and Hastie, 2005).

[1] for boolean satisfiability problems.
[2] for constraint logic programming.

- Nondominated-filter to the number of bases versus the testing or training error.

While FFX does not use GP directly, it will become evident that its aims and design are GP-influenced.

I will compare FFX to a competent GP-SR approach on a set of real-world problems. I will see that FFX returns simpler models, has comparable or better prediction on unseen data, and is completely deterministic. Figure 13-4 summarizes the key result of this paper. Furthermore, I will show how to successfully scale FFX to real-world problems having >1000 input variables, which to my knowledge is the most input variables that any SR technique has attacked[3].

The rest of this paper is organized as follows. Section 2 describes the SR problem. Section 3 describes pathwise regularized learning. Section 4 describes the FFX algorithm, and section 5 presents results using the algorithm. Section 6 scales up FFX, guided by theory. Section 7 gives results using the scalable FFX algorithm. Section 8 gives related work in GP and elsewhere. Section 9 concludes.

2.   SR Problem Definition

Given: X and y, a set of $\{x_j, y_j\}, j = 1..N$ data samples where x_j is an n-dimensional point j and y_j is a corresponding output value. Determine: a set of symbolic models $M = m_1, m_2, \ldots$ that provide the Pareto-optimal tradeoff between minimizing model complexity $f_1(m)$ and minimizing expected future model prediction error $f_2 = E_{x,y}L(m)$ where $L(m)$ is the squared-error loss function $y - m(x)^2$. Each model m maps an n-dimensional input x to a scalar output value $\hat{y}$, i.e., $\hat{y} = m(x)$. Complexity is *some* measure that differentiates the degrees of freedom between different models; I use the number of basis functions.

I restrict myself to the class of generalized linear models (GLMs) (Nelder and Wedderburn, 1972). A GLM is a linear combination of N_B basis functions $B_i; i = 1, 2, ..., N_B$:

$$\hat{y} = m(x) = a_0 + \sum_{i=1}^{N_B} a_i * B_i(x) \tag{13.1}$$

3.   Background: Pathwise Regularized Learning

Least-squares (LS) learning aims to find the values for each coefficient a_i in Equation (13.1) that minimize $||y - X*a||^2$, where the X and y are training data.

---

[3]To be precise: attacked directly, without pre-filtering input variables or transforming to a smaller dimensionality.

Therefore LS learning aims to minimize training error; it does not acknowledge testing error (future model prediction error). Because it is singularly focused on training error, LS learning may return model coefficients a where a few coefficients are extremely large, making the model overly sensitive to those coefficients. This is overfitting.

Regularized learning aims to minimize the model's sensitivity to overfit coefficient values, by adding minimization terms that are dependent solely on the coefficients: $||a||^2$ or $||a||_1$. This has the implicit effect of minimizing expected future model prediction error. The overall problem formulation is:

$$a^* = minimize \; ||y - X * a||^2 + \lambda_2 ||a||^2 + \lambda_1 ||a||_1 \qquad (13.2)$$

Including both regularization terms is an *elastic net* formulation of regularized learning (Zou and Hastie, 2005)[4]. To make the balance between λ_1 and λ_2 explicit, we can set $\lambda_1 = \lambda$ and $\lambda_2 = (1 - \rho) * \lambda$, where λ is now the regularization weight, and ρ is a "mixing parameter."

A *path* of solutions sweeps across a set of possible λ values; returning an a for each λ. Interestingly, we can start at a *huge* value of λ, where all a_i are zero; then work towards smaller λ, uniformly on a log scale. Figure 13-1 illustrates: the path starts on the far left, and the with λ decreasing (going right), coefficients a_i take nonzero values one at a time.

An extremely fast variant of pathwise elastic nets was recently developed / rediscovered: coordinate descent (Friedman et al., 2010). At each point on the path, coordinate descent solves for coefficient vector a by: looping through each a_i one at a time, updating the a_i through a trivial formula while holding the rest of the parameters fixed, and repeating until a stabilizes. For speed, it uses "hot starts": at each new point on the path, coordinate descent starts with the previous point's a.

Some highly useful properties of pathwise regularized learning are:

- Learning speed is comparable or better than LS.
- Unlike LS, can learn when there are fewer samples than coefficients $N < n$.
- Can learn thousands or more coefficients.
- It returns a whole *family* of coefficient vectors, with different tradeoffs between number of nonzero coefficients and training accuracy.

For further details, we refer the reader to (Zou and Hastie, 2005; Friedman et al., 2010).

---

[4]The middle term (quadratic term, like ridge regression), encourages correlated variables to group together rather than letting a single variable dominate, and makes convergence more stable. The last term (l_1 term, like lasso), drives towards a sparse model with few coefficients, but discourages any coefficient from being too large. $||a||_1 = \sum_i |a_i|$.

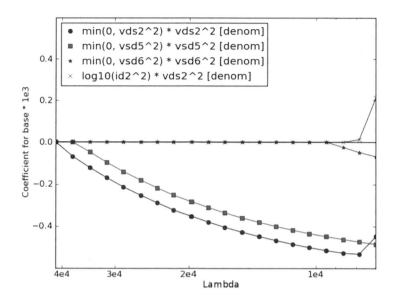

Figure 13-1. A path of regularized regression solutions: each vertical slice of the plot gives a vector of coefficient values a for each of the respective basis functions. Going left to right (decreasing λ), each coefficient a_i follows its own path, starting at zero then increasing in magnitude (and sometimes decreasing).

4. FFX Algorithm

The FFX algorithm has three steps, which I now elaborate.

FFX Step One. Here, FFX generates a massive set of basis functions, where each basis function combines one or more interacting nonlinear subfunctions.

Table 13-1 gives the pseudocode. Steps 1-10 generate univariate bases, and steps 11-20 generate bivariate bases (and higher orders of univariate bases). The algorithm simply has nested loops to generate all the bases. The *eval* function (line 5, 9, and 18) evaluates a base b given input data X; that is, it runs the function defined by b with input vectors in X. The *ok*() function returns $False$ if any evaluated value is inf, - inf, or NaN, e.g., as caused by divide-by-zero, log on negative values, or negative exponents on negative values. Therefore, *ok* filters away all poorly-behaving expressions. Line 16 means that expressions of the form $op() * op()$ are not allowed; these are deemed too complex.

FFX Step Two. Here, FFX uses pathwise regularized learning (Zou and Hastie, 2005) to identify the best coefficients and bases when there are 0 bases, 1 base, 2 bases, and so on.

Table 13-2 gives the pseudocode. Steps 1-2 create a large matrix X_B which has evaluated input matrix X on each of the basis functions in B. Steps 3-4

Table 13-1.   Step One: GenerateBases()

Inputs: X #input training data
Outputs: B #list of bases

\# Generate univariate bases
1. $B_1 = \{\}$
2. for each input variable $v = \{x_1, x_2, \ldots\}$
3.   for each exponent $exp = \{0.5, 1.0, 2.0\}$
4.   let expression $b_{exp} = v^{exp}$
5.   if $ok(eval(b_{exp}, X))$
6.   add b_{exp} to B_1
7.   for each operator $op = \{abs(), log_{10}, \ldots\}$
8.   let expression $b_{op} = op(b_{exp})$
9.   if $ok(eval(b_{op}, X))$
10.   add b_{op} to B_1

\# Generate interacting-variable bases
11. $B_2 = \{\}$
12. for $i = 1$ to $length(B_1)$
13.   let expression $b_i = B_1[i]$
14.   for $j = 1$ to $i - 1$
15.   let expression $b_j = B_1[j]$
16.   if b_j is not an operator # disallow $op() * op()$
17.   let expression $b_{inter} = b_i * b_j$
18.   if $ok(eval(b_{inter}, X))$
19.   add b_{inter} to B_2
20. return $B = B_1 \cup B_2$

---

determine a log-spaced set of N_λ values; see (Zou and Hastie, 2005) for motivations here. Steps 5-16 are the main work, doing pathwise learning. At each iteration of the loop it performs an elastic-net linear fit (line 11) from $X_B \mapsto y$ to find the linear coefficients a. As the loop iterates, N_{bases} tends to increase, because with smaller λ there is more pressure to explain the training data better, therefore requiring the usage of more nonzero coefficients. Once a coefficient value a_i is nonzero, its magnitude tends to increase, though sometimes it will decrease as another coefficient proves to be more useful in explaining the data.

FFX step two is like standard pathwise regularized learning, *except* that whereas the standard approach covers a whole range of λ such that all coefficients eventually get included, FFX stops as soon as there are more than $N_{max-bases}$ (e.g., 5) nonzero coefficients (line 9). Naturally, this is because in the SR application, expressions with more than $N_{max-bases}$ are no longer interpretable. In practice, this makes an enormous difference to runtime; for example, if there are 7000 possible bases but the maximum number of bases is 5, and assuming that coefficients get added approximately uniformly with decreasing λ, then only 5/7000 = 1/1400 = 0.07% of the path must be covered.

Table 13-2. Step Two: PathwiseLearn()

Inputs: X, y, B #input data, output data, bases
Outputs: A #list of coeffcient-vectors

\# Compute X_B
1.   for $i = 1$ to $length(B)$
2. $X_B[i] = \text{eval}(B[i], X)$

\# Generate λ_{vec} = range of λ values
3. $\lambda_{max} = max(|X^T y|)/(N * \rho)$
4. $\lambda_{vec} = logspace(log_{10}(\lambda_{max} * eps), log_{10}(\lambda_{max}), N_{\lambda})$

\# Main pathwise learning
5. $A = \{\}$
6. $N_{bases} = 0$
7. $i = 0$
8. $a = \{0, 0, \ldots\}$ #length n
9.   while $N_{bases} < N_{max-bases}$ and $i < length(\lambda_{vec})$
10. $\lambda = \lambda_{vec}[i]$
11. $a = elasticNetLinearFit(X_B, y, \lambda, \rho, a)$
12. N_{bases} = number of nonzero values in a
13.   if $N_{bases} < N_{max-bases}$
14.   add a to A
15. $i = i + 1$
16. return A

In short, the special property of pathwise regularized learning, to start with zero coefficients and incrementally insert them (and therefore insert bases), reconciles extremely well with the SR objectives trading off complexity versus accuracy with an upper bound on complexity. To a GP practitioner, it feels like doing a whole multi-objective optimization for the cost of a single LS solve.

FFX Step Three. Here, FFX filters the candidate functions to a nondominated set that trades off number of bases and error.

Table 13-3 gives the pseudocode. Steps 1-8 take the coefficients and bases determined in previous FFX steps, and simply combine them to create a set of candidate models M_{cand}. Steps 9-13 apply standard nondominated filtering to the models, with objectives to minimize complexity (number of bases) and error.

Rational Functions Trick. For maximum coverage of possible functions, FFX leverages a special technique inspired by (Leung and Haykin, 1993) to include rational functions, with negligible extra computational cost. The general idea is: learning the coefficients of a rational function can be cast into a linear

Table 13-3. Step Three: NondominatedFilter()

Inputs: A, B # coefficient vectors, bases
Outputs: M # Pareto-optimal models

Construct candidate models
1. $M_{cand} = \{\}$
2. for $i = 1$ to length($\|A\|$)
3. $a = A[i]$
4. $a_0 = a[0]$ # offset
5. a_{nz} = nonzero values in a (ignoring offset)
6. B_{nz} = expressions in B corr. to nonzero values in a
7. m = model(a_0, a_{nz}, B_{nz}), following eqn. (13.1)
8.   add m to M_{cand}

Nondominated filtering
9. $f_1 = numBases(m)$, for each m in M_{cand}
10. $f_2 = testError(m)$ or $trainError(m)$, for each m in M_{cand}
11. J = nondominatedIndices(f_1, f_2)
12. $M = M_{cand}[j]$ for each j in J
13. return M

regression problem, solved with linear regression, then back-transformed into rational function form. Let us elaborate:

A rational function has the form:

$$\hat{y} = m(\boldsymbol{x}) = \frac{a_0 + \sum_{i=1}^{N_{BN}} a_i * B_i(\boldsymbol{x})}{1.0 + \sum_{i=N_{BN}+1}^{N'_B} a_i * B_i(\boldsymbol{x})} \tag{13.3}$$

where N'_B is the number of numerator bases (N_{BN}) plus the number of denominator bases (N_{BD}).

Let us perform simple algebraic manipulations to transform this problem. First, we multiply both sides by the denominator:

$$y * \left(1.0 + \sum_{i=N_{BN}+1}^{N'_B} a_i * B_i(\boldsymbol{x})\right) = a_0 + \sum_{i=1}^{N_{BN}} a_i * B_i(\boldsymbol{x}) \tag{13.4}$$

Then we expand the left-hand side:

$$y + \sum_{i=N_{BN}+1}^{N'_B} a_i * B_i(\boldsymbol{x}) * y = a_0 + \sum_{i=1}^{N_{BN}} a_i * B_i(\boldsymbol{x}) \tag{13.5}$$

where $B_i(\boldsymbol{x}) * y$ is element-wise multiplication, i.e., $B_i(\boldsymbol{X}_j) * y_j$ for each data point j. Now, subtract to isolate y on the left-hand side:

$$y = a_0 + \sum_{i=1}^{N_{BN}} a_i * B_i(\boldsymbol{x}) - \sum_{i=N_{BN}+1}^{N_B'} a_i * B_i(\boldsymbol{x}) * y \qquad (13.6)$$

Finally, let us define a new set of basis functions.

$$B_i' = \left\{ \begin{array}{ll} B_i & i \le N_{BN} \\ B_i * y & otherwise \end{array} \right\} \qquad (13.7)$$

At the end of FFX step 1, we had N_B basis functions. Before we start step 2, we insert all N_B functions into both the numerator and denominator; therefore $N_{BN} = N_{BD} = N_B$, and $N_B' = 2 * N_B$. We redefine the basis functions according to Equation (13.7). Then, all the subsequent FFX steps are performed with these new basis functions. Once the coefficients are found, the final model is extracted by applying the algebraic manipulations in reverse: Equation (13.6), then Equation (13.5), then Equation (13.4).

This concludes the description of the FFX algorithm. Note that for improved scalability, FFX must be adapted according to section 6.

5. Medium-Dimensional Experiments

This section presents experiments on medium-dimensional problems. (Section 7 will give higher-dimensional results.)

Experimental Setup

Problem Setup. I used a test problem used originally in (Daems et al., 2003) for posynomial fitting, but also studied extensively using GP-based SR (McConaghy and Gielen, 2009). The aim was to model performances of a well-known analog circuit, a CMOS operational transconductance amplifier (OTA). The goal was to find expressions for the OTA's performance measures: low-frequency gain (A_{LF}), phase margin (PM), positive and negative slew rate (SR_p, SR_n), input-referred offset voltage (V_{offset}), and unity-gain frequency (f_u)[5].

Each problem has 13 input variables. Input variable space was sampled with orthogonal-hypercube Design-Of-Experiments (DOE) (Montgomery, 2009), with scaled $dx = 0.1$ (where dx is % change in variable value from center value), to get 243 samples. Each point was simulated with SPICE. These points were used as training data inputs. Testing data points were also sampled with DOE and 243 samples, but with $dx = 0.03$. Thus, this experiment leads to somewhat localized models; we could just as readily model a broader design space, but

---

[5]We log-scale f_u so that learning is not wrongly biased towards high-magnitude samples of f_u.

this allows us to compare the results to (Daems et al., 2003). I calculate normalized mean-squared error on the training data and on the separate testing data:

$$nmse = \sqrt{\sum_i ((\widehat{y}_i - y_i)/(max(\mathbf{y}) - min(\mathbf{y}))^2)}$$

FFX Setup. Up to $N_{max-bases}$=5 bases are allowed. Operators allowed are: $abs(x)$, $log_{10}(x)$, $min(0, x)$, $max(0, x)$; and exponents on variables are $x^{1/2}$ (=$\sqrt{(x)}$), x^1 (=x), and x^2. By default, denominators are allowed; but if turned off, then negative exponents are also allowed: $x^{-1/2}$ (=$1/\sqrt{(x)}$), x^{-1} (=$1/x$), and x^{-2} (=$1/x^2$). The elastic net settings were $\rho = 0.5$, $\lambda_{max} = max|\mathbf{X}^T\mathbf{y}|/(N * \rho)$, $eps = 10^{-70}$, and N_λ=1000.

Because the algorithm is not GP, there are no settings for population size, number of generations, mutation/crossover rate, selection, etc. I emphasize that the settings in the previous paragraph are very simple, with no tuning needed by users.

Each FFX run took ≈5 s on a 1-GHz single-core CPU.

Reference GP-SR Algorithm Setup. CAFFEINE is a state-of-the-art GP-based SR approach that uses a thoughtfully-designed grammar to constrain SR functional forms such that they are interpretable by construction. Key settings are: up to 15 bases, population size 200, and 5000 generations. Details are in (McConaghy and Gielen, 2009). Each CAFFEINE run took ≈10 minutes on a 1-GHz CPU.

Experimental Results

This section experimentally investigates FFX behavior, and validates its prediction abilities on the set of six benchmark functions.

FFX Data Flow. To start with, I examine FFX behavior in detail on a test problem. Recall that FFX has three steps: generating the bases, pathwise learning on the bases, and pruning the results via nondominated filtering. I examine the data flow of these steps on the A_{LF} problem.

The first step in FFX generated 176 candidate one-variable bases, as shown in Table 13-4. These bases combined to make 3374 two-variable bases, some of which are shown in Table 13-5. This made a total of 3550 bases for the numerator; and another 3550 for the denominator[6].

The second FFX step applied pathwise regularized learning on the 7100 bases (3550 numerator + 3550 denominator), as illustrated in Figure 13-1 (previously shown to introduce pathwise learning). It started with maximum lambda (λ), where all coefficient values were 0.0, and therefore there are 0 (far left of figure). Then, it iteratively decreased λ and updated the coefficient estimates. The first

---

[6]See "Rational Functions Trick" in section 4.

Table 13-4. For FFX step 1: The 176 candidate one-variable bases.

$v_{sg1}^{0.5}$, $abs(v_{sg1}^{0.5})$, $max(0, v_{sg1}^{0.5})$, $min(0, v_{sg1}^{0.5})$, $log_{10}(v_{sg1}^{0.5})$, v_{sg1}, $abs(v_{sg1})$, $max(0, v_{sg1})$, $min(0, v_{sg1})$, $log_{10}(v_{sg1})$, v_{sg1}^2, $max(0, v_{sg1}^2)$, $min(0, v_{sg1}^2)$, $log_{10}(v_{sg1}^2)$, $v_{gs2}^{0.5}$, $abs(v_{gs2}^{0.5})$, $max(0, v_{gs2}^{0.5})$, $min(0, v_{gs2}^{0.5})$, $log_{10}(v_{gs2}^{0.5})$, v_{gs2}, $abs(v_{gs2})$, $max(0, v_{gs2})$, $min(0, v_{gs2})$, $log_{10}(v_{gs2})$, v_{gs2}^2, $max(0, v_{gs2}^2)$, $min(0, v_{gs2}^2)$, $log_{10}(v_{gs2}^2)$, $v_{ds2}^{0.5}$, $abs(v_{ds2}^{0.5})$, $max(0, v_{ds2}^{0.5})$, $min(0, v_{ds2}^{0.5})$, $log_{10}(v_{ds2}^{0.5})$, v_{ds2}, $abs(v_{ds2})$, $max(0, v_{ds2})$, $min(0, v_{ds2})$, $log_{10}(v_{ds2})$, v_{ds2}^2, $max(0, v_{ds2}^2)$, $min(0, v_{ds2}^2)$, $log_{10}(v_{ds2}^2)$, $v_{sg3}^{0.5}$, $abs(v_{sg3}^{0.5})$, $max(0, v_{sg3}^{0.5})$, $min(0, v_{sg3}^{0.5})$, $log_{10}(v_{sg3}^{0.5})$, v_{sg3}, $abs(v_{sg3})$, $max(0, v_{sg3})$, $min(0, v_{sg3})$, $log_{10}(v_{sg3})$, v_{sg3}^2, $max(0, v_{sg3}^2)$, $min(0, v_{sg3}^2)$, $log_{10}(v_{sg3}^2)$, $v_{sg4}^{0.5}$, $abs(v_{sg4}^{0.5})$, $max(0, v_{sg4}^{0.5})$, $min(0, v_{sg4}^{0.5})$, $log_{10}(v_{sg4}^{0.5})$, v_{sg4}, $abs(v_{sg4})$, $max(0, v_{sg4})$, $min(0, v_{sg4})$, $log_{10}(v_{sg4})$, v_{sg4}^2, $max(0, v_{sg4}^2)$, $min(0, v_{sg4}^2)$, $log_{10}(v_{sg4}^2)$, $v_{sg5}^{0.5}$, $abs(v_{sg5}^{0.5})$, $max(0, v_{sg5}^{0.5})$, $min(0, v_{sg5}^{0.5})$, $log_{10}(v_{sg5}^{0.5})$, v_{sg5}, $abs(v_{sg5})$, $max(0, v_{sg5})$, $min(0, v_{sg5})$, $log_{10}(v_{sg5})$, v_{sg5}^2, $max(0, v_{sg5}^2)$, $min(0, v_{sg5}^2)$, $log_{10}(v_{sg5}^2)$, $v_{sd5}^{0.5}$, $abs(v_{sd5}^{0.5})$, $max(0, v_{sd5}^{0.5})$, $min(0, v_{sd5}^{0.5})$, $log_{10}(v_{sd5}^{0.5})$, v_{sd5}, $abs(v_{sd5})$, $max(0, v_{sd5})$, $min(0, v_{sd5})$, $log_{10}(v_{sd5})$, v_{sd5}^2, $max(0, v_{sd5}^2)$, $min(0, v_{sd5}^2)$, $log_{10}(v_{sd5}^2)$, $v_{sd6}^{0.5}$, $abs(v_{sd6}^{0.5})$, $max(0, v_{sd6}^{0.5})$, $min(0, v_{sd6}^{0.5})$, $log_{10}(v_{sd6}^{0.5})$, v_{sd6}, $abs(v_{sd6})$, $max(0, v_{sd6})$, $min(0, v_{sd6})$, $log_{10}(v_{sd6})$, v_{sd6}^2, $max(0, v_{sd6}^2)$, $min(0, v_{sd6}^2)$, $log_{10}(v_{sd6}^2)$, i_{d1}, $abs(i_{d1})$, $max(0, i_{d1})$, $min(0, i_{d1})$, i_{d1}^2, $max(0, i_{d1}^2)$, $min(0, i_{d1}^2)$, $log_{10}(i_{d1}^2)$, $i_{d2}^{0.5}$, $abs(i_{d2}^{0.5})$, $max(0, i_{d2}^{0.5})$, $min(0, i_{d2}^{0.5})$, $log_{10}(i_{d2}^{0.5})$, i_{d2}, $abs(i_{d2})$, $max(0, i_{d2})$, $min(0, i_{d2})$, $log_{10}(i_{d2})$, i_{d2}^2, $max(0, i_{d2}^2)$, $min(0, i_{d2}^2)$, $log_{10}(i_{d2}^2)$, $i_{b1}^{0.5}$, $abs(i_{b1}^{0.5})$, $max(0, i_{b1}^{0.5})$, $min(0, i_{b1}^{0.5})$, $log_{10}(i_{b1}^{0.5})$, i_{b1}, $abs(i_{b1})$, $max(0, i_{b1})$, $min(0, i_{b1})$, $log_{10}(i_{b1})$, i_{b1}^2, $max(0, i_{b1}^2)$, $min(0, i_{b1}^2)$, $log_{10}(i_{b1}^2)$, $i_{b2}^{0.5}$, $abs(i_{b2}^{0.5})$, $max(0, i_{b2}^{0.5})$, $min(0, i_{b2}^{0.5})$, $log_{10}(i_{b2}^{0.5})$, i_{b2}, $abs(i_{b2})$, $max(0, i_{b2})$, $min(0, i_{b2})$, $log_{10}(i_{b2})$, i_{b2}^2, $max(0, i_{b2}^2)$, $min(0, i_{b2}^2)$, $log_{10}(i_{b2}^2)$, $i_{b3}^{0.5}$, $abs(i_{b3}^{0.5})$, $max(0, i_{b3}^{0.5})$, $min(0, i_{b3}^{0.5})$, $log_{10}(i_{b3}^{0.5})$, i_{b3}, $abs(i_{b3})$, $max(0, i_{b3})$, $min(0, i_{b3})$, $log_{10}(i_{b3})$, i_{b3}^2, $max(0, i_{b3}^2)$, $min(0, i_{b3}^2)$, $log_{10}(i_{b3}^2)$

Table 13-5. For FFX step 1: Some candidate two-variable bases (there are 3374 total).

$log_{10}(i_{b3}^2)*i_{d2}^2$, $log_{10}(i_{b3}^2)*i_{b1}^{0.5}$, $log_{10}(i_{b3}^2)*i_{b1}$, $log_{10}(i_{b3}^2)*i_{b1}^2$, $log_{10}(i_{b3}^2)*i_{b2}^{0.5}$, $log_{10}(i_{b3}^2)*i_{b2}$,
$log_{10}(i_{b3}^2) * i_{b2}^2$, $log_{10}(i_{b3}^2) * i_{b3}^{0.5}$, $log_{10}(i_{b3}^2) * i_{b3}$, $log_{10}(i_{b3}^2) * i_{b3}^2$

(and 3364 more)

base to get a nonzero coefficient was $min(0, v_{ds2}^2) * v_{ds2}^2$ (in the denominator). At a slightly smaller λ, the second base to get a nonzero coefficient was $min(0, v_{sd5}^2) * v_{sd5}^2$ (also in the denominator). These remain the only two bases for several iterations, until finally when λ shrinks below 1e4, a third base is added. A fourth base is added shortly after. Pathwise learning continued until the maximum number of bases (nonzero coefficients) was hit.

The third and final FFX step applies nondominated filtering to the candidate models, to generate the Pareto Optimal sets that trade off error versus number of bases (complexity). Figure 13-3 shows the outcome of nondominated filtering, for the case when error is training error, and for the case when error is testing error. Training error for this data is higher than testing error because the training data covers a broader input variable range ($dx = 0.1$) than the testing data ($dx = 0.03$), as section 5 discussed.

Extracted Whitebox Models. Table 13-6 shows the lowest test-error functions extracted by FFX, for each test problem. First, we see that the test errors are all very low, <5% in all cases. Second, we see that the functions themselves are fairly simple and interpretable, at most having two basis functions. For

Genetic Programming Theory and Practice IX

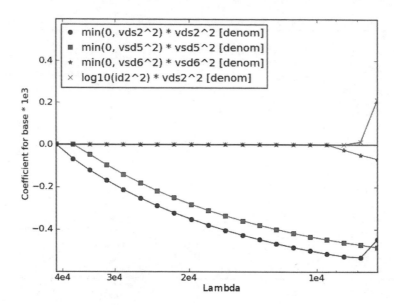

Figure 13-2. For FFX step 2: Pathwise regularized learning following on A_{LF}.

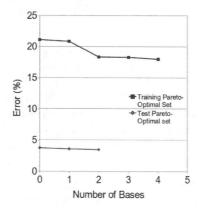

Figure 13-3. For FFX step 3: results of nondominated filtering to get the Pareto optimal tradeoff of error versus number of bases, in modeling A_{LF}. Two cases are shown: when error is on the training data, and when error is on testing data.

A_{LF}, PM, and SR_n, FFX determined that using a denominator was better. I continue to find it remarkable that functions like this can be extracted in such a computationally lightweight fashion. For SR_p, FFX determined that the most predictive function was simply a constant (2.35e7). Interestingly, it combined univariate bases of the same variable to get higher-order bases, for example $min(0, v_{ds2}^2) * v_{ds2}^2$ in A_{LF}.

Table 13-6. Functions with lowest test error as extracted by FFX, for each test problem. Extraction time per problem was ≈5 s on a 1-GHz machine.

Problem	Test error (%)	Extracted Function
A_{LF}	3.45	$\dfrac{37.020}{1.0-1.22e\text{-}4*min(0,v_{ds2}^2)*v_{ds2}^2-4.72e\text{-}5*min(0,v_{sd5}^2)*v_{sd5}^2}$
PM	1.51	$\dfrac{90.148}{1.0-8.79e\text{-}6*min(0,v_{sg1}^2)*v_{sg1}^2+2.28e\text{-}6*min(0,v_{ds2}^2)*v_{ds2}^2}$
SR_n	2.10	$\dfrac{-5.21e7}{1.0-8.22e\text{-}5*min(0,v_{gs2}^2)*v_{gs2}^2}$
SR_p	4.74	$2.35e7$
V_{offset}	2.16	$-0.0020 - 1.22e\text{-}23 * min(0, v_{gs2}^2) * v_{gs2}^2$
$log_{10}(f_u)$	2.17	$0.74 - 1.10e\text{-}5 * min(0, v_{sg1}^2) * v_{sg1}^2$ $+1.88e\text{-}5 * min(0, v_{ds2}^2) * v_{ds2}^2$

Recall that what FFX does is designed to not just return the function with the lowest error, but a whole set of functions that trade off error and complexity. It does this efficiently by exploiting pathwise learning. Table 13-7 illustrates the Pareto optimal set extracted by FFX for the A_{LF} problem.

Table 13-7. Pareto optimal set (complexity vs. test error) for A_{LF} extracted by FFX.

Test error (%)	Extracted Function
3.72	37.619
3.55	$\dfrac{37.379}{1.0-6.78e\text{-}5*min(0,v_{ds2}^2)*v_{ds2}^2}$
3.45	$\dfrac{37.020}{1.0-1.22e\text{-}4*min(0,v_{ds2}^2)*v_{ds2}^2-4.72e\text{-}5*min(0,v_{sd5}^2)*v_{sd5}^2}$

Prediction Abilities. Figure 13-4 compares FFX to GP-SR, linear models, and quadratic models in terms of average test error and build time. The linear and quadratic models took <1 s to build, using LS learning. GP-SR and FFX predict very well, and linear and quadratic models predict poorly. GP-SR has much longer model-building time than the rest. In sum, FFX has the speed of linear/quadratic models with the prediction abilities of GP-SR.

Table 13-8 compares the test error for linear, quadratic, FFX, and GP-SR models; plus the approaches originally compared in (McConaghy and Gielen, 2005): posynomial (Daems et al., 2003), a modern feedforward neural network (FFNN) (Ampazis and Perantonis, 2002), boosting the FFNNs, multivariate

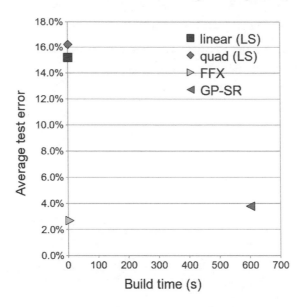

Figure 13-4. Average test error (across six test problems) versus build time, comparing linear, quadratic, FFX, and GP-SR

adaptive regression splines (MARS) (Friedman, 1991), least-squares support vector machines (SVM) (Suykens et al., 2002), and kriging (gaussian process models) (Sacks et al., 1989). Lowest-error values are in bold.

From Table 13-8, we see that of all the modeling approaches, FFX has the best average test error; and best test error in four of the six problems, coming close in the remaining two.

6.   FFX Scaling

Experimental Setup

So far, I have tested FFX on several problems with 13 input variables. What about larger real-world problems? I consider the real-world integrated circuits listed in Table 13-9. The aim is to map process variables to circuit performance outputs. Therefore, these problems have hundreds or thousands of input variables.

The data was generated by performing Monte Carlo sampling: drawing process points from the process variables' pdf, and simulating each process point using Hspice^{TM}, to get output values. The opamp and voltage reference had 800 Monte Carlo sample points, the comparator and GMC filter 2000, and bitcell and sense amp 5000. The data is chosen as follows: sort the data

Table 13-8. Test error (%) on the six medium-dimensional test problems.

Approach	A_{LF}	PM	SR_n	SR_p	V_{offset}	f_u	Avg.
Linear (LS)	17.2	11.9	15.6	20.5	7.1	19.0	15.21
Quadratic (LS)	18.5	12.2	15.7	22.7	7.4	20.9	16.23
FFX (this work)	3.5	**1.5**	**2.1**	**4.7**	2.2	**2.2**	**2.69**
GP-SR	**2.8**	2.6	3.9	7.4	1.0	5.0	3.78
Posynomial	6.5	9.7	78.0	31.0	**0.8**	5.9	21.98
FFNN	5.0	6.8	9.5	8.2	2.9	9.3	6.93
Boosted FFNN	5.3	2.8	9.7	14.0	1.4	10.0	7.19
MARS	4.4	1.8	5.4	7.2	1.2	9.4	4.88
SVM	11.5	5.8	4.1	10.0	1.8	12.7	7.64
Kriging	7.3	3.8	5.1	8.9	2.2	7.3	5.75

according to the y-values; every 4th point is used for testing; and the rest are used for training[7].

Table 13-9. Twelve higher-dimensional test problems across six circuits.

Circuit	# Devices	# Input Variables	Outputs Modeled
opamp	30	215	AV (gain), BW (bandwidth) PM (phase margin), SR (slew rate)
bitcell	6	30	$cell_i$ (read current)
sense amp	12	125	$delay$, pwr (power)
voltage reference	11	105	$DVREF$ (difference in voltage), PWR (power)
GMC filter	140	1468	$ATTEN$ (attenuation), IL
comparator	62	639	BW (bandwidth)

Initial Scaling Experiments

I ran FFX on the larger circuit problems. In the larger circuits, it failed miserably, getting out-of-memory errors.

To understand why, we can analyze FFX's computational complexity.

[7]This is faster than cross-validation, yet gives consistent, reliable answers.

FFX Computational Complexity

Let us determine the computational complexity of FFX, for each step. This can be viewed as the core theory for FFX.

Step One. Let e be the number of exponents and o be the number of nonlinear operators. Therefore the number of univariate bases per variable is $(o + 1) * e$. (The $+1$ is when no nonlinear operator is applied; or, equivalently, unity). With n as the number of input variables, then the total number of univariate bases is $(o+1)*e*n$. With N samples, the univariate part of step one has a complexity of $O((o+1)*e*n*N)$. Since e and o are constants, this reduces to $O(n*N)$. The number of bivariate bases is $p = O(n^2)$, so the bivarate part of step one has complexity $O(n^2 * N)$.

Step Two. The cost of an older elastic-net pathwise technique, LARS, was approximately that of one LS fitting according to p.93 of (Hastie et al., 2008). Since then, the coordinate descent algorithm (Friedman et al., 2010) has been shown to be 10x faster. Nonetheless, I will use LS as a baseline. With p input variables, LS fitting with QR decomposition has complexity $O(N * p^2)$. Because $p = O(n^2)$, FFX has approximate complexity $O(N * n^4)$.

Step Three. Reference (Deb et al., 2002) shows that nondominated filtering has complexity $O(N_o * N_{nondom})$ where N_o is the number of objectives, and N_{nondom} is the number of nondominated individuals. In the SR cases, N_o is a constant (at 2) and $N_{nondom} \leq N_{max-bases}$ where $N_{max-bases}$ is a constant (≈ 5). Therefore, FFX step three complexity is $O(1)$.

The complexity of FFX is the maximum of steps one, two, and three; which is $O(N * n^4)$. $\square$

Given this, the fact that FFX hits limits of computational resources when n is large is not surprising. In the largest circuit, $n = 1468$, therefore $n^4 = 4.64\text{e}12$.

Modifying FFX for Scalability

We can improve FFX to have a computational complexity $O(N * n^2)$, as follows. I adapt the procedure in Table 13-1 to be stepwise: first learn univariate coefficients; then only combine the $k \leq O(\sqrt{n})$ most important basis functions with each other for candidate bivariate coefficients; then learn the coefficients on the combinations of most-important univariate bases. This means that each linear learning has $\leq O(n)$ basis functions; therefore overall complexity is $O(N * n^2)$.

This adaptation can be seen as a "batch" approach to stepwise-forward regression like that in MARS (Friedman, 1991).

I took another cue from MARS to improve model flexibility, by adding *hinge* basis functions $max(0, x - thr)$, and $max(0, thr - x)$. These operators add "turn off" to some regions of input space and focus on remaining regions. For each hinge operator at each variable x_j, I allowed 5 different threshold values thr, uniformly distributed from $minx_j + 0.2 * (maxx_j - minx_j)$ to $minx_j + 0.8 * (maxx_j - minx_j)$; where $minx_j$ and $maxx_j$ are the minimum and maximum values seen for x_j in all training samples.

In preliminary experiments, I found that FFX would give a more thorough sets of results if I re-ran it on different high-level settings as shown in Table 13-10, and merged the results.[8]

Table 13-10. FFX runs on each of these settings, and merges the results.

Inter-actions	Denom-inator	Expon-entials	Log/Abs Operators	Hinge Functions	Notes
					linear
Y					quadratic
		Y	Y	Y	
	Y	Y	Y	Y	
Y				Y	
Y	Y				
Y	Y			Y	
Y		Y	Y		
Y			Y		
Y			Y	Y	

FFX settings were like in section 5, except up to 250 bases were allowed. The overall runtime per problem was $\approx$30 s on a single-core 1-GHz CPU.

7. High-Dimensional Experiments

This section presents results using the scaled-up FFX, on the high-dimensional modeling problems described in section 6.

Table 13-11 shows the lowest test error found by FFX, compared to other approaches. FFX always gets the lowest test error, and many other approaches failed badly. FFX did find it easier to capture some mappings than others.

Figure 13-5 shows the trade-off of equations, for each modeling approach. Each dot represents a different model, having its own complexity and test error. For a given subplot, the simplest model is a constant, at the far left. It also has the highest error. As new bases are added (higher complexity), error drops. The curves have different signatures. For example, we see that when the opamp BW model (top center) gets 2 bases, its error drops from 6.8% to 1.9%. After that, additional bases steadily improve error, until the most complex model having 31 bases has 1% error. Or, for opamp PM (top right), there is little reduction in error after 15 bases.

---

[8]This, of course, can be trivially parallelized.

Table 13-11. Test error (%) on the twelve high-dimensional test problems. The quadratic model failed because it had too samples for the number of coefficients. GP-SR and FFNN failed, either because test error was ≫100% or model build time took unreasonably long (several hours).

Approach	opamp *AV*	opamp *BW*	opamp *PM*	opamp *SR*	bitcell *cell$_i$*	sense amp *delay*
Lin (LS)	1.7	1.3	1.3	3.2	12.7	3.4
Quad (LS)	FAIL	FAIL	FAIL	FAIL	12.5	3.5
FFX	**1.0**	**0.9**	**1.0**	**2.0**	**12.4**	**3.0**
GP-SR	FAIL	FAIL	FAIL	FAIL	FAIL	FAIL
FFNN	FAIL	FAIL	FAIL	FAIL	FAIL	FAIL

Approach	sense amp *pwr*	voltage reference *DVREF*	voltage reference *PWR*	GMC filter *ATTEN*	GMC filter *IL*	comparator *BW*
Lin (LS)	3.5	2.4	22.8	16.4	17.3	27.2
Quad (LS)	2.9	2.8	40.4	FAIL	FAIL	FAIL
FFX	**2.7**	**1.0**	**2.0**	**7.0**	**8.5**	**17.0**
GP-SR	FAIL	FAIL	FAIL	FAIL	FAIL	FAIL
FFNN	FAIL	FAIL	FAIL	FAIL	FAIL	FAIL

In many modeling problems, FFX determined that just linear and quadratic terms were appropriate for the best equations. These include the the simpler opamp *PM* functions, GMC filter *IL*, GMC filter *ATTEN*, opamp *SR* (for errors > 2.5%), and bitcell *cell$_i$*. But in some problems, FFX used more strongly nonlinear functions. These include voltage reference *DVREF*, sense amp *delay*, and sense amp *pwr*. Let us explore some models in more detail.

Table 13-12 shows some functions that FFX extracted for opamp *PM*. At 0 bases is a constant, of course. From 1 to 4 bases, FFX adds one more linear base at a time, gradually adding resolution to the model. At 5 bases, it adds a base that has both an $abs()$ operator, and an interaction term: $abs(dvthn) * dvthn$. It keeps adding bases up to a maximum of 46 bases. By the time it gets to 46 bases, it has actually started using a rational model, as indicated by the $/(1+\ldots)$ term.

Table 13-13 shows some functions that FFX extracted for voltage reference *DVREF*. It always determines that a rational with a constant numerator is the best option. It uses the hinge basis functions, including interactions when 3 or more bases are used. It only needs 8 bases (in the denominator) to capture error of 0.9%. Of the 105 possible variables, FFX determined that variable

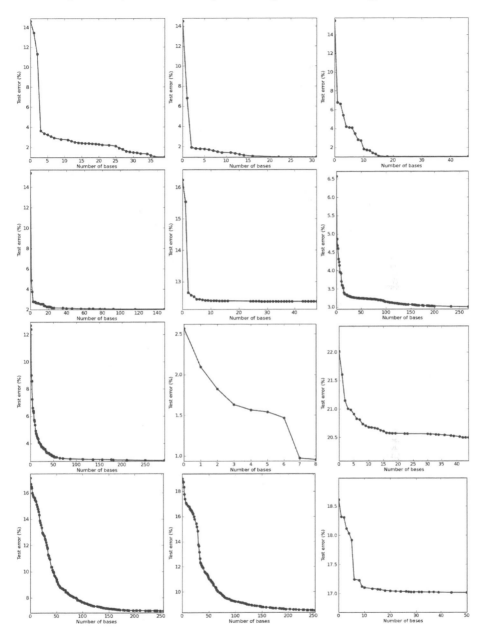

Figure 13-5. Test error versus Complexity. Top row left-to-right: opamp AV, opamp BW, opamp PM. Second-from-top row: opamp SR, bitcell $cell_i$, sense amp $delay$. Third-from-top row: sense amp pwr, voltage reference $DVREF$, voltage reference PWR. Bottom row: GMC filter $ATTEN$, GMC filter IL, comparator BW.

$dvthn$ was highly useful, by reusing it in many ways. $dvthp$ and dxw also had prominence.

Table 13-12. Equations for opamp PM, extracted by FFX.

# Bases	Test error (%)	Extracted Function
0	15.5	59.6
1	6.8	$59.6 - 0.303 * dxl$
2	6.6	$59.6 - 0.308 * dxl - 0.00460 * cgop$
3	5.4	$59.6 - 0.332 * dxl - 0.0268 * cgop + 0.0215 * dvthn$
4	4.2	$59.6 - 0.353 * dxl - 0.0457 * cgop + 0.0403 * dvthn - 0.0211 * dvthp$
5	4.1	$59.6 - 0.354 * dxl - 0.0460 * cgop - 0.0217 * dvthp + 0.0198 * dvthn + 0.0134 * abs(dvthn) * dvthn$
$\vdots$	$\vdots$	$\vdots$
46	1.0	$(58.9 - 0.136 * dxl + 0.0299 * dvthn - 0.0194 * max(0, 0.784 - dvthn) + \ldots)/(1.0 + \ldots)$

Table 13-13. Equations for voltage reference $DV\,REF$, extracted by FFX.

# Bases	Test error (%)	Extracted Function
0	2.6	512.7
1	2.1	$504/(1.0 + 0.121 * max(0, dvthn + 0.875))$
2	1.8	$503 - 199 * max(0, dvthn + 1.61) - 52.1 * max(0, dvthn + 0.875)$
$\vdots$	$\vdots$	$\vdots$
8	0.9	$476/(1.0 + 0.105 * max(0, dvthn + 1.61) - 0.0397 * max(0, -1.64 - dvthp) * max(0, dvthn + 0.875) - \ldots)$

8.   Related Work

Related Work in GP

Some GP papers use regularized learning. (McConaghy and Gielen, 2009) runs gradient directed regularization on a large set of enumerated basis functions, and uses those to bias the choice of function building blocks during GP search. FFX is similar, except it does not perform GP after regularized learning, and does not exploit pathwise learning to get a tradeoff. (Nikolaev and Iba, 2001) and (McConaghy et al., 2005) use ridge regression and the PRESS statistic, respectively, as part of the individual's fitness function.

Some GP research recasts SR from tree-valued problems towards vector-valued optimization problems. (O'Neill and Brabazon, 2006) cast SR into a string-based space, then solve it with a differential-evolution (DE) variant of grammatical evolution (O'Neill and Ryan, 2003). (McConaghy and Gielen, 2006) cast SR into a vector-valued Euclidian space, but solve it with a combination of vector-valued and traditional tree-valued operators in an EA framework. (Fonlupt and Robilliard, 2011) and others cast SR into a vector-valued Euclidian space, then solve it with vector-valued DE. (Korns, 2010) casts SR into a vector-valued space, and solves with Particle Swarm Optimization. (Topchy and Punch, 2001) and others cast the sub-problem of learning SR coefficients into traditional real-valued optimization problems as the inner loop of memetic learning; the outer loop remains GP-style search.

There are several approaches that recast general tree-valued search into simpler spaces; (Rothlauf, 2006) is a good starting point.

Shifting towards deterministic behavior, Estimation of Distribution Algorithms (EDAs) are sometimes framed as "derandomized" algorithms (Hansen and Ostermeier, 2001)[9]. EDAs have been applied to tree-based search; a recent example is (Looks, 2006). Variance-reduction techniques have also been used to derandomize EAs, such as (Teytaud and Gelly, 2007).

(O'Reilly, 1995) is a thorough example of doing tree-based search with non-evolutionary algorithms (hill climbing, simulated annealing).

Of course, none of these approaches are really *that* closely related to FFX. FFX dispenses with selection, mutation, and crossover. It has no individuals, and no population. At its core, it simply casts SR as one (or two) convex optimization problems, and solves them with off-the-shelf algorithms.

GLMs and Universal Approximation

Researchers familiar with generalized linear models (GLMs) may see FFX "merely" as a particular choice of "basis expansions"; for example (Hastie et al., 2008) suggests possible expansions including $log(x_j)$ and $\sqrt{x_j}$. The benefit of this, of course, is that GLM theory applies directly to FFX. However, this sells FFX short; consider the usefulness of other "merely GLM" techniques like CART (with indicator-style bases), MARS (with hinge-function bases), and SVMs (with kernel bases). Their usefulness is precisely due to a particular choice of basis functions, with appropriate algorithmic support framework, and a thoughtfully-chosen application. In my case, the choice of basis functions is driven from an SR perspective; the algorithmic support framework makes special use of the pathwise regularized learning, and includes nondominated filtering; the application is the SR-derived aim to generate whitebox models trading off prediction error versus complexity; and finally the scalable variant of FFX has "batch" stepwise-forward regression and hinge functions.

---

[9]The authors claim CMA-ES is a "completely" derandomized algorithm, but that is not quite accurate, because CMA-ES still relies on drawing samples from a pdf. To be *completely* derandomized, an algorithm has to be deterministic.

FFX shares a related philosophy with SVMs: transform a lower-dimensional set of n linear bases to a much larger set of bases $n_{new} \gg n$; then apply linear learning on this larger set, but prune them down (in the case of SVMs, to a set of "support vectors"). Of course, the distance calculation in SVM basis function of $\|x - x_{svi}\|$ for support vector i is not naturally interpretable, so does not apply to SR problems.

With a sufficiently broad choice of basis functions, FFX would be a universal approximator. But as already discussed, the aim of *specific* GLM techniques is to thoughtfully choose basis functions that reflect their aims. FFX's basis functions FFX are not sufficiently general to give FFX universal approximation. Hinge functions help, but to make FFX fully universal we would need to add more threshold values, and allow iteration to higher orders (similar to MARS). Of course, doing this hurts interpretability.

FFX is not a panacea: because its functional form is not naturally a universal approximator, there will be classes of SR problems that it handles poorly. For example, it cannot tune the coefficients $\{w_0, w_1\}$ inside a nonlinear basis function like $sin(w_0 + w_1 * x_1)$. This is not unlike other "technologies": linear regression can only competently handle linear and weakly nonlinear models; convex optimization can only handle unimodal problems; and so on. But what they trade off for flexibility, they gain in speed and reliability. To my knowledge, of the regression "technologies" that output interpretable models, FFX covers the broadest class of functions. And as we have seen, even with these restrictions, FFX is extremely competitive with GP-SR in finding accurate models on real-world data.

9.   Conclusion

This paper presented FFX, a new SR technique that approaches "technology" level speed, scalability, and reliability. Rather than evolutionary learning, it uses a recently-developed technique from the machine learning literature: pathwise regularized learning (Friedman et al., 2010). FFX applies pathwise learning to an enormous set of nonlinear basis functions, and exploits the path structure to generate a set of models that trade off error versus complexity. FFX was verified on six real-world medium-sized SR problems: average training time is ≈ 5 s (compared to 10 min with GP-SR), prediction error is comparable or better than GP-SR, and the models are at least as compact. FFX was scaled up to perform well on real-world problems with >1000 input variables. Due to its simplicity and deterministic nature, FFX's computational complexity could readily be determined: $O(N * n^2)$; where N is number of samples and n is number of input dimensions.

A python implementation of FFX, along with the real-world benchmark datasets used in this paper, are available at trent.st/ffx.

FFX's success on a problem traditionally approached by GP raises several points. First, stochasticity is not necessarily a virtue: FFX's deterministic nature means no wondering whether a new run on the same problem would work. Second, this paper showed how doing SR does not have to mean doing GP. What about other problems traditionally associated with GP? GP's greatest virtue is perhaps its convenience. But GP is not necessarily the only way; there is the possibility of dramatically different approaches. The problem may be reframed to be deterministic or even convex. As in the case of FFX for SR, there could be benefits like speed, scalability, simplicity, and adoptability; plus a deeper understanding of the problem itself. Such research can help crystallize insight into what problems GP has most benefit, and where research on GP might be the most fruitful; for example, answering specific questions about the nature of evolution, of emergence and complexity, and of computer science.

10. Acknowledgment

Funding for the reported research results is acknowledged from Solido Design Automation Inc.

References

Ampazis, N. and Perantonis, S. J. (2002). Two highly efficient second-order algorithms for training feedforward networks. *IEEE-EC*, 13:1064–1074.

Boyd, Stephen and Vandenberghe, Lieven (2004). *Convex Optimization*. Cambridge University Press, New York, NY, USA.

Castillo, Flor, Kordon, Arthur, and Villa, Carlos (2010). Genetic programming transforms in linear regression situations. In Riolo, Rick, McConaghy, Trent, and Vladislavleva, Ekaterina, editors, *Genetic Programming Theory and Practice VIII*, volume 8 of *Genetic and Evolutionary Computation*, chapter 11, pages 175–194. Springer, Ann Arbor, USA.

Daems, Walter, Gielen, Georges G. E., and Sansen, Willy M. C. (2003). Simulation-based generation of posynomial performance models for the sizing of analog integrated circuits. *IEEE Trans. on CAD of Integrated Circuits and Systems*, 22(5):517–534.

Deb, Kalyanmoy, Pratap, Amrit, Agarwal, Sameer, and Meyarivan, T. (2002). A fast and elitist multiobjective genetic algorithm: Nsga-ii. *IEEE Transactions on Evolutionary Computation*, 6:182–197.

Fonlupt, Cyril and Robilliard, Denis (2011). A continuous approach to genetic programming. In Silva, Sara et al., editors, *Proceedings of the 14th European Conference on Genetic Programming, EuroGP 2011*, volume 6621 of *LNCS*, pages 335–346, Turin, Italy. Springer Verlag.

Friedman, J. H. (1991). Multivariate adaptive regression splines. *Annals of Statistics*, 19(1):1–141.

Friedman, Jerome H., Hastie, Trevor, and Tibshirani, Rob (2010). Regularization paths for generalized linear models via coordinate descent. *Journal of
Statistical Software*, 33(1):1–22.

Hansen, N. and Ostermeier, A. (2001). Completely derandomized self-
adaptation in evolution strategies. *Evolutionary Computation*, 9(2):159–195.

Hastie, Trevor, Tibshirani, Robert, and Friedman, Jerome (2008). *The elements
of statistical learning: data mining, inference and prediction*. Springer, 2
edition.

Kim, Minkyu, Becker, Ying L., Fei, Peng, and O'Reilly, Una-May (2008). Constrained genetic programming to minimize overfitting in stock selection. In
Riolo, Rick L., Soule, Terence, and Worzel, Bill, editors, *Genetic Programming Theory and Practice VI*, Genetic and Evolutionary Computation, chapter 12, pages 179–195. Springer, Ann Arbor.

Korns, Michael F. (2010). Abstract expression grammar symbolic regression.
In Riolo, Rick, McConaghy, Trent, and Vladislavleva, Ekaterina, editors,
Genetic Programming Theory and Practice VIII, volume 8 of *Genetic and
Evolutionary Computation*, chapter 7, pages 109–128. Springer, Ann Arbor,
USA.

Koza, John R. (1992). *Genetic Programming: On the Programming of Computers by Means of Natural Selection*. MIT Press, Cambridge, MA, USA.

Langley, Pat, Simon, Herbert A., Bradshaw, Gary L., and Zytkow, Jan M. (1987).
Scientific discovery: computational explorations of the creative process. MIT
Press, Cambridge, MA, USA.

Leung, Henry and Haykin, Simon (1993). Rational function neural network.
Neural Comput., 5:928–938.

Looks, Moshe (2006). *Competent Program Evolution*. Doctor of science, Washington University, St. Louis, USA.

McConaghy, Trent, Eeckelaert, Tom, and Gielen, Georges (2005). CAFFEINE:
Template-free symbolic model generation of analog circuits via canonical
form functions and genetic programming. In *Proceedings of the Design Automation and Test Europe (DATE) Conference*, volume 2, pages 1082–1087,
Munich.

McConaghy, Trent and Gielen, Georges (2005). Analysis of simulation-driven
numerical performance modeling techniques for application to analog circuit optimization. In *Proceedings of the IEEE International Symposium on
Circuits and Systems (ISCAS)*. IEEE Press.

McConaghy, Trent and Gielen, Georges (2006). Double-strength caffeine: fast
template-free symbolic modeling of analog circuits via implicit canonical
form functions and explicit introns. In *Proceedings of the conference on
Design, automation and test in Europe: Proceedings*, DATE '06, pages 269–
274, 3001 Leuven, Belgium, Belgium. European Design and Automation
Association.

McConaghy, Trent and Gielen, Georges G. E. (2009). Template-free symbolic performance modeling of analog circuits via canonical-form functions and genetic programming. *IEEE Transactions on Computer-Aided Design of Integrated Circuits and Systems*, 28(8):1162–1175.

McConaghy, Trent, Vladislavleva, Ekaterina, and Riolo, Rick (2010). Genetic programming theory and practice 2010: An introduction. In Riolo, Rick, McConaghy, Trent, and Vladislavleva, Ekaterina, editors, *Genetic Programming Theory and Practice VIII*, volume 8 of *Genetic and Evolutionary Computation*, pages xvii–xxviii. Springer, Ann Arbor, USA.

Montgomery, Douglas C. (2009). *Design and analysis of experiments*. Wiley, Hoboken, NJ, 7. ed., international student version edition.

Nelder, J. A. and Wedderburn, R. W. M. (1972). Generalized linear models. *Journal of the Royal Statistical Society, Series A, General*, 135:370–384.

Nikolaev, Nikolay Y. and Iba, Hitoshi (2001). Regularization approach to inductive genetic programming. *IEEE Transactions on Evolutionary Computing*, 54(4):359–375.

O'Neill, Michael and Brabazon, Anthony (2006). Grammatical differential evolution. In Arabnia, Hamid R., editor, *Proceedings of the 2006 International Conference on Artificial Intelligence, ICAI 2006*, volume 1, pages 231–236, Las Vegas, Nevada, USA. CSREA Press.

O'Neill, Michael and Ryan, Conor (2003). *Grammatical Evolution: Evolutionary Automatic Programming in a Arbitrary Language*, volume 4 of *Genetic programming*. Kluwer Academic Publishers.

O'Reilly, Una-May (1995). *An Analysis of Genetic Programming*. PhD thesis, Carleton University, Ottawa-Carleton Institute for Computer Science, Ottawa, Ontario, Canada.

Riolo, Rick, McConaghy, Trent, and Vladislavleva, Ekaterina, editors (2010). *Genetic Programming Theory and Practice VIII*, Genetic and Evolutionary Computation, Ann Arbor, USA. Springer.

Rothlauf, Franz (2006). *Representations for genetic and evolutionary algorithms*. Springer-Verlag, pub-SV:adr, second edition. First published 2002, 2nd edition available electronically.

Sacks, Jerome, Welch, William J., Mitchell, Toby J., and Wynn, Henry P. (1989). Design and analysis of computer experiments. *Statistical Science*, 4(4.409–435):409–427.

Schmidt, Michael D. and Lipson, Hod (2006). Co-evolving fitness predictors for accelerating and reducing evaluations. In Riolo, Rick L., Soule, Terence, and Worzel, Bill, editors, *Genetic Programming Theory and Practice IV*, volume 5 of *Genetic and Evolutionary Computation*, chapter 17, pages –. Springer, Ann Arbor.

Smits, Guido F., Vladislavleva, Ekaterina, and Kotanchek, Mark E. (2010). Scalable symbolic regression by continuous evolution with very small populations. In Riolo, Rick, McConaghy, Trent, and Vladislavleva, Ekaterina, editors, *Genetic Programming Theory and Practice VIII*, volume 8 of *Genetic and Evolutionary Computation*, chapter 9, pages 147–160. Springer, Ann Arbor, USA.

Suykens, J. A. K., Gestel, T. Van, Brabanter, J. De, Moor, B. De, and Vandewalle, J. (2002). *Least Squares Support Vector Machines*. World Scientific, Singapore.

Teytaud, Olivier and Gelly, Sylvain (2007). Dcma: yet another derandomization in covariance-matrix-adaptation. In *Proceedings of the 9th annual conference on Genetic and evolutionary computation*, GECCO '07, pages 955–963, New York, NY, USA. ACM.

Topchy, Alexander and Punch, William F. (2001). Faster genetic programming based on local gradient search of numeric leaf values. In Spector, Lee et al., editors, *Proceedings of the Genetic and Evolutionary Computation Conference (GECCO-2001)*, pages 155–162, San Francisco, California, USA. Morgan Kaufmann.

Zou, Hui and Hastie, Trevor (2005). Regularization and variable selection via the elastic net. *Journal Of The Royal Statistical Society Series B*, 67(2):301–320.

Index

(1+1)GP, 117
90/10 crossover, 70
Adaptive Tarpeian method, 77
Affine arithmetic, 99, 103
Alpha-beta, 24
Ambitious objectives, 40
Antibodies, 7
Architecture-altering operations, 3–4, 9
Arguments, 3–4, 9
Aristotle, 2
Artificial ant, 57, 63, 69
    benchmark, 47
Autoconstructive evolution, 6
Automatically defined
    functions, 3–4, 9
    macros, 4
Backgammon, 17, 19–20
Baptism, 2
Batch Recombination, 216
Behavior space, 45
Behaviour, 71
Benchmark
    design, 173
    problem, 256
Benchmarks, 173
Binary decision diagrams, 63
Binding, 1, 7
Biocomputing and Developmental Systems Group, xxvii
Biped locomotion, 47
Bloat, 212
Bloat control, 77
Boolean, 57
Boolean problems, 66
Brain Computer Interfaces, 77
Brood Recombination, 216
Building blocks hypothesis, 40
CDP, 199
Center for the Study of Complex Systems, xxvii
Checkers, 22
Chess, 17, 19–20
Cinel Caterina, 77
Code-manipulation instructions, 5
Code reuse, 5

Coevolution, 31, 42
Combinators, 4–5, 9
Complexity, 53
Component mapping, 58
Comprehensive Domestic Product, 199
Computational complexity, 114, 126, 250, 256
Computational Evolution, 154
Computational Genetics Laboratory, xxvii
Convex, 235, 255–257
    optimization, 235, 255–257
Co-routines, 4
CRAFTY, 20
Critical Technologies Inc, xxvii
Crossover, 126
Crossover Bias theory, 212
Customized Scoring In Symbolic Regression
    Search, 201
Deception, 38
Definition
    ARC, 196
    IDP, 196
Definitions, 2
Derandomized algorithm, 255
Deterministic, 235–237, 255–257
De Vasconcelos J. A., 97
Distance, 60
    distortion, 59
Diversity, 62, 125
    maintenance, 41
Domain specific knowledge, 173
Download, 63
Dubbing, 2
Dynamic
    fitness, 5
    limits, 216
DynOpEq, 213–215
Elastic net, 238, 244
Encoding, 57, 66
Epistasis, 59, 154
Estimation of Distribution Algorithm, 255
Even Parity, 66
Evolution of cooperation, 7–8
Evolved Analytics, xxvii
Exaptation, 43

Extended phenotype, 62
Fast Function Extraction, 236–237, 239–241,
    243–245, 247–252, 254–257
FFX, 236–237, 239–241, 243–245, 247–252,
    254–257
Finite state machine, 63
Fisher Jonathan M., 153
Fitness
    cases, 66
    clouds, 59
    distance correlation, 59
    landscape, 41
Flat distribution, 211
FlatOpEq, 221
FlatOpEq2, 221
FreeCell, 17, 28–29
Frege Gottlob, 2
Functions, 3, 9
Galván-Lopéz Edgar, 57
Generalized linear model, 237, 255–256
Genetic Epidemiology, 154
Genetic Finance LLC, xxvii
Genetics Squared, xxvii
Genotype, 57
Genotype-phenotype mapping, 58, 71
Genotypic step-size, 60, 71
GLM, 237, 255–256
GP adoption, 236
Grammars, 2
Grow mutation, 215
HaikuBot, 21
Hamming distance, 66
Harrington Kyle, 1
Hedonic
    modeling, 173
    modeling validation, 174
    response, 173
Helmuth Thomas, 1
Heuristic function, 26
Hierarchy, 2
Hill Douglas P., 153
Holland John, 3, 7, 13
Human-competitive results, 5
HVL mutation, 116
Hyper-heuristic, 27
Indexed memory, 3
Inexact matching, 7
Integrated circuit, 243, 248
Interval
    arithmetic, 99, 103
    methods, 98
Introns, 24
Iteration, 4
Iterative-deepening, 25
Kidd La Creis, 153
Korns Michael, xxvii, 129, 195
Koza John, 9

Kripke Saul, 2
Labels, 1
Lagrange distribution of the second kind, 212
Lambda expressions, 2
Landscape autocorrelation, 59
Lasso, 238
Lavender Nicole, 153
Lawnmower problem, 9–10
Least-squares regression, 235, 237
Lehman Joel, 37
Linear
    functions, 124
    programming, 235
    regression, 235, 237–238, 242
Linkage, 59
Lisp, 5, 8, 13
Locality, 57, 59
Local optima, 41
Looks Moshe, 97
Lose checkers, 17, 22
Majority, 66
MAJORITY, 120
Martin Brian, 1
McConaghy Trent, 235
McDermott James, 57
Measuring
    bloat, 226
    flatness, 223
Meta-genetic programming, 6
Metropolis-Hastings, 67
Mill John Stuart, 2
Minimax, 25
Modular
    architecture, 3, 6, 11–13
Modularity, 1, 5, 9–10
Modules, 2, 4, 11
Moore Jason H., xv, 153
Multi-objective, 125, 237–238, 241, 244–245, 247,
    250, 255
Multi-Objective Evolutionary Algorithms, 42
Multiple phenotypes, 58
Multiplexer, 66
MutOpEq, 213, 215
Names, 1–3, 5, 7, 11
Natural evolution, 39–40, 53
NEAT, 46
Negative slope coefficient, 59
Neighbourhood, 60
Neumann Frank, 113
Neural networks, 109
Neuroevolution, 45
Neutrality, 67, 73
Neutral network, 41
Noel Pierre-Luc, 173
Non-objective search, 39, 42, 53
Novelty
    metric, 44

search, 39, 44, 52
Objective-based search, 40, 53
Obstacle-avoiding robot problem, 10–13
O'Neill Michael, 57
Operator-distance coherence, 60
Operator Equalisation, 212–213
ORDER, 119
O'Reilly Una-May, xiii, 113, 173
Parity, 5
Parsimony, 124
Pathwise regularized learning, 236, 238–241, 244–245, 247, 250, 254–256
Pennachin Cassio, 97
Phenotype, 57, 62, 71–72
Phenotype-fitness mapping, 58, 71
Phenotype-phenotype mapping, 58, 71
Phenotypic distance, 60
Picbreeder, 43
Policies, 27
Policy, 17
Poli Riccardo, 77
Population, 125
Problem difficulty, 40, 57, 59
Program bloat, 47
Programming languages, 1
Prostate Cancer, 154
Protected operators, 102
Pubeval, 20
PushGP, 1, 4–5, 9–10, 13
Push programming language, 1, 4–5, 9
Random search, 71
RankOpEq, 223
RARS, 17
Rational functions, 241–243, 252
Real-world problems, 237, 248, 256
Recursion, 4, 9
Regularized learning, 236, 238–241, 244, 246, 254–256
Ridge regression, 238, 254
Riolo Rick, xv
Robocode, 17, 19, 21
Robot Auto Racing Simulator, 32
Robot navigation, 1
Rush Hour, 17, 25
Russell Bertrand, 2
Salvaris Mathew, 77
Scalability, 235–237, 243, 255–257
Scope and extent, 2, 13
Self-validated numerics, 98
Semantics, 57, 62, 71
Sensory evaluation process, 174
Sensory map, 173
 2-piecewise linear, 178
 construction, 176
 design steps, 177
 invariants, 177

linear, 178
naive, 176
n-piecewise linear, 178, 184
rational, 177
smooth, 178
Sensory science, 173
Serendipity, 39
Shadow Economy
 Definition, 196
Shadow Economy
 Method to Estimate
  Currency Demand, 197
  Expenditure Surveys, 197
  MIMIC Model, 197
  Physical Input, 197
Shrink mutation, 215
Silva Sara, 211
Simon Herbert, 2
Sipper Moshe, 17
SORTING, 116, 121
Spector Lee, 1
Sponsors, xxvii
SR, 236–237, 240–241, 243–244, 247, 250, 252, 254–257
Stack-based genetic programming, 1, 4
Stanley Kenneth O., 37
Static program analysis, 102
 asymptotes, 102
 output bounds, 102
Step limit, 9
Stepping stones, 38, 44
Step-size, 58
Stochastic, 255, 257
Strategy, 19
String-edit distance, 64
Subtree mutation, 67
Support vector machines, 109
Symbolic regression, 71, 97, 103, 236–237, 240–241, 243–244, 247, 250, 252, 254–257
 benchmarks, 173
 linear scaling, 103
Tags, 1, 3, 6–11, 13
Taxi-driver's distance, 65
Technology, 235–236, 256
Theory, 250
Third Millenium, xxvii
Time series prediction, 105
Tolerance, 7
Truscott Philip D., 195
Truth table, 66
University of Michigan, xxvii
Vanneschi Leonardo, 211
Veeramachaneni Kalyan, 173
Visualization, 154
Vladislavleva Ekaterina, xv
Wagner Markus, 113
Wind forecasting, 108